Vulnerable Workers: Psychosocial and Legal Issues

WILEY SERIES ON STUDIES IN OCCUPATIONAL STRESS

Series Editors

Professor Cary L. Cooper
Manchester School of Management,
University of Manchester
Institute of Science and Technology

Professor S. V. Kasl
Department of Epidemiology
School of Medicine
Yale University

A Behavioural Approach to the Management of Stress
H. R. Beech, L. E. Burns and B. F. Sheffield

Living Abroad: Personal Adjustment and Personal Policy in the Overseas Setting
Ingemar Torbiorn

The Mechanisms of Job Stress and Strain
John P. R. French, Jr., Robert D. Caplan and R. Van Harrison

Noise and Society
Edited by Dylan M. Jones and Antony J. Chapman

Job Stress and Blue Collar Work
Edited by Cary L. Cooper and Michael Smith

Stress and Health: Issues in Research Methodology
Edited by Stan V. Kasl and Cary L. Cooper

Stress in Health Professionals
Edited by Roy Payne and Jenny Firth-Cozens

Causing, Coping and Consequences of Stress at Work
Edited by Cary L. Cooper and Roy Payne

Job Control and Worker Health
Edited by Steven L. Sauter, Joseph J. Hurrell, Jr. and Cary L. Cooper

Employment, Stress and Family Functioning
Julian Barling

Stress and Challenge at the Top: The Paradox of the Successful Executive
James Campbell Quick, Debra L. Nelson and Jonathan D. Quick

Vulnerable Workers: Psychosocial and Legal Issues
Edited by Marilyn J. Davidson and Jill Earnshaw

Further titles in preparation

Vulnerable Workers: Psychosocial and Legal Issues

Edited by

Marilyn J. Davidson

and

Jill Earnshaw

University of Manchester Institute of Science and Technology, UK

JOHN WILEY & SONS

Chichester · New York · Brisbane · Toronto · Singapore

Other Wiley Editorial Offices

John Wiley & Sons, Inc., 605 Third Avenue,
New York, NY 10158-0012, USA

Jacaranda Wiley Ltd, G.P.O. Box 859, Brisbane,
Queensland 4001, Australia

John Wiley & Sons (Canada) Ltd, 22 Worcester Road,
Rexdale, Ontario M9W 1L1, Canada

John Wiley & Sons (SEA) Pte Ltd, 37 Jalan Pemimpin #05-04,
Block B, Union Industrial Building, Singapore 2057

Library of Congress Cataloging-in-Publication Data:

Vulnerable workers : psychosocial and legal issues / edited by Marilyn J. Davidson and Jill Earnshaw.
p. cm. — (Wiley series on studies in occupational stress)
Includes bibliographical references and index.
ISBN 0-471-92759-7 (hard)
1. Discrimination in employment—Great Britain. 2. Employee rights—Great Britain. 3. Handicapped—Employment—Great Britain. 4. AIDS (Disease)—Patients—Employment—Great Britain. 5. Sexual harassment—Great Britain. 6. Sex discrimination in employment—Great Britain. 7. Part-time employment—Great Britain. 8. Blacks—Employment—Great Britain. 9. Discrimination in employment—Law and legislation—Great Britain. 10. Labor laws and legislation—Great Britain. I. Davidson, Marilyn. II. Earnshaw, Jill. III. Series.
HD4903.5.G7V85 1991
331.13'3'0941—dc20 90-12597
CIP

British Library Cataloguing in Publication Data:

Vulnerable workers : psychosocial and legal issues – (Wiley series on studies in occupational stress)
1. Handicapped personnel. Social minority personnel
I. Davidson, Marilyn J. II. Earnshaw, Jill, *1947–*
331.59

ISBN 0-471-92759-7

Typeset by Photo·graphics, Honiton, Devon
Printed and bound by Biddles Ltd, Guildford, Surrey

Contents

List of Contributors

RANDHIR AULUCK	*Senior Lecturer, Women and Work Programme, Coventry Polytechnic, Coventry, UK*
DOUGLAS D. BAKER	*Associate Professor of Management, College of Business and Economics, Washington State University, Pullman, Washington, USA*
GEOFFREY BINDMAN	*Solicitor and Honorary Visiting Professor in Law, University College London and formerly Legal Adviser to the Commission for Racial Equality, UK*
MARILYN J. DAVIDSON	*Senior Lecturer in Organizational Psychology, Manchester School of Management, University of Manchester, Institute of Science and Technology, Manchester, UK*
BRIAN DOYLE	*Senior Lecturer in Law, Department of Business and Management Studies, University of Salford, Salford, UK*
JILL EARNSHAW	*Lecturer in Law, Manchester School of Management, University of Manchester, Institute of Science and Technology, Manchester, UK*
VIVIENNE GAY	*Barrister, London, UK*
PAUL ILES	*Director of Diploma in Management Programme, Open Business School, Open University, Milton Keynes, UK*
CECLIA KITZINGER	*Senior Lecturer in Psychology, Polytechnic of East London, London, UK*
PATRICIA LEIGHTON	*Reader in Law, Anglia Higher Education College and Visiting Research Fellow, Institute of Manpower Studies, Brighton, UK*

SONIA LIFF — *Lecturer, Department of Management Studies, Loughborough University, UK*

MARTIN F. MCHUGH — *Professor of Psychology and Head of Department of Psychology, University College, Galway, Ireland*

BRIAN W. NAPIER — *Digital Professor of Information Technology, Law Centre for Commercial Law Studies, Queen Mary and Westfield College, London, UK*

PETER J. PACE — *Principal Lecturer in Law, Department of Law, Manchester Polytechnic, Manchester, UK*

KATE PAINTER — *Principal Research Officer, Middlesex Polytechnic, Criminology Centre, Enfield, UK*

ANNA STALLARD — *Senior Clinical Psychologist, Ruchill Hospital, Glasgow, UK*

DAVID E. TERPSTRA — *Hearin-Hess Professor of Business Administration, School of Business Administration, The University of Mississippi, Mississippi, USA*

GILL WHITTING — *Senior Researcher, ECOTEC Research and Consulting Ltd, Birmingham, UK*

STEVEN WILLBORN — *Professor of Law, College of Law, University of Nebraska, Lincoln, Nebraska, USA*

Editorial Foreword to the Series

This book, *Vulnerable Workers: Psychosocial and Legal Issues*, is the seventeenth* book in the series of *Studies in Occupational Stress*. The main objective of this series of books is to bring together the leading international psychologists and occupational health researchers to report on their work on various aspects of occupational stress and health. The series will include a number of books on original research and theory in each of the areas described in the initial volume, such as Blue Collar Stressors, The Interface Between the Work Environment and the Family, Individual Differences in Stress Reactions, The Person–Environment Fit Model, Behavioural Modification and Stress Reduction, Stress and the Socio-technical Environment, The Stressful Effects of Retirement and Unemployment and many other topics of interest in understanding stress in the workplace.

We hope these books will appeal to a broad spectrum of readers—to academic researchers and postgraduate students in applied and occupational psychology and sociology, occupational medicine, management, personnel, and law—and to practitioners working in industry, the occupational medical field, mental health specialists, social workers, personnel officers, lawyers and others interested in the health of the individual worker.

Cary L. Cooper,
University of Manchester Institute of Science and Technology
Stanislav V. Kasl,
Yale University

*Three earlier titles are now out of print.

Preface

There has been a growing awareness that certain groups of workers are more disadvantaged than others at work. This book attempts to explore the legal and psychosocial issues involved in the employment of some of these groups.

Indeed, we believe that this publication has been aptly timed. Recently, the President of the United States has signed into law the Disabilities Act of 1990, covering 43 million Americans with physical and mental disabilities. This volume also coincides with a decade when North American, European and British firms are facing a growing shortage of workers. Increasingly, organisations will be hiring 'minority group' employees and workers with disabilities, and they will need to understand them better in order to utilise them more effectively in the workforce. Furthermore, we are on the verge of Europe 1992, and it will be necessary for organisations to become more global and to understand more fully the psychosocial and legal issues relating to vulnerable workers.

MARILYN J. DAVIDSON
JILL EARNSHAW
University of Manchester, UK

Chapter 1

Vulnerable Workers: An Overview of Psychosocial and Legal Issues

Jill Earnshaw and Marilyn J. Davidson, University of Manchester Institute of Science and Technology, UK

WHAT MAKES PEOPLE VULNERABLE AT WORK?

Vulnerability is a relative term; it would be impossible to draw a sharp distinction between those who are vulnerable at work and those who are not. In fact, there are perhaps few workers who would not describe themselves as vulnerable in some aspect of employment—whether it be lack of job security, the potential risk of accident, industrial disease or stress, exploitation in terms of pay or unequal opportunity in the job market. Vulnerability also connotes different things to different people; lawyers, economists, sociologists would doubtless hold differing views as to what is meant by 'vulnerable' workers. (Leighton and Painter, 1987a).

What sort of factors operate to make people vulnerable at work? Paradoxically, the law itself may do so. Over the last 25 years there has been a sharp increase in legislation affecting the rights of those at work, and indeed much of it has been of a protectionist nature. The Redundancy Payments Act of 1965 provided statutory compensation for those whose job was lost by reason of redundancy; the Health and Safety at Work Act 1974 aimed to protect the health, safety and welfare of *everyone* at work, and the Sex Discrimination Act 1975 and Race Relations Act 1976 provided protection against unlawful discrimination. However, many of the employment protection rights now re-enacted in the Employment Protection (Consolidation) Act 1978 such as the right to a redundancy payment, maternity rights, and most importantly, the right not to be unfairly dismissed, are *not* available to everyone at work. They are provided only to 'employees'. While it may be reasonable to exclude the genuinely self-employed

Vulnerable Workers: Psychosocial and Legal Issues. Edited by M. J. Davidson and J. Earnshaw

businessman or woman who merely provides services for others as an independent contractor, numerous examples exist of people who could not in the true sense of the words be regarded as 'their own boss' and yet failed in their claim to employee status. Furthermore, in the absence of a statutory definition of a 'contract of employment' (which implies employee status) the courts have been left to decide cases on an individual basis with confusing and sometimes inconsistent results. Thus in two recent cases, homeworkers regarded by their employer as self-employed, were found to be employees (*Airfix Footwear* v. *Cope* [1978] ICR 1210; *Nethermere* (*St Neots*) v. *Gardiner and Taverna* [1983] IRLR 103) yet a regular casual who had worked for 52 weeks for 42 hours a week for Trusthouse Forte was held to be self-employed. Such *ad hoc* decisions on so crucial an issue are undesirable and it has been argued that a radical change of approach is necessary (Hepple, 1986).

Even those deemed to be 'employees' have further hurdles to clear. Most employment protection rights are available only to employees who satisfy a qualifying period of continuous employment which in many cases (e.g. unfair dismissal, redundancy) is two years. Many temporary and casual workers thus fall outside the net. Furthermore, those who work less than 16 hours per week are generally excluded (unless they have worked for at least five years for eight or more hours per week), which as Patricia Leighton discusses in Chapter 9.2, immediately puts many part-time workers at a huge disadvantage. The rationale for thereby creating a 'core' of permanent, full-time employees who are provided with employment protection while denying it to the growing part-time, casual, temporary and contracted-out 'peripheral' workforce is obscure. In effect, the law has made vulnerable those most in need of protection, for in many cases such peripheral workers are already disadvantaged in lack of access to occupational benefits provided for full-time employees, and in lack of trade union support. At least a third of workers now fall outside basic labour law rights (Leighton and Painter, 1987b).

However, a case of great significance in its potential for challenging the hours restriction in UK law recently came before the European Court of Justice (see Chapter 9.2). The Court found that a German sick pay scheme limited to those employed for at least 10 hours per week discriminated against women (who dominate the part-time workforce) and was therefore contrary to Community law. The UK government may be forced to think again in terms of its eligibility rules for employment protection.

Vulnerability at work may also arise simply through a worker's inherent physical characteristics or emotional make-up. In Chapter 4.1, Martin McHugh discusses the psychosocial issues concerning some of the major types of disability such as blindness, deafness and epilepsy but he also points out that '. . . every person is handicapped in the sense of being unable to do some things which others can manage' (p. 69). Not everyone can type at 70 words per minute, however much they apply themselves; not everyone possesses the skills and qualities of leadership and decision making of a managing director. Obviously, however, those with severe disabilities are bound to be disadvantaged simply by being unable even to compete on the same footing as those without handicap, and as Brian Doyle describes in Chapter 4.2, it has in fact been found necessary to provide sheltered employment for some of these individuals. Victims of AIDS arguably fall into a fairly special category in that the extent of their disability at work is likely to be uncertain, but will inevitably be compounded by the enormous psychological and emotional problems of coming to terms with a terminal, and socially unacceptable illness.

For some groups of workers, vulnerability stems not from an incapacity to do the job but from the attitudes and prejudices of others. The generalised assumptions made about women, for example, which have acted to their detriment in employment are widely recognised—and still acted upon. 'Working mothers are unreliable, they constantly take time off', 'There's no point training young women, they'll just leave to have babies', 'Women don't possess management qualities'—these are just a number of the views on which employment decisions are based. Some chapters of this book explore the vulnerability of other groups who face similar ignorance and consequent discrimination, such as ethnic minority workers, gays, lesbians and transsexuals. In many cases employers' own bigotory and prejudice is added to by their fears, real or imagined, of unfavourable reactions on the part of clients or indeed the public. A solicitor may refuse to brief a female barrister because the client does not believe a woman can do the job as well as a man; homosexual teachers may be dismissed because parents' outrage at their continued employment is assumed; a black worker may be denied promotion because the employer fears a backlash from the union.

It should not be forgotten that disabled workers face not only their physical limitations and structural barriers at work, but that they too may be the victims of ignorance and prejudice. Many people, for example, seem automatically to link severe physical handicap with mental handicap, and conditions such as epilepsy are particularly susceptible to myths associated with 'fits'. Fear of AIDS can make even the most rational individual tempted into beliefs wholly at variance with scientific evidence, and as Napier points out in Chapter 5.2

> . . . there is a need to distinguish between advice which tells us how good, responsible and reasonable citizens should respond to the risks associated with

> AIDS, and that which predicts the likely response of the courts and tribunals to the employment-related problems likely to be encountered . . .
> (p. 141)

A person may be vulnerable at work in terms of the physical risks of injury, accident or disease which the job entails. Some people do jobs which are inherently dangerous such as steel erectors, coal-miners or deep sea divers. Others may work with dangerous machinery or be susceptible to industrial diseases such as asbestosis, dermatitis, industrial deafness or certain forms of cancer. For many years, legislation such as the Factories Acts and the Mines and Quarries Act have existed to lay down standards and reasonable precautions to be taken in order to safeguard the workers. However, despite such legislation the level of industrial accidents has remained unacceptably high, and actions for personal injuries by workers against their employers are a common feature of the civil courts. It was concern about accident statistics and the somewhat fragmented and patchy nature of the legislative provisions which concerned the Robens Committee and led to the passing of the Health and Safety at Work Act in 1974. The Act covered everyone at work and aimed at prevention rather than cure by a policy of informing and educating the workforce, and trade union representatives in particular, so as to involve workers in taking care for their own safety. Part of the continuing problem lies in enforcement, however. The number of inspectors is inadequate for the enormous number of establishments involved, so that those who choose to disregard the law may go unnoticed unless a major accident occurs.

Injury may not of course be suffered accidentally; intentional violence against employees appears to be on the increase in a number of jobs. Social workers, teachers, nurses, ambulance staff and public transport staff all run the risk of physical violence or verbal abuse, the impact of which has both short-term and long-term effects. Sexual harassment too, while not necessarily on the increase, has been increasingly recognised as a threat to individuals at work, and its unlawfulness under the Sex Discrimination Act 1975 confirmed. In their more serious forms both sexual and racial harassment may easily constitute various kinds of criminal assault, though the terms also encompass verbal abuse or gestures which would not possess a criminal element.

Vulnerability is of course also a function of the economic, social and political climate of the day, and therefore cannot be a static concept. Those workers who face discrimination at work will be even more disadvantaged at a time of economic recession or in the pruning of manpower due to the inexorable march of technological advances. Worker vulnerability increased as the protectionist policies of the 1970s gave way to the deregulation and survival-of-the-fittest attitudes of the 1980s. Conversely the position of women in the labour market has improved as women's working, and more particularly, the employment of married women has become socially acceptable. Women workers arc not only increasing in numbers, but they are beginning to find their way into jobs such as train-driver or airline pilot—jobs which it would have been unthinkable for them to hold a generation ago.

Needless to say, vulnerable workers can be utilised politically to satisfy the needs of the government of the day. It is well known that during the Second World War women were encouraged to fill the employment gaps left by men, and state nurseries were provided free of charge. When the war ended, women were pressured into returning to domestic duties and the nurseries were closed down. In the 1960s when there was full employment, immigration policies exploited the influx of black workers, channelling them into jobs which their white contemporaries found unappealing. Employers were happy to take on black workers as road-sweepers, bus conductors and in low level jobs in the health service, but the professions were largely closed to them. Even now, the demographic changes taking place, due to the subsequent shortage of young school-leavers, are causing the government to alert employers to the availability of more mature recruits, and in particular women returning after raising a family, as a valuable resource. The tide may turn again in the not-too-distant future, however; the potential for opportunity being heralded is unlikely to lead to a permanent state of affairs.

HOW IS VULNERABILITY RECOGNISED?

Some aspects of vulnerability are easily measured by statistical methods. Earnings surveys, for example, show clearly that in terms of pay, women remain a disadvantaged group. Figures comparing gross hourly earnings, excluding overtime, reveal that in 1989 women's average earnings were 76.0% of men's (HMSO, 1989c), though as may be expected the figure is considerably lower, at 67.6% if gross weekly earnings including overtime are compared. Statistics also show the gap appears to be narrowing; the figures for average earnings, for instance, were 74.9% in 1988 and 73.4% in 1987. Similarly, in Chapter 6, the level of violent incidents against certain occupational groups such as social workers and health service personnel is indicated by the results of various surveys, though Kate Painter warns that massive under-reporting is likely to make the official figures inaccurate.

Vulnerability ought also to be reflected in unemployment figures. If certain sections of the economically active population are over-represented among the unemployed, then that is some indication that those sections may be disadvantaged at the point of recruitment. Between 1985 and 1986, surveys carried out on economically active people with disabilities showed disproportionately high rates of unemployment: 27% of men and 20% of women surveyed were unemployed (HMSO, 1989a). Further unemployment statistics are discussed by Brian Doyle in Chapter 4.2, where it is also shown that employment rates of disabled persons who had undergone rehabilitation are significantly lower at a time when unemployment in general is higher.

Information regarding the vulnerability of workers subject to discrimination is revealed by examination of reported industrial tribunal cases. Throughout this book, in the chapters on sexual harassment, part-timers, the disabled, homosexuals and AIDS victims, individual authors have, by analysing tribunal decisions, illustrated many aspects of vulnerability. They point out the negative management attitudes to employment of certain groups, the sort of adverse treatment meted out to those groups while in employment, and the factors which may bring about their dismissal. Other cases can show how management policies such as age limitations, or preferential selection of part-timers for redundancy, may have an adverse impact on women, and how word-of-mouth recruitment can disadvantage ethnic minority workers. Statistics relating to tribunal cases should however be approached with caution. The fact of an increase of 50% in race discrimination cases (from 40 to 61) in 1987–88 (*Employment Gazette*, 1989) should be read in conjunction with two other statistics: first that successful race cases as a proportion of cases heard by tribunals increased by only 6%; and secondly that the proportion of such cases withdrawn, conciliated or otherwise disposed of, rose from 56% to 63%. Furthermore, many workers suffering discrimination will be dissuaded from making a tribunal claim at all, whether through lack of funds or information about procedure, fear of publicity or victimisation, or simply the realisation that modest financial compensation is unlikely to prove a worthwhile remedy.

An increasing number of employers, notably those in the public sector, have accepted that promoting equality of opportunity can only be done effectively if the ethnic composition of the workforce is monitored. Such monitoring aims to highlight areas where discrimination may be occurring, for example at the point of recruitment or in promotion, and also to assess progress being made by equal opportunity policies. Leicester City Council began monitoring in 1977 and by 1982 had noted that particularly in certain areas of work, black people were not applying for jobs in the numbers which could be expected (considering the ethnic composition of the local population). As a result, many changes were made to recruitment policies including a ban on word-of-mouth recruitment and telephone interviewing, and external as well as internal advertising of all vacancies. By 1985 the monitoring statistics showed an increase in the ethnic minority workforce, from 9% to 12% of council employees, though the uneven spread of this increase across various posts led to further positive action steps (Equal

Opportunities Review, 1989b). In 1988, in what was regarded as a landmark decision (*West Midlands Passenger Transport Executive* v. *Singh* [1988] IRLR 186) the Court of Appeal ruled that statistics such as those gathered by ethnic monitoring could be used as evidence pointing to discrimination against a particular ethnic group. For example, such figures might show a significantly lower promotion rate for black workers in a particular firm, and therefore support the claim of a black applicant who argues that *he* or *she* has been discriminated against. Though such a ruling is good news for those seeking to prove discrimination, it is greatly to be hoped that it will not act as a disincentive to employers who carry out monitoring, or are considering its use, on the basis that it may later be used against them.

Vulnerability which can be measured in terms of numbers is relatively easy to identify. However, vulnerability may also manifest itself in ways which are not so easily documented—in stress, isolation, job dissatisfaction and even physical symptoms and absence from work. In Chapter 6 Kate Painter discusses the physical and psychological effects of violence and threatened violence at work such as headaches, nausea and digestive problems, feelings of guilt and loss of confidence. Similarly the emotional outcomes of sexual harassment are reported in Chapter 7.1, outcomes which include tension, anxiety, anger, depression and the physical consequences of such emotional stress. Personal relationships with others in the workplace and even within the family may also be affected. Celia Kitzinger (Chapter 8.1) describes the sense of alienation and anxiety felt by homosexual men and women at work as a result of leading what they see as a 'double' life. She points out the tensions which may arise where the partner of a homosexual man or woman resents the secrecy imposed on the relationship by the need to maintain a heterosexual front at work.

Thus vulnerability may be something easy to isolate—the lack of a job, low pay, failure to climb the promotional ladder. Illness and absence from work may even be recognised as stress related now that greater awareness exists of the physical outcomes of psychological factors (Cooper, Cooper and Eaker, 1988). However, some aspects of vulnerability are extremely difficult to recognise—how can 'isolation' be measured, or 'anxiety' which does not manifest itself in physical symptoms? For some workers, being vulnerable may simply mean an unpleasant working environment or a lack of job satisfaction—vulnerability such as this is unlikely to be reflected in statistics.

VULNERABLE GROUPS OMITTED

This book does not claim to give comprehensive coverage of all those who may be described as vulnerable at work, even if that were theoretically possible. Rather, it aims to illustrate some of the different types of vulnerable worker. A chapter has not been devoted to 'women' as a vulnerable group *per se* even though there would be few who would argue that equality of opportunity between the sexes has been achieved. As we have seen, women's earnings still lag behind those of men. Furthermore, segregated employment remains common, and though women's presence in the workforce continues to increase, women tend to predominate in the lower paid jobs. Even where women work in occupations traditionally regarded as 'women's work', such as hairdressing, catering and the clothing industry, the top jobs are dominated by men (Davidson, 1987).

There were two reasons for omitting a chapter on women. The first was one of space. So much can be, and has been, written about women at work (e.g. Davidson and Cooper, 1987) that it was felt the constraints of a single chapter would have made meaningful coverage dubious. The second, related, reason was that certain aspects of women's vulnerability is covered in other chapters. Sonia Liff and Patricia Leighton in Chapters 9.1 and 9.2 deal with the problems faced by part-timers, who are predominantly women. Women are more likely than men to be the victims of violence and especially of sexual harassment and therefore Chapters 6 and 7 focus more on women than on men. In Chapter 3, Steven Willborn describes how Title VII of the Civil Rights Act of 1964 has been used to develop the law on sex discrimination and sexual harassment in the United States, which led in fact to a parellel development in the United Kingdom. Thus 'direct' and 'indirect' discrimination under the Sex Discrimination Act 1975 follows very closely the concepts of 'disparate treatment' and 'disparate impact' at the heart of US sex discrimination law. Finally the commitment of the European Community to equal treatment between men and women is described in Chapter 2. The interpretation of Community law by the European Court of Justice, and the application of Article 119 ('equal pay for equal work') of the Treaty of Rome, along with the Equal Pay Directive of 1975 and Equal Treatment Directive of 1976, by our domestic courts, has in fact had a profound effect in the United Kingdom, and on at least two occasions has forced a change in national legislation.

As previously mentioned, the demographic changes of the 1990s promise an improvement for women as employers perceive the need to woo them back to work after having families and to accommodate their domestic commitments by more flexible patterns of working. The future may look a little more rosy, but it remains to be seen whether the demographic changes will bring about progress for women in a way that legislating for equal opportunities failed to do.

A group of workers who could clearly be described as vulnerable are immigrant workers, especially those who are still illegal. This is a very vulnerable group with no employment rights whatsoever and is a problem particularly prevalent in the United States. Another vulnerable section of workers (which can often include illegal immigrants) are the homeworkers. Sincc they are often regarded as self-employed they lack employment protection rights, and even if they are treated as employees many will work part time, with the consequent disadvantages described in Chapters 9.1 and 9.2. Homeworkers are likely to feel isolated and lacking in support, and the inherent fragmentation of their jobs geographically is likely to imply very low levels of unionisation. They can be subject to fluctuations in work and pay (which rarely offers benefits such as holiday pay) and suffer health hazards in terms of materials, equipment, or in the improper adaptation of the home as a workplace.

Traditionally, homeworking was low status, insecure work in manufacturing industry but today, less than a third of homeworkers in England and Wales are carrying out manufacturing jobs. In particular, working from home with new technology is on the increase, especially by women who have young children at home. The majority of new technology homeworkers are either applying computer programming skills or working for companies in the computing fields. Nevertheless, with women homeworkers having a history of earning less than the going rate and being exploited generally, there is concern that this new group may suffer a similar fate (Davidson, 1987; Davidson and Cooper, 1987).

Mention should also be made of the vulnerability of older workers. Though the naive outsider might very well assume that as workers become older, gaining experience and skill, they would become more valued, more highly prized, this is not the case. Age discrimination is common in the United Kingdom. A recent survey (Equal Opportunities Review, 1989a) found that of 11500 job advertisements monitored in the *Sunday Times, Personnel Management* and four London 'free' magazines, over 27% stated an age preference. A glance at one day's national newspaper by the present writers revealed nine job adverts specifying 'preferred' ages or an upper age limit, and in all but one, which stated 'You are probably about thirty-four to forty-two', the highest age mentioned was 35. In an era when even the highest paid jobs may be threatened by redundancy, such limitations must be dispiriting in the extreme. In addition, they fail to take account both of women returners, who are likely to have taken time off during their late twenties or early thirties, and of the growing numbers of people who do not see a job as a lifetime commitment and may wish, perhaps following retraining, to make a mid-career change.

In 1988 Philip Walker, a print manager who is now 55 and unemployed formed the Company Against Age Discrimination in Employment (CAADE). Of its 2000 members, 95% are former business executives, for many of whom divorce, ill-health and even suicide were the results of being unable to find employment. One senior manager who had been out of work for 14 months described his experience

> I started applying for jobs I could do standing on my head and eventually dropped my sights considerably. But after two hundred applications I had no joy whatosever . . . So far I've spent £3000 on chasing jobs to no avail . . . Last April I had a nervous breakdown out of frustration and fear of losing the roof over our heads . . . What angers me is that I'm a damn good marketing man with a lot to offer, but nobody will give me a chance to prove it because I'm over 50.
>
> (Silk, 1990)

Unlike the United States and Canada, the United Kingdom has no law expressly prohibiting discrimination on grounds of age, though age restrictions which adversely affect women as opposed to men may be unlawful under the Sex Discrimination Act 1975. An upper age limit of 35, for example, would disadvantage considerable numbers of women returning to work having taken time off to have families, and unless such restriction were justified by the employer, could constitute 'indirect discrimination'. The House of Commons Employment Committee recently ruled out legislation against age discrimination, endorsing instead the CBI view that persuasion is preferable to legislation (HMSO, 1989b). The CBI feels that the decline in the numbers of young people entering the labour market will force employers to seek recruits from older workers, and there are signs that this may indeed be the case. A number of organisations are taking steps to target their recruitment campaigns towards the more mature end of the population; Dixon Stores Group, for example, has introduced a national scheme aimed specifically at the over forties and Tesco is encouraging applications from those aged 55 or over. Even the Inland Revenue has raised the upper age limit for graduate recruits to the tax inspectorate from 36 to 52.

However, opening up jobs as cashiers in supermarkets is unlikely to be of much avail to the out-of-work business executives such as Philip Walker and other CAADE members. Yet the government, despite lobbying from pressure groups such as the Association for Retired Persons and Age Works, seems firmly set against legislation, and Private Members' bills to outlaw age discrimination have so far met with no success in Parliament. In refusing to take action, the government is arguably failing to abide by the 1980 International Labour Organization (ILO) Older Workers Recommendation which provides that members should take measures for the prevention of discrimination against older workers in employment.

Age may not be the only factor affecting a worker's chances of equality of opportunity. Those with a criminal conviction often find employers unwilling to take them on. While it may be difficult to criticise a bank for failing to hire a convicted embezzler as a teller, or to criticise a bus company which refuses to take on bus drivers who have driving offences, in many cases the refusal is based simply on prejudice. The conviction may have little, if any relevance to the ability to do the job. Furthermore, the Rehabilitation of Offenders Act 1974, which aimed to remove the stigma of conviction from those who subsequently 'went straight', by regarding a conviction as 'spent' after the appropriate rehabilitation period, has proved largely ineffective. In particular, its lack of enforcement provisions means that though it is unlawful to refuse to recruit (or to dismiss) a person on the basis of a spent conviction, that person has no legal remedy (see also Chapter 8.2, p. 246).

THE AIMS OF THIS BOOK

Employers have to discriminate. They have to make employment decisions which involve making choices between workers. In an ideal world such decisions would be based purely on merit, but in reality subconscious bias, financial considerations, industrial relations implications and, at worst, outright bigotry, may affect their views. This book seeks to explore the legal provision (or lack of it) which aims to protect or to provide for workers who are disadvantaged or discriminated against. It also highlights the psychosocial issues involved in the employment of 'vulnerable' workers.

The contributors to each chapter review the relevant contemporary up-to-date literature/case law and legislation and issues pertaining to their specific chapter subject. In some cases complete chapters will cover both psychosocial and legal implications whereas in others, chapters are divided into two, with different authors reviewing the psychosocial and legal issues.

CHAPTER STRUCTURE AND CONTENT

The book is divided into four main parts. Part I presents a cross-cultural perspective of vulnerable workers in the European Community and the United States. Part II concentrates on the psychosocial and legal issues relevant to two groups of workers who are particularly vulnerable in terms of physical and health disabilities, namely the disabled and sufferers of HIV and AIDS. Part III deals with three types of workers who are susceptible to physical or verbal abuse or victimisation generally, i.e. victims of violence at work, victims of sexual harassment at work, and homosexuals and transsexuals at work. The final part covers two groups of vulnerable workers whose numbers do not justify their commonly assigned 'minority' label, i.e. part-time workers and job sharers, and black and ethnic workers.

In Chapter 2, Gill Whitting questions the European Community (EC) attitude to vulnerable workers. Firstly, she outlines current EC objectives followed by the EC commitment with regard to equal treatment of men and women, the disabled, ethnic workers, social protection and social security, combating poverty, reducing unemployment, and the economic and social implications of migration. Clearly, the EC commitment to vulnerable workers is limited through the powers which the EC has to influence practices in the member states. However, where legislation is in existence, as is the case for equal treatment between men and women, she points out that the EC has more power over member states especially through the work of the European Court of Justice. For some sections of workers such as the disabled, EC migrants and women, the EC commitment is greater. Nevertheless, certain groups such as migrants and refugees from Third World countries are totally excluded. Moreover, the author believes the use of such avenues as the European Social Fund may fail to target successfully vulnerable workers, due to the fact that these groups are often identified in fairly broad terms, e.g. the 'long-term unemployed'.

In Chapter 3, Steven Willborn provides a psychosocial and legal perspective on vulnerable workers in the United States. This chapter proposes a method of analysis for identifying groups of vulnerable workers, discusses the psychosocial consequences of vulnerability, and reviews the legal protections provided to vulnerable workers in the United States. He asserts that compared to workers in other Western industrialised countries, workers in the United States have only limited employment protection rights. Furthermore, workers usually rely on unions to provide protection despite the fact that less than 18% of American workers today are members of unions. He also suggests that certain structural aspects of the labour market can directly or indirectly play a significant role in either increasing or decreasing the vulnerability of groups of workers. For example, the effect of the tax structure discourages married women from fully participating in the labour market; workers' compensation laws fail to create incentives for employers to protect workers from violence at work; and architectural barriers can act as a literal structural impediment for disabled workers. As is a common theme running throughout this book, in the United States legal protections directed towards vulnerable workers have been enacted in a haphazard way, both geographically and the way in which certain groups have been excluded.

In Chapter 4.1, Martin McHugh looks at the psychosocial issues surrounding the plight of disabled workers. Here, the terms disabled and handicapped are used interchangeably, although it should be noted that the term generally adopted in the United States is 'the disabled'. The concept of normalisation, i.e. when handicapped individuals are encouraged to participate in life as far as they are able on a normal, culturally valued basis, is a generally accepted desirable goal. Unfortunately, the social integration of handicapped people into the community has not always proved successful, due often to inadequate preparation. The author also points out that due to the stigma attached to certain disabilities such as drug addiction and psychiatric illnesses, it has been estimated that half those eligible never register as disabled, fearing that it would worsen their employment opportunities.

Methods concerning the preparation and evaluation of rehabilitation programmes are also reviewed, as well as the role of new technology and the disabled worker. The author then goes on to discuss the problems commonly experienced by the disabled ranging from emotional disturbances and accident proneness to interrupted schooling. Some of the major types of disability discussed include alcoholism, epilepsy, deafness, blindness, heart disease, motor deficits and severe learning disorders. Martin McHugh also makes the important observation that the economic recession and reduction in funding for certain training programmes sometimes results in them being abandoned and this can cause disabled individuals, such as the moderately handicapped, to regress to their former state of lethargy.

In Chapter 4.2, Brian Doyle discusses the legal issues raised by disabled employment. This also includes an examination of disabled workers' rights regarding equal treatment and employment opportunities, as well as an analysis of job security laws and employment protection affecting the group. Clearly, disabled people like many of the other vulnerable worker groups, suffer from both structural and institutional discrimination—a fact which both McHugh and Doyle believe should be more fully recognised by the population as a whole. Brian Doyle argues that legal reforms are necessary on three levels. Firstly, they should include a degree of positive action such as affirmative action planning, contract compliance, reasonable accommodation and outreach requirements, and equal opportunities audits. Secondly, as the experience in the United States illustrates, it may be necessary to undertake separate legislative interventions in order to guarantee disabled rights. Finally, he proposes a certain amount of reverse discrimination especially in relation to employment for the severely disabled. Here, he also refers to West German and French legislation which includes a role for reserved occupations and a strengthened quota system. None the less, he concludes that stronger legislation alone is not enough, and that political and economic power must also be utilised in order to enfranchise disabled workers.

Chapter 5 focuses on the most recently categorised groups of vulnerable workers, namely those who are HIV positive and workers with AIDS. In Chapter 5.1, Anna Stallard presents factual information about the virus and emphasises the present and future seriousness of the epidemic. She goes on to discuss the psychological and social consequences of having HIV, and the implications of being an HIV worker. Employees with HIV and AIDS may be susceptible to some form of impairment in their job performance and attendance.

Furthermore, psychological distress and social isolation can be enhanced by prejudice, ignorance and fear of AIDS. Not surprisingly, due to such problems, many HIV workers decide not to divulge their illness to their employer. However, she makes the important point that the period between becoming infected and becoming ill can be a very long period of time and indeed, an HIV positive employee may never become ill.

The author proposes important guidelines for employers in terms of individual counselling for HIV employees as well as staff training and education for his or her colleagues. She also recommends that a carefully drafted workplace policy on HIV could ensure appropriate action is taken. The last part of Anna Stallard's review concerns the role of the counsellor and HIV positive clients. It becomes obvious that counselling, guidance and education from an early stage (including initial testing) can be an important tool in helping to decrease the distress experienced by people who turn out to be HIV positive.

The legal issues surrounding AIDS employees are explored in Chapter 5.2 by Brian Napier. He discusses what specific legal protections are available in domestic law in terms of recruitment, conditions of employment and dismissal. Questions are posed such as whether measures to exclude from employment certain categories of high risk individuals of one sex (typically male homosexuals) will amount to unlawful discrimination against men as a whole. The rights and duties of an employer in respect of an employee who is found or suspected to be a carrier of the AIDS virus are also raised. The author concludes that the response of employment law to the AIDS phenomenon is far from clear. What is needed is for judges to provide authoritative guidance on how the law of contractual obligations, tortious liability and unfair dismissal will adapt to the particular problems related to AIDS. In addition, although Brian Napier views the prospect as unlikely, he believes in principle that there is no reason why legislation prohibiting discrimination against AIDS sufferers (actual and suspected), should not be enacted in Britain.

Chapter 6, which opens Part III on vulnerable workers in terms of victimisation, focuses on violence and vulnerability in the workplace. Kate Painter investigates the causes, extent and impact of violence upon employees as well as presenting some of the legal and social policies being adopted to prevent it. In particular, she concentrates on violence which occurs in the public sector and the impact of violence on working women—a highly vulnerable group.

All the evidence supports the contention that violence at work is on the increase. Besides a wide range of occupations being at risk, throughout the public sector certain groups of workers are more vulnerable to violent attacks than others. Even within the same professions, geographical location and specific job can heighten or decrease the risk factor. For example, a survey of social workers found that one in four working in inner city areas was assaulted at work each year compared to one in ten social workers as a whole. Furthermore, residential social workers were also more at risk of violence compared to their community counterparts. The author also illustrates how the impact of either threatened or actual violence has detrimental effects both for individual workers and the organisation.

While Kate Painter acknowledges that there are no simple solutions to preventing violence at work, she does outline a number of effective preventive strategies which are usually locally based and specifically focus on high risk employees and workplaces. These initiatives include recording and reporting procedures, training programmes which teach staff how to diffuse and contain violence, situational and social prevention such as security measures and victim support systems. In addition, she suggests that more use could be made of existing support networks.

Three possible legal responses to violence at work stemming from employment law are highlighted. These include the law relating to employment protection rights, the statutory duties placed on employers by the Health and Safety at Work Act and the employer's common law obligation to take reasonable care of an employee. However, like many other vulnerable groups, victims of violence appear to have scanty legal protection in practice. Kate Painter concludes that the real long-term solution lies in understanding the underlying causes of violence which must be seen in relation to the wider political and economic climate. In her words

> The last decade has not only seen an upward spiral in recorded and perceived risks of violence within the workplace, it has also been a time in which chaotic labour market practices and government policies have economically and socially marginalised whole sections of the population while simultaneously reducing the rights of those in work.
>
> (p. 177)

Kate Painter emphasises that women are vulnerable to violence in the workplace due to their powerlessness and sensitivity. As well as experiencing physical and non-physical violence, women experience sexual harassment and incivilities that men seldom encounter. Indeed, this issue is further developed in Chapter 7. David Terpstra and Douglas Baker in Chapter 7.1 examine some of the negative psychological/emotional, physiological/medical, social/interpersonal, and work-related outcomes experienced by the victims of sexual harassment. The events and processes leading up to these outcomes are also assessed with the aid of a model. This model for the study of sexual harassment includes the order and stages of investigation, namely—the antecedents of sexual harassment, behaviours exhibited by harassers, behaviours as perceived by harassers, immediate reactions of harassers, and finally psychological, physiological, social and work-related outcomes. As the review is limited primarily to US literature, a predominantly American perspective is presented.

These authors stress that the seriousness of the problem of sexual harassment and its negative effects both on victims and organisations, should not be underestimated. Individual victims of sexual harassment can experience a wide range of negative psychological and physiological outcomes while organisations can suffer due to the cost of reduced productivity, sick leave payments, and the costs of replacing employees who leave their jobs. In the United States, the costs to organisations due to litigation resulting from sexual harassment can also be high.

Not surprisingly, one of the proposed recommendations aimed at reducing the negative effects of sexual harassment includes stronger legislation. The authors suggest that the focus of future legislation might be directed more towards prevention, and a number of organisational and individual actions aimed at reducing the problem of sexual harassment are proposed (see also Davidson and Earnshaw, 1990).

In Chapter 7.2 Vivienne Gay writes about the past and future legal issues relating to sexual harassment. To date, in Britain no legislation specifically renders sexual harassment unlawful. Even so, some degree of judicial awareness of the existence of sexual harassment may be isolated, stemming from the overlap of the tort of assault and battery with the crime of assault. Despite a recent proposal by Michael Rubenstein to produce a Directive on sexual harassment, the European Parliament has only instructed the European Commission to draw up a code of practice on the issue, with a view to monitoring its adaption and effect—a move which the author suggests may be a 'form of benign cold storage'.

She recognises that the most recent development is in the application of the Sex Discrimination Act 1975 to make employers liable for their own acts and for the acts of their employees when a woman is subjected to sexual harassment, and examines this development in depth. While acknowledging the problems of proof associated with conduct committed when perpetrator and victim were alone together, Vivienne Gay states that tribunals have tended to believe women's complaints rather than accept their harassers' denials. However, from the point of view of obtaining an effective remedy, victims of sexual harassment need to show employer responsibility for the unlawful acts of the harasser. In view of the difficulties involved in proving that these acts were committed 'in the course of employment' such as to make the employer vicariously liable, she suggests a solution may be to bring an action against both harasser and employer jointly, alleging that the latter has 'aided an unlawful act' under s.42 of the

Sex Discrimination Act. Unlike the American experience, levels of damages have tended not to be high and the author emphasises the importance of support needed whenever an applicant brings a case in order to help decrease inevitable distress. Taking into account all of these issues, in the final analysis, she posits that there is now a clear, well-established legal route to a remedy for the employee who has suffered sexual harassment at work.

In Chapter 8.1 Celia Kitzinger investigates the psychological, social and personal/political issues related to being gay or lesbian at work. She explores the numerous problems associated with people who conceal their homosexuality at work as well as those who 'come out' and decide to disclose their sexuality. The reactions of heterosexuals to such disclosures are also highlighted with case study examples and the final section proposes ways of combating 'heterosexism' at work.

The author believes that heterosexism will not be alleviated by simply challenging individual attitudes but that employment methods and practices which discriminate against homosexuals need to be addressed by those responsible for organisational policies and personnel issues. Promotion and recruitment procedures should be examined, along with employees' contracts and conditions of service. For instance, pension schemes or relocation allowances often exclude a same-sex partner and compassionate leave is usually limited to the spouse and blood relatives of the employee. Indeed, she refers to one recent review of a large voluntary organisation which revealed 11 regulations in its written conditions of service which clearly excluded lesbians and gays from their provisions.

The author concludes that it is in the interest of *all* individuals irrespective of their sexual preferences to challenge heterosexism in and out of the workplace. Until anti-homosexuality is eradicated in the workplace, homosexuals will be subject to possible discrimination, threats and assaults and will continue to be 'vulnerable workers'.

In Chapter 8.2 Jill Earnshaw and Peter Pace write not only about the legal issues surrounding homosexuals at work, but also those which relate to transsexual employees. In Britain there is no legislation which outlaws discrimination on grounds of sexual orientation. In contrast, the authors note that a number of American state laws not only prohibit discrimination on sexual orientation but also on such criteria as personal appearance, and arrest record.

The widespread ignorance and prejudice surrounding homosexuality is often even greater in relation to transsexualism. When applying for a job, some employers insist on viewing birth certificates, a practice which could be a cause of great concern to transsexuals. As yet, there is no provision whereby in the United Kingdom transsexuals can apply for a revision of their birth certificate to accord with the desired gender. On an even more pessimistic note, a review of numerous industrial tribunal cases, reveals that dismissals due to sexual orientation certainly happen and unfair dismissal claims have a low chance of success. According to Earnshaw and Pace 'The present lack of legal protection for homosexuals and transsexuals cannot be justified!' (p. 256).

Part IV of this book deals with two groups of vulnerable workers whom we have categorised as belonging to the 'major' minorities. These are employees who while making up a substantial proportion of the workplace, are often labelled 'minorities' and tend not to enjoy equal employment rights and opportunities. In Chapter 9.1 Sonia Liff presents the current and future opportunities for part-time workers, 80% of whom are women who are likely to be married with dependent children. It seems ironic that while part-time work is the major area of job growth and employers are being encouraged to introduce more flexible working conditions in order to counteract demographic trends and skill shortages, part-timers are still disadvantaged.

Throughout this chapter the author takes the stance that the situation of women part-time workers can only be understood by presenting a gendered analysis of both the construction of jobs and employee relations. For example, she provides some mock definitions of what is commonly accepted as 'a proper job', e.g. around 40 hours per week with 'a proper wage' in the manufacturing sector and usually done by male workers. Hence, from these definitions, it is very difficult for women (particularly part-time workers) to be accepted as proper workers doing proper jobs.

She discusses the interdependence of part-time working and domestic commitments and argues that any attempts to adjust the domestic division of labour more equally, are undermined by the continuing *differences* between women's and men's hours of work. The limited availability of part-time work is seen as being instrumental in perpetuating occupational segregation by sex and subsequently hampering gains in 'equal opportunities'.

Although there appear to be some positive developments by employers in response to demographic trends and skill shortages associated with new technology, Sonia Liff concludes that they are generally not targeted at part-time workers. Part-time working continues to be available in sectors dominated by women. In addition, although more flexible hours, career breaks and in some instances childcare, are being introduced (particularly in the finance sector and the health sector), in some cases they are only available to women in the higher grades. While the unequal division of domestic labour in the home persists and employers continue to view part-time workers as low-status and less-committed employees not doing a 'proper job', she believes they will never attain equal opportunities as far as training, promotion and wages are concerned.

Patricia Leighton, in Chapter 9.2, addresses the legal vulnerability of part-timers and also questions whether job sharing could be the solution. The author points out that the tradition of deliberate exclusion of those working less than a fixed number of hours per week (mentioned earlier in this chapter) began in the mid-1960s with the first major protective statute, and she estimates that over 50% of part-timers presently have no legal protection in relation to unfair dismissal and redundancy payments. Furthermore, the author emphasises that managerial policies have also perpetrated the downgrading of part-timers. Part-timers have fewer occupational benefits such as pension schemes, holiday and sick pay and are often treated differently regarding recruitment and induction, social and fringe benefits and health and safety at work arrangements. However, on a more optimistic note, the author acknowledges that there has been a gradual improvement in occupational benefits and pressure has been increasing within the European Community through the European Social Charter, urging fairer treatment of part-time and temporary workers.

Finally, the process of establishing job share schemes is investigated from the premise that here is a part-time work option which could also provide opportunities and security comparable to full-time positions. In fact, in the United Kingdom, job sharing has increased rapidly during the past couple of years both in the private and public sectors. It becomes evident that while job sharing has not yet combated all of the disadvantages associated with part-time work, clearly there are a number of advantages. Unlike the majority of part-time jobs, job sharing can include senior positions and also present opportunities to challenge managerial assumptions. Research studies indicate that practical problems can often be overcome by individuals' commitment and motivation, and progress on organisation of the workload and occupational benefits has been great. Predictably, the author also maintains that adjustments to fiscal policies and legislation are needed and she doubts whether legal changes will proceed beyond the minimum of those required by the European Community.

Chapters 10.1 and 10.2 explore the experience of black and ethnic workers in the United Kingdom and the present and future legal issues. In Chapter 10.1 Paul Iles and Randhir Auluck examine issues related to black people (i.e. people of Asian, African and Caribbean descent) and employment and emphasise that the response from employers, academics and researchers in terms of these people's experiences has been limited. Particular attention is directed towards an analysis of employment patterns and variations in relation to black/white and male/female employees.

Around 4.6% of the British population of working age are black but unemployment rates are much higher for these workers compared to their white counterparts. The authors review a number of surveys of black workers which illustrate considerable disparities in pay and working conditions to the disadvantage of both black men and women. Recent studies also highlight the greater difficulties faced by black people in Britain in obtaining professional employment. Moreover, the authors make the interesting observation that findings in American studies of black managers resemble those often reported for white women managers in Britain.

The main organisational responses to the perceived constraints experienced by black employees are also considered in some detail. These initiatives include recruitment practices, performance appraisal schemes and positive action programmes. The authors conclude that what is needed is compatible change within all formal and informal structures and systems of organisations if black workers are to attain equal opportunities in all areas of employment.

In Chapter 10.2 Geoffrey Bindman questions where the law is going in relation to ethnic minority workers in the United Kingdom. He suggests that the legal protection required is not against unequal application of the law to ethnic minority workers in comparison to whites, but rather the need of legal protection against unequal treatment by others. Here, he includes employers and those in positions of power such as the police, estate agents and public authorities.

In common with all the other vulnerable groups of workers included in this book, unequal treatment of black and other ethnic minorities has been largely ignored by the law. In fact, it was not until 1965 that the first anti-discrimination law was introduced in Britain and it did not include employment. The Race Relations Act 1968 was the first statute which brought racial discrimination in employment within the scope of the law. Although the Act retained the Race Relations Board as the exclusive resource for the investigation and settlement of complaints, if a 'suitable body of persons' were available to investigate the complaint (an industrial body set up by unions and management), then it had to refer to that body instead of the Board. The author highlights the ineffectiveness of this system and the law was re-modelled in the Race Relations Act 1976. The new framework filled several loopholes and also introduced three new principles which included an equal right to sue (i.e. a victim could take legal proceedings in the ordinary courts of law), it included indirect as well as direct discrimination, and it gave the new Commission for Racial Equality (CRE—which replaced the Race Relations Board) much wider powers of investigation.

A review of a number of studies indicates that this law has not dramatically reduced discrimination. As well, the author notes that to date, there have been no more than a few hundred individuals a year gaining redress or being rescued from the consequences of discrimination by the law. He suggests that the limited impact of the law has been reflected in the build-up of tensions and existence of unsatisfied grievances in relationships between black youths and the police in particular communities such as Brixton.

Geoffrey Bindman concludes that the objectives of the anti-discrimination law have largely not been met. He feels that the price of discrimination for the employer has to be made far more costly both in terms of facing a serious risk of being found out and subsequent high financial penalties. In his view, the greatest weakness of the 1976 Act is the complexity and ultimate futility of the CRE's formal investigative powers. Even the CRE's constructive recommendations are only of value to ethnic minority workers if they receive backing of a government which is prepared to put them into effect. Unfortunately, the author illustrates that not only has the present British government's attitude been totally negative, but it is unwilling to consider a new, more effective Race Relations Act. Geoffrey Bindman hopes that either the present or the next government will introduce a new Race Relations Act which he would prefer to be even tougher than the one suggested by the CRE.

CONCLUSION

The contributors to this book have made a number of very important recommendations to improve the long-term plight of vulnerable workers. As Steven Willborn states in his review of the situation in the United States, while vulnerable workers will probably always exist, there are numerous ways in which their vulnerability, and the negative psychological and social consequences of vulnerability, can be reduced. Where vulnerable groups lack protection from discrimination such as the victims of AIDS, or the disabled, contributors see no reason why legislation outlawing such discrimination should not be passed. Others recommend alterations to existing law, for example to give part-timers employment protection rights on a par with their full-time colleagues. And for some, the answer is to be found in tougher sanctions so that financial considerations, if not humanitarian ones, will make the price of discrimination too high.

Of course, legislation alone is unable to redress completely the vulnerability of certain individuals in the labour market. Legislation needs to be backed up by codes of practice giving guidance on how to make the law a reality, and by equal opportunities policies which are clearly thought out and put effectively into practice. Without the commitment of management to such policies and to the initiation of training programmes dealing with, for example, the needs of the disabled, methods of handling violence at work or how to avoid subconscious bias in employment decisions, the law's penetration can only be slight.

Nor is this enough; education at a much earlier stage of a person's life is necessary if the vicious circle of ignorance and prejudice is to be broken. Pressure for a change in traditional assumptions and practices has already been brought to bear by the impact of European Community law and the decisions of the European Court of Justice. The European Community Social Charter emphasises the importance of combating every form of social exclusion and discrimination. We believe the evidence presented in this book, illustrating the plight of vulnerable workers, clearly advocates that the British government can no longer continue to resist EC powers to make the Charter operative. What is needed is both more rational and comprehensive legal protection for vulnerable workers backed up by strong commitment from national governments; political and economic power must be forthcoming and utilised in order to influence the attitudes, understanding and behaviour of employers and work colleagues.

REFERENCES

Cooper, C.L., Cooper, R.D. and Eaker, L.H. (1988). *Living with Stress*, Penguin Books, London.

Davidson, M.J. (1987). Women and employment. In P. Warr (ed.) *Psychology at Work*, pp. 223–46, Penguin Books, London.

Davidson, M.J. and Cooper, C.L. (eds) (1987). *Women and Information Technology*, Wiley, Chichester.

Davidson, M.J. and Earnshaw, J. (1990). Policies, practices and attitudes towards sexual harassment in UK organisations, *Personnel Review*, **19**(3).

Employment Gazette (1989). May.

Equal Opportunities Review (1989a). Age discrimination: over the hill at 45? *EOR*, **25**, 10.

Equal Opportunities Review (1989b). Working for race equality at Leicester City Council, *EOR*, **25**, 15.

Hepple, B. (1986). Restructuring employment rights, *Industrial Law Journal*, **5**(2).

HMSO (1989a). *Disabled Adults: Services, Transport and Employment.*

HMSO (1989b). *Employment Committee Second Report: The employment patterns of the over 50s*, Vol. 1.

HMSO (1989c). *New Earnings Survey*, Part A.

Leighton, P. and Painter, R. (eds) (1987a). Vulnerable workers in the UK labour market: Some challenges for labour law, *Employee Relations*, **9**(5).

Leighton, P. and Painter, R. (1987b). Who are vulnerable workers? *Employee Relations*, **9**(5), 3–8.

Silk, B. (1990). Pressing for a new deal to fortify the over 40s, *Sunday Times*, 7 January 1990.

PART I

Vulnerable Workers: A Cross-Cultural Perspective

Chapter 2

Vulnerable Workers: What is the European Community Commitment?

Gill Whitting, ECOTEC, Research and Consulting Ltd, Birmingham, UK

INTRODUCTION

This chapter provides an overview of the European Community (EC) commitment to vulnerable workers. The first part of the chapter is a brief introduction to current EC objectives; the second part outlines, under seven main headings, the EC commitment to vulnerable workers:

- Equal treatment of men and women
- Independence for people with disabilities
- Social protection and social security
- Combating poverty
- Reducing unemployment
- Other employment and unemployment measures
- The economic and social implications of migration

The third part discusses some of the main limitations of this commitment. As far as possible, the chapter will refer to the groups of workers discussed in later sections of this book: workers with physical and health disabilities; vulnerability in terms of victimisation; part-time workers (mainly women); and ethnic workers.

The views expressed are those of the author and do not necessarily reflect the opinions of the European Commission or other Community institutions.

Vulnerable Workers: Psychosocial and Legal Issues. Edited by M. J. Davidson and J. Earnshaw

CURRENT EC OBJECTIVES

The EC enters the 1990s with the primary aim of completing the Internal Market by 1992. It is anticipated that the location and nature of work will undergo certain changes and that these changes will generate economic and social costs which will fall upon particular geographical areas and population groups. The Commission of the European Communities (CEC) warns that progress towards the Internal Market is likely to involve new patterns of 'social exclusion and marginalisation'; the 'appearance of new forms of poverty'; and the consequential development of 'pathological social behaviour' (European Commission, 1988). However, it is difficult to predict precisely how the Internal Market will affect the labour market, and the consequences for those in work or seeking work across the 12 member states. In any case, the factors that contribute to vulnerability with respect to work are *not necessarily new*. Currently there are approximately 44 million people living in poverty in the EC (O'Higgins and Jenkins, 1989), and 10% unemployed (Labour Force Survey, 1988). These are indications of the extent of deprivation and discrimination that many population groups experience.

Other demographic and social trends will also begin to have an impact on the relative position of groups of workers. For example, the predicted decline in the population and the changing demographic structure may increase the possibility of a new immigration policy in order to boost the numbers of workers necessary to sustain the required level of economic activity. The growing number of single parents (mainly women) will result in varying socio-economic circumstances for this group with varying demands for full-time and part-time work. A predicted increase in the number of people suffering from AIDS may also place at risk a significant number of workers (see COM (88) 268 Final).

There is no evidence to suggest that those who are vulnerable now—ill or disabled people, migrants and refugees, black and other minority ethnic groups, part-time workers, lone mothers, the low paid—will fare any differently under the terms and conditions of the Internal Market post-1992. The emphasis on increased worker mobility and flexibility for the employer may intensify the competition for jobs and worsen the position for those who are already vulnerable. Or, demands on the labour market may create new opportunities for workers who are currently vulnerable to precarious employment or even unemployment. Two factors are clear, however. Firstly, the groups of workers who are vulnerable within the EC are by no means homogeneous; secondly, the consequences of the Internal Market and the outcomes of current demographic, social and economic trends will not be uniform. These pose particular problems for the kinds of strategies and responses to deal with vulnerability.

VULNERABLE WORKERS: AN OVERVIEW

Despite the EC's solid *economic* foundation and rationale, thc CEC, as one of the social partners, has argued for *social* cohesion to ensure the success of the completion of the Internal Market. The Commission is particularly concerned to reverse the trend towards the polarisation of geographical areas and population groups and to reduce inequalities. The commitment to vulnerable workers is expressed through a variety of measures, for example, legislation, financial assistance, action programmes, networks, the funding of research, and so on. In some instances these are components of one broad policy as is the case for the EC's commitment to equal opportunities: the psychosocial and legal commitments are expressed in a broad action programme comprising both legislation and parallel positive action. Policies and actions for disabled workers depend more on non-legislative measures to promote recruitment, training and good practice. Some of the main laws, programmes and actions that target vulnerable workers are discussed below. These cover equal treatment of men and women, independence for people with disabilities, social protection and social security, combating poverty, reducing unemployment, and the economic and social implications of migration.

Equal Treatment of Men and Women

The EC's commitment to equality between men and women goes back to Article 119 of the Treaty Establishing the European Economic Community, with subsequent legislation based on the Social Action Programme of 1974 which aimed to achieve 'equality between men and women as regards access to employment and vocational training and advancement as regards working conditions, including pay . . . and to ensure that the family responsibilities of all concerned may be reconciled with job aspirations' (Council Resolution, 21.2.74).

In legal terms, the EC's commitment to equal opportunities is founded upon three main equality Directives (Docksey, 1987): the Equal Pay Directive adopted in 1975 was designed to implement the principle of equal pay for men and women; the Equal Treatment Directive adopted in 1976 guarantees the principle of equal treatment for men and women in access to employment, vocational training and promotion, and working conditions; the 1978 Directive concerns the progressive implementation of the principle of equal treatment for men and women in statutory social security schemes. Two futher Directives have been adopted in 1986; to extend the principle of equal treatment to occupational social security schemes, and to men and women in self-employed occupations including agriculture, and the protection of self-employed women during pregnancy and maternity. The Commission drafted a Directive on Parental Leave and Leave for Family Reasons; this is before the Council of Ministers and has not been adopted owing mainly to the opposition of the UK government to legal intervention in this area (Moss, 1988). A Draft Directive was also prepared on Voluntary Part-time and Temporary Work but again this has so far been unsuccessful. There is also a proposal for a Directive on the burden of proof in the area of equal pay and equal treatment for women and men. This has not been adopted, due to opposition from the United Kingdom. In addition, the Commission has been asked in a study on sexual harassment to prepare a Directive on the prevention of sexual harassment at work which would have as its aim protecting workers against the risk of sexual harassment and encouraging employers to establish and maintain working environments free of sexual harassment. However, in the Commission's view, sexual harassment is contrary to the already-existing Equal Treatment Directive, but it felt that a code of practice on the subject would be advisable.

The Commission oversees existing legislation and develops current policy through the establishment of Community Action Programmes on the Promotion of Equal Opportunities for Women. The First Programme ran from 1982 to 1985. As well as monitoring the existing legislation, it introduced the concept of positive action in favour of women. The current programme, the Medium Term Community Programme on Equal Opportunities for Women 1986–1990, is developing the same themes. The work of the Action Programmes is described below. These address both the legal and psychosocial issues with respect to women as vulnerable workers.

The Commission's First Programme covered two types of action (CEC, Women of Europe, No. 9): one aimed at strengthening the rights of the individual, as a means of achieving equal treatment; the other at the practical achievement of equal opportunities, particularly by means of positive action. The following actions were included:

- Reinforcing and monitoring application of the Directives
- Legal redress in respect of equal treatment
- Revision of national and Community protective legislation
- Equal treatment in matters of social security
- Application of the principle of equal treatment to self-employed women and to women in agriculture, particularly in family enterprises
- Taxation and the employment of women
- Parental leave, leave for family reasons
- Protection of women during pregnancy and motherhood
- Integration into working life
- Vocational choices
- Desegregation of employment

- Analysis of trends in female employment
- Application of the principle of equal treatment to women immigrants
- Sharing of occupational, family and social responsibilities
- Development of public attitudes

One of the results of the First Programme was the setting up of a network of independent experts from all member states to monitor the practical and legal implementation of Directives, and to note obstacles and cases of discrimination. There are now five networks working under the Second Action Programme. These cover the application of the equality Directives, women in the labour force, the diversification of vocational choices, childcare, and women in local employment initiatives. Apart from these networks, a number of other expert groups cover areas such as women in broadcasting, positive action, and equal opportunities in education and training.

The Commission considered it necessary to maintain these actions and the objectives for the Second, medium-term Programme were defined as follows (CEC, Women of Europe, No. 23):

— to consolidate rights under Community law, particularly by improving the application of existing provisions and adopting the proposals under examination;
— to follow up and develop action launched under the 1982–85 Action Programme, in particular the networks for contacts and exchanges which represent a new form of social dialogue in this area, and which have made a very positive contribution;
— to intensify efforts to involve all those concerned through a broader dialogue and a consciousness-raising campaign aimed at the people involved and at a wider target public;
— to develop and intensify support for specific actions, in particular those intended to develop women's employment;
— to develop and adopt such action, in particular with regard to the most vulnerable and/or disadvantaged categories;
— to examine the situation in the new member states of the Community;
— to continue and strengthen positive action at the level of Community staff policy.

The Commission is currently concentrating on seven main actions: improved application of existing provisions, education and training, employment, new technologies, social protection and social security, sharing of family and occupational responsibilities, and increasing awareness and changing attitudes.

One of the recent developments is the huge growth in take-up of an EC start-up grant for women wishing to create their own businesses or local employment initiatives. This was introduced in 1983 under the First Action Programme. An essential condition for eligibility is that the business supported must create *jobs and incomes* for women (CEC V/1476/87).

Independence for People with Disabilities

Since 1981—the United Nations International Year of Disabled People—the Commission has developed within one programme, a range of actions which contribute to the ideal of independent living. A Bureau established in May 1982 oversees policies and actions in favour of disabled people. The first EC Action Programme for Disabled People was launched in 1983. The Programme itself pursues three main objectives:

- — to encourage policy development, and wherever possible to take a lead in this by means of a planned series of policy initiatives;
- — to establish a Community-wide system for the acquisition and exchange of information on disability problems, using new technology for this purpose;
- — to promote and facilitate innovation, the exchange of experience and the dissemination of good practice, with particular attention to the activities of associations of disabled people, to the work of rehabilitation professionals, and to services and cooperations undertaken at local level.

A network of 19 district projects was established as a major part of this First Programme. Actions involved a wide range of local agencies.

With reference to disabled people as workers, the Council of Ministers has adopted, as one of the first policy measures emanating from the Bureau, an employment recommendation. The recommendation proposes that a wide range of interdependent measures is required in the employment sector, for example, quota legislation (see Chapter 4.2 dealing specifically with disability) and incentives to employers to recruit disabled people. Parallel initiatives emphasise the role of research, the development of information systems and greater participation by disabled people in the development and implementation of policies. The recommendation includes a Model Code of Positive Action.

The Commission has also considered the relations that exist between employment, vocational rehabilitation and social security schemes. The Commission insists on the principle that 'Rehabilitation comes before benefit'; this implies an insistence on the need to develop coherence between employment policy and benefit policy in the disability field. The Commission is convinced that there are possibilities to reduce the number of disabled people dependent on social security by modifying social security schemes or by improving their application. These possibilities include the adoption of more preventive actions, the removal of disincentives and a clearer statement that individuals have a right to vocational rehabilitation (*Social Europe*, 1986).

The latest stage in the work on disability is the Second European Community Action Programme for Disabled People. It is known as the HELIOS Programme: 'Handicapped People in the European Community living Independently in an Open Society' (HELIOS, 1989). It aims to continue, develop and expand the work of the first programme. The objectives specify the development of a Community approach based on the best innovatory experience in the member states. One of the priorities concerns transport problems for people with restricted mobility. Other policy proposals will concern access to public buildings, school integration and the impact of new technology. HELIOS is continuing to develop the dialogue and exchange of information between non-governmental organisations at a Community level.

The vocational needs of disabled women and the needs of carers are identified as groups requiring special attention.

Social Protection and Social Security

The EC's role in social protection is limited to, firstly, identifying the issues of common concern, and secondly, *coordinating* what member states are doing. There is considerable opposition by member states within the current economic climate, to consider *harmonising* social protection schemes across the Community. Nevertheless, the Commission is concerned that beyond the 1990s, with the completion of the Internal Market, the economic and social climate will require a greater *approximation* of social protection schemes.

The Commission has selected three social security problem areas of interest to all member states: the financing of current or projected needs in terms of social protection expenditure; the implications of demographic trends; and the increasing problem of marginalisation affecting a considerable number of people in the member states. The Commission recognises the interdependence of these problems.

'For society to take charge, through its social protection schemes, of the social risks arising from economic changes resulting from the restructuring of the labour market (unemployment and social exclusion) or the consequences of the ageing of the population (in terms of expenditure on health care for the elderly and aged, pensions and new services for this category) would inevitably lead to a considerable increase in compulsory social charges' (Com 87/230 Final).

On the basis of the existence of common interests, the Commission recommended that member states proceed with a discussion at Community level on the objectives to be fixed for social protection schemes beyond the 1990s. These are the common interests (Com 87/230 Final):

(1) *Financing* Social security schemes are under pressure from two quarters: the growth in expenditure resulting from persistent high unemployment, and changing demographic structures, which are increasing the pressure on old-age and sickness insurance sectors. The flow of incoming revenue is also slowing down. Governments have been forced to impose higher compulsory levies, the bulk of which is used for social protection. Not only the amounts of compulsory social charges are being criticised but also the way in which these charges are levied. Social security contributions are calculated and paid on the basis of wages received, leading to higher labour costs and possibly even contributing to unemployment. Alternative ways of raising money have so far proved to be elusive, although various types of financing have been considered. These include: the relative importance of taxes and contributions linked to value added/direct/indirect taxation; the effects of alternatives on the labour market; the implications for business (particularly small businesses); the financial stability of different schemes; the likelihood of fraud; the effects on the redistribution of income; the funding of pensions (instead of financing from current income).

(2) *Demographic problems* Birthrates are declining and this is likely to continue. There is no current policy to increase the immigration rate. If current trends are maintained, the population of the Community will cease to grow in about 15 years time and then begin to decline slowly. The increases in the proportion of old people will continue slowly for another 20 years and accelerate sharply from 2005 to 2010 onward.

   The short-term consequences may mean less public expenditure on young people but an increase in expenditure, particularly on health, for older people. There are a number of uncertain economic effects on the level and structure of consumption and changes in the volume and quality of savings and investment.

   Long term, the ageing of the working population will produce strains as regards the cost of labour, a decline in geographical and vocational mobility and a sharp drop in the rate at which the active population is renewed. There may be a need for a migration policy in the more distant future.

(3) *Marginalisation* Budgetary restrictions often lead public authorities to exclude young unemployed persons, at national or local level, from

social protection or to restrict the duration or level of entitlement for other categories of unemployed persons. Another hard-hit category is that of working people, aged over 50, who are the first to lose their jobs as a result of industrial restructuring. Public assistance schemes are no longer in a position to take over where social security schemes leave off.

The Commission also associates marginalisation with the increasing instability of the family situation. In the absence of individual rights, social protection which is based on the rights enjoyed by the 'spouse', is threatened when marriage breaks down, with consequences for children.

The Commission also recognises that large groups in the population are insufficiently aware of their rights, how to exercise them and how to get assistance from appropriate authorities.

Combating Poverty

The EC's Second Programme to Combat Poverty drew to a close at the end of 1989; a 'third' follow-on programme 'to foster the economic and social integration of the least privileged groups' is now in operation (Com (88) 826). The Second Programme, an action research programme, was organised around a number of theme groups. The groups included the long-term unemployed, the young unemployed, elderly people, single parents, migrants, urban and rural areas, and a 'marginals' groups that focused mainly on homeless people. The Programme comprised 91 funded projects carrying out activities and services to combat various forms of poverty (Room, Laczko and Whitting, 1990).

The follow-on programme is not structured in the same way. The major part of the resources will be allocated in the first instance to 'geographical areas'. Projects have been selected for their capacity to demonstrate *integrated* strategies to combat poverty in all its widely varying aspects. The intention is to support high risk groups in the selected geographical areas for a period of five years.

Reducing Unemployment

One of the Community objectives established by the Single European Act is that of strengthening economic and social cohesion, in particular by reducing disparities between the various regions and the backwardness of the least-favoured regions (Cmnd 372, 1988). This includes the achievement of equalisation between levels of employment in the various regions. Regional unemployment rates range from 3% to over 30%. Over the last 10 years, the unemployment rate in the Community has remained almost constant at around 11% of the labour force. The unemployment rate for those under 25 years is over 22%; 50% of unemployed workers have been unemployed for more than one year, and 30% for more than two years (European Commission, 1988). The EC main measures to strengthen economic and social cohesion are the Structural Funds. These are the European Regional Development Fund (ERDF), the European Social Fund (ESF) and the European Agricultural Guidance and Guarantee Fund (EAGGF).

All three funds have undergone substantial reform as part of the progress towards 1992 (Com (88) 500 Final). There are five priority objectives for the Funds:

- Promoting the development and structural adjustment of the less developed regions (objective 1).
- Converting the regions, frontier regions or part of regions (including employment areas and urban communities) seriously affected by industrial decline (objective 2).
- Combating long-term unemployment (objective 3).
- Facilitating the occupational integration of young people (objective 4).
- With a view to the reform of the Common Agricultural Policy, speeding up the adjustment of agricultural structures (objective 5a) and promoting the development of rural areas (objective 5b).

The ESF is more specifically targeted towards vulnerable groups. It is essentially a job-training and job-creation fund which can finance operations concerning: vocational training, recruitment and wage subsidies, resettlement and social or vocational integration for geographically mobile workers, and services and technical advice concerned with job creation. The ESF will contribute uniquely to objectives 1, 2, 3, 4 and 5b but its main activities will be concerned with the long-term unemployed (objective 3) and young people aged between the compulsory school-leaving age and 25 (objective 4).

With respect to long-term unemployment, the ESF is called on to assist training for those affected, to strengthen the link between training and labour market requirements, to influence the labour market through subsidies for recruitment or creation or self-employed activities, and to make available information and counselling.

With respect to the unemployment of young people, ESF measures also emphasise the need to combine training with work experience and to encourage initiatives aimed at promoting training for new qualifications. Under the new guidelines, schemes will be given preferential treatment if they target population groups, or categories of workers, experiencing special difficulties in the labour market. Three special categories are cited:

— the integration of disabled people in the open economy;
— integration of women in occupations where they are substantially under-represented; where operations are carried out for them in connection with initiatives by public or private bodies supplementing general operations carried out by the member states in the context of the national vocational training system;
— training of migrant workers in the three years following their immigration, or to facilitate their return to a member state.

Other Employment and Unemployment Measures

The pursuit of employment objectives at Community level through specific policies has taken a variety of forms. These include legislation, policy guidelines, direct actions through programmes, cooperation between member states and information and exchange systems (Employment in Europe, 1989).

Legislation is important in relation to certain aspects of employment policies covered by the Treaty. The principal areas concern the free movement of people (see p. 36), the assurance of equal opportunities between men and women (see earlier discussion), health and safety at work, and some aspects of contractual employment relationships.

Policy guidelines have addressed many of the problems of employment and unemployment including the special problems experienced by young people, the long-term unemployed and women in the labour market.

A range of action programmes exist, dealing both with employment issues and training or education. Two programmes directly targeted on employment problems are a local employment development programme, LEDA, and an action programme against long-term unemployment, ERGO.

Cooperation between the member states is facilitated through regular meetings of the Directors-General of Employment of the member states, and the equivalents responsible for vocational training. The core of the Community's effort in the field of vocational training is the pursuit of its responsibilities under the Treaty of Rome (Article 128) to lay down general principles for the implementation of a common training policy.

The Community's ability to monitor and analyse trends in employment and to exchange information of all kinds is assisted through a range of documentation and information systems. These include MISEP, ELISE, EURYDICE and SEDOC. The employment implications of the Internal Market are the focus of a new intitiative called SYSDEM: European System of Documentation on Employment.

The Economic and Social Implications of Migration

The rights of workers to move freely within the EC is enshrined in the Treaty Establishing the European Economic Community, and subsequent Community legislation. Directive 68/360 abolishes restrictions on movement and residence within the community for workers of member states and their families. Workers also have a right to remain in a member state after having been employed there (Regulation 1251/70). *Guaranteeing* the conditions for the free movement and equal treatment of workers is a major principle of completing the Internal Market. Workers includes all workers who transfer within the Community including manual workers, professionals; those unemployed are (for the most part) not covered. Four basic principles underly the coordination of social security schemes in all member states:

(1) Equality of treatment covering both contributions and rights.
(2) Totalisation and aggregation of insurance periods across different member states where relevant.
(3) Payments of benefits, although unemployement and health benefits are not exportable.
(4) Determination of which legislation is applicable (the legislation belonging to which member state). This is to avoid duplication, on the one hand, and no entitlement, on the other hand.

While it is hard to foresee any further harmonisation of social protection insurance and benefits, there is an attempt to coordinate what member states are doing to assist the freedom of movement for workers.

Migrant women

A vastly different situation exists for migrant women entering the EC whose rights, in the majority of cases and in the majority of countries, are derived from those of their husbands. The relevant legislation normally relates to workers, whereas women migrate as family members and dependants. For this reason, migrant women are particularly vulnerable in fields such as employment, vocational training and welfare provisions and family law (*Social Europe*, 1988). The Commission is addressing the needs of migrant women as part of its Action Programmes on Equal Opportunities. It has been possible for the Commission to take stock of the legal and administrative forms of discrimination in respect of access to employment for immigrant women, the measures put forward by the member states of the Community as regards training, and the position of immigrant women in the labour market.

Racial discrimination

The EC prohibits discrimination on grounds of nationality. The European Parliament held a special inquiry into Racism and Fascism which resulted in a Parliamentary Resolution in January 1986. This led to the first ever 'joint declaration' between the Council of Ministers, European Parliament and Commission in June 1986. It expressly condemns all forms of racial discrimination and calls on governments to take preventive measures (Drury, 1987).

EXTENT AND LIMITATIONS

The EC commitment to vulnerable workers raises three sets of issues:

(1) The political and financial possibilities of influencing the position of vulnerable workers within member states.
(2) The extent and success of *targeting* by EC policies and programmes of action.
(3) The concept of 'integrated action' and implications for vulnerable workers.

Political and Financial Possibilities

The EC has certain powers by which it can seek to influence the policies of member states; member states have certain rights of 'sovereignty' that preserve their independence. In Community law, vulnerable groups such as migrant workers who have lost their jobs, or women who feel they are being unequally treated, are able to assert their rights in the knowledge that EC legislation exists to protect them. But even when legislation exists, the strength of the commitment will depend on how successfully the laws have been applied and implemented within a member state, and how far the EC can perform a role in extending the actions of a member state (Meehan and Whitting, 1988). The United Kingdom provides a good example. In the early stages of implementation, the European influence on the development of British sex discrimination and equal pay legislation was relatively weak. More recently the European Court of Justice has played a major role in confirming and extending the UK policy commitment (McCrudden, 1987).

In other spheres of social policy, for example social protection and social security, where legislation is limited to *coordination* rather than *harmonisation*, the differences across the Community must be taken into account. There are differences between the 'North' and the 'South' of the

Community, between countries and between regions. Social security systems are not so well developed in some countries as they are in others. For example, it may be a tradition in southern countries for the 'family' to provide social security where formal systems are lacking. Individuals who lose the security of family networks will become particularly vulnerable. In these countries, social security measures are not at a stage of development that invites or assists change. The role of the family is one way of evaluating the stage of development. But there are many other factors that also influence the impact of EC measures: the relationship between central and local government in managing benefits, the role of the private or voluntary sectors, the extent of decentralisation for policy responsibility, and so on.

The Commission is aware that social protection policies have dramatic effects on the lives of individuals and particular social groups; moreover, the trends in social security provision, for example in the United Kingdom, are leading to greater marginalisation of the poor. Social protection will continue to be high on the agenda of the European Commission. But measures in this area have to be formulated in relation to EC employment and labour market strategies, equal treatment and anti-discrimination policies, anti-poverty programmes and policies, and the development of family policies. The implementation structures for achieving change across the Community, in the longer term, are still a matter for debate. The case for a guaranteed minimum income, community wide, is a part of this broader policy discussion (O'Higgins, 1988).

There is also a financial aspect to commitment which raises the question of whether it is possible to assist vulnerable workers given that the size of the resources available is minute in relation to the scale of the problem. While this has to some extent been addressed with respect to the Structural Funds where quite substantial budgets have been doubled in the process of reform, the increased sums proposed for the EC's Third Action Programme for least privileged groups remain small relative to the problem. The management of both the European Social Fund and the 'Third Programme' referred to above relies on the availability of matching funds which is not always forthcoming in all countries. There are considerable differentials here. For example in countries where local government is weak, local projects find it harder to attract the necessary matching funds.

The future role of the EC in committing resources to assist vulnerable workers will, in part, depend on the relative importance given to social policy in the progression towards 1992. The first issue relates to the analysis of economic and social change. To what extent does the understanding of inequality take account of economic and social factors? The Commission, among others, is arguing strongly that European integration requires the *development of economic and social policies in tandem* in order for the Internal Market to be completed. For example, vulnerable workers will be assisted to take part in the process of integration through the development and targeting of special measures in employment, training and social protection. The second issue goes a stage further by considering the *unintended consequences* of the Internal Market for those workers who become vulnerable and who would benefit from social policies. There is strong opposition by some countries, including the United Kingdom, to accept that integration requires the development of policies other than economic policies; indeed, arguments are made by the UK government that social measures would *impede* progress towards European integration. The attitude of the UK government is at the forefront of the debate over the Community Charter of Basic Social Rights for Workers—'The Social Character' (*Social Europe* 1/90).

The Extent and Success of Targeting

A main component of the EC commitment to vulnerable workers is the identification of population groups and the targeting of legislation, actions and resources. Examples include the European Social Fund, principally aimed at the long-term unemployed and the young unemployed; the second European Programme to Combat Poverty which included five population groups; and the special measures developed within the programme of initiatives for disabled people. Given the critical importance of current EC policy developments, the time is ripe to ask whether these groups are the right ones—is there a more effective way of allocating resources—and what factors determine successful targeting? Who are the vulnerable workers within the EC? Is the EC committed to some groups more than others? What are the trends in the way resources are targeted?

High unemployemnt and changes in the labour market have undermined the ability of societies to protect their weaker members. This has affected disabled people, women bringing up children on their own, migrants and refugees, the 'settled' black population and other minority ethnic groups. Young people are also at particular risk. Many are now chronically dependent on social assistance and basic welfare. Other social trends, combined with forms of discrimination and harassment present within the workplace, place pressures on gays and lesbians, workers suffering from AIDS, and workers (mainly women) who experience sexual advances and abuse. This list however glosses over the variation of circumstances—in socio-economic status, in culture and ethnicity, in ability and disability, in experience—and subsequently of needs. To what extent can the EC commitment address this heterogeneity, given that the member states themselves are also heterogeneous and at various stages of social, economic and political development?

This chapter shows that the EC is more sensitive to particular population groups: for example women, disabled people, migrants are frequently targeted. There is minimal commitment to workers who are gay or lesbian, to workers with AIDS, to elderly workers, to travellers, and to workers made redundant towards the end of their working lives. The question of discrimination against 'homosexuals' in the workplace is not specifically provided for under the Treaty; the Commission has indicated to the European Parliament that complaints by gay or lesbian workers, or their organisations, should be addressed to the authorities responsible for the protection of human rights (*Official Journal*, C317/38). Community action against AIDS includes preventive work, medical and health research and an EEC/ACP technical and financial aid programme (COM (88) 268 Final).

The differences within population groups, for example in relation to women—the varying needs of single women, older women, migrant women, lone mothers—are addressed by the EC through research and, where finances permit, through the programmes of action. The challenge to the development of EC equal treatment legislation is to embrace the varying definitions and uses in the practical application of the law.

The success of targeting resources does however rely on the way in which population groups are identified. For example, research has revealed the different histories and experiences of lone mothers (Millar, 1987). Lone mothers comprise women who have never married, women whose husbands have died, and divorced and separated women. In addition to cultural, religious or ethnic differences, these groups will have varying access to income, housing, childcare, social services, and so on. Well-targeted services are those that are tailor-made to suit the characteristics and social well-being of a population group. For example, the single parent projects in the Second Programme to Combat Poverty included training schemes run especially for lone women, with children, who were living in poverty. The training schemes were successful because they met the psychosocial needs of participant women—the schemes felt 'safe' because they did not emphasise 'failings' and 'weaknesses'—and because they provided essential childcare and were conveniently timetabled (Whitting and Quinn, 1989).

The EC commitment to migrant workers is an example of targeting that excludes certain black and minority ethnic groups because of different histories and patterns of migration, even though they too experience severe forms of discrimination within the labour market. The imperative for the EC is to enhance geographical mobility within the EC and to protect workers and their families who migrate between member state countries. Workers who migrate to the EC from outside the EC do not have access to the same rights. The term 'migrant' also excludes the 'settled' black communities, for example the black population who have lived in the United Kingdom (e.g. in Liverpool) for hundreds of years, but who none the less suffer from deprivation and discrimination. A further and growing category is the number of Third World refugees, men and women, arriving in the EC. Given the preoccupation with 1992, one of the fears is that groups in the population will be carefully categorised according to changing economic needs: 'This most privileged group are the citizens (people with permanent rights), followed by denizens (people with legal status of a temporary nature) and, at the bottom, the helots, undocumented workers with no rights' (Alibhai, 1989).

Another way of discussing the outcomes of EC policy commitment to vulnerable workers, in this case the use of the European Social Fund, is to assess how equally the resources are in practice allocated across the member states. To date, the resources of ESF have principally been used by a small number of countries and mainly the early entrants to the Community. The current changes in the use of the ESF will to some extent address these past inequalities. Future allocations will be based as much on the needs of geographical areas as on the needs of population groups; the trend is also to target most resources on groups defined by unemployment status, e.g. long-term unemployed and the young unemployed, rather than groups in the population defined by their socio-economic status, e.g. lone mothers, disabled people, migrants. Women, disabled people and migrants are special categories (see p. 35) but this consideration is rather secondary to the main priorities.

Conceptual and Organisational Policy Issues

As the EC moves towards 1992, with the primary aim of enhancing economic and social cohesion, greater emphasis is being given to integrated *area* development. One example is the way in which the Structural Funds are being concentrated on the most deprived regions of the EC. The aim is to combine resources and to coordinate actions so as to meet the economic and social demands of member states. Plans are being prepared by member states in conjunction with regional and local tiers of government; these will be discussed and agreed by the Commission. These policy developments place an emphasis on geographical areas, as the basis for resource allocation, that may have consequences for meeting the needs of vulnerable groups of workers. The effectiveness of the Commission in policy development also depends, to a major extent, on the financial resources and staffing at its disposal, which are already severely stretched in many of the areas discussed in this chapter.

Both the European Social Fund and the proposals for the Third Action Programme 'for least privileged groups' give a greater priority to area deprivation than before. The success of integrated operations will depend on the plans that are negotiated and agreed between various levels of government and the Commission. But in certain countries, the opportunities for groups and organisations at the local level to participate may be absent. For example, local organisations may not have the level of organisation and contacts to enable them to participate in the planning machinery, or they may not be invited to do so. These organisations may include the individuals and projects that are in touch with the circumstances and needs of vulnerable workers. Not all countries have governments, or planning powers, that are able to provide data and information about local labour markets and vulnerable workers; in these circumstances, the problems of targeting those vulnerable in the labour market may increase. In theory, the moves towards integrated area development can involve participative action, not only in the carrying out of projects but also in the conceptualisation and planning of strategies. The EC may have to make a commitment to *community development* as well as economic development to ensure that the views of marginalised groups are included in integrated development policies and programmes (Whitting, O Cinneide, Mylonakis, 1989).

CONCLUSIONS

The EC commitment to vulnerable workers is expressed through legislation, programmes of action, financial grants, the funding of research, the creation of networks, and various measures to promote good practice. The limitations of this commitment arise primarily through the powers which the EC has to influence practices in the member states. This is particularly so for those policy areas, e.g. income maintenance, that remain the responsibility of national governments in member state countries. Where EC legislation exists as is the case for equal treatment between men and women, the EC is able to exert greater influence over member states particularly with the assistance of the European Court of Justice. The EC commitment is more developed for some groups of workers, e.g. women, EC migrants and disabled people. Other groups are excluded, e.g. migrants and refugees from Third World countries, or their needs are hidden, e.g. migrant women who *derive* rights from their husbands. The success of targeting vulnerable workers, for example, through the use of the European Social Fund, may be reduced because groups are identified broadly by unemployment status: the young unemployed, the long-term unemployed, rather than distinguishing between socio-economic circumstances. Research into the situation of vulnerable groups illustrates the heterogeneity of circumstances and needs which can be used to support arguments for more specific targeting, e.g. young homeless people, or for recognising the existence of 'double' discrimination, e.g. black women caring for children on their own. However, there is a trend within the policies of the Community—integrated area development—which gives a high priority to the inequalities between regions rather than between communities and individuals. It is not clear how, in practice, policies and actions for *areas* will filter down to the individuals and communities who live in those areas. The EC may need to make a greater commitment to community development to ensure that the interests of vulnerable workers are included in these plans of action and expenditure. For the future, the EC commitment to vulnerable workers may depend on the emphasis given to social policy as a means of achieving European integration in the longer term. The adoption recently of the Social Charter by the European Council (8.12.89) is a landmark in the further development of an EC social policy. And the Commission has also pressured its Action Programme relating to the implementation of the Social Charter. Legislation is especially important in this regard; without it EC powers are dependent on the decisions of national governments and *their* views on the social dimension of the Internal Market and *their* commitment to population groups who are marginalised or excluded from mainstream society.

REFERENCES

Alibhai, Y. (1989). Community Whitewash, *Guardian*, 23 January.

CEC V/1476/87, *Women's Local Employment Initiatives*.

CEC, Women of Europe, No. 9 : *Equal Opportunities—Action Programme 1982–1985*.

CEC, Women of Europe, No. 23.

Cmnd 372 (1988). *The Single European Act*, HMSO.

Com (800) 500 Final, Back-up policies: Reform of the structural funds.

Com (87) 230 Final, Problems of social security—Common interests in the member states.

COM (88) 268 Final, *Community Action Against AIDS in 1987*, 17 May.

Com (88) 826 Final, Establishing a medium-term community action programme to foster the economic and social integration of the least privileged groups.

Council Resolution 21.2.74 establishing a Social Action Programme, Official Journal 1974, C13/2.

Docksey, C. (1987). The European Community and the promotion of equality. In McCrudden (ed.) *Women, Employment and European Equality Law*, Eclipse.

Drury, E. (1987). *European Community Policies and Actions of Relevance to the Second EC Programme to Combat Poverty*, Working Paper No. 30, Centre for the Analysis of Social Policy, University of Bath. August.

Employment in Europe (1989). Directorate General V, CEC.

European Commission (1988). 1148, *The Social Dimension of the Internal Market*, September.

HELIOS (1989). *CEC Programme for Disabled People*, First Magazine of the HELIOS Programme.

Labour Force Survey (1988). EUROSTAT.

McCrudden (ed.) (1987). *Women, Employment and European Equality Law*, Eclipse.

Meehan and Whitting (1988) (eds) Gender and public policy, Special issue of *Policy and Politics*, **17**(4).

Millar, J. (1987). Lone Mothers. In Millar and Glendinning (eds) *Women and Poverty in Britain*, Wheatsheaf.
Moss, P. (1988). *Consolidated Report of the European Childcare Network*, CEC.
Official Journal C 317/38, Written Question No. 1/88 on the subject of discrimination against homosexuals at the workplace.
O'Higgins, M. (1988). Horizon 1992 and the Guarantee of a Minimum Income, paper to a European Seminar CRESGE/EEC, Tilques, October.
O'Higgins, M. and Jenkins, S. (1989). Poverty in Europe, Paper presented at EUROSTAT Seminar on poverty statistics, Nordwijk-an-Zee, The Netherlands, October.
Room, G., Laczko, F. and Whitting, G. (1990). *Action to Combat Poverty*, Final Report, University of Bath, Centre for the Analysis of Social Policy.
Social Europe (1986). Supplement No. 7.
Social Europe (1988). Supplement No. 2.
Social Europe 1/90, Special Issue on the Social Charter.
Whitting, G., O Cinneide, S. and Mylonakis, D. (1989). In Diana Robbins (ed.) *Integrated Area Development and the Mobilisation of Local Resources*, Working Paper No. 40, University of Bath, Centre for the Analysis of Social Policy.
Whitting, G. and Quinn, J. (1989). Women and work: preparing for an independent future. In Meehan and Whitting (eds) Gender and public policy, op. cit.

Chapter 3

Vulnerable Workers in the United States: A Psychosocial and Legal Perspective

Steven L. Willborn, University of Nebraska, USA

INTRODUCTION

Vulnerable workers, like the poor, will always be with us. But vulnerable workers are especially visible in the United States today. During the Reagan years, the working poor—those who remain below the poverty line even though they work regularly—constituted a steadily increasing proportion of the working population. This chapter will discuss the status of vulnerable workers in the United States. The chapter will propose an analysis for identifying groups of vulnerable workers, discuss the psychosocial consequences of vulnerability, and review the legal protections provided to vulnerable workers in the United States.

IDENTIFYING THE VULNERABLE WORKER

Worker vulnerability is a relative concept. Under a broad definition, all workers are vulnerable. Workers are subject to such a variety of hazards, ranging from relatively minor irritants (such as inconvenient working hours) to major calamities (such as the loss of a job), that no worker can feel completely immune. And the hazards strike very broadly. One out of every six American workers in 1986 was unemployed for at least one week—and 1986 was not a bad year economically (Mellor and Parks, 1988). The hazards can strike even workers who seem relatively well protected, as workers in the automobile and meat packing industries learned during the recession in the early 1980s (Freeman and Medoff, 1984, pp. 55–7).

Workers in the United States enjoy only quite limited protection from most of the common vulnerabilities, certainly as compared to workers in

Vulnerable Workers: Psychosocial and Legal Issues. Edited by M. J. Davidson and J. Earnshaw

other Western industrialized countries. Workers often rely on unions to provide protection. In the United States, however, less than 18% of workers today are members of unions, fewer than at any time since 1936, and less than 25% are covered by collective bargaining agreements (Summers, 1985; Willborn, 1988). The protections provided by unionization cover a much higher proportion of workers in other countries. In Sweden, for example, 90% of blue collar workers and 80% of white collar workers are represented by unions and in Australia 88% of all workers are represented by unions (Flanagan, 1987; Mitchell, 1984).

Workers in the United States also receive fairly limited protection from the government. This is evident not only from the shop floor, but also from the ivory tower. From the shop floor, basic protection that is commonly provided by statute in other countries, such as protection from unjust discharge or the right to take parental leave, is only beginning to gain a precarious acceptance in the United States (Gould, 1988; Maternity Leave Policies, 1988; Dowd, 1986; Estreicher, 1985). From the ivory tower, the most prestigious journals publish articles calling for a radical non-involvement by the government in labor relations (Epstein, 1983, 1984).

But even within a country like the United States where workers in general are fairly vulnerable, or perhaps especially in such a country, there are certain groups of workers who are particularly vulnerable. Minorities, women, the disabled, homosexuals and transsexuals, part-time workers, older workers, victims of violence at work, and other groups are even more subject to workplace hazards than others.

Vulnerable workers can be identified analytically by focusing on three interacting factors. First, a group's level of vulnerability depends on the ability of employers to distinguish at low cost between group members and non-members. Employers might distinguish between group members and non-members based on personal characteristics (e.g. on the race and sex of workers); on where the work is done (e.g. homeworkers); on the hours of work (e.g. part-time workers); or even on characteristics of the employer itself (e.g. employees of small employers and agency workers). If a group has a tendency to be vulnerable based on the other factors discussed below, one would expect the level of vulnerability of groups which are easy for employers to identify (minorities, for example) to be greater than the level of vulnerability of groups which present distinguishability problems (homosexuals, for example).

A group's level of vulnerability also depends on ideas or preconceptions about the group that might cause employers (or others) to discriminate against the group. A group would be vulnerable, for example, if employers had a taste for discrimination against that group (Becker, 1971) or if the productivity of the group was lower than the productivity of other groups from which employers might hire and information on individual productivity was expensive to obtain (Arrow, 1972, 1973). Indeed, a group would be vulnerable even if the actual productivity of the group was equal to or greater than the productivity of other groups, if employers *thought* the productivity of the group was lower than the productivity of other groups and it was expensive for the employer to obtain information on actual productivity (Phelps, 1972; Arrow, 1973). The level of vulnerability of a group depends on the commonness and intensity of these types of ideas or preconceptions about the group. For example, if the taste for discrimination against homosexuals were greater than the taste for discrimination against other groups, homosexuals may be more vulnerable than other groups despite the difficulties in determining group membership.

Finally, a group's level of vulnerability depends on structural aspects of the labor market. Certain groups of workers may be vulnerable because the labor market is structured in ways that are disadvantageous to them. Disabled workers may be vulnerable, for example, if workplaces are physically inaccessible to them. Or female workers may be vulnerable if tax laws discriminate against secondary earners within families (who are disproportionately female) or if the availability of childcare is limited (because women disproportionately are expected to be the primary caretakers of children) (Davis, 1988; Bloom and Steen, 1988). Thus, even if employers cannot or do not care to distinguish between vulnerable group members and non-members and even if employers do not explicitly discriminate against a vulnerable group, the group may be vulnerable if the structure of the labor market presents special impediments to full participation by group members.

The level of vulnerability created by the interplay of these three factors can be assessed by comparing the treatment of groups in the labor market. Black workers in the United States, for example, appear to be more vulnerable than other workers based on a number of labor market indicators. Compared to other workers, black workers are paid less, the non-monetary characteristics of their jobs are less desirable, their employment rate is lower, and their unemployment rate is dramatically higher (Jencks *et al.*, 1988; Mellor and Parks, 1988; National Committee on Pay Equity, 1987). Thus, with respect to black workers, the labor market seems to indicate that black workers are distinguishable from other workers at a low cost, that the disadvantageous ideas or preconceptions about them as workers are fairly common and/or intense, and that there are structural aspects of the labor market that are disadvantageous to them.

This type of analysis promises to provide guidance on legal strategies that might protect vulnerable workers. The analysis can do a good job of isolating groups of workers who need protection and then the law can be used to counteract the three factors that in combination cause the group to be vulnerable.

PSYCHOSOCIAL CONSEQUENCES OF VULNERABILITY

The psychosocial consequences of vulnerability are, in part, surprising. As this section will indicate, the social consequences of vulnerability are not surprising. Vulnerable workers generally receive lower pay and have higher rates of unemployment and these social effects, in turn, create other undesirable social consequences, such as reduced access to medical care and lower health levels. But the psychological consequences of vulnerability do not match up so easily with one's intuitions. Studies on the effect of vulnerability on psychological health indicate that there are some adverse consequences, but that the consequences are less widespread than one would expect.

The social consequences of vulnerability are a result, in large part, of the labor market consequences of vulnerability. These labor market consequences are perhaps most visible in terms of the pay vulnerable workers receive for their work. As the following examples indicate, vulnerable workers earn less than other workers. For full-time, year-round workers in 1986, for example, the earnings of women were 64.3% of those of men and the earnings of black men (70.7%), black women (56.8%), Hispanic men (64.8%), and Hispanic women (53.4%) were all significantly less than the earnings of white men (National Committee on Pay Equity, 1987). Older data for the disabled indicate that the median annual earnings of the severely disabled and mildly disabled were 33.4% and 77.5%, respectively, of those of persons who were not disabled. The economic disadvantages of the disabled do not disappear if monies received from government support programs are added to their earned income. In 1978, the total incomes of the severely disabled and mildly disabled were 52.9% and 81.2%, respectively, of the total income of persons who were not disabled (Burkhauser and Haveman, 1982). The earnings of part-time workers are also indicative of vulnerability; the median hourly earnings of men and women working part time in 1979 were 51.2% and 80.7%, respectively, of the equivalent earnings of full-time workers (US Department of Labor, 1983). Although statistics on the relative earnings of all vulnerable groups cannot be presented here because of space limitations, the statistics here and later in this chapter are representative of the labor market treatment of other groups of vulnerable workers.

The focus on the earnings of vulnerable workers relative to other workers both understates and overstates the labor market disadvantages of vulnerable workers. Relative earnings understate the disadvantages of vulnerable workers because they generally do not include portions of the compensation package which may be even more disadvantageous to vulnerable workers. Reports of earnings, for example, generally do not include the value of vacation and sick leave, employer-provided health and life insurance, or employer contributions to pension plans. Some vulnerable workers, such as part-time workers, are often not eligible for these types of compensation at all or receive them in reduced amounts (Blau and Ferber, 1986), while others, such as women and minorities, receive less of this type of compensation, in part because they work disproportionately for firms and in industries with low benefit levels (Rothstein, Knapp and Liebman, 1987). Moreover, earnings do not include benefits that, properly speaking, are not a part of the compensation package at all, but that nevertheless are real economic benefits. For example, the chances for promotion of some vulnerable workers are much less than the chances of other workers either because of the type of job held by vulnerable workers (e.g. part-time workers) or because of the personal characteristics of vulnerable workers (e.g. older workers) (Blau and Ferber, 1986; Hall, 1986).

The focus on earnings, however, may also overstate the labor market disadvantages of vulnerable workers. Economic theory predicts that the earnings of groups will be equal only if the groups are equally productive (Becker, 1971). Thus, if vulnerable workers are less productive than other workers, the gross difference in earnings between vulnerable workers and other workers may overstate the labor market disadvantages of vulnerable workers to the extent that the difference is caused by lower productivity. Studies that have been done on the relative productivity of vulnerable workers, most notably studies on women and the disabled, indicate that a portion of the difference in earnings between vulnerable workers and other workers is due to productivity differences, but that most of the difference cannot be explained in terms of productivity (Willborn, 1986; Burkhauser and Haveman, 1982; Treiman and Hartmann, 1981).

The labor market disadvantages of vulnerable workers, then, cannot be quantified precisely. Nevertheless, there is no doubt that vulnerable workers are subject to identifiable, significant, and roughly quantifiable labor market disadvantages.

These labor market disadvantages translate into other types of social disadvantages. Since most people in the United States obtain health insurance through their employment, the labor market disadvantages translate into lower access to the health care system. And lower access to the health care system translates into lower health levels, sometimes shockingly lower health levels. Black babies in the United States, for example, are three times as likely as white babies to be born to a mother who has had no prenatal care and are more than twice as likely to die during the first year of life (National Urban League, 1989). The labor market disadvantages also translate into other less tangible, but no less real, social disadvantages. For example, work that is identified with an individual vulnerable worker is evaluated more harshly (Treiman and Hartmann, 1981) and jobs that are dominated by vulnerable workers have less prestige than other jobs (Bose, 1985).

Vulnerable workers, then, are socially disadvantaged not only in relation to material well-being and its direct by-products (such as improved health), but also because of the manner in which they and their work are treated by others, because they and their work do not receive the respect and dignity that they deserve.

The labor market disadvantages of vulnerability do not translate so directly into psychological disadvantages. Certainly, there are psychological disadvantages to vulnerability. Victims of violence at work experience a variety of negative psychological reactions including depression, anxiety, increased stress and loss of job motivation (Terpstra and Baker, 1988). And unemployment, which is suffered disproportionately by vulnerable workers, causes poorer psychological health including symptoms such as anxiety, depression and insomnia (Brenner and Bartell, 1983; Warr, 1983; Jahoda, 1981). Moreover, several studies indicate that job stress is likely to be a more severe problem for vulnerable workers than for other workers. For example, several studies indicate that women, one group of vulnerable workers, are more likely to suffer from stress and that working in low-level jobs, which are held disproportionately by vulnerable workers, tends to increase stress levels (McLaughlin, Cormier and Cormier, 1988; Russell, Altmaier and Van Velzen, 1987; Jick and Mitz, 1985; Shamir, 1980).

At the same time, however, there are indications that vulnerable workers are healthier psychologically than one would expect them to be based on their position in the labor market. Research on the relationship between occupational characteristics and job satisfaction establishes that pay, occupational control (e.g. autonomy, responsibility, supervisory status), and occupational complexity (e.g. skill level, lack of repetition) are all associated with higher levels of job satisfaction. Increases in these job characteristics are also associated with a reduction in adverse psychological symptoms such as depression, anxiety, and neurotic illness. (For a review, see Adelman, 1987) Since vulnerable workers disproportionately hold positions with low levels of pay, control and complexity, one would expect their levels of job satisfaction and psychological health to be relatively low. But that is not the case. Bokemeier and Lacy (1986), for example, found that, although women were paid less than men and worked under less desirable working conditions, there was no difference in job satisfaction between men and women. Other researchers have found that part-time workers, despite their many disadvantages in the labor market, exhibit levels of job satisfaction that are equal to or greater than the levels exhibited by full-time workers (Eberhardt and Shani, 1984; Logan, Reilly and Roberts, 1973). Similar findings have been reported for minority workers and older workers (Pond and Geyer, 1987; Landy, 1985). This apparent anomaly is explained by the lower expectations of vulnerable workers. Vulnerable workers accept and are satisfied with smaller rewards than other workers; as a result, their level of job satisfaction is higher than one might expect and that tends to protect them from some of the psychological disadvantages of vulnerability (Major, 1987).

Vulnerable workers, then, exhibit some adverse psychological symptoms that seem to flow from the effects of their vulnerability. But vulnerable workers in general seem to enjoy a psychological hardiness that one would not expect given their employment circumstances.

VULNERABLE WORKERS AND THE LAW

Vulnerable workers, and indeed all workers, are significantly affected by a wide range of laws, including many that are ordinarily thought to be fairly tangential to the workplace. As a result, the legal structure of the workplace must be viewed broadly to encompass the effects of all these laws on vulnerable workers. This broad view, however, is especially difficult in the United States because employment law in this country is so fractured. Legislative bodies at the federal, state and local levels have enacted literally hundreds of laws to regulate various aspects of the employment relationship and state courts in the past few years have increasingly applied common law concepts to employment issues creating 50 new common laws of employment. This multitude of sources for employment law results not only in a complex of overlapping, and sometimes conflicting, substantive requirements, but also in a maze of procedural requirements and a variety of possible remedies. As one commentator put it, employment law in the United States is changing 'from a troublesome thicket to an impenetrable jungle' (Summers, 1988). The jungle will be partially pruned in this chapter by focusing on the groups of vulnerable workers that are emphasized in this volume: disabled workers, workers with AIDS (including workers with the HIV virus or AIDS-related complex), women (especially as victims of sexual harassment), homosexuals, part-time workers, workers who suffer from violence at work, and ethnic minorities.

Interfering With the Ability to Distinguish Between Group Members and Non-Members

Since a group's level of vulnerability depends, in part, on the ability of employers to distinguish at low cost between group members and non-members, one way in which the law can protect vulnerable workers is by making it more difficult for employers to make that distinction. The ability of the law to do that effectively, of course, depends to some extent on the nature of the particular vulnerable group. For some groups, such as women and ethnic minorities of the groups we are considering, employers can make the distinction between group members and non-members without explicit enquiry, so it is more difficult for the law to interfere with the employer's ability to distinguish (although as we shall see it is still possible to do so in a limited way). For other groups, such as workers with AIDS and homosexuals, it is difficult for employers to make the distinction without explicit enquiry, so potentially the law could be quite effective. For still other groups, such as part-time workers, the distinction between group members and non-members is in important respects a function of the law, so the law could be very effective in reducing vulnerability.

For groups such as women and ethnic minorities, the ability of the law to make it difficult for employers to distinguish between group members and non-members is fairly limited. Nevertheless, there are ways in which the law can make it marginally more difficult for employers to distinguish. In hiring, for example, large employers could be required or encouraged to exclude identifying information from the paper record of applicants upon which hiring decisions are made. (In the United States, most employers are required to maintain records of the race and sex of their applicants, but those records can be maintained separately from the record upon which the hiring decisions is made.) In that way, decision makers who do not meet applicants personally (e.g. decision makers who initially screen applicants on the basis of their résumés) would be less likely to be able to distinguish between group members and non-members. In the United States, many employers utilize some variant of this type of hiring process, not because the law requires it directly (although it could), but because the law creates incentives indirectly to do so. That is, the law imposes significant costs on employers that discriminate against women and ethnic minorities and this type of procedure reduces the likelihood of discrimination (and its consequent costs) at some stages of the hiring process. Nevertheless, the value of this type of mechanism is fairly limited primarily for two reasons: (1) even without an explicit indication, in many cases decision makers in the hiring process will be able to distinguish between group members and non-members based on other information in the record, such as the name of the applicant or where the applicant lives; and (2) the mechanism can be used only in fairly limited circumstances, e.g. it generally cannot be used with respect to promotions because the decision makers are too familiar with the candidates, or by small employers.

When it is difficult for employers to distinguish between group members and non-members, the law can be effective in reducing vulnerability by enhancing that natural difficulty. This group is perhaps best exemplified by workers with AIDS (including workers with the HIV virus or AIDS-related complex). In the United States, there are at least four types of legal regulation that, even though not always promulgated primarily for this purpose, have the effect of making it difficult for employers to identify workers with AIDS. First, laws in every state that protect the confidentiality of the physician–patient relationship in general, make it difficult for employers to obtain information on workers with AIDS (Zelin, 1986). Second, there are laws in at least two states (California and Wisconsin) that specifically protect the confidentiality of AIDS tests. Third, there are statutes in at least three states (Florida, Massachusetts and Wisconsin), ordinances in several municipalities (e.g. San Francisco), and several court cases (especially with respect to public and unionized employers) that make it illegal for employers to test employees or applicants for AIDS (Achtenberg, 1987). And fourth, there are a variety of laws that make it illegal for employers to discriminate against workers with AIDS. (These laws will be discussed later in this section.) As discussed in the previous paragraph, these laws create incentives for employers to refrain from attempting to identify workers with AIDS. The incentives, however, should be more effective with respect to workers with AIDS because the factors that limit the effectiveness of this process with respect to women and ethnic minorities are not as likely to be present. In sum, since the vulnerability of workers with AIDS depends in part on the ability of employers to identify them, all of these legal impediments help to reduce the vulnerability of workers with AIDS.

Homosexuals are another group of vulnerable workers that employers have difficulty in identifying. In fact, homosexuals would seem to pose greater identification difficulties for employers than workers with AIDS because there is no medical test available that employers can use to make the distinction. Nevertheless, the laws in the United States make it easier for employers to identify homosexuals than workers with AIDS and, indeed, perhaps easier than to identify women and ethnic minorities. The reason for this is that the laws prohibiting discrimination against homosexuals are much more limited than the laws protecting any of these other groups. (The laws and their limitations will be discussed later in this Chapter.) As a result, employers do not have the fairly strong incentives that are present with respect to other groups to refrain from asking about the sexual preferences of workers or from seeking to find out in other ways. Although workers do have the option of attempting to hide their sexual preferences by lying if employers ask, exercising that option does not lead to the most comfortable of working environments and the lying itself may be cause for discharge if discovered, even in jurisdictions where it is illegal to discriminate on the basis of sexual preference (*Jimerson* v. *Kisco Co., Inc.*, 542 F.2d 1008 (8th Cir. 1976)). These differences in the identifiability of homosexuals and workers with AIDS, both vulnerable groups that pose identification problems for employers, emphasize the important role the law can play with respect to this contributing factor to vulnerability.

For other groups of vulnerable workers, such as part-time workers, some of the significant distinctions between members and non-members are direct functions of the law. Part-time workers are vulnerable in large part because several of the legal protections enjoyed by other workers are not extended to them. In the United States, for example, part-time workers are not entitled to the same protection as other workers under laws such as the Equal Pay Act that requires equal pay for equal work, the Fair Labor Standards Act that establishes minimum wages, and the Employee Retirement Income Security Act that requires employer-sponsored pension plans to meet certain minimum standards (Chamallas, 1986; Coleman, 1985). The definition of part-time worker in statutes such as these is a direct product of the law; it is either contained in the statute itself and/or in regulations or cases interpreting the statute. There are, of course, other ways in which part-time workers are vulnerable. In the United States, employers are generally not required by law to provide health insurance or vacation or sick leave for any employees and yet employers generally do provide those benefits for full-time employees, but not for part-time employees, based on the employer's own definition of full- and part-time work. The law could be very effective in reducing these types of vulnerabilities by modifying the definitions of part-time work that are direct products of the law and by restricting the ability of employers to draft their own definitions in other areas.

In summary, vulnerability can be reduced by making it more difficult for employers to distinguish between members and non-members of vulnerable groups. There are many ways in which the law can be fashioned to do this, but the effectiveness of laws with this aim depends to a considerable extent on the nature of the vulnerable group.

Protecting Vulnerable Groups from Discrimination

Another way in which the law can protect vulnerable groups of workers is by attempting to shield them from the discrimination that results from disadvantageous ideas or preconceptions about the group. In the United States, and elsewhere, this has been the most common use of the law to address the problems of vulnerable workers. But this type of protection has not been extended equally to all groups of vulnerable workers.

Of the groups emphasized in this volume, women and ethnic minorities receive the most extensive protection. At the federal level, Title VII of the Civil Rights Act of 1964 makes it illegal for an employer to discriminate against either of these groups. Thus, if an employer thinks that women as a group are less productive workers than men, Title VII makes it illegal for an employer to discriminate against women based on that preconception except in the rarest of circumstances. Title VII forbids not only employer actions based on an explicit or implicit intention to discriminate against women or ethnic minorities ('disparate treatment' discrimination), but it also makes it illegal for an employer, even in the absence of an adverse intention, to use criteria for making employment decisions that disproportionately exclude women and minorities from consideration unless the criteria are justified by good business reasons ('disparate impact' discrimination). (The most important disparate treatment cases are *McDonnell Douglas Corp.* v. *Green*, 411 U.S. 792 (1973) and *Teamsters* v. *United States* 431 U.S. 324 (1977). The most important disparate impact cases are *Griggs* v. *Duke Power Co.*, 401 U.S. 424 (1971) and *Wards Cove Packing Company, Inc.* v. *Atonio*, 109 S.Ct. 2115 (1989)). For a good general review of Title VII and of other less important federal laws protecting women and minorities from discrimination, see Sullivan, Zimmer and Richards, 1988.

Literally hundreds of state and local employment discrimination laws supplement the protections of Title VII for women and ethnic minorities, often filling in gaps in the protection provided by federal law. An important limitation of Title VII, for example, is that it only applies to employers that employ 15 or more employees. Thus, only about 20% of all employers and 85% of all employees in the United States are covered by Title VII (Report of the President, 1988). Most of the state and local employment discrimination laws extend to smaller employers, thus expanding the protections of women and minorities. Under the state laws, for example, employers in Minnesota and Wisconsin are covered if they have at least one employee, in New York if they have at least four employees, in California if they have at least five employees, and in Massachusetts if they have at least six employees. All but three states have employment discrimination laws protecting women and/or ethnic minorities; most states have more than one law (Dean, Roberts and Boone, 1984). In addition, hundreds of local ordinances have been enacted which prohibit employment discrimination against women and minorities.

The treatment of women under the employment discrimination laws has often posed special problems. These problems have generally been resolved in a way that eases the vulnerability of women to some extent, but fails to protect them completely. Consider, for example, the problem of sexual harassment in the workplace. In a 1986 case, the United States Supreme Court accepted an expansive definition of sexual harassment: Sexual harassment is 'unwelcome' sexual advances or verbal or physical contact of a sexual nature (*Meritor Savings Bank* v. *Vinson*, 477 U.S. 57 (1986)). The Court rejected the defendant's claim in the case that since the plaintiff had voluntarily had sexual intercourse with her supervisor, the supervisor's advances had not constituted sexual harassment. The Court said the correct enquiry was not whether the plaintiff's actual participation in sexual intercourse was voluntary, but whether the advances were unwelcome. But the Court also said that to be actionable under Title VII, sexual harassment either had to affect directly a term or condition of the victim's employment (e.g. it had to result in the loss of a promotion or pay rise) or it had to be sufficiently severe or pervasive to create an abusive working environment. Moreover, in sexual harassment cases alleging an abusive working environment, an employer could avoid liability if it had an acceptable policy against harassment and adequate procedures for pursuing violations of the policy. Thus, although women in the United States receive significant protections from sexual harassment, the Supreme Court at the same time leaves women legally vulnerable to conduct which, under its own definition of the term, *is* sexual harassment. Other important issues for women, such as issues relating to pregnancy and wage discrimination, have also been resolved by reducing, but not eliminating, the vulnerability of women (*California Federal Savings & Loan Association* v. *Guerra*, 107 S.Ct. 683 (1987); *Wimberly* v. *Labor and Industrial Relations Commission*, 107 S.Ct. 821 (1987); *American Nurses Ass'n* v. *Illinois*, 783 F.2d 716 (7th Cir. 1986)).

A generous interpretation of Title VII would provide protection for homosexuals and transsexuals that is equivalent to the protections received by women and ethnic minorities. Title VII prohibits employment discrimination based on 'sex' and homosexuals have argued that that term should be interpreted so as to encompass sexual preferences as well as biological sex. To date, however, every federal court that has addressed the issue has ruled that homosexuals and transsexuals are not protected by Title VII's ban on sex discrimination (*DeSantis* v. *Pacific Telephone and Telegraph Co.*, 608 F.2d 327 (9th Cir. 1979)). State laws that prohibit sex discrimination in employment have also been interpreted so as not to extend protection to homosexuals and transsexuals (*Gay Law Students Association* v. *Pacific Telephone and Telegraph Co.*, 24 Cal. 3d 458, 595 P.2d 592 (1979)). As a general matter, then, employers in the United States can discriminate against homosexuals and transsexuals. There are, however, a few areas of the country where this type of discrimination is prohibited. Wisconsin is the only state with a law prohibiting discrimination against homosexuals and transsexuals and there are two to three dozen local ordinances that cover this type of discrimination (Pearldaughter, 1979). In addition, although there is still a great deal of uncertainty in the area and the Supreme Court has indicated that it is not likely to be sympathetic (*Bowers* v. *Hardwick*, 478 U.S. 186 (1986)), the Constitution *may* prohibit public employers from discriminating against homosexuals and transsexuals (*BenShalom* v. *Marsh*, 703 F.Supp. 1372 (E.D. Wis. 1989); *Watkins* v. *U.S. Army*, 847 F.2d 1329 (9th Cir. 1988), withdrawn en banc, 875 F.2d 699 (9th Cir. 1989)).

Disabled workers, like homosexuals and transsexuals, receive protections from a patchwork of federal and state laws and local ordinances. At the federal level, the most significant legislation is the Rehabilitation Act of 1973. The Rehabilitation Act in some ways provides fairly generous employment protections for workers with handicaps. The Act contains a broad definition of the protected class. The Act's protections apply to 'individual[s] with handicaps', which is defined as persons who have a physical or mental impairment which substantially limits one or more major life activities, who have a record of such an impairment (even if they are not currently impaired), or who are regarded as having such an impairment (even if they do not currently have or never have had such an impairment). The Supreme Court has recently interpreted this definition liberally. In *School Board of Nassau County* v. *Arline* 480 U.S. 273 (1987), the Supreme Court held that a person who suffers from a physical or mental impairment is not removed from coverage under the Rehabilitation Act simply because the person's impairment is contagious. The Rehabilitation Act is also generous in the scope of its anti-discrimination obligation. Under the Act, workers with handicaps are protected from employment discrimination to the extent they can, with reasonable accommodation, perform the essential functions of the job. Thus, workers with handicaps are protected even if they cannot perform all of the tasks required by a job, so long as they can perform the 'essential' or 'necessary' job tasks (*Simon* v. *St Louis County*, 656 F.2d 316 (8th Cir. 1981)) and employers are under an affirmative obligation to make reasonable accommodations to enable workers with handicaps to perform the job (*Stutts* v. *Freeman*, 694 F.2d 666 (11th Cir. 1983)).

Unfortunately, the generous provisions of the Rehabilitation Act are largely undercut by the limited coverage of the Act. The Act applies only to three fairly limited types of employers: (1) to federal agencies as employers; (2) to employers that have contracts with the federal government in excess of $2500; and (3) to employers that receive federal financial assistance (but only to the programs or activities of those employers that actually receive the federal financial assistance) (Civil Rights Restoration Act of 1987; *United States Department of Transportation* v. *Paralyzed Veterans*, 477 U.S. 597 (1986)). Because of this limited coverage, the vast majority of workers in the United States are not protected from handicap discrimination under federal law. (There is currently legislation in Congress that would, in essence, extend the protections of the Rehabilitation Act to employees in the private sector, but at the time of writing it is not clear whether the proposed legislation will be enacted into law.)

The protections received by those workers who are covered by the Rehabilitation Act are also limited by procedural and remedial shortcomings. Some workers covered by the Act cannot sue their employers directly in federal court for handicap discrimination, but instead must file complaints with the Department of Labor (*Rogers* v. *Frito-Lay, Inc.*, 611 F.2d 1074

(5th Cir.), *cert. denied*, 449 U.S. 889 (1980)). Workers are entitled only to very limited judicial review of adverse decisions of the Department of Labor. (*Moon* v. *United States Department of Labor*, 747 F.2d 599 (11th Cir. 1984); *Presinzano* v. *Hoffman La Roche, Inc.*, 726 F.2d 105 (3rd Cir. 1984)). Even when workers can file in federal court and they are successful on the merits, full relief may not be available. Compensatory relief, for example, may not be available at all if disparate impact discrimination provides the basis of liability (Flaccus, 1986, pp. 315–17). (Federal employees with claims of handicap discrimination do not suffer from these shortcomings. They are entitled to the same remedies and procedures as federal employees with claims under Title VII.)

When federal law proves to be inadequate, disabled workers may be protected under state law. Forty-eight states have laws prohibiting employment discrimination against workers with handicaps. Five of the state laws prohibit discrimination only by state agencies and recipients of state funds, but the remaining state laws prohibit discrimination by private employers. In 43 states, then, there are large classes of workers with handicaps who are protected by a state anti-discrimination law, but who do not fall within the protection of the federal Rehabilitation Act.

Despite their broader coverage, most of the state laws prohibiting discrimination against workers with handicaps provide inadequate protection. The state laws are inadequate in a variety of ways. First, many of the state laws are restrictive in what they consider to be a handicap. The New Hampshire statute, for example, excludes handicaps caused by illness and the Arizona statute excludes handicaps that are first manifested after the age of 18. Only 17 of the state statutes define handicap as broadly as the Rehabilitation Act. Second, many of the state statutes provide protection only if the disabled worker can perform all of the tasks required by the job. The statutes, then, are more restrictive than the Rehabilitation Act which provides protection if the worker can perform 'essential' or 'necessary' job functions. The protections contained in 26 of the state statutes are limited in this way. Third, many of the state statutes require less from employers to accommodate workers with handicaps than is required by the Rehabilitation Act. The Rehabilitation Act requires employers to make reasonable accommodations for workers with handicaps, to the extent the accommodations would not cause the employer undue hardship. Nineteen of the state statutes do not require employers to make any accommodations at all for workers with handicaps. Of the other 25 statutes, none is more generous to workers with handicaps than the federal Rehabilitation Act (all of the statutes use the Rehabilitation Act's 'undue hardship' criterion to limit the employer's duty to accommodate), but several are less generous. In Minnesota, for example, only employers with 50 or more employees are under a duty to make reasonable accommodations for workers with handicaps. (This discussion of state handicap discrimination laws draws heavily upon a thorough survey by Flaccus, 1986.)

In summary, the federal Rehabilitation Act provides fairly strong employment protections for disabled workers, but because the Act only applies to a few types of employers the vast majority of disabled workers are not covered by the Act. Most states also have laws that protect disabled workers from employment discrimination and the coverage of those statutes, in most instances, is considerably broader than the coverage of the Rehabilitation Act. In most cases, however, the state statutes provide significantly less protection to covered workers than the Rehabilitation Act does. Only eight of the state statutes provide protection equivalent to the protection provided by the Rehabilitation Act. As with homosexuals and transsexuals, then, the protection received by disabled workers in the United States depends as much on where and for whom they work as it does on the ability of the disabled person to be a productive worker.

Workers with AIDS in the United States are in a very similar position to disabled workers. Although the issue is by no means settled, most courts in the United States that have considered the issue have found that persons with AIDS are handicapped within the meaning of that term in the Rehabilitation Act. Indeed, the cases to date have held that persons with AIDS are handicapped, within the meaning of that term in the Rehabilitation Act, even if they are asymptomatic (*Doe* v. *Dalton Elementary School*, 694 F.Supp. 440 (N.D. Ill. 1988); *Thomas* v. *Atascadero Unified School District*, 662 F.Supp. 376 (C.D. Cal. 1987)). As a result, workers with AIDS are protected from employment discrimination to the extent their employer is covered by the Rehabilitation Act, but, as indicated above, most employers are not covered by the Act. As with disabled workers, the state laws prohibiting handicap discrimination may provide supplemental protection for workers with AIDS. Twenty states have indicated that their handicap discrimination laws cover workers with AIDS and another 13 states have indicated that, although the issue of whether AIDS is a handicap is not yet resolved under their laws, they will accept AIDS-related discrimination complaints (Achtenberg, 1987, pp. 15–16). In addition to these laws that might protect workers with AIDS as one subcategory of disabled workers, in at least five states and in several local jurisdictions, there are laws that specifically prohibit employment discrimination on the basis of AIDS (Achtenberg, 1987).

Part-time workers, the last group of vulnerable workers under consideration here, are protected the least from disadvantageous ideas or preconceptions about the group. Employers in the United States are, in general, not prohibited from discriminating against part-time workers. There are a few scattered statutes which provide protections for narrow categories of workers, such as a federal statute that requires the federal government to provide *pro rata* health benefits for its part-time employees and an Ohio statute that requires *pro rata* sick leave for part-time school employees in that state. But, in general, employers are permitted to discriminate against part-time employees in many, if not most, aspects of the employment relationship—in wages and fringe benefits, in layoffs, in access to other jobs, etc. (Chamallas, 1986).

In the United States, then, the law is commonly used to prohibit employers from acting on disadvantageous ideas or preconceptions about vulnerable groups. Vulnerable groups receive some protection from these laws, but the extent of the protection varies considerably. Some groups receive more protection than other groups and greater protections are provided in some states and localities than in other areas of the country.

Protecting Vulnerable Groups by Changing the Structure of the Labor Market

A group may also be vulnerable if the labor market is structured in ways that are disadvantageous to it. The structure of the labor market is the result of a complex array of rules that apply to a variety of decisions related to employment (such as decisions concerning hiring, training, compensation, and capital investment) and that are made by an assortment of different actors (corporations, unions, government) (Doeringer and Piore, 1975). The structure of the labor market includes not only rules that apply directly to employment, such as labor relations and employment discrimination laws, but also rules such as tax laws that, although more tangential to employment, affect the employment-related decisions of workers and employers. The complexity of the relationships between all of the rules that constitute the structure of the labor market make rational and comprehensible analysis very difficult. And yet, because the structure is not neutral between groups, it is clear that labor market structure can be a significant contributor to the vulnerability of particular groups. This section will present a brief introduction to a few of the ways in which labor market structures can operate to disadvantage vulnerable workers.

The structure of the labor market in a very literal sense can disadvantage disabled workers. Architectural barriers that make the workplace inaccessible to disabled workers increase the vulnerability of that group of workers. There are a variety of laws at the federal and state level that require employers to increase the accessibility of the workplace to disabled workers, but many of the laws have only limited coverage (e.g. many apply only to publicly funded buildings and facilities) and many apply only to future construction but not to existing buildings and facilities (Clelland, 1978; Nicolai and Ricci, 1977). Thus, architectural barriers are one example of a structural impediment that can increase the vulnerability of a group of workers.

There are several aspects of the structure of the labor market, using the term in a less literal sense, that increase the vulnerability of women. Consider, for example, the effect of the tax structure in the United States on the vulnerability of married women as workers. The tax structure discourages married women from fully participating in the labor market because it omits the value of unpaid work in the home from the tax base (thus artificially increasing the value of that work) and because it taxes the market earnings of married women at the highest marginal tax rate of their spouses (thus decreasing the after-tax earnings married women receive from market work) (Davis, 1988). These disincentives are enhanced by the difficulty women workers in the United States have in obtaining reliable childcare at a reasonable cost. More than a quarter of non-working mothers with preschool children said they would work if reasonably priced childcare were available and 13% of working women with preschool children said they would work more hours if better childcare were available. The labor market in the United States is not structured to accommodate the needs of workers (predominantly women) with childcare responsibilities. Only 1.6% of private employers offer employer-sponsored day care and only 3.1% assist with childcare expenses (Bloom and Steen 1988). (Childcare, however, is currently a hot political issue, so the labor market in the United States may be more accommodating to women with children in the near future.) The disincentives to participate fully in the labor market created by these structural aspects of the labor market have a ripple effect that magnifies their importance. Women are less likely to participate in the labor market because of these structural disincentives which means they are less likely to invest in skills valued in the labor market, less likely to acquire tenure either in their particular job or in the labor market generally, and more likely to assume responsibility for non-market work in the household. All of these factors, in turn, make it even less likely that women will participate in the labor market.

Structural aspects of the labor market also increase the vulnerability of potential victims of violence at work. Workers' compensation laws in the United States, for example, fail to create incentives for employers to protect workers from violence at work. The workers' compensation laws immunize employers from tort suits by workers who suffer from violence on the job, but require employers to compensate these workers only at a level significantly below the full economic and non-economic costs caused by the violence. Employers, for instance, are required to compensate workers for only a portion of lost wages and are not required to provide any compensation at all for non-economic losses, such as pain and suffering, which are likely to be particularly significant in cases involving victims of violence at work

(Shroeder, 1986). As a result, since employers are not liable for most of the losses resulting from violence at work, they are not sufficiently encouraged to take steps that might reduce the problem (Victor, 1982).

Structural aspects of the labor market, then, can play a significant role, both directly and indirectly, in increasing (or decreasing) the vulnerability of groups of workers such as women, disabled workers, and potential victims of violence at work.

CONCLUSION

Although vulnerable workers will always be with us, there are ways in which their vulnerability, and the adverse social and psychological consequences of vulnerability, can be reduced. The law can make it difficult to identify vulnerable workers, it can make it illegal for employers to discriminate against vulnerable workers, and it can shape the structure of the labor market so that it does not disadvantage vulnerable workers.

In the United States, the law has been used in all of these ways to address the special barriers faced by vulnerable workers. The legal protections, however, have been enacted in a haphazard fashion. Some groups of vulnerable workers have been protected, others have not. Protections are provided in some areas of the country, but not in other areas. Analyzing the common problems of vulnerable workers as a class, as this book does, is an important first step in providing a more rational and comprehensive set of legal protections for vulnerable workers.

REFERENCES

Achtenberg, R., (ed.) (1987). *Sexual Orientation and the Law*, Clark Boardman, New York.

Adelman, P.K. (1987). Occupational complexity, control, and personal income: their relation to psychological well-being in men and women, *Journal of Applied Psychology*, **72**, 529–37.

Arrow, K. (1972). Models of job discrimination. In A.H. Pascal (ed.) *Racial Discrimination in Economic Life*, pp. 83–102, D.C. Heath, Lexington, Massachusetts.

Arrow, K. (1973). The theory of discrimination. In O. Ashenfelter and A. Rees (eds), *Discrimination in Labor Markets*, pp. 3–33, Princeton University Press, Princeton, New Jersey.

Becker, G.S. (1971). *The Economics of Discrimination*, University of Chicago Press, Chicago.

Blau, F.D. and Ferber, M.A. (1986). *The Economics of Women, Men, and Work*, Prentice-Hall, Englewood Cliffs, New Jersey.

Bloom, D.E. and Steen, T.P. (1988). Why child care is good for business, *American Demographics*, **10**, 22–7, 58–9.

Bokemeier, J.L. and Lacy, W.B. (1986). Job values, rewards, and work conditions as factors in job satisfaction among men and women, *Sociological Quarterly*, **28**, 189–204.

Bose, C.E. (1985). *Jobs and Gender: A Study of Occupational Prestige*, Praeger, New York.

Brenner, S.O. and Bartell, R. (1983). The psychological impact of unemployment: a structural analysis of cross-sectional data, *Journal of Occupational Psychology*, **56**, 129–36.

Burkhauser, R.V. and Haveman, R.H. (1982). *Disability and Work: The Economics of American Policy*, Johns Hopkins University Press, Baltimore.

Chamallas, M. (1986). Women and part-time work: the case for pay equity and equal access, *North Carolina Law Review*, **64**, 709–75.

Clelland, R. (1978). *Section 504: Civil Rights for the Handicapped*, American Association of School Administrators, Arlington, Virginia.

Coleman, B.J. (1985). *Primer on Employee Retirement Income Security Act*, Bureau of National Affairs, Washington, DC.

Davis, L.A. (1988). A feminist justification for the adoption of an individual filing system, *Southern California Law Review*, **62**, 197–252.

Dean, V., Roberts, P. and Boone, C. (1984). Comparable worth under various federal and state laws. In H. Remick (ed.) *Comparable Worth and Wage Discrimination*, pp. 238–66, Temple University Press, Philadelphia.

Doeringer, P.B. and Piore, M.J. (1975). Unemployment and the 'Dual Labor Market', *Public Interest*, **38**, 67–79.

Dowd, N.E. (1986). Maternity leave: Taking sex differences into account, *Fordham Law Review*, **54**, 699–765.

Eberhardt, B.J. and Shani, A.B. (1984). The effects of full-time versus part-time employment status on attitudes toward specific organizational characteristics and overall job satisfaction, *Academy of Management Journal*, **27**, 893–900.

Epstein, R.A. (1983). A common law for labor relations: A critique of the new deal labor legislation, *Yale Law Journal*, **92**, 1357–1408.

Epstein, R.A. (1984). In defense of the contract at will, *University of Chicago Law Review*, **51**, 947–82.

Estreicher, S. (1985). Unjust dismissal laws: Some cautionary notes, *American Journal of Comparative Law*, **33**, 310–23.

Flaccus, J.A. (1986). Handicap discrimination legislation: With such inadequate coverage at the federal level, can state legislation be of any help?, *Arkansas Law Review*, **40**, 261–326.

Flanagan, R.J. (1987). Efficiency and equality in Swedish labor markets. In B.P. Bosworth and A.M. Rivlin (eds) *The Swedish Economy*, pp. 125–84, Brookings Institution, Washington, DC.

Freeman, R.B. and Medoff, J.L. (1984). *What Do Unions Do*? Basic Books, New York.

Gould, W.B. (1988). Job security in the United States: Some reflections on unfair dismissal and plant closure legislation from a comparative perspective, *Nebraska Law Review*, **67**, 28–55.

Hall, R.H. (1986). *Dimensions of Work*, Sage Publications, Beverly Hills, California.

Jahoda, M. (1981). Work, employment, and unemployment: Values, theories, and approaches in social research, *American Psychologist*, **36**, 184–91.

Jencks, C. *et al*. (1988). What is a good job? A new measure of labor-market success, *American Journal of Sociology*, **93**, 1322–57.

Jick, T.D. and Mitz, L.F. (1985). Sex differences in work stress, *Management Review*, **10**, 408–20.

Landy, F.J. (1985). *Psychology of Work Behavior*, 3rd edn, Dorsey Press, Chicago.

Logan, N., O'Reilly, C. and Roberts, K.H. (1973). Job satisfaction among part-time employees, *Journal of Vocational Behavior*, **3**, 33–41.

Major, B. (1987). Gender, justice and the psychology of entitlement. In P. Shaver and C. Hendrick (eds) *Review of Personality and Social Psychology: Vol. 7, Sex and Gender*, pp. 124–48, Sage, Beverly Hills.

Maternity leave policies: An international survey (1988). *Harvard Women's Law Journal*, **11**, 171–95.

McLaughlin, M., Cormier, L.S. and Cormier, W.H. (1988). Relation between coping strategies and distress, stress, and marital adjustment of multiple-role women, *Journal of Counseling Psychology*, **35**, 187–93.

Mellor, E.F. and Parks, W. (1988). A year's work: Labor force activity from a different perspective, *Monthly Labor Review*, **111**, 13–18.

Mitchell, D.J.B. (1984). The Australian labor market. In R.E. Caves and L.B. Krause (eds) *The Australian Economy: A View from the North*, pp. 127–93, George Allen & Unwin, Sydney.

National Committee on Pay Equity (1987). Briefing paper on the wage gap, unpublished memo.

National Urban League (1989). *The State of Black America, 1989*, Urban League, Washington, DC.

Nicolai, D.F. and Ricci, W.J. (1977). Access to buildings and equal employment opportunity for the disabled: Survey of state statutes, *Temple Law Quarterly*, **50**, 1067–85.

Pearldaughter, A. (1979). Employment discrimination against lesbians: Municipal ordinances and other remedies, *Golden Gate University Law Review*, **8**, 537–58.

Phelps, E.S. (1972). The statistical theory of racism and sexism, *American Economic Review*, **62**, 659–66.

Pond, S.B. and Geyer, P.D. (1987). Employee age as a moderator of the relation between perceived work alternatives and job satisfaction, *Journal of Applied Psychology*, **72**, 552–7.

Report of the President (1988). *The State of Small Business*, US Government Printing Office, Washington, DC.

Rothstein, M.A., Knapp, A.S. and Liebman, L. (1987). *Cases and Materials on Employment Law*, Foundation Press, Mineola, New York.

Russell, D.W., Altmaier, E. and Van Velzen, D. (1987). Job-related stress, social support, and burnout among classroom teachers, *Journal of Applied Psychology*, **72**, 269–74.

Shamir, B. (1980). Between service and servility: Role conflict in subordinate service roles, *Human Relations*, **33**, 741–56.

Schroeder, E.P. (1986). Legislative and judicial responses to the inadequacy of compensation for occupational disease, *Law and Contemporary Problems*, **49**, 151–82.

Sullivan, C.A., Zimmer, M.J. and Richards, R.F. (1988). *Employment Discrimination*, 2nd edn, Little, Brown, Boston.

Summers, C.W. (1985). What we should teach in labor law: The need for a change and a suggested direction. In *The Park City Papers*, Labor Law Group, Park City, Utah.

Summers, C.W. (1988). Labor law as the century turns: a changing of the guard, *Nebraska Law Review*, **67**, 7–27.

Terpstra, D.E. and Baker, D.D. (1988). A hierarchy of sexual harassment, *Journal of Psychology*, **121**, 599–605.

Treiman, D.J. and Hartmann, H.I. (1981). *Women, Work, and Wages: Equal Pay for Jobs of Equal Value*, National Academy Press, Washington, DC.

US Department of Labor, Women's Bureau (1983). *Time of Change: 1983 Handbook on Women Workers*, US Government Printing Office, Washington, DC.

Victor, R.B. (1982). *Workers' Compensation and Workplace Safety: The Nature of Employer Financial Incentives*, Rand Institute for Civil Justice, Santa Monica.

Warr, P.B. (1983). Work, jobs, and unemployment, *Bulletin of the British Psychological Society*, **36**, 305–11.

Willborn, S.L. (1986). *A Comparable Worth Primer*, D.C. Heath, Lexington, Massachusetts.

Willborn, S.L. (1988). Labor law without labor, *Wisconsin Law Review*, **1988**, 547–60.

Zelin, J.E. (1986). Physician's tort liability for unauthorized disclosure of confidential information about patient, *American Law Reports (ALR)* 4th, **48**, 668–713.

PART II

Vulnerable Workers: Physical and Health Disabilities

Chapter 4.1

Disabled Workers: Psychosocial Issues

Martin F. McHugh, University College, Galway, Ireland

TERMINOLOGY

Lord Snowdon once remarked: 'Just because someone is disabled doesn't mean he or she doesn't have a range of other talents. If you mention the names of Milton, Beethoven and Nelson, probably the last thing you would think they had in common was that they were disabled' (Smyth, 1981). From another perspective, every person is handicapped in the sense of being unable to do some things which others can manage.

Following the World Health Organizations's (1980) classification, Haggard (1985) suggests that 'Disability refers to a reduced repertoire of generally valuable biological, physical or social skills . . . . Handicap refers to the reduced personal, social, educational, economic and cultural opportunities available as a consequence'. Although Finkelstein (1985), a Council Member of Disabled People's International, regards these definitions as unacceptable, they accord with common usage. Since they refer to closely associated forms of vulnerability, the terms are often used interchangeably, as here (Sculnick, 1988).

STIGMATIZATION OF THE DISABLED

Those who have particular difficulty in coping are often stigmatized, whether their disabilities be physical, intellectual, emotional, social or vocational (Croxen, 1983).

As Safilios-Rothschild (1966) indicates, the amount of stigma attached to various disabilities seems to depend on notions with regard to their causes; the values a given society places on mental and physical health; the visibility, alarming aspect or unaesthetic quality of the defect; the part of the body affected; the pervasiveness, severity and assumed contagiousness of the illness; and the barrier the handicap poses for interpersonal communication.

Vulnerable Workers: Psychosocial and Legal Issues. Edited by M. J. Davidson and J. Earnshaw

People, even the disabled themselves, sometimes 'distinguish those whose disability has been acquired "honourably", such as loss of a limb in battle, from those injured by accident, while the latter are differentiated from those who are congenitally crippled' (Cohen and Clark, 1979, p. 354).

NORMALIZATION

In Britain in the early 1940s the successful inclusion of many mentally handicapped people in the war effort indicated that it might be feasible to train them in a range of other vocational skills (Brown and Hughson, 1987, p. 2).

Later came the concept of normalization or, in Wolfensberger's (1983) term, 'social role valorization', whereby 'handicapped individuals are helped to grow and participate in life, as far as they can, on a normal [i.e. culturally valued] basis' (Brown and Hughson, 1987, p. 7). Originating in Scandinavia (Grunewald, 1969), normalization is now accepted world-wide as a desirable goal. Unfortunately, however, it has sometimes resulted in the dumping of vulnerable persons on the community without adequate preparation (Esgrow, 1978) and to their consequent harm (Rollin, 1980; Wilder, 1982; Moore, 1985; Leighton, 1988).

The British Psychological Society's view (1984) has been that: 'The goals of community care need to be defined more precisely, in terms of desired change in the relevant patients . . . the methods which are to be employed to achieve these outcomes must be specified . . . the proposed programmes should be evaluated' in clearly detailed ways (p. 378). Furthermore, 'any evaluation . . . must take account of the effects of the programmes not merely on the patients themselves, but upon the families of those living at home (Wing and Greer, 1980) and on other parts of the social and health system (e.g. the probation service and general practice)' (p. 379).

Moving patients out into the community does not guarantee that they will have any more social contact with the non-handicapped than they had when in the institution (Markova, Jahoda and Cattermole, 1988). Indeed, Stevens (1989) refers to the ongoing debate as to 'whether care in the community would be optimal for all patients/clients'. Nevertheless, Dooley-Groarke (1985) and Felce (1988) have demonstrated how successful community integration can be in the Irish and British contexts respectively, if the mentally handicapped are appropriately trained not only in vocational but also in home living and social skills and in use of leisure time. Toomey and O'Callaghan (1983), McGinley (1986) and McLoone (1988) provide corroborating evidence.

Yet even in those cases social integration of the handicapped into the community fell short of the ideal.

ASSESSING COMMUNITY ATTITUDES

Community attitudes towards such vulnerable persons are not easily probed, however. McConkey (1988) points out that, apart from the problem of securing representative samples of the public willing to state their opinions, and the difficulty of finding reliable measures of such disclosures, there is the vexed issue of the extent to which private feelings find expression in frank statements and overt actions.

Questions about attitudes must at the very least be simply worded, unambiguous, realistic, unbiased, specific, and supplemented by observation and accurate recording of behaviour.

CHANGING COMMUNITY ATTITUDES

The do's and don'ts of trying to change public attitudes towards the disabled have been thoroughly discussed by McConkey and McCormack (1983). The following account is largely drawn from their insightful analysis, some supplementary points being taken from Threlkeld (1983), Stevens (1986), Anonymous (1986), Duran (1987) and Solomon and Wagel (1988).

Amelioration of attitudes can be attempted by:

- providing relevant, succinct, lucid, credible, practical and accurate information (especially when this is done through opinion leaders by a friendly, non-dogmatic person who has the disability in question);
- giving opportunity for experiential learning through group projects and individual role play (e.g. by getting an able-bodied person actually to go round a factory or neighbourhood in a wheelchair);
- arranging contacts between disabled and non-disabled persons.

Since contacts sometimes reinforce rather than reduce prejudice, it is desirable to allay anxieties and fears on both sides beforehand. Any possible unease about the meeting can be reduced if the able-bodied are briefed in advance on how to behave towards the handicapped or (better still) are shown videos of successful interactions. Contacts are usually more successful if they are made on an equal-footing basis, involve some shared enjoyable activity in pleasant surroundings, and (where possible) allow the disabled to speak for themselves and show what they can do.

Whether the planned intervention be a publicity campaign, opportunity for experiential learning, or arranged contact, it is important to assess the views of the targeted group of the community beforehand and afterwards to determine what, if any, change of attitude has occurred and how the programme might be improved. Very practical advice on ways of measuring such 'consumer reactions' is given by McConkey and McCormack (1983) and by McConkey (1988).

Managers, supervisors and employees are affected, of course, by the general public's attitudes towards the handicapped, but also by special considerations. In the mind of even the most humanitarian employer the cost/benefits of habilitation (especially as reflected in training expenses, productivity, and turnover of employees) must loom large (McHugh and O'Donoghue, 1980; Schapire and Berger, 1984; Gallivan, 1986; Hill, Mehnert and Lederer, 1987).

HANDICAPPED ACHIEVERS: A SOURCE OF INSPIRATION?

Gifted individuals who have coped with a personal handicap have done much to improve the public image of the disabled. Physical disability, or what Alfred Adler (1907) termed 'organ inferiority', may be overcome directly in some cases or else 'compensated for' indirectly.

Thus, to take the world of music as an example, the blind composers Handel and Delius (Griffiths, 1986) continued composing with the aid of amanuenses. Similarly, Paul Wittgenstein, who lost his right arm in the First World War, resumed his career as a professional pianist by commissioning works for the left hand such as Ravel's Piano Concerto in D major (Demuth, 1947); while Cyril Smith, after one of his arms was paralysed by a stroke, likewise persisted as a concert pianist by joining his wife Phyllis Sellick in playing three-handed arrangements of musical compositions. Robert Schumann may be taken as an instance of indirect compensation for disability. When he permanently damaged two fingers by injudicious use of a mechanical practising aid (Taylor, 1985), he found fulfilment and success in composing works many of which were popularized by his wife, the pianist Clara Wieck Schumann.

Even if on a less lofty plane, there are in every community inspiring examples of those who treat their own disabilities as a challenge, and thereby arouse public interest in, and sympathy and support for, their fellow disabled who may be finding it more difficult to adjust. From his own experience of growing up with a severe handicap, Kanga (1990) concluded that 'the only thing that makes you stronger is seeing somebody like you achieving something large. Then you know how much is possible and you reach out, further than you ever thought you could'.

But, although such examples may be stimulating for some, they can be counter-productive for others. For example, they can arouse unrealistic expectations in relatives, and can be discouraging to the disabled themselves. Unlike Helen Keller, most blind-and-deaf persons do not have an inspiring

Anne Sullivan constantly available, nor do they have the potential of graduating from Radcliffe College with honours!

MEASURES WHICH BACKFIRE

Measures intended to help the handicapped may have the opposite effect. Quota schemes, if imposed rather than voluntary, can create resentment on the part of employers and, particularly when jobs are scarce, hostility from able-bodied workers (Cooper, 1968). Designation of certain occupations as solely open to the disabled can adversely affect the status of such jobs in the eyes not only of the public but of the handicapped themselves (Hill, 1983). The need to fill a quota of disabled workers can also lead to mere token employment (Willis, 1987). Witness the case of the 32-year-old man confined to a wheelchair who has been left idle on the staff of a telecommunications firm in Milan for nearly 10 years. According to a report by the Rome correspondent of the *Daily Telegraph* (5 July 1989), this man is taking his firm to court to demand he be given actual work to do.

Cohen and Clark (1979, p. 354) claim that 'there is evidence that there are about as many unregistered disabled as registered. Reluctance to be stigmatized as "disabled" is one reason for failing to apply to be placed on the register'. People who suffer from psychiatric illness, are drug addicts or have AIDS may actually fear (with some justification) that, if they were registered as disabled, that would worsen their chances of employment.

Similarly, invalidity benefits can have unintended effects (Greenblum and Bye, 1987). As Willetts (1989) points out, 'if you are a GP in a town with high unemployment and someone comes in with a bad back saying he cannot work, you may be inclined to assess him as disabled so he can get a higher benefit than if he was simply unemployed'. This may help to explain why recipients of invalidity benefit in Britain nearly doubled during the past decade.

To prevent disability allowances discouraging job seeking, the welfare package announced by Mr Tony Newton, Social Services Secretary, on 10 January 1990, contained a proposed new Disability Employment Credit which, it is hoped, 'will help about 50 000 partly incapacitated people to take low-paid jobs without losing their entitlement to cash' (Hibbs, 1990).

PREPARATION AND EVALUATION OF HABILITATION PROGRAMMES

Successful habilitation depends on the enthusiastic cooperation of skilled staff from a variety of backgrounds. As Cullen (1988) indicates, their training should feature role play, modelling, feedback and incentives more than traditional lectures. Cullen also notes that the rehabilitation procedures most likely to be implemented by staff are those they have seen to be not only effective but also simple, flexible, and inexpensive in time and effort.

The evaluation of rehabilitation programmes has been considered by Hughson and Brown (1988). The main points in their excellent discussion are:

Rehabilitation programmes should have precise goals involving the imparting of skills critical for independent life and work. Advance specification of standards helps to ensure the health, safety and welfare of rehabilitees. Programmes may be evaluated by participants or outside observers. Observers tend to be more objective but less knowledgeable than participants, and their recommendations may not meet with as much acceptance. Research can focus on the feelings, attitudes, decisions and actions of those engaged in the rehabilitation programme, or it can concentrate on the programme's outcomes (such as the number of rehabilitees placed in jobs). Baseline measures must be taken. Where possible, a control group should be included. Evaluators should not be stakeholders in the projects. Views of rehabilitation staff and of the disabled trainees ought to be canvassed. Long- as well as short-term effects of the programme should be assessed by a variety of techniques such as interviews, questionnaires, rating scales, tests, direct observation, video and audio recordings, as well as by concrete cost/benefit indices (such as productivity, absenteeism, turnover). The reliability and validity of all these measures must be established.

By and large, the effectiveness of a programme can be judged by the levels of ability and stability to which it raises the rehabilitee.

DISABILITY AND THE NEW TECHNOLOGIES

As Hurley (1989) points out, the new technologies include computer-assisted design and manufacture, programmable robotics, office automation (including word processors) and computer-assisted learning. Increasingly, computer-controlled machinery will take the place of the labourer, machine minder, and tradesman, though unskilled and semi-skilled individuals may continue to work in 'the service industries . . . transport and delivery . . . the leisure industry . . . agriculture, fisheries, conservation and security' (p. 372). There will be 'a shift from manual bodily-dependent work, towards more mental ideas-dependent work' (p. 373). As a result, more and more work will be done from home through a link to a central computer; and there will be considerable flexibility of working hours and days.

Such developments will suit the severely disabled in many ways (Williams, 1988). Flack (1981) feels the minicomputer will give the home-bound handicapped greater contact with the outside world, though fear has been expressed that it will cause them to have fewer face-to-face meetings with other people. Whatever the outcome in that respect, it can hardly be denied that, since the traditional work of disabled persons confined to home tended to be restricted to such unstimulating activities as packaging or toy assembly, the coming of the minicomputer has considerably expanded the vocational horizons of such persons.

A news item in *The Psychologist* (Anonymous, 1989) reveals that Royal Earlswood Hospital, Redhill, has a microcomputer network for use by its mentally handicapped residents. The reporter claims that 'microcomputers are ideal for educational use in such settings, as learning is self-paced, with immediate feedback, and small increases in task difficulty can be programmed. Many clients have improved their numeracy and literacy, as well as enjoying less easily quantifiable benefits in areas like quality of life and self-esteem' (p. 120).

Cybernetic aids permit people with motor handicap to use a remote-control electric typewriter by means of a keyboard operated by almost any part of the body which the individual can move, whether it be finger, elbow, fist, foot, toe, tongue, eyelid or head with stylus attached. As Anastasi (1979, p. 207) notes, 'the same types of keyboards can be adapted to operate telephones, computers or other home, office or factory equipment'.

Since most vocational aptitude tests have been designed for non-handicapped job applicants able to write, see, hear and speak, they are unsuitable for many disabled persons. Through computer-based assessment, however, such difficulties can often be obviated, since, as Wilson (1987) points out, 'tests can be presented visually or aurally (using a voice-over system or synthetic speech) and a variety of response media can be used'.

During his recent interview with disabled Professor Stephen Hawking, however, Kanga (1990) noted that 'it was a disadvantage of the Professor's voice synthesizer that it could convey no inflection, no shades or tone'.

Another invention with potential yet to be fully realized is the Optacon which allows the blind to read directly from the printed page. The Optacon consists of a camera which records the visual images and a tactile stimulator which converts these into vibrations which can be felt by the fingertip. This device gets round the bulkiness and production costs of braille, as Anastasi (1979) observes, but the rate of reading achievable with it seems to be slower. More promising are attempts to convert scanned text into synthesized speech (Vincent, 1986).

PROBLEMS COMMONLY EXPERIENCED BY THE DISABLED

The secondary effects of a severe disability may be more disruptive than the primary. There is often an emotional disturbance for which counselling or psychotherapy may be needed if the handicapped person is to develop a realistic and constructive attitude towards his or her disability. The deaf-and-blind Helen Keller would not have benefited from Anne Sullivan's insightful teaching, gone on to obtain an Honours BA, and embarked on a distinguished career as writer and lecturer, had her governess not first discovered psychologically sound ways of controlling that little spitfire's rages. '"I saw clearly", wrote Anne, "that it was useless to try to teach [Helen] language or anything else until she learned to obey me"' (Lash, 1980, pp. 53–5).

The problems of the handicapped are often compounded by interrupted schooling. Disabled persons who are poorly educated can only secure unskilled (often physically demanding) jobs which may further damage their health. The educational handicap may well prove more serious than any physical limitations of the individual. So, hospital-based teachers and home tutors are often as important as medical, nursing, and paramedical personnel for the treatment of young people suffering from chronic illness.

If vocational potential is to be inferred from workshop performance (as is often done), it is important that the training or rehabilitation workshop should be large enough to offer a variety of jobs demanding a range of skills, rather than be limited to simple assembly tasks. Furthermore, as Griffiths (1975) points out, work content should be realistic and work tempo set by supervisors drawn from industry. Not all workshops meet these requirements.

CURRENT ISSUES REGARDING SPECIFIC TYPES OF HANDICAP

Space only permits touching on psychosocial issues in some of the major types of disability, namely:

- epilepsy,
- deafness,
- blindness,
- heart disease,
- alcoholism,
- motor deficits, and
- severe learning difficulties

Epilepsy

As Wallechinsky and Wallace (1978, p. 1103) record, some epileptics can function at a very high level (witness Julius Caesar, Berlioz, Byron,

Swinburne, Dostoievsky, Flaubert, van Gogh, de Maupassant, Paganini, Pascal, Peter the Great, Pope Pius IX, Cardinal Richelieu).

Yet many jobs are quite unsuitable for those who are liable to grand mal seizures or even frequent petit mal attacks. Melin (1969) maintains that epileptics subject to loss of consciousness should not be employed near high-tension electric current, hot surfaces, dangerous chemicals, or deep vats. They should not work on ladders or scaffolding or drive vehicles. Neither should they be in charge of small children or other dependent individuals.

To this we may add that solitary jobs and those involving handling fragile objects are also contraindicated.

The strains of shiftwork, particularly of 'the nightwatch' (Gibbons, 1989), are probably best avoided. Keane's findings (1990) suggest that the job should not make heavy demands on the severe epileptic's memory.

Despite such restrictions, the occupational horizons of the average epileptic have expanded well beyond the agricultural employment that was once so strongly recommended. Take, for example, Chaplin's (1987) prospective study of 300 civil servants with this disability, 200 of whom were 'recent recruits'. Chaplin's laudable aim is 'to formulate guidelines for employers to aid the support and development of people with epilepsy'.

As Taylor and Taylor (1967, p. 179) emphasize, 'understanding and sympathy are especially important in the early stages of a new job when the excitement of starting . . . might precipitate seizures that do not recur when the initial adjustment is past'. The same authors note, however, that employers may be concerned by the disorganization of the workplace a seizure can cause, by the difficult personality of some epileptics, and by their alleged accident proneness.

New drugs are improving seizure control, but problems at work can arise when epileptics fail to adhere to prescribed medication.

Deafness

'Over 20 000 people in the UK have severe to total acquired deafness. Of these, about 7000 [are] under 60 [years old]' (Cowie and Stewart, 1987, p. 141).

If highly motivated and otherwise gifted, even the severely deaf can sometimes cope exceptionally well with jobs that seem to demand hearing. Contemporary examples are percussionist Evelyn Glennie; Bryan Kneale, Professor of Sculpture at the Royal Academy of Art, who was almost 'stone' deaf from the age of 14 until a recent operation; and Jack Ashley whose 23-year career as a lip-reading Member of Parliament included, as Comfort (1989) notes, spells as Parliamentary Private Secretary to Mrs Barbara Castle and Lord Ennals.

Rittersporn (1986) gives 'sound' arguments for employing the deaf! Improvements in early diagnosis, hearing aids, and speech therapy have boosted their vocational prospects. So has the introduction of cochlear implants (Thornton, 1986). In the United States the advancement of the deaf in the professions has been greatly facilitated by the existence of Gallaudet College, whereas Britain lacks a third-level educational facility with special provision for the deaf. A deaf employee can mind a machine or take dial readings as well as a worker with normal hearing can—sometimes even better because of not being so easily distracted. Also, deafness can be a positive asset in noisy jobs such as riveting or pneumatic drilling (Taylor and Taylor, 1967). Care, however, should be taken not to damage residual hearing.

Some forms of deafness have associated disabilities (such as anomalous colour vision or liability to dizziness) which clearly have vocational implications. The tinnitus (or ringing in the ears), so movingly expressed in Smetana's autobiographical String Quartet 'From My Life', torments many deaf people.

Cowie, Douglas-Cowie and Stewart (1987) highlight the differences in adjustment associated with various forms of hearing loss. Retarded linguistic and intellectual development in children congenitally deaf may be more serious than the sensory handicap itself. In cases of acquired deafness in adult life there may be loss of social contact, a feeling of being left out of discussions and decision making, embarrassment at misunderstandings, denial of the disability, suspiciousness, irritability, or even what Kyle (1985) refers to as 'a massive psychological crisis which is the more likely with the greater degree of hearing loss and the greater suddenness of onset' (p. 139).

Kyle goes on to point out (p. 140): 'Onset is normally gradual. The National Study of Hearing (IHR, 1981) suggests that [in Britain] only 25 per cent of those with a hearing problem have actually obtained a hearing aid. Reduction in sound information may create problems for an individual years before they realise the extent of their loss. In that time, difficulties at work . . . will be matched by stress at home'.

Blindness

To be independently mobile the blind must be able to detect obstacles and find their way around. A guide dog can anticipate dangers and follow familiar routes, but only a minority of the blind can cope with ownership of such dogs. The long cane is a cheaper option, the sonic torch a more sophisticated revealer of surroundings. Tactile maps with raised lines and symbols can aid direction finding.

Traditional crafts for the blind (such as basket making) cannot readily compete with modern mass production, but opportunities of semi-skilled work have arisen in new industries such as plastics. In some countries the blind have been making notable advances at the highest occupational levels. Spain can boast not only of Joaquin Rodrigo (world-famous composer of Concierto de Aranjuez) but also of the brilliant young business man Miguel Duran who has just been named as managing director of one of Spain's three new commercial television networks (Brown, 1990). For many blind persons, however, interpersonal communication still remains a daunting problem.

As Kemp (1981) attests, the blind cannot avail of such cues to other people's feelings as facial expression, posture or gestures. It is not easy for them to recognize who in a group is actually speaking, and they are prone to develop 'blindisms', i.e. socially unacceptable behaviour such as eye-ball rolling or not facing the speaker. Kemp (1981, p. 82) mentions ways of eradicating 'blindisms' and of improving conversational ability, self-presentation and social judgement. He also records attempts to enhance ability to localize sound, and to teach facial expression to the blind through myoelectric feedback.

Heart Disease

Taylor and Taylor (1967) draw attention to the ironical fact that teenagers with heart conditions are often excluded from sedentary jobs in offices because of the strict health requirements of superannuation schemes, whereas the same young people can get dangerously strenuous work in, say, the building industry without any medical examination whatever. If the heart trouble develops later in life, the 'white collar' employee can often return to his previous occupation, but the labourer may have to seek lighter (and less well paid) work as a messenger or watchman. Moreover, employers who would pride themselves on having a blind telephonist or a one-armed welder may not be as sympathetic towards someone with the hidden disability of heart disease.

Because his or her illness may not have obvious external symptoms, the person with a bad heart may feel embarrassed at having to refuse repeatedly to climb stairs or do any heavy lifting, and may worry unduly about being considered a malingerer (Cohen and Clark, 1979). Kent and Dalgleish (1986, p. 146) note that in Britain about 50% of myocardial infarction patients never resume employment, and that many of these 'become invalids through psychological and social rather than cardiac problems'.

Clearly, with patients who may have justifiable fear of sudden death or another attack, the rehabilitation counsellor has to steer a difficult course 'between encouragement of invalidism and premature return to work' (Cohen and Clark, 1979, p. 356).

Alcoholism

At least half a million people in England and Wales engage in alcohol abuse (Donnan and Haskey, 1977). Prevalence is even higher among the Irish and the Scots (Madden, 1979). One Scottish firm discovered that 14% of its managers were alcoholics (Gray, 1969). Women and young people seem to be increasingly at risk (Johnson, 1987).

The temptation to over-indulge in alcohol is particularly strong in those whose work is stressful, solitary, close to a drink supply, or not closely supervised (Plant, 1979).

Physical sequelae of prolonged heavy drinking of alcohol can include brain and liver damage, tumours, circulatory and muscular disorders; while psychological correlates range from memory loss, anxiety, jealousy, hallucinations to suicidal tendencies (Madden, 1979). Moss and Davies (1967) found that, in one English county, drinking had disrupted the work performance of 52% of male alcoholics (though just over 4% of them actually became unemployable or had to take early retirement). Excessive drinking can lead to absenteeism and interfere with promotion prospects. In the United States, 40% of industrial fatalities and 47% of industrial accidents have been attributed to alcohol abuse (Quayle, 1983).

Small wonder, then, that the often unsatisfactory work history of alcohol abusers deters some employers from hiring them or leads those employers to offer only low-level jobs apt to undermine the already poor self-esteem of alcoholics (Wolkstein, 1979).

Excessive drinking is often concealed not only by alcoholics themselves but also by their relatives and mates, yet 'the worst thing the colleagues of a problem drinker can do is to cover up for lateness, inefficiencies and botch-ups at work', since alcoholics 'do not usually learn by merely being told to drink less, but from the hard experience of last warnings, financial penalties and even dismissals'. Also, if the drinking problem becomes known before it is well developed, the employer is not forced to impose extreme sanctions but can instead exert sympathetic pressure on affected employees to avail themselves of rehabilitation opportunities which have some prospect of success (Heather and Robertson, 1985, pp. 251–2).

Concealment of his or her problem can deprive the alcoholic of the invaluable support of an understanding colleague who would help during crises and lessen pressures to participate in after-work drinking sessions. Nevertheless, heavy drinkers who are unable or unwilling to identify themselves publicly can be helped by 'a whole range of telephone, postal, written, audio—or video—taped communications' such as the Scottish Health Education Group's self-help manual (Heather and Robertson, 1985, pp. 234–5).

In ex-addicts, who do not reveal their drinking histories to prospective employers, maintaining a fictional identity entails continuous fear of exposure and an inability to relax socially. On the other hand, those who reveal their past may suspect they are being closely monitored as a result, and may feel uneasy about the possibility that information about their chequered careers may leak out to other staff. So it must be borne in mind that, for many reformed alcoholics, getting a job is just the first hurdle to overcome on their way back to recovery. Other pressures will develop, especially in the competition for promotion (Wolkstein, 1979).

Some of the problems caused by excessive drinking in business and industry would be largely preventable if all employers followed the good example of US firms like Ford and Heinz in banning alcohol from their canteens and dining rooms (Madden, 1979). In France and Germany, and to a lesser extent in the United Kingdom, it is government policy to promote non-availability of alcohol in the workplace (Health and Safety Executive, 1981). The United States has now implemented the Drug-Free Workplace Act of 1988.

However, even if strong drink is unavailable at work, the habit of alcohol abuse obviously can develop in leisure time for a variety of reasons. Because of the disparate emotional needs and levels of functioning of addicts, it has proved hard to individualize rehabilitation services to the optimal extent (Wolkstein, 1979). Moreover, in alcoholism therapy, the controversy has not yet been resolved between the advocates of complete abstinence (e.g. Alcoholics Anonymous) and those, such as Sanchez-Craig *et al.* (1984), who argue that controlled drinking should be the goal.

Nearly 25 years ago, Madden (1967) described how sympathetic and enlightened the British Civil Service was in handling those of its personnel who had alcohol or drug dependency problems. He later (1979) noted that more and more firms were developing programmes for the identification and treatment of employees who drink too much. Commenting on Wiegand's (1972) finding that recovery rates for alcoholics in programmes run by companies in North America were a remarkably high 50% to 70%, Madden (1979, p. 87) suggests that 'the satisfactory results possibly arise because the alcoholics, being in employment, possess some stability of personality, are in the early stages of dependence, and have much to lose if they continue to drink excessively'.

Employee Assistance Programmes (which have mostly developed out of Occupational Alcoholism Programmes) are now widespread in the United States (Masi, 1984; MacLeod, 1985). As Farkas (1989, p. 1488) points out: 'Returns on investment in EAPs have been said to range from 2:1 to 20:1, with savings coming in the form of increased worker attendance, reduced health plan utilization, and greater job site productivity (e.g. Klarreich, Di Giuseppe, and Di Mattia, 1987)'. That being so, it seems likely that only unjustified scepticism about the effectiveness of treatment, or else fear of a prolongation of the economic recession, can hinder the spread of the Employee Assistance Programme idea.

Motor Deficits

In some cultures those with marked physical handicaps are apt to encounter prejudice. The dwarfish Indian author Firdaus Kanga (who suffers from brittle bone disease and is confined to a wheelchair) reports (1990) that he was told 'you have to pay for sins from your previous life'.

Among those with severe motor handicaps, the cerebral palsied pose special placement problems. In their case, as Rosen, Clark and Kivitz (1977) observe, 'many occupations available even to the mentally handicapped must be ruled out because of physical limitations' (p. 77). However, Floor and Rosen (1976) showed that these physical limitations are not always as important a determinant of potential as other factors such as intelligence.

The last-mentioned study also revealed that cerebral palsy sufferers with high IQ can quickly become bored with routine work and unstimulating workmates; and it indicated that group homes for the spastic 'should be located close to feasible work situations to reduce transportation difficulties' (p. 97).

In their study of 119 teenagers suffering from cerebral palsy or spina bifida, Anderson and Clarke (1983) found that 18 months after leaving school only a third were in open employment. For many of the rest the alternative was a day centre more geared to the needs of the elderly.

Those bored unemployed youngsters and the contrasting instances of Christy Brown, author of *My Left Foot* (1972); of Christopher Nolan, winner of the Whitbread Biography Award for *Under the Eye of the Clock* (1987); and of Stephen Hawking, Professor of Gravitational Physics at the University of Cambridge and author of the best-selling *A Brief History of Time* (1988); all these cases taken together should make us wonder how much talent is going to waste in the frail bodies of those with severe motor impairment.

People with Severe Learning Difficulties

The life span of mentally handicapped persons continues to increase, so more and more of them will be looking for jobs at a time when machines are replacing unskilled workers.

'Farming, which years ago provided a field of employment for many of the retarded, has become so specialized that persons who would have been employed in the past have a difficult time finding employment at all now' (Katz and Felton, 1965, p. 257).

Nevertheless, there is still some repetitive unskilled work available which those with severe learning difficulties can find very fulfilling, but which brighter individuals would tend to regard as intolerably tedious. So turnover may well be less in the former group (Clements, 1987).

As far back as the mid-1960s, the mildly mentally handicapped were showing in workshops such as those of Cork Polio and General Aftercare Association that they were capable of operating woodworking machinery efficiently to make furniture, and that their accident rate was remarkably low since they never removed safety guards from the dangerous equipment (unlike 'more intelligent' machinists who sometimes do so out of a sense of bravado or to get a better view of the work surface).

Marshall's (1985) investigation revealed a much higher awareness and use of their own memory skills by the mentally handicapped than had been previously reported. Research by Slevin (1986) showed that provision of photographic cues can enable severely mentally handicapped young adults to master a relatively complex construction task more quickly than would otherwise be the case.

Many other examples, such as McHugh (1969), Carney (1983) and Ashman (1988), could be cited to demonstrate that the employment potential of people with severe learning difficulties is constantly improving through higher aspirations for them and improvements in training procedures, so much so that one mentally handicapped man in Britain, Joey Deacon by name, has published his autobiography; a British girl with Down's syndrome has passed her car driving test; a Down's syndrome youth in the United States has become a screen actor.

What a pity, then, that in the former country the 1980s, when the ability to develop the vocational potential of those with limited ability is greater than ever before, should also be the decade when, as Mittler (1984, p. 224) sadly records, 'it is sometimes argued that it is not justifiable to train mentally handicapped people for work or to spend resources on trying to find them jobs when well over 3 million non-handicapped people are unemployed'. Mittler goes on to lament that 'some mentally handicapped people still find it difficult to get access to wheelchairs, mobility and hearing aids, walking aids, glasses and other prosthetic devices, as well as to the services of physiotherapists and speech therapists, on the grounds that "they are unlikely to be able to benefit"'.

Another tragic consequence of the economic recession is that even where groups such as Carney's (1983) moderately mentally handicapped females have, through operant conditioning techniques, made significant gains in aspects of self-help (such as domestic duties, grooming, shopping) and in self-occupation (workshop activities), they are apt to regress to their former state of lethargy and over-dependency, when funds and staff are unavailable to maintain the programme.

CONCLUSION

Transfer of severely handicapped persons from institutional to community care can be non-beneficial, even harmful, unless desired goals are clearly defined, methods to achieve them specified, and programme impact monitored.

For improvement of community attitudes towards the disabled to be brought about, suitable information should be provided through opinion leaders; opportunities should be given for experiential learning of what it is like to be handicapped; and contacts should be arranged between disabled and non-disabled persons.

Since contacts can reinforce prejudice, it is important to allay anxieties and fears on both sides beforehand. Ideally, contacts should involve some shared enjoyable activity in pleasant surroundings. Pre- and post-measures of relevant feelings should be taken. Such soundings necessitate great sensitivity and expertise because of the problem of securing representative samples of the public willing to state their opinions, and the vexed issue of the extent to which private feelings find expressions in frank statements and overt actions.

Even the most humanitarian employers have to take into account not only community attitudes but also the cost/benefits of habilitation (in terms of training expenses, productivity and turnover). Handicapped achievers can be inspiring examples, but can also arouse unrealistic expectations in the disabled and their relatives. Measures intended to help the handicapped can backfire. Examples discussed are quota schemes, reserved occupations, and registration of the disabled. In some circumstances disability allowances can discourage job seeking. Hence the proposed Disability Employment Credit scheme.

Successful habilitation requires enthusiastic staff. Their training should feature role play, modelling, feedback and incentives more than traditional lectures. Staff are most likely to implement habilitation procedures which they see to be effective, simple, flexible and inexpensive in time and effort. Programmes should aim at imparting specific skills necessary for independent life and work.

Evaluation of programmes may be done by participants or external observers. The latter tend to be more objective but less aware of what is going on; and their recommendations may not be readily acceptable.

Research can focus on the feelings or actions of those engaged in the habilitation programme, or focus on the programme's outcomes (such as the number of rehabilitees placed in jobs). Baseline measures are essential, and a control group desirable. Evaluators should not be personally or financially involved in the projects. Opinions of staff and of the disabled trainees ought to be sought. Long- as well as short-term effects of the programme should be examined by a variety of techniques (such as interviews, questionnaires, rating scales, tests, direct observation, video- and audio-recordings) as well as by cost/benefit indices (such as productivity, absenteeism, turnover). The reliability and validity of all these measures must be established.

The minicomputer will mean redundancy for many unskilled and some skilled workers, but will greatly extend the vocational potential of the home-bound handicapped, though it may also reduce the amount of face-to-face contact they have with other people. Microcomputer networks are increasing the learning capacity (and correlatively the self-esteem) of mentally handicapped persons in institutions like Royal Earlswood Hospital, Redhill. Keyboards depressed by almost any part of the body which the individual can move enable people with severe motor handicaps to operate electric typewriters, telephones, computers or other home, office or factory equipment. Traditionally, vocational aptitude tests are designed for the able-bodied, but computer-based modes of assessment can be applied to those whose disabilities prevent them from writing, seeing, hearing or speaking. Some aids for the handicapped, like the Optacon for the blind, have potential yet to be fully realized. More promising are attempts to convert scanned text into synthesized speech, even though such speech lacks intonation for communication of feelings.

The secondary effects of a severe disability may be more disruptive than the primary. Counselling or psychotherapy may be needed for emotional disturbance. Tutoring in hospital or home may be essential to compensate for interrupted schooling of young persons who are chronically ill. Training or rehabilitation workshops do not always offer a sufficiently large range of useful and stimulating jobs to test vocational potential. Work tempo in such workshops should be set by supervisors drawn from industry.

Psychosocial issues in some of the major types of disability have been reviewed in this chapter and include the occupational constraints advised for severe epileptics detailed. The excitement of starting a new job can precipitate seizures. New drugs are improving seizure control, but prescribed medication is not always taken.

Improvements in early diagnosis, hearing aids and speech therapy have boosted the vocational prospects of the deaf, as have cochlea implants. Advancement of the deaf in the professions is facilitated in the United States by the existence of a third-level college for them. The deaf can be less distractible employees and be less disturbed by noisy surroundings, but some forms of deafness have associated disabilities, such as dizziness, which narrow employment possibilities. The effects of congenital deafness on language development, and the impact of deafness acquired in adult life on social adjustment, need to be counteracted.

Mobility of the blind is facilitated by guide dogs, long canes, sonic torches and tactile maps, but traditional 'blind' crafts are dying out, though new industries like plastics are to some extent replacing them. Despite cited successes in high-level occupations, for many blind people interpersonal communication remains a daunting problem. Reference is made to new ways of eradicating 'blindisms' and of improving conversational ability, self-presentation and social judgement.

Employers may not always be as sympathetic towards an employee with a hidden disease like heart trouble as towards one with more overt symptoms. It is relatively easy for the 'white collar' worker to return to his or her job after cardiac illness. The labourer, however, may have to seek lighter and less well paid work. Employees with heart disease may feel suspected of malingering. It is difficult for rehabilitation counsellors to steer a proper course between encouraging invalidism and prompting premature return to work by people with a bad heart.

Employers may not be willing to offer the alcoholic a responsible job, as they are well aware that excessive drinking can cause absenteeism, poor job performance and industrial accidents, even fatalities. Concealment of his or her problem by the alcoholic, relatives and colleagues prevents early (and more likely to be successful) remedial action, and can lead to continuous fear of exposure. However, a self-confessed alcoholic may resent being under constant surveillance. For reformed alcoholics the getting of a job is just one stage on the way back and often brings in its train new pressures (e.g. competition for promotion). Non-availability of alcohol in the workplace is an important preventive measure. Therapy is not helped by the controversy between the advocates of complete abstinence and those for whom controlled drinking is the aim. Programmes for the identification and treatment of employees who drink too much, such as the Employee Assistance Programmes, seem cost-effective so should continue spreading despite scepticism about the treatment in some quarters.

Some people with severe motor deficits can perform at a very high level, although a high proportion have their talents unused despite technological advances in their favour. High-IQ spastics can quickly become bored with routine work or unstimulating workmates.

People with marked learning difficulties can find fulfilment in repetitive unskilled work which brighter individuals would quickly abandon, but with automation such jobs are becoming scarcer. The employment potential of persons with mental handicap is increasing with higher aspirations for them and improvements in training methods. Yet they are sometimes denied aids and treatments, available to others, on the grounds that they are unlikely to benefit. Recent cuts in staff and funds have meant the collapse of successful training programmes for some mentally handicapped persons who have consequently reverted to lethargy and over-dependency.

The Earl of Lytton once observed: 'Genius does what it must, and Talent does what it can'. It is up to all of us—employers, employees and the rest—to ensure that the talents, great or small, of handicapped persons can find at least as free and full expression in the work situation as the talents of more fortunate able-bodied individuals.

REFERENCES

Adler, A. (1907). *Study of Organ Inferiority and its Psychical Compensation* (translated by S. Jeliffe), Nervous and Mental Disease Publishing Co., New York.

Akerlind, I., Hörnquist, J.O. and Bjurulf, P. (1988). Prognosis in alcoholic rehabilitation: The relative significance of social, psychological and medical factors, *International Journal of the Addictions*, **23**, 1171–95.

Anastasi, A. (1979). *Fields of Applied Psychology*, 2nd edn, McGraw-Hill, New York.

Anderson, E. and Clarke, L. (1983). *Disability in Adolescence*, Methuen, London.

Anonymous (1986). Hiring the handicapped: Overcoming physical and psychological barriers in the job market, *Journal of American Experience*, **62**, 13–19.

Anonymous (1989). Microcomputers and mental handicap, *The Psychologist*, **2**(3), 120.

Ashman, A.F. (1988). Improving the cognitive competence of intellectually disabled adolescents, *The British Psychological Society Abstracts*, 39.

British Psychological Society, The (1984). Evidence to the House of Commons Social Service Committee on community care, with special reference to the adult mentally ill and mentally handicapped, *Bulletin of The British Psychological Society*, **37**, 378–80.

Brown, C. (1972). *My Left Foot*, Secker & Warburg, London.

Brown, R.A. and Hughson, E.A. (1987). *Behavioural and Social Rehabilitation and Training*, Wiley, Chichester.

Brown, T. (1990). Spain's new TV station chooses blind boss, *Daily Telegraph*, 13 January.

Carney, J. (1983). Behaviour Modification of the Mentally Handicapped, M.Sc. thesis, Department of Psychology, University College, Galway.

Chaplin, J.E. (1987). Health, safety and performance at work of people with epilepsy, *Bulletin of The British Psychological Society*, **40**, A70.

Clements, J. (1987). *Severe Learning Disability and Psychological Handicap*, Wiley, Chichester.

Cohen, B., Anthony, W.A. and Kennard, W.A. (1986). Opening the workplace to the psychologically disabled, *Business and Health*, **3**(4), 9–11.

Cohen, J. and Clark, J.H. (1979). *Medicine, Mind and Man*, Freeman and Co., Reading and San Francisco.

Comfort, N. (1989). 'Superhuman' Jack Ashley to retire, *Daily Telegraph*, 8 February.

Cooper, N.E. (1968). The funding and creating of employment opportunities,

Seminar Report, pp. 59–66, C.S.E. and I.S.R.D., Gothenburg.
Cowie, R.I.D. and Stewart, P. (1987). Acquired deafness and the family: A problem for psychologists, *The Irish Journal of Psychology*, **8**, 138–54.
Cowie, R., Douglas-Cowie, E. and Stewart, P. (1987). The experience of becoming deaf. In J.G. Kyle (ed.) *Adjustment to Acquired Hearing Loss*, Centre for Deaf Studies, Bristol.
Croxen, M. (1983). Prejudice and disability: An overview and introduction, *Bulletin of The British Psychological Society*, **36**, A52.
Cullen, C. (1988). A review of staff training: The emperor's old clothes, *The Irish Journal of Psychology*, **9**(2), 309–23.
Demuth, N. (1947). *Ravel*, Dent, London.
Dijkstra, A. (1986). Turnover among new employees with physical and mental disabilities because of unsuccessful socialization in sheltered workshops, *International Journal of Rehabilitation Research*, **9**(2), 129–37.
Donnan, S. and Haskey, J. (1977). Alcoholism and cirrhosis of the liver. In *Population Trends*, **7**, 18–24, HMSO, London.
Dooley Groarke, A.M. (1985). *Community Integration*, Woodlands Centre, Galway.
Duran, E. (1987). Overcoming people barriers in placing severely aberrant autistic students in work sites and community, *Education*, **107**(3), 333–7.
Esgrow, C. (1978). Placement and follow-up as part of the rehabilitation process, *Journal of Practical Approaches to Developmental Handicap*, **2**, 5–8.
Farkas, G.M. (1989). The impact of federal rehabilitation laws on the expanding role of employee assistance programs in business and industry, *American Psychologist*, **44**(12), 1482–90.
Felce, D. (1988). Evaluating the extent of community integration following the provision of staffed residential alternatives of institutional care, *The Irish Journal of Psychology*, **9**(2), 346–60.
Finkelstein, V. (1985). Concepts of impairment, disability and handicap, Letter to the editors, *Bulletin of The British Psychological Society*, **38**, 263.
Flack, J. (1981). Minicomputers and the disabled user, *Bulletin of The British Psychological Society*, **34**, 209.
Floor, L. and Rosen, M. (1976). New criteria of adjustment for the cerebral palsied, *Rehabilitation Literature*, **37**(9), 268–74.
Fralick, P.C. and Brochu, S. (1988). The Canadian Forces Europe lifeskills program, *Alcoholism Treatment Quarterly*, **5**, 191–208.
Gallivan, M. (1986). Disabled workers can stabilize staff turnover, *Hospitals*, **60**(9), 154.
Gibbons, H. (1989). The nightwatch: Cognitive correlates of nightwork in a student nurse sample, Paper read at the First European Congress of Psychology, Amsterdam, 2–7 July.
Gray, J. (1969). The Scottish experiment, *Journal of Alcoholism*, **4**, 461–6.
Greenblum, J. and Bye, B. (1987). Work values of disabled beneficiaries, *Social Security Bulletin*, **50**(4), 67–74.
Griffiths, P. (1986). *Encyclopaedia of 20th-Century Music*, Thames and Hudson, London.
Griffiths, R.D.P. (1975). Vocational guidance conducted with psychiatric patients, *Bulletin of The British Psychological Society*, **28**, 427–36.
Grunewald, K. (1969). *The Mentally Retarded in Sweden*, National Board of Health and Welfare, Stockholm.
Haggard, M.P. (1985). Concepts of impairment, disability and handicap, *Bulletin of The British Psychological Society*, **38**, 83.

Hawking, S.W. (1988). *A Brief History of Time*, Bantam Books, London.
Health and Safety Executive (1981). *The Problem Drinker at Work*, HMSO, London.
Heather, N. and Robertson, I. (1985). *Problem Drinking*, Penguin Books, Harmondsworth.
Hibbs, John (1990). Extra £200m in aid for the disabled, *Daily Telegraph*, 11 January.
Hill, M. (1983). *Understanding Social Policy*, 2nd edn, Blackwell and Robertson, Oxford.
Hill, N., Mehnert, T. and Lederer, E. (1987). The merits of hiring disabled persons, *Business and Health*, **4**(4), 42–4.
Hughson, E.A. and Brown, R.I. (1988). The evaluation of adult rehabilitation programmes, *The Irish Journal of Psychology*, **9**(2), 249–63.
Hurley, J. (1989). The new technologies and the changing nature and organization of work, *The Irish Journal of Psychology*, **10**(3), 368–80.
Institute of Hearing Research (1981). Population study of hearing disorders in adults, *Journal of the Royal Society of Medicine*, **74**, 819–27.
Johnson, D.G. (1987). Correlates of Adolescent Alcohol Involvement, M.A. thesis, Department of Psychology, University College, Galway.
Kanga, F. (1990). A meeting of two remarkable men, *Sunday Correspondent*, 21 January.
Katz, A.H. and Felton, J.S. (eds) (1965). *Health and the Community*, Free Press, New York.
Keane, A.M. (1990). An Investigation of Inter-ictal Learning and Memory in Epileptic Outpatients, Ph.D. thesis, Department of Psychology, University College, Galway.
Kemp, N.J. (1981). Social psychological aspects of blindness: A review, *Current Psychological Reviews*, 68–89.
Kent, G. and Dalgleish, M. (1986). *Psychology and Medical Care*, 2nd edn, Baillière Tindall, London.
Kirton, M. (1989). Cognitive style and alcoholics: A comment on Robertson *et al.*, *Psychological Reports*, **65**, 456–8.
Klarreich, S.H., Di Giuseppe, R. and Di Mattia, D.J. (1987). Cost effectiveness of an employee assistance programme with rational-emotive therapy, *Professional Psychology: Research and Practice*, **18**, 140–4.
Kyle, J.G. (1985). Deaf people: Assessing the community or the handicap, *Bulletin of The British Psychological Society*, **38**, 137–41.
Kyle, J.G. and Pullen, G. (1984). *Young Deaf People in Employment: Report to M.R.C.*, University School of Education, Bristol.
Lash, J.P. (1980). *Helen and Teacher: The Story of Helen Keller and Anne Sullivan Macy*, Penguin Books, Harmondsworth.
Leighton, A. (ed.) (1988). *Mental Handicap in the Community*, Woodhead-Faulkner, London.
MacLeod, A.G.S. (1985). EAPs and blue collar stress. In C.L. Cooper and M.J. Smith (eds) *Job Stress and Blue Collar Work*, pp. 185–93, Wiley, Chichester.
Madden, J.S. (1967). Alcoholism and drug dependency in the Civil Service, *British Journal of Addiction*, **62**, 403.
Madden, J.S. (1979). *A Guide to Alcohol and Drug Dependence*, Wright, Bristol.
Markova, I., Jahoda, A. and Cattermole, M. (1988). Towards truly independent living, *The Psychologist*, **1**(10), 397–9.
Marshall, J. (1985). An Experimental Study of Metamemory and Interrogative Strategy Training, Maintenance and Far Generalization in the Mentally Handicapped, Ph.D. thesis, Department of Psychology, University College, Galway.

Masi, D. (1984). *Designing Employee Assistance Programs*, AMACOM, New York.

McConkey, R. (1988). Assessing community attitudes, *The Irish Journal of Psychology*, **9**(2), 373–88.

McConkey, R. and McCormack, B. (1983). *Breaking Barriers: Educating People about Disability*, Souvenir Press, London.

McGinley, P. (ed.) (1986). *Research and Practice in the Service of People with Learning Difficulties*, Brothers of Charity Services, Galway.

McHugh, M.F. (1969). Some applications and limitations of operant conditioning in the training of so-called ineducable children. In M.F. McHugh (ed.) *Proceedings of the Fourth International Seminar on Special Education*, pp. 65–70, International Society for Rehabilitation of the Disabled, New York.

McHugh, M.F. and O'Donoghue, A. (1980). *Employment and the Disabled: Part 1, Principles; Part 2, Practice*. Report commissioned by The Industrial Training Authority, Dublin.

McLoone, J. (1988). The development of services for people with mental handicap in Ireland: The contribution of psychologists, *The Irish Journal of Psychology*, **9**(2), 205–10.

Melin, K.-A. (1969). Practical aspects of employing people with epilepsy. *Proceedings of the 11th World Congress of Rehabilitation International*, pp. 54–7, N.R.B./I.S.R.D., Dublin.

Mittler, P. (1984). Quality of life and services for people with disabilities, *Bulletin of The British Psychological Society*, **37**, 218–25.

Moore, P.J. (1985). Learned Helplessness in Developmentally Disabled Adults: An Examination of the Mediating Influence of Normalization Processes, Ph.D. thesis, Department of Psychology, The Queen's University, Belfast.

Moss, M.C. and Davies, E.B. (1967). *A Study of Alcoholism in an English County*, Geigy, London.

Nathan, P.E. (1986). What do behavioural scientists know—and what can they do—about alcoholism, *Nebraska Symposium on Motivation*, **34**, 1–25.

Nolan, Christopher (1987). *Under the Eye of the Clock*, Weidenfeld and Nicolson, London.

Plant, M. (1979). *Drinking Careers*, Tavistock, London.

Quayle, D. (1983). American productivity: The devastating effect of alcoholism and drug abuse, *American Psychologist*, **38**, 454–8.

Rittersporn, B. (1986). Employ the deaf: It's sound advice, *Worklife*, **4**(6), 14.

Robertson, I. and Heather, N. (1985). *So You Want to Cut Down Your Drinking*?, Scottish Health Education Group, Edinburgh.

Rollin, H.R. (1980). The right to care: The plight of the chronic schizophrenic in the community. In H.R. Rollin (ed.) *Coping with Schizophrenia*, Burnett Books, London.

Rome Correspondent (1989). 'Worker' sick of being paid for doing nothing, *Daily Telegraph*, 5 July.

Rosen, M., Clark, G.R. and Kivitz, M.S. (1977). *Habilitation of the Handicapped*, University Park Press, Baltimore.

Safilios-Rothschild, C. (1966). Social prejudice against the sick and disabled, *Abstracts of Tenth World Congress of the International Society for Rehabilitation of the Disabled*, pp. 181–2, I.S.R.D., New York.

Sanchez-Craig, M., Annis, H., Bornet, A. and McDonald, K. (1984). Random assignment to abstinence and controlled drinking: Evaluation of a cognitive behavioral program for problem drinkers, *Journal of Consulting and Clinical Psychology*, **52**, 390–403.

Schapire, J.A. and Berger, F. (1984). Responsibilities and benefits in hiring the handicapped, *Cornell Hotel and Restaurant Administration Quarterly*, **24**(4), 59–67.

Sculnick, M.W. (1988). Defining disability: What is a 'handicap'?, *Employment Relations Today*, **15**(2), 87–106.

Slevin, M. (1986). The Utility of Photographic Cues in Training Severely Mentally Handicapped Young Adults on a Complex Vocational Task, M.A. thesis, Department of Psychology, University College, Galway.

Smyth, B. (1981). Help!, *Radio Times*, London, 3–9 January.

Solomon, B. and Wagel, W.H. (1988). Spreading the word on new technologies for people with disabilities, *Personnel*, **65**(7), 14–18.

Stevens, A. (1989). The politics of caring, *The Psychologist*, **2**(3), 110–11.

Stevens, G.E. (1986). Exploding the myths about hiring the handicapped, *Personnel*, **63**(12), 57–60.

Taylor, R. (1985). *Robert Schumann: His Life and Work*, Panther Books, London.

Taylor, W.W. and Taylor, I.W. (1967). *Services for Handicapped Youth in England and Wales*, I.S.R.D., New York.

Thornton, A.R. (1986). Estimation of the number of patients who might be suitable for cochlear implant and similar procedures, *British Journal of Audiology*, **20**, 221–9.

Threlkeld, R.M. (1983). Hiring the disabled: An attempt to influence behavioral intentions through a media presentation, *Rehabilitation Psychology*, **28**(2), 105–14.

Toomey, J.F. and O'Callaghan, R.J. (1983). Adult status of mentally retarded pupils from special education. Part two: Social adaptation, *International Journal of Rehabilitation Research*, **6**, 301–12.

Vincent, T. (1986). Communication and blind people: Some experiences with new technology in education, *Bulletin of The British Psychological Society*, **39**, A89.

Wallechinsky, D. and Wallace, I. (1978). *The People's Almanac*, 2nd edn, Bantam Books, New York.

Wiegand, R.A. (1972). Alcoholism in industry, *British Journal of Addiction*, **67**, 181–7.

Wilder, J. (1982). The ill on the streets, *The Health Service*, 24 December.

Willetts, D. (1989). Cutting through the shackles of disability, *Sunday Correspondent*, 17 December.

Williams, J.M. (1988). Technology and the disabled, *Personnel Administrator*, **33**(7), 81–3.

Willis, R. (1987). Mainstreaming the handicapped without tokenism, *Management Review*, **76**(3), 42–8.

Wilson, S.L. (1987). Psychological assessment of people with varying degrees of physical disability, *Bulletin of The British Psychological Society*, **40**, A35.

Wing, J.K. and Greer, C. (1980). Schizophrenia at home. In H.R. Robbin (ed.) *Coping with Schizophrenia*, Burnett Books, London.

Wolfensberger, W. (1983). Social role valorization: A proposed new term for the principle of normalization, *Mental Retardation*, **21**(6), 234–9.

Wolkstein, E. (1979). The former addict in the work place. In B.S. Brown (ed.) *Addicts and Aftercare*, pp. 103–14, Sage, London.

World Health Organization (1980). *International Classification of Impairment, Disability and Handicap*, WHO, Geneva.

Chapter 4.2

Disabled Workers: Legal Issues

Brian Doyle, University of Salford, UK

INTRODUCTION

In this chapter, the legal issues raised by disabled employment are discussed. The foundations of modern disabled employment policy are laid and the legal definition of disability explained. Disabled persons' entry into the labour market is considered, and the problem of countering discrimination, while promoting acceptance in recruitment and selection, is addressed. Disabled workers' rights to equal treatment and employment opportunities are examined, followed by analysis of employment protection and job security laws affecting disabled persons. Finally, in so far as labour law is found to be wanting in reducing the employment vulnerability of disabled people, the desirability and shape of future law reform is reflected upon.

The Justification for Disabled Employment Laws

The justification for legislating for disabled employment has been advanced by Berkowitz and Hill (1986):

> Disability imposes individual and social costs. With the onset of a potentially disabling condition, an individual experiences both economic and psychic losses as he or she faces restricted choices. The individual may suffer pain, incur increased medical costs, lose income, and face societal prejudice. Society may lose the output of an otherwise productive worker and use its resources for medical care and rehabilitation. A firm may lose its investment in the hiring and training of that worker.

The nature and severity of disability disqualifies many individuals from economic activity. Nevertheless, disabled workers can be handicapped by ignorance, fear and prejudice of employers and 'able-bodied' workers (Lyth, 1973; Walker, 1982). Entry to and participation in the labour market is

Vulnerable Workers: Psychosocial and Legal Issues. Edited by M. J. Davidson and J. Earnshaw

obstructed by structural and institutional barriers erected by the norms of the non-disabled world and maintained by the legacy of past discrimination. Like women and minority groups, disabled workers often experience unequal employment opportunities, limited rights at work and reduced job security. Therein lies the employment vulnerability of persons with disabilities.

International labour standards recognize this vulnerability and furnish some support for the guarantee of disabled employment rights. The United Nations Declaration on the Rights of Disabled Persons expresses the right of disabled people to

> economic and social security and to a decent level of living, . . . [and] according to their capabilities, to secure and retain employment or to engage in a useful, productive and remunerative occupation.

The International Labour Organization requires governments to formulate and implement policies for vocational rehabilitation and disabled employment, to promote equal employment opportunities in competitive employment and to permit positive discrimination in favour of disabled workers (Convention No. 159 and Recommendation No. 168 of 1983). The European Social Charter mandates signatory states

> to take adequate . . . measures to encourage employers to admit disabled persons to employment.

The European Communities' Recommendation on the Employment of Disabled People exhorts member states to take all appropriate measures to promote fair employment and vocational training opportunities for disabled people (note also the EC Charter of Fundamental Social Rights).

In Britain, however, disabled employment rights have been more often the product of political pragmatism than of international obligation. Recent research (Martin, Meltzer and Elliot, 1988; Martin and White, 1988; Martin, White and Meltzer, 1989) estimates that there are 2.3 million disabled adults below pension age in Britain (cf. National Audit Office, 1987; Birkett and Worman, 1988; Prescott-Clarke, 1990). Of these, only 31% were in paid employment, compared with 69% for the general population, while the rate and length of disabled unemployment is twice that for the population in general (Manpower Services Commission, 1982; Parker, 1983; NAO, 1987).

The Tomlinson Principles

Post-war British employment policy conceded to disabled people limited recognition of a right to work. Government acknowledged that their exclusion from the labour force reduced productive capacity and increased social costs (Tomlinson, 1943). Disabled persons were seen to have a justifiable claim to competitive employment and, given the opportunity, to be capable of normal working lives without institutional or sheltered protection. The objective was

> to secure for the disabled their full share, within their capacity, of such employment as is ordinarily available.

Measures to promote opportunity and negate prejudice were essential, but the creation of employment for disabled workers and the extension of preference to them, without regard to individual ability and production efficiency, were ruled out.

These principles formed the basis of the Disabled Persons (Employment) Act 1944. A decade later, the law was found to be without need of radical change (Piercy, 1956), and only minor amendments were effected in 1958. Since then, there have been changes in the composition of the disabled population and advances in medical science and health care. Increases in unemployment and novel demand for a skilled and flexible workforce have accompanied developments in technology and in the range of disablement assistance and benefits. While the aspirations of disabled people have changed, subsequent reviews of disabled employment services have rarely questioned the Tomlinson philosophy (MSC, 1978a, 1982, 1986).

A recent reassessment of this philosophy found continuity in the approach to disabled employment provision and endorsed the justification for helping disabled people in the employment field (National Advisory Council on Employment of Disabled People, 1986). The fundamental policy was reiterated: that

> access of disabled people to training and to jobs and their development within organisations should be based on their capacities as individuals, properly and fairly assessed . . . [and that] . . . disabled people for whom special employment provision has been arranged should enjoy the same employment rights as other workers.

A strong case was recognized that

> legislation properly designed and applied is an essential tool, particularly when supported by persuasive action, for helping the employment prospects of disabled people.

A change in emphasis in disabled employment policy, away from statutory compulsion and towards the promotion of voluntary equal opportunity practices, is illustrated by contemporary developments (DE, 1990).

The Legal Concept of Disability

Disability denotes a physical or mental condition substantially modifying daily life functions without destroying the ability to work (Weiss, 1974). Tomlinson (1943) defined disability by reference to the handicap it created in obtaining suitable employment. That definition covered disablements of all kinds and from all causes, excluding those of a minor or temporary character. A distinction between handicaps produced by disability and those resulting from other disadvantages was drawn. The definition was subjective, rather than dependent upon objective medical criteria, but recognized that handicap is a changing social construct resulting from the interaction of person and environment.

For the purposes of the 1944 Act, a disabled person is defined as

> a person who, on account of injury, disease, or congenital deformity, is substantially handicapped in obtaining or keeping employment, or in undertaking work on his own account, of a kind which apart from that injury, disease or deformity would be suited to his age, experience and qualifications.

Registration as disabled under the Act is voluntary and eligibility is determined in the light of medical and other relevant evidence. Disability must be likely to continue for at least 12 months and the applicant must be otherwise employable. Proof of registration is afforded by a certificate, commonly known as a 'green card'. A disabled person may be removed from the register upon ceasing to satisfy the registration criteria, or as a result of unreasonable failure to attend or complete vocational rehabilitation or training, or because of an unreasonable and persistent refusal of suitable work, or by application for deregistration.

It is believed that the register

> encourages the view that disabled people are a separate and stereotyped category of human being rather than individuals with diverse and changing needs.
>
> (NACEDP, 1986)

Registration can stigmatize and highlight disabilities rather than abilities, while producing a risk of permanent categorization as disabled. The status of registered disabled person is the basis for certain, although not all, disabled employment rights. Nevertheless, numbers of registered disabled persons have declined steadily since 1944. Between 1950 and 1986, the *registered* disabled population declined from 936000 to 389000, which constitutes about 1% of the workforce (NAO, 1987; cf. Martin, White and Meltzer, 1989; Prescott-Clarke, 1990), although simultaneously the number of disabled persons registered for social welfare purposes was rising (Topliss and Gould, 1981; Whitehead, 1981). The decline in the number of registered disabled persons is variously ascribed to ignorance of the legislation, lack of incentive to register for perceived ineffective rights, the availability of many services regardless of registration, individuals' self-perception of their status, or plain dislike of the concept of registration (MSC, 1981a; NAO, 1987; Prescott-Clarke, 1990).

The individual should bear the burden of proving membership of a protected class, but disabled persons ought not to be asked to register their status in order to enjoy basic human rights. A legal redefinition of disability must precede enfranchisement of disabled workers. In the United States, disabled persons constitute a broadly defined protected class (Chapter 3), while Canadian and Australian legislation exemplifies disability definitions sufficiently precisely to exclude negative judicial interpretation, but is flexible enough to recognize disability as a product of self-definition and social construction (Doyle, 1987b). These comparative perspectives point a way forward.

ENTRY INTO THE LABOUR MARKET

For many disabled persons, entry or re-entry to the labour market is restricted by impairment or disability, lack of skills or qualifications, and income insecurity during the transition from disabled unemployment to rehabilitated employment. Labour market access may be encouraged via a combination of vocational resettlement, rehabilitation and training; social security and income maintenance measures; and provision of non-competitive or sheltered employment (Haveman, Halberstadt and Burkhauser, 1984; Habeck *et al.*, 1985; Berkowitz and Hill, 1986). In Britain, these facilities are the product of an uneven patchwork of legal regulation, administrative action and voluntary effort (McCrostie and Peacock, 1984).

Vocational Resettlement, Rehabilitation and Training

The 1944 Act provided various services targeted at disabled persons. Resettlement of disabled workers is the responsibility of Disablement Resettlement Officers (DROs), who act as a conduit between disabled persons and the rehabilitation and training services, while the Disablement Advisory Service advises and liaises with employers. The significance of this role in assisting disabled persons into employment cannot be overestimated (Robbins, 1982). Disabled people are recognized as having priority in and are encouraged to use mainstream training and employment services, freeing the DRO to provide a more specialist service (MSC, 1982). In 1985–86, 18000 disabled persons were placed into employment by a DRO, a further

37400 by mainstream employment services, and an estimated 22300 through the self-service facilities of Jobcentres (NAO, 1987; cf. DE, 1990).

Vocational rehabilitation facilitates the re-entry into employment of the long-term unemployed, among whom disabled people are represented disproportionately. The origins of the employment rehabilitation services lie in interim arrangements made during the Second World War for recruiting previously unemployed disabled workers to industrial vacancies left by military conscription (Cornes, 1982). The Tomlinson recommendations (1943) led to establishment upon a statutory footing of an Employment Rehabilitation Service and a network of Employment Rehabilitation Centres, whose objectives include improving physical capacity, restoring confidence and assessing the rehabilitee's chances of permanent resettlement (Darnbrough and Kinrade, 1981). Registration under the 1944 Act is not a precondition to participation in the rehabilitation services, and non-disabled persons unemployed for reasons other than work shortage may also be able to take advantage.

ERC success in restoring disabled persons to the labour market is in inverse proportion to the prevailing rate of unemployment (MSC, 1981b; Cornes, 1982). In 1975, within six months of completing rehabilitation, 45% of rehabilitees were employed and 55% unemployed (Greaves and Massie, 1979). A decade later, within three months of completing rehabilitation, only 40% went into employment and 60% undertook further training or remained unemployed (NAO, 1987). Vocational rehabilitation has had low expectations of disabled persons' abilities (Greaves, 1969; Greaves and Massie, 1979), and ERC provision has been geographically uneven, the proportion of non-disabled clients significantly high, and reference of disabled job seekers to an ERC by Jobcentres spasmodic (Employment Rehabilitation Research Centre, 1984; NAO, 1987). Although not immune from criticism, vocational rehabilitation has made important contributions to the employability of disabled workers and assisted their access to the labour market. A recent review of rehabilitation services is likely to lead to improved, increased coverage of such services and to the reorientation of their aims and objectives towards disabled clients (Committee of Public Accounts, 1988; DE, 1990).

Government has been under a duty since 1973 to make appropriate arrangements for vocational training to assist disabled persons to enter the labour market on equal terms with other workers. Training scheme rules have been applied less restrictively in respect of disabled persons, who have also enjoyed some priority in course allocation and, in appropriate cases, access to professional training (Piercy, 1956; MSC, 1978a; Darnbrough and Kinrade, 1981). In 1985–86, some 6000 disabled persons were placed on the Youth Training Scheme (YTS) and 3600 on adult training schemes (NAO, 1987). However, there is evidence that persons with certain disabilities continue to be handicapped by lack of employment training and become trapped in their unskilled or semi-skilled status (Whaley *et al.*, 1986; Royal National Institute for the Deaf, 1987). With renewed emphasis upon strategies to assist the long-term unemployed, training assistance for disabled persons is now a high priority (DE, 1988a; 1990).

Social Security and Income Maintenance

Where disability results in diminished employment status, reduced earnings and additional costs, disabled people must look to the state for income maintenance and substitution (Walker, 1981; Brown, 1984; Alcock, 1987). The national insurance scheme provides income replacement for employed disabled persons in the form of short-term statutory sick pay and invalidity benefit payable during continued work incapacity. Under the industrial injuries scheme, employed earners who suffer injury (or disease) at work receive a disablement pension paid on a sliding scale according to degree of disablement, and a reduced earnings allowance to make up the difference between what they are now capable of earning and projected earnings but for disablement. Entitlement to invalidity benefit and reduced earnings allowance accrued by demonstrating incapacity for work or loss of earning capacity, whereas entitlement to disablement pension under the industrial injuries scheme is assessed by reference to the degree of impairment or loss of faculty. Many disabled people can work but cannot earn enough to support themselves, while others may not have a sufficient record of employment to qualify for national insurance benefits. They must look to severe disablement allowance, the extra costs benefits of attendance, mobility and invalid care allowances, and to means-tested benefits.

Transition from unemployment to competition in the labour market via part-time employment is hampered by the operation of the benefits system. The system does not allow for many disabled persons who fall between the stools of complete work incapacitation and full employability. Except in the case of the industrial injuries scheme, part-time work can lead to the loss of state benefits. Weekly earnings over a relatively low threshold temporarily result in disentitlement to benefit and, if the work is not therapeutic, entitlement to benefit may be stopped altogether on the ground of capability for work. If invalidity benefit claimants work for more than eight weeks between two periods of incapacity for work, they have to spend 28 weeks on statutory sick pay (or sickness benefit) at a lower rate than invalidity benefit, before requalifying. This is

> a disincentive . . . to try working until they are sure they are fit to go back to work (Social Security Advisory Committee, 1988).

McDonnell and Weale (1984) speculate that the elasticity of supply of disabled workers might be affected by social security payments acting as a disincentive to enter the labour market (cf. Robbins, 1982; Leonard, 1986; Worrall and Butler, 1986). Thus the value of disability benefits may lead to a larger number of people redefining themselves as disabled and withdrawing from an unstable labour market, rather than lose hard won entitlement to benefits and sacrifice income support by taking low paid employment. Equally, however, it may not be the value of the benefits which acts as an employment disincentive, but rather the abrupt loss of them (Simpkins and Tickner, 1978). In either case, the number of recipients of invalidity benefit has risen in recent years, as unemployment grew and disabled people with a marginal capacity for work became unable to compete in the labour market (SSAC, 1988).

A larger number of disabled persons could be brought to full participation in the labour market through a combination of flexible or part-time employment and income maintenance provision (Davoud, 1980; Topliss, 1982; Lonsdale and Walker, 1984). Grover and Gladstone (1981) observe that

> if part-time and shared working is to become a reality, it is essential that the financial disincentives are removed, that the principle of partial incapacity is acknowledged and a sliding scale of benefits clawback is introduced . . . People who have been out of work for a certain period by reason of illness or disability should be able, as of right, to work to their limited capacity and to retain a decreasing proportion of benefit.

As has been seen, at present

> most invalidity benefits are geared to non-workers rather than to those individuals who occupy a place somewhere in the grey area between total incapacity and complete capacity for work
>
> (Lonsdale and Walker, 1984).

This has led many commentators to argue for a comprehensive disability income (Disability Alliance, 1975, 1987; Mitchell, 1986; Disablement Income Group, 1987). This might include a partial invalidity benefit, which can supplement part-time earnings, and a reducing scale of benefits as earned income increases from open employment. Provision could be made for a universal non-means-tested benefit, based upon the degree of disability, as a compensatory payment to recognize the extra costs of being disabled; an invalidity pension payable to those incapable of earning employed income (with provision being made for partial incapacity); and special allowances to reflect the special needs produced by certain disabilities (Topliss, 1979, 1982).

The EC Recommendation suggests that measures should be taken to ensure that benefit systems do not act as disincentives to part-time employment, trial periods of employment or gradual take-up of a job or return to it where this is desirable to disabled workers and employers (see also NACEDP, 1986). The SSAC (1988) rejects the argument that substantial improvements in incapacity benefits would have adverse effects on work and rehabilitation incentives. The introduction of an integrated disablement allowance, payable at a variety of rates, as income replacement and extra disability-related costs assistance is recommended. The linking rule for invalidity benefit should be extended to at least 13 weeks, it is proposed, so as to encourage people who are on benefit to test their capacity for work without losing the safety net of benefit entitlement should they find it impossible to continue working. The devising of a means-tested benefit to supplement incomes of disabled people who work but are not fully able to support themselves, entitlement to which would be based on an assessment of disability similar to that of the industrial injuries scheme, is also mooted (SSAC, 1988). In response, a new disability employment credit supplementing a revised disability allowance has been proposed (Department of Social Security, 1990).

Non-Competitive and Sheltered Employment

Tomlinson (1943) identified the need to provide sheltered employment for a minority of disabled persons unlikely, due to the nature or severity of their disability, to be capable of open employment for a substantial period or at all. The 1944 Act mandates the provision of facilities, to enable registered disabled persons with severe disabilities, who are unable in the open labour market to obtain employment or to compete on comparable terms with able-bodied persons, to be trained and to work or be employed under special conditions. Sheltered employment provision is undertaken by local authorities, approved voluntary bodies, and Remploy Ltd (Edwards, 1958; Van de Vliet, 1984). Approximately 17000 severely disabled people are employed under sheltered conditions (NAO, 1987) but, contrary to the expectations of Tomlinson (1943), only 1% of disabled persons in sheltered employment achieve a transition into open employment (MSC, 1982).

The organizational, financial and managerial efficiency of sheltered employment provision has been often criticized (DE, 1973b; Morgan and Makeham, 1978; NACEDP, 1986; NAO, 1987). The risks of segregation and stigmatization of disabled workers in sheltered employment must also be accounted for. Integration must be a key objective of any transitional and supported employment policy (Lonsdale and Walker, 1984). At the same time, the division of disabled persons into those capable of competing in open employment and those for whom sheltered employment is the only option must be seen for the over-simplification that it is.

The Sheltered Placement Scheme (SPS) meets some of these criticisms. It provides integrated employment opportunities for severely disabled persons in open employment (Wood, 1986; DE, 1988b). Local authorities, voluntary bodies or Remploy Ltd sponsor a registered disabled person who satisfies the condition of severe disability. The sponsor pays the individual a wage for work done under contract for a host company which provides the work and training. The host company pays the sponsor for the work done by the individual based upon actual output measured against the notional costs of employing an able-bodied worker to do the work. The sponsor may also be subsidized from government funds. Further development of sheltered employment constitutes an alternative approach to disabled employment opportunity (Thornton and Maynard, 1986), and may be defensible on both economic and political grounds (Jones and Cullis, 1988; Prescott-Clarke, 1990; DE, 1990).

COUNTERING DISCRIMINATION AND PROMOTING EMPLOYABILITY

The Quota Scheme

The 1944 Act obliges employers of at least 20 workers to employ registered disabled persons up to a standard quota currently fixed at 3%. Although not binding upon the Crown, government departments have accepted that the principle of the quota applies to them (Cabinet Office, 1985). For the purpose of calculation, workers employed for less than 10 hours per week are disregarded, while those working less than 30 hours per week count as half a unit. Disabled persons employed by a host employer under the SPS do not count towards satisfaction of that employer's quota. On application by a particular employer, the quota percentage applicable to that employer may be reduced for up to 12 months where the employer's circumstances dictate.

If an employer is not employing the quota of registered disabled persons at times when vacancies occur, vacancies must be allocated for this purpose. An employer shall not employ or offer to employ any person other than a registered disabled person (unless, for example, where complying with an unfair dismissal re-employment order), if immediately after employing such other person the employer is below quota. The legality of the employment of a person resulting in breach of the statutory quota scheme is unaffected, but contravention of this duty is a criminal offence. The statutory quota does not apply to the filling of vacancies by an employer with an exemption permit. These are issued if expedient in the light of the nature of the employment vacancies, and the qualifications and suitability for that work of available registered disabled persons; or if there are no (or insufficient numbers of) registered disabled persons available for that work. A permit may authorize the employment in identified occupations of named individuals or a specified number of non-registered individuals. Alternatively, a bulk permit may allow the employment of a specified number of workers during the following six months, although the employer is still notionally (although not legally) bound to notify vacancies and consider sympathetically registered disabled persons available during the permit's currency.

It is estimated that the scheme covers 59% of the employed population and applies to some 34000 employers (NAO, 1987). However, the proportion of employers fulfilling quota has fallen between 1965 and 1986 from 53% to 27%, while the number of employers below quota holding permits has risen from 28% to 56%. Between 1979 and 1986, the percentage of the workforce registered as disabled in employments covered by the quota scheme fell from 1.8% to 1.0% in the private sector and from 1.3% to 0.8% in the public sector. On 1987 figures, no government department or county council met the quota and the record of local government is generally poor. Bulk permits now represent 98% of all permits issued. The quota scheme has been characterized as 'ineffective, unenforceable and incapable of achieving its aim' (NAO, 1987; Committee of Public Accounts, 1988).

The enforcement of the scheme is perhaps most controversial. Employers must keep records, open to inspection, relating to the employment of registered disabled persons and quota compliance, and ought to make annual returns to Jobcentres whose staff regularly draw the quota obligation to employers' attention. DRO and DAS teams carry out some 2000 inspections per year and infringing employers can expect follow-up visits (NAO, 1987). However, only 10 prosecutions (eight successful) have been brought during the history of the scheme. In any event, the penalties for breach of the quota may be of little deterrence to employers ignoring their statutory obligations, as was recognized by an unsuccessful attempt to raise them in the Companies (Disabled Employees Quota) bill 1986. Undoubtedly, the inability of employers to meet the quota in principle, consequent upon the decline in the numbers of registered disabled persons, makes enforcement academic. Previous attempts to enforce the quota more rigorously only resulted in employers putting pressure on *existing* employees to register rather than leading to new engagements (NAO, 1987). Zealous enforcement of the law is seen to be counter productive to the coterminous strategies for placement of disabled persons into employment. Emphasis is upon education, advice and encouragement rather than prosecution (DE, 1990).

Despite this catalogue of weaknesses, the quota has shown remarkable durability and has survived largely because of the symbolic significance attached to it (Bolderson, 1980). The quota has even been shown to be an attainable goal, albeit not without difficulties, given requisite political and managerial will (Industrial Relations Services, 1989). A decision on the future of the scheme is expected shortly (DE, 1990). Earlier reviews (DE, 1973a; MSC, 1979, 1981a, 1985) have considered that retention of the quota would require an amended scheme, which might include reducing the quota to a realistic target, allowing employers to count all disabled workers regardless of registration, abolishing exemption permits, and providing incentives in the form of subsidies or favourable taxation treatment to employers of disabled people. More radically, the enforcement of the quota via levies against recalcitrant employers has been urged, an approach favoured in a number of European models (Brooke-Ross, 1984; Floyd and North, 1986; IRS, 1988c).

Each option attracts simultaneous support and reservation (Lonsdale and Walker, 1984; Gladstone, 1985). It may be that the political and legislative rationale for the statutory scheme has been undermined (McDonnell and Weale, 1984; Jones and Cullis, 1988), leaving abolition inevitable (DE, 1990). It was suggested that the quota should be replaced by a general statutory duty, linked to a code of practice, requiring employers to promote the employment of disabled people (MSC, 1981a). This proposal did not attract political support (Employment Committee, 1981. 1982). A Code of Good Practice on the Employment of Disabled People was produced by the MSC in 1984 but, without the statutory framework of the original proposal, is deprived of legal status and is devoid of sanctions to underpin it.

Reserved Occupations

Certain classes of employment may be reserved for registered disabled persons on the grounds that they afford specially suitable disabled employment opportunities. The employment of passenger electric lift attendant and car park attendant have been singled out as reserved occupations. Any employer, whether or not otherwise subject to the quota scheme, who engages or employs a person other than a registered disabled person in such reserved occupations commits an offence, subject to parallel exceptions to those in the quota scheme. Registered disabled persons employed in reserved occupations do not count towards the fulfilment of the employer's statutory quota.

The abandonment of the reserved occupations provision has been recommended (MSC, 1981a). Tomlinson (1943) did not intend that the scheduled occupations should become regarded as the proper employment objective of disabled persons without regard to individual intelligence or capacity. They tend to reinforce the prejudice that disabled workers are only capable of low grade, low paid employment and

> should not form part of any policy which is seriously attempting to improve the lot of workers with disabilities.
>
> (Lonsdale and Walker, 1984)

Yet,

> practical realities, rather than philosophical arguments, point to the need to continue the scheme
>
> (Employment Committee, 1981)

in a time of high disabled unemployment.

Measures of Reasonable Accommodation

The employability of disabled persons can be promoted if an employer is willing to take measures of reasonable accommodation at the workplace (Collignon, 1986). Making adaptations to premises and equipment can remove many of the structural and environmental barriers which produce employment handicap. The Chronically Sick and Disabled Persons Act 1970 requires employers to make reasonable and practicable provision for the needs of disabled persons using any premises provided by them. This obligation encompasses access to and within the workplace, car parking facilities and sanitary conveniences. When provisions of the Disabled Persons Act 1981 are brought into force, employers will be obliged to make appropriate provision in these areas in conformity with the Code of Practice for Access for the Disabled in Buildings. Grants are available for adaptation to premises or equipment in order that disabled employees, who would otherwise have no chance of finding alternative work in the near future, might enjoy equal terms and conditions with able-bodied employees doing the same work. In addition, registered disabled employees may be lent special tools or equipment other than would be needed ordinarily by non-disabled co-workers. The employment of certain visually handicapped workers is also encouraged by meeting in part the costs of providing part-time readers to assist them at work.

The Job Introduction Scheme may also be seen as a measure of reasonable accommodation. This allows an employer to employ a disabled worker on a trial basis for up to six weeks with a subsidy against the worker's wages. This applies to an existing, newly disabled employee or a potential employee introduced by a DRO where there are doubts about the individual's employability. While the scheme is intended to assist the disabled worker's integration into the employer's core workforce, the worker may be dismissed if proving unsuitable for the job. A further measure of assistance is the Fares to Work Scheme under which registered disabled workers may be given financial assistance to meet commuting expenses.

EMPLOYMENT PROTECTION AND JOB SECURITY

The nature of disability and attendant discrimination or disadvantage often dictates the employment status of disabled persons. For example, while part-time employment may be a gateway to the labour market for many disabled people, it is also a separate source of their vulnerability. Disabled persons in employment generally enjoy or are denied statutory employment protection rights upon an equal footing with other workers. The discussion of employment vulnerability of marginal, atypical and 'minority' workers may be particularly relevant to the experience of economically active disabled people.

Employment Security and Registered Disabled Persons

Under the 1944 Act, it is an offence to dismiss a registered disabled person without reasonable cause if, as a result, an employer subject to the quota would fall (or remain) below quota. Contravention of the Act does not otherwise affect the legality of the contractual termination, although the dismissed worker may have breach of contract or unfair dismissal remedies. Equally, it does not follow that an unreasonable dismissal in breach of the 1944 legislation will be an unfair dismissal under the Employment Protection (Consolidation) Act 1978. In practice, these provisions provide scant employment security for disabled workers. The case for strengthening them has been met by the proposition that unfair dismissal laws provide more appropriate protection (MSC, 1979).

Disability and Unfair Dismissal

Disabled employees enjoy equal employment protection with able-bodied employees where the conditions of unfair dismissal legislation are satisfied (Income Data Services, 1986; IRS, 1988a, 1988b). In most cases, protection from unfair dismissal only applies where the disabled person has been employed continuously by the employer under a contract of employment for two years. Disabled workers may be particularly vulnerable to dismissal during the initial period of employment and thus may not qualify for employment protection. This may be so where, anticipating possible discrimination in recruitment, selection or employment, the fact or extent of a disability is concealed from the employer. Pre-employment screening frequently attempts to identify disabilities, and disabled applicants may show understandable reticence in disclosing their status, even where the employer does not intend the fact of disability to influence the selection process. An employer who dismisses an employee who has concealed a disability in such circumstances would not have to justify the dismissal if within the first two years of employment and, at common law, may be able to defend dismissal on the grounds of misrepresentation or serious contractual breach. A failure to disclose a disability could in some circumstances be a breach of the employee's statutory duty to take reasonable care for his or her own health and safety and for those who may be affected by these acts or omissions, and to cooperate with the employer so that the employer might comply with the Health and Safety at Work, etc., Act 1974.

Once the disabled employee has acquired two year's service, however, an employer will need to justify a dismissal relating to disability and demonstrate fair and reasonable actions in treating it as a reason for dismissal. If disability is a cause of the employee's work falling below standard, dismissal by reason of incapability or conduct may be justifiable. Nevertheless, the employer must act fairly and reasonably in treating the diminution of performance as a reason for dismissal. If the employee's disability was known to the employer on engagement, the employer may be taken to have implicitly accepted lower expectations of performance and the decision to dismiss must be judged accordingly. The employee should be given an opportunity to improve, further assistance or training may be appropriate, and consultation with the employee and any mentor could be required. Considerations of safety of the employee and fellow employees may be part of the equation, allowing the employer to dismiss for some other substantial reason. There may be a statutory duty under health and safety law to volunteer disability information if it is relevant to the health and safety of the employee or others (IRS, 1988a, 1988b). Discovery of deliberately concealed disability may justify dismissal in such circumstances as a serious breach of the employment relationship.

The dismissal of newly disabled employees requires special care and attention. The Code of Good Practice espouses the principle of retention in employment, while the extent of the disability and opportunities for rehabilitation, retraining and reasonable accommodation are examined. Nevertheless, if the employee's ability to carry out *contractual* duties is seriously impaired, dismissal on grounds of incapability can be considered. The importance of following fair procedure in handling the dismissal cannot be understated. An employer would be expected to act upon the basis of medical opinion on the extent and effect of the disability, and an assessment by the DAS might also be sought. Consultation with the employee should follow, so that the employee can draw the employer's attention to any relevant facts which might influence the decision to dismiss or retain. This is particularly the case where the employee disputes the conclusions of the medical evidence, and the employee should be allowed the opportunity to bring other evidence to bear. Before a decision to terminate employment is taken, the employer should consider whether measures of reasonable accommodation (such as available alternative employment, adjustments to the job, and appropriate assistance or aids) might promote retention of the employee. However, in the final analysis, the employer is allowed to take managerial decisions based upon the available medical advice.

Other considerations can apply where the reason for dismissal is not the disability itself but absenteeism caused by it. Short-term absences should be easily discounted. Long-term absence caused by disability, however, might lead to a conclusion that the employment contract has been frustrated. Where redundancy arises, although registered disabled employees might be entitled to special consideration, disabled employees generally are entitled only to be treated upon their merits when selection criteria are applied, though it would be unusual for selection purely on the basis of disability status to be fair.

EQUAL OPPORTUNITIES IN EMPLOYMENT

The EC Recommendation 1986 urges member states to take all appropriate measures to promote fair opportunities for disabled people in the field of employment and vocational training. In the absence of anti-discrimination or equal opportunities legislation, however, the expectation of disabled employees to equality of employment opportunity rests upon frail foundations.

Disability and Safety Legislation

Employers' obligation under health and safety law are often used to justify employment discrimination against disabled persons or as the basis for compromising their employment rights out of fear, often baseless, that the nature of such employees' disabilities make them a safety risk to themselves, their fellow workers or third parties. At common law, employers owe a duty of reasonable care to provide for the occupational health and safety of their employees. In exercising that duty of care towards a disabled employee, the employer must take into account the greater risk and degree of injury faced by employees with particular disabilities. This may lead to the employer needing to take additional steps or precautions to ensure the safety of disabled workers than might otherwise apply to their able-bodied colleagues. For example, the need for enhanced training or closer supervision of some disabled employees might be called for. This analysis is underlined by the Health and Safety at Work, etc., Act 1974 which indicates that the employer has a duty to the workforce to provide safe fellow employees, and a duty to third parties not to expose their health and safety to risk through the activities of the employer's business.

Disability, Low Pay and Wage Inequality

The segregation of disabled workers in low paid employment provides further evidence of their vulnerability (Jordan, 1979). Low earnings of those employed in sheltered and rehabilitative employment are especially remarkable (Lonsdale and Walker, 1984). Under the Wages Council Act 1979 employers could be permitted to pay disabled workers less than the statutory fixed minimum rate. This provision was repealed by the Wages Act 1986 but, given the low rates of pay in wages council industries, this is a small concession. The possible abolition of the wages councils by repeal of the statutory minimum wages machinery in the Wages Act 1986 (DE, 1988c) is likely to contribute to wage inequality bearing especially hard upon disabled people.

Disabled employees' rights to equal pay with their able-bodied comparators is not a *legal* issue which has been aired to any great extent in this country. Recent evidence (Martin and White, 1988) shows that both male and female full-time disabled employees earn less than full-time employees in the general population, and that the differences could not be explained merely by differences in hours worked. The average gross earnings of male and female disabled adults are respectively 81% and 88% of earnings in the working population, while the comparable figures for average hourly pay are 84% and 91%, with internal variation according to manual or non-manual status (cf. Prescott-Clarke, 1990). These figures correlate with evidence from the United States suggesting that disabled workers' wages are 16% less than other workers (Johnson and Lambrinos, 1985), and supporting the hypothesis that wage discrimination is a product of prejudice, not simply lower productivity (Johnson and Lambrinos, 1987). Earlier studies point to occupational segregation, employment status and working hours as being significant indicators of disabled earnings inequality (Buckle, 1971; Jordan, 1979; Lonsdale and Walker, 1984). Where women and other minorities may seek some remedy against the indirectly discriminatory effects of these variables, disabled persons enjoy no legal rights to equal treatment in employment terms.

Developing Equal Opportunity Policies

The Companies Act 1985 requires companies employing more than 250 people to publish in the directors' annual report a statement of corporate policy on the employment of disabled persons. The statement must describe *any* policy applied by the company for giving full and fair consideration to job applications from disabled people (having regard to their particular aptitudes and abilities), for continuing the employment of (and arranging appropriate training for) employees who become disabled during employment with the company, and for training, career development and promotion of disabled persons employed by the company. Unless the directors have taken all reasonable steps to ensure that such a statement is included in the annual report, a failure to publish a corporate disability employment policy is an offence. This aside, the creation of a climate for equal opportunities relies upon voluntary, extra-legal provisions.

In 1977, the government launched a major programme to encourage and to educate employers about the employment of disabled persons. Following a review of disabled employment services (MSC, 1982), the Disablement Advisory Service was established to promote progressive personnel policies and practices in respect of disabled people. Under the Fit for Work Award Scheme, annual awards are made to employers who, by their record and performance, have promoted equal opportunities for disabled people at work. The Code of Good Practice addresses employers' concerns about employing disabled persons and explains the desiderata of recruiting and selecting disabled applicants. Employers are advised on considerations and needs which may affect disabled employees, including questions of induction, health and safety, integration into the workforce, training and promotion opportunities, redundancy and the rights of newly disabled employees. The Code is also an important source document for assisting employers to devise, coordinate and implement policy towards disabled workers. Undoubtedly, a number of employers have given attention to policy (IDS, 1981; Doyle, 1987a; Birkett and Worman, 1988; Leach, 1989) and employing disabled people has been seen as being 'good for business'. However, the effect of these various initiatives to educate and encourage employers to extend equal opportunities to disabled workers is hard to gauge (cf. DE, 1990).

The Case for Equal Opportunities Legislation

Discrimination and disadvantage faced by disabled workers in recruitment and selection, terms and conditions (including pay, benefits and career progression), and employment security have been demonstrated over time (Sainsbury, 1970; Shearer, 1981; Topliss, 1982; Large, 1982; Locker, 1983; Fry, 1986). The case for anti-discrimination legislation was first put by Snowdon (1976) and legislative models for the promotion of disabled equal employment opportunity have been canvassed (MSC, 1981a) but received little political support (Employment Committee, 1981, 1982; DE, 1990).

However, the case for equal opportunity legislation has become increasingly compelling (TUC, 1988) and is supported by many disabled people (MSC, 1978b; Townsend, 1981; Graham, Jordan and Lamb, 1990).

One possible legislative model would be to prohibit employment discrimination in all aspects of the employment relationship on the grounds of disability by adopting the paradigm of sex and race discrimination statutes. The anti-discrimination model has been adopted in a number of jurisdictions to provide either particular protective legislation for disabled people or comprehensive and integrated legislation which addresses disability alongside other incidents of social discrimination. The United States' federal Rehabilitation Act 1973 exemplifies the first of these approaches (Chapter 3) as does earlier state legislation in Australia (Nothdurft and Astor, 1986). The second approach is more prevalent and is seen in state laws in the United States (see Chapter 3), in Canadian federal and provincial legislation, and in recent consolidating legislation in Australian states.

It will be necessary, in addition, to consider what forms of positive action or positive discrimination might be included in such legislation. Such positive measures are necessary once it is recognized that disabled people suffer from institutional and structural discrimination (Rebell, 1986) such that, even if tomorrow no further acts of disability discrimination were to be committed, disabled persons would continue to experience disadvantage for many years to come (Cornes, 1984). Intervention would be necessary on three levels. First, any reform must contain a degree of positive action: such as contract compliance, affirmative action planning, equal opportunity management audits, reasonable accommodation and outreach requirements. The US federal Rehabilitation Act 1973 provides the best, but not sole, example of such intervention (see Chapter 3). Second, as the experience in the United States demonstrates, it may be necessary to undertake separate legislative intervention to guarantee disabled rights in education, employment, transport, income maintenance and public access (*Georgetown Law Journal*, 1973). Third, a degree of reverse discrimination, especially in employment, might be countenanced on behalf of those for whom full integration in a competitive society is impossible because of the severity of their disability. A role for reserved occupations and a strengthened quota system, borrowing from the experience of West German or recent French legislation (IRS, 1988c), might be envisaged, as would continued sheltered employment, improved rehabilitation and placement services, increased provision of aids and facilities, and comprehensive income maintenance.

CONCLUSION

If equal opportunity legislation is one way ahead for disabled workers' rights, the limitations of legal formulae must be recognized (*Harvard Law*

Review, 1984). Legislation cannot hope completely to redress the vulnerability of disabled people in the labour market, and political and economic power must be used to enfranchise disabled workers (Acton, 1981; Bordieri and Comninel, 1987). The anti-discrimination model may only be capable of containing overt discrimination while defusing such social pressure for radical change in favour of disabled persons as may exist (Oliver, 1984, 1985, 1986). Yet, as in the United States (Weiss, 1974), recognition in law that disabled persons are a disadvantaged group in the employment field is a necessary, but not sufficient, condition to mandate remedial action and equal rights. Statutory commitment to equal opportunities and equal treatment can assist the integration of this minority group. Furthermore, labour law solutions to the problems of low pay, job insecurity and marginal employment, and legal developments towards alternative employment opportunities, will contribute to the improved socio-economic status of disabled people.

GLOSSARY

DAS	Disablement Advisory Service
DE	Department of Employment
DRO	Disablement Resettlement Officer
EC	European Communities
ERC	Employment Rehabilitation Centre
ERS	Employment Rehabilitation Service
IDS	Income Data Services
IRS	Industrial Relations Services
MSC	Manpower Services Commission
NACEDP	National Advisory Council on Employment of Disabled People
NAO	National Audit Office
SPS	Sheltered Placement Scheme
SSAC	Social Security Advisory Committee
UN	United Nations

REFERENCES

Acton, N. (1981). Employment of disabled persons: where are we going?, *International Labour Review*, **120**(1), 1–14.

Alcock, P. (1987). *Poverty and State Support*, Longman, London.

Berkowitz, M. and Hill, M.A. (1986). Disability and the labor market: an overview. In M. Berkowitz and M.A. Hill (eds) *Disability and the Labor Market: Economic Problems, Policies and Programs*, pp. 1–28, ILR Press, Ithaca.

Birkett, K. and Worman, D. (1988). *Getting on with Disabilities: An Employer's Guide*, IPM, London.

Bolderson, H. (1980). The origins of the disabled persons employment quota and

its symbolic significance, *Journal of Social Policy*, **9**(2), 169–86.
Bordieri, J.E. and Comninel, M.E. (1987). Competitive employment for workers with disabilities: an international perspective, *Journal of Rehabilitation*, **53**(3), 51–7.
Brooke-Ross, R. (1984). The disabled in the Federal Republic of Germany, *Social Policy and Administration*, **18**(2), 172–8.
Brown, J.C. (1984). *Disability Income Part 2: The Disability Income System*, Policy Studies Institute, London.
Buckle, J.R. (1971). *Handicapped and Impaired in Great Britain Part II: Work and Housing of Impaired Persons in Great Britain*, (Office of Population Censuses and Surveys: Social Survey Division: Report M418), HMSO, London.
Cabinet Office (1985). *Code of Practice: Employment of Disabled People*, Management and Personnel Office, London.
Collignon, F.C. (1986). The role of reasonable accommodation in employing disabled persons in private industry. In M. Berkowitz and M.A. Hill (eds) *Disability and the Labor Market: Economic Problems, Policies and Programs*, pp. 196–241, ILR Press, New York.
Committee of Public Accounts (1988). *Employment Assistance to Disabled Adults* (House of Commons: 21st Report from the Committee of Public Accounts: Session 1987–88: HC Paper 144), HMSO, London.
Cornes, P. (1982). *Employment Rehabilitation: The Aims and Achievements of a Service for Disabled People*, MSC Employment Service (Employment Rehabilitation Service), Sheffield.
Cornes, P. (1984). *The Future of Work for People with Disabilities: A View from Great Britain*, (International Exchange of Experts and Information in Rehabilitation Monograph 28), World Rehabilitation Fund, New York.
Darnbrough, A. and Kinrade, D. (1981). The disabled person and employment. In D. Guthrie (ed.) *Disability: Legislation and Practice*, pp. 52–81, Macmillan, London.
Davoud, N. (1980). *Part-time Employment: Time for Recognition, Organisation and Legal Reform*, Multiple Sclerosis Society, London.
Department of Employment (1973a). *The Quota Scheme for Disabled People: Consultative Document*, DE, London.
Department of Employment (1973b). *Sheltered Employment for Disabled People: Consultative Document*, HMSO, London.
Department of Employment (1988a). *Training for Employment*, HMSO, London.
Department of Employment (1988b). *The Employment Service: An Evaluation of the Sheltered Placement Scheme*, HMSO, London.
Department of Employment (1988c). *Wages Councils: 1988 Consultation Document*, DE, London.
Department of Employment (1990). *Employment and Training for People with Disabilities: Consultative Document*, DE, London.
Department of Social Security (1990). *The Way Ahead: Benefits for Disabled People* (Cm. 917), HMSO, London.
Disability Alliance (1975). *Poverty and Disability: The Case for a Comprehensive Income Scheme for Disabled People*, Disability Alliance, London.
Disability Alliance (1987). *Poverty and Disability: Breaking the Link*, Disability Alliance, London.
Disablement Income Group (1987). *Disablement Income Group's National Disability Income*, DIG, London.

Doyle, B. (1987a). Employing disabled workers: the framework for equal opportunities, *Equal Opportunities Review*, **12**, 5–10.

Doyle, B. (1987b). Disabled workers, employment vulnerability and labour law. In P. Leighton and R.W. Painter (eds) *Vulnerable Workers in the UK Labour Market: Some Challenges for Labour Law, Employee Relations*, **9**(5), 20–9.

Edwards, J. (1958). Remploy: an experiment in sheltered employment for the severely disabled in Great Britain, *International Labour Review*, **77**(2), 147–59.

Employment Committee (1981). *The MSC's Review of the Quota Scheme for the Employment of Disabled People* (House of Commons: 2nd Report: Session 1981–82. HC Paper 27), HMSO, London.

Employment Committee (1982). *The MSC's Review of the Quota Scheme for the Employment of Disabled People: Observations by the Government on the 2nd Report of the Committee in Session 1981–82*, (House of Commons: 6th Special Report: Session 1981–82. HC Paper 556), HMSO, London.

Employment Rehabilitation Research Centre (1984). *Proposals for the Development of the Manpower Services Commission's Rehabilitation Service*, ERRC, London.

Floyd, M. and North, K. (1986). Quota schemes and the assessment of employment handicap in Britain and West Germany, *Disability, Handicap and Society*, **1**(3), 291–9.

Fry, E. (1986). *An Equal Chance for Disabled People? A Study of Discrimination in Employment*, Spastics Society, London.

Georgetown Law Journal (1973). Abroad in the land: legal strategies to effectuate the rights of the physically disabled, *Georgetown Law Journal*, **61**(6), 1501–23.

Gladstone, D.E. (1985). Disabled people and employment, *Social Policy and Administration*, **19**(2), 101–11.

Graham, P., Jordan, A. and Lamb, B. (1990). *An Equal Chance Or No Chance? A Study of Discrimination Against Disabled People in the Labour Market*, Spastics Society, London.

Greaves, M. (1969). *Work and Disability: Some Aspects of the Employment of Disabled Persons in Great Britain*, British Council for Rehabilitation of the Disabled, London.

Greaves, M. and Massie, B. (1979). *Work and Disability 1979*. Disabled Living Foundation, London.

Grover, R. and Gladstone, F. (1981). *Disabled People—A Right to Work*?, Bedford Square Press/National Council for Voluntary Organisations, London.

Habeck, R., Galvin, D., Frey, W., Chadderdon, L. and Tate, D. (1985). *Economics and Equity in Employment of People with Disabilities: International Policies and Practices*, UCIR Michigan State University, East Lansing.

Harvard Law Review (1984). Employment discrimination against the handicapped and section 504 of the Rehabilitation Act: an essay on legal evasiveness, *Harvard Law Review*, **97**(4), 997–1015.

Haveman, R.H., Halberstadt, V. and Burkhauser, R.V. (1984). *Public Policy Toward Disabled Workers: Cross-National Analyses of Economic Impacts*, Cornell University Press, Ithaca.

Income Data Services (1981). *Employing Disabled People* (IDS Study 255), IDS, London.

Income Data Services (1986). Employing the disabled, *IDS Brief*, **335**, 7–10.

Industrial Relations Services (1988a). Disabled employees, *Industrial Relations Legal Information Bulletin*, **345**, 2–11.

Industrial Relations Services (1988b). Disabled employees: the legal position, *Equal Opportunities Review*, **20**, 8–15.

Industrial Relations Services (1988c). Employment of the disabled, *European Industrial Relations Review*, **175**, 17–23.

Industrial Relations Services (1989). Only people with disabilities need apply, *Equal Opportunities Review*, **23**, 22–5.

Johnson, W.G. and Lambrinos, J. (1985). Wage discrimination against handicapped men and women, *Journal of Human Resources*, **20**(2), 264–77.

Johnson, W.G. and Lambrinos, J. (1987). The effect of prejudice on the wages of disabled workers, *Policy Studies Journal*, **15**(3), 571–90.

Jones, P. R. and Cullis, J.G. (1988). Employment of the disabled: a rationale for legislation in the United Kingdom, *International Review of Law and Economics*, **8**(1), 37–49.

Jordan, D. (1979). *A New Employment Programme Wanted for Disabled People*, Disability Alliance/Low Pay Unit, London.

Large, P. (1982). *Committee on Restrictions Against Disabled People: Report*, HMSO, London.

Leach, B. (1989). Disabled people and the implementation of local authorities' equal opportunities policies, *Public Administration*, **67**, 65–77.

Leonard, J.S. (1986). Labor supply incentives and disincentives for disabled persons. In M. Berkowitz and M.A. Hill (eds) *Disability and the Labor Market: Economic Problems, Policies and Programs*, pp. 64–94, ILR Press, Ithaca.

Locker, D. (1983). *Disability and Disadvantage: The Consequences of Chronic Illness*, Tavistock Publications, London.

Lonsdale, S. and Walker, A. (1984). *A Right to Work: Disability and Employment*, Disability Alliance/Low Pay Unit, London.

Lyth, M. (1973). Employers' attitudes to the employment of the disabled, *Occupational Psychology*, **47**, 67–70.

Manpower Services Commission (1978a). *Developing Employment and Training Services for Disabled People*, MSC, London.

Manpower Services Commission (1978b). *Attitudes of the Disabled to Employment Legislation: Main Report*, MSC/Research Surveys of Great Britain Ltd, London.

Manpower Services Commission (1979). *The Quota Scheme for the Employment of Disabled People: A Discussion Document*, MSC, London.

Manpower Services Commission (1981a). *Review of the Quota Scheme for the Employment of Disabled People: A Report*, MSC, Sheffield.

Manpower Services Commission (1981b). *Employment Rehabilitation: A Review of the Manpower Services Commission's Employment Rehabilitation Services*, MSC, London.

Manpower Services Commission (1982). *Review of Assistance for Disabled People: A Report to the Commission*, MSC, London.

Manpower Services Commission (1985). *Quota Scheme for the Employment of Disabled People: Working Group Report on Suggestions for Improving the Scheme's Effectiveness*, MSC, Sheffield.

Manpower Services Commission (1986). *Jobcentre Staff's Perception of their Services to Disabled People*, MSC, Sheffield.

Martin, J., Meltzer, H. and Elliot, D. (1988). *The Prevalence of Disability Among Adults* (Office of Population Censuses and Surveys (Social Survey Division): OPCS Surveys of Disability in Great Britain Report 1), HMSO, London.

Martin, J. and White, A. (1988). *The Financial Circumstances of Disabled Adults Living in Private Households* (Office of Population Censuses and Surveys (Social Survey Division): OPCS Surveys of Disability in Great Britain Report 2), HMSO, London.

Martin, J., White, A. and Meltzer, H. (1989). *Disabled Adults: Services, Transport and Employment* (Office of Population Censuses and Surveys (Social Survey Division): OPCS Surveys of Disability in Great Britain Report 4), HMSO, London.
McCrostie, M.J. and Peacock, A. (1984). Disability policy in the United Kingdom. In R.H. Haveman, V. Halberstadt and R.V. Burkhauser (eds) *Public Policy Toward Disabled Workers: Cross-National Analyses of Economic Impacts*, pp. 517–73, Cornell University Press, Ithaca.
McDonnell, R. and Weale, A. (1984). Regulating for equal employment opportunities: the case of the disabled quota, *Journal of Law and Society*, **11**(1), 105–14.
Mitchell, P. (1986). *Constructing a National Disability Income*, RADAR: London.
Morgan, P.L. and Makeham, P. (1978). *Economic and Financial Analysis of Sheltered Employment* (DE Research Paper No. 5), DE, London.
National Advisory Council on Employment of Disabled People (1986). *Report of the Working Party on the Principles Underlying Employment Provisions for Disabled People*, NACEDP, London.
National Audit Office (1987). *Department of Employment and Manpower Services Commission: Employment Assistance to Disabled Adults: Report by the Comptroller and Auditor General*, (HC Paper 367), HMSO, London.
Nothdurft, J. and Astor, H. (1986). Laughing in the dark: anti-discrimination law and physical disability in New South Wales, *Journal of Industrial Relations*, **28**(3), 336–52.
Oliver, M. (1984). The politics of disability, *Critical Social Policy*, **11** (winter), 21–32.
Oliver, M. (1985). Discrimination, disability and social policy. In C. Jones and M. Brenton (eds) *The Year Book of Social Policy in Britain 1984-85*, pp. 74–99, Routledge and Kegan Paul, London.
Oliver, M. (1986). Social policy and disability: some theoretical issues, *Disability, Handicap and Society*, **1**(1), 5–17.
Parker, S. (1983). *The Disabled Unemployed: A Survey Carried Out On Behalf of the Manpower Services Commission*, Office of Population Censuses and Surveys (Social Survey Division), London.
Piercy (Lord) (1956). *Report of the Committee on the Rehabilitation, Training and Resettlement of Disabled Persons* (Cmd. 9883), HMSO, London.
Prescott-Clarke, P. (1990). *Employment and Handicap*, Social and Community Planning Research, London.
Rebell, M.A. (1986). Structural discrimination and the rights of the disabled, *Georgetown Law Journal*, **74**(5), 1435–89.
Robbins, D. (1982). *The Chance To Work: Improving Employment Prospects For Disabled People*, Disablement Income Group Charitable Trust, London.
Royal National Institute for the Deaf (1987). *Communication Works: An RNID Inquiry into the Employment of Deaf People*, RNID, London.
Sainsbury, S. (1970). *Registered As Disabled*, Bell, London.
Shearer, A. (1981). *Disability: Whose Handicap*?, Blackwell, Oxford.
Simpkins, J. and Tickner, V. (1978). *Whose Benefit*?, Economist Intelligence Unit: London.
Snowdon (Earl of) (1976). *Integrating the Disabled: Volume 1: Report of the Working Party on Integration of the Disabled*, National Fund for Research into Crippling Diseases: Horsham.
Social Security Advisory Committee (1988). *Benefits for Disabled People: A Strategy for Change*, HMSO, London.
Thornton, C. and Maynard, R. (1986). The economics of transitional employment

and supported employment. In M. Berkowitz and M.A. Hill (eds) *Disability and the Labor Market: Economic Problems, Policies and Programs*, pp. 142–70, ILR Press, Ithaca.

Tomlinson, G. (1943). *Report of the Interdepartmental Committee on the Rehabilitation and Resettlement of Disabled Persons* (Cmd. 6415), HMSO, London.

Topliss, E. (1979). *Provision for the Disabled*, 2nd edn, Blackwell, Oxford.

Topliss, E. (1982). *Social Responses to Handicap*, Longman, London.

Topliss, E. and Gould, B. (1981). *A Charter for the Disabled*, Blackwell, Oxford.

Townsend, P. 1981. Employment and disability: the development of a conflict between state and people. In A. Walker and P. Townsend (eds) *Disability in Britain: A Manifesto of Rights*, pp. 52–72, Martin Robertson, Oxford.

Trades Union Congress (1988). *Bill of Rights for People with Disabilities: Consultation Paper*, TUC, London.

Van de Vliet, A. (1984). How Remploy made whole, *Management Today*, September, 54–61 and 133.

Walker, A. (1981). Disability and income. In A. Walker and P. Townsend (eds) *Disability in Britain: A Manifesto of Rights*, pp. 31–51, Martin Robertson, Oxford.

Walker, A. (1982). *Unqualified and Underemployed: Handicapped Young People and the Labour Market*, Macmillan, London.

Weiss, S. (1974). Equal employment and the disabled: a proposal, *Columbia Journal of Law and Social Problems*, **10**(4), 457–96.

Whaley, J., Mattison, C., Dodd, A. and Mullins, D. (1986). *A Sense of Purpose: A Study of Visually Handicapped People and Their Search for Work*, Royal National Institute for the Blind, London.

Whitehead, A. (1981). Identification of the disabled person. In D. Guthrie (ed.) *Disability: Legislation and Practice*, pp. 116–140, Macmillan, London.

Wood, D. (1986). *Sheltered Employment*, Social and Community Planning Research, London.

Worrall, J.D. and Butler, R.J. (1986). Some lessons from the workers' compensation program. In M. Berkowitz and M.A. Hill (eds) *Disability and the Labor Market: Economic Problems, Policies and Programs*, pp. 95–123, ILR Press, Ithaca.

Chapter 5.1

HIV Positive Workers and Workers with AIDS: Psychosocial and Counselling Issues

Anna Stallard, Ruchill Hospital, Glasgow, UK

INTRODUCTION

It is likely that AIDS will cease to be an unusual illness occurring only among specific members of our community. It will affect ordinary people in all spheres of life including work. People with HIV infection and AIDS are vulnerable to psychological distress and social isolation. Workers with HIV and AIDS are likely to suffer from some degree of impairment to their performance and attendance. Ignorance, prejudice and fear of AIDS can lead to thoughtless behaviour among colleagues, friends and employers which only serves to worsen its psychosocial effects. In this chapter the seriousness of the epidemic is outlined. Factual information about the virus is provided along with discussion of the psychological and social implications of having HIV, HIV at work and counselling issues.

AIDS was first identified in 1981. Some homosexual men were showing an unusual immune deficiency, manifesting itself in the form of infections, ordinarily easy to overcome (Shilts, 1987). Amidst a new sense of freedom from restrictions on the expression of sexuality, an ideal climate was created for accelerated spread of infection. People with many partners, engaging in unprotected anal sex were especially at risk.

The impact of the disease cannot be underestimated. The number of people known to be infected with HIV in Britain on 31 March 1989 was 10259, while the number of people with AIDS was 2192 (CDS, 1989a 1989b). The number infected who are not yet ill, represent the large and unseen part of the epidemic which will move inexorably onwards producing many more cases of AIDS over the next few years. In the absence of behaviour changes, the virus will continue to spread. Many workplaces will

Vulnerable Workers: Psychosocial and Legal Issues. Edited by M. J. Davidson and J. Earnshaw

be affected. AIDS will become part of our lives in the same way that tuberculosis was a feature of everyday life in the early decades of this century.

It is difficult to comprehend the scope of the problem until we understand the nature of the pattern of spread. Imagine a pond in which there is a tiny patch of lilies, hardly noticeable at one end. Each day it doubles in size. Two lilies, then four, then eight, then sixteen—not occupying much space in the pond. It is only when the patch reaches a certain size, that it will fill the pond rapidly. The patch would grow from one-eighth to one-quarter to one-half until it has covered the pond. The first stages in growth may have taken weeks but the final stages from one-eighth to completely full take only four days.

HIV has the potential to spread in the same way, seeming to start slowly but reaching a point as it did in New York and Edinburgh when spread increased in a rapid and uncontrollable manner among intravenous drug users (Robertson *et al.*, 1986). One person with HIV passes the virus to another person, each of them passes it to two others making four. These four pass the virus to four more people and so on . . . slow spread at first increasing in speed as the number of infected individuals increases. Obviously this is simplifying matters. Luckily, few people have large numbers of sexual partners and the virus does not always pass easily from one person to another—there are couples in which one partner is HIV positive and the other negative, who have been having unprotected sexual intercourse for months (Perroni, Albertoni and Soscia, 1989). There is no room for complacency however; the virus can spread from one person to another after only one sexual encounter. People with HIV can pass through stages of being more infectious than at other times, and there is a possibility that some strains of the virus may be more infectious than others.

'Don't Die of Ignorance' was the catch phrase of one British campaign encouraging us to find out more about AIDS. Ignorance may have contributed to the explosive growth of HIV infection such as that observed in New York and Edinburgh in the early 1980s. Certainly, education and consequent behaviour change have slowed down the spread (Becker and Joseph, 1988). Unfortunately this is not always the case. Years after the cause of HIV spread became well known, in 1988 over a six-month period, the number of HIV positive drug users in Bangkok has risen from just a few per cent to nearly half of intravenous drug users (Plansringarm *et al.*, 1989). This could happen elsewhere, given the right conditions.

Even if the virus spreads at the slower pace more typical of most countries in the world, The World Health Organization estimates that during the 1990s, the number of new infections of HIV will increase two- or three-fold (CDS, 1989c).

In New York large numbers of hospital beds are occupied by AIDS patients. The health care system in many areas of the United States is under enormous pressure—patients sometimes have to wait days in the emergency areas for beds. Therefore the impact of AIDS on New York health professionals has been profound: it has changed the nature of the work in which they are engaged; it has dramatically increased their workload; and it has raised considerations of occupational risk (Pittman-Lindeman, Miller and Sowa, 1989). Many individuals' lives are touched by the illness. It has been estimated that 10% of US firms have an HIV positive employee (Anon., 1988). It is a matter of time before British experiences will be similar.

The economic impact in terms of lost working time is likely to be enormous. For example, Carwein and Ray (1989) calculated that Nevada's 209 AIDS cases reported in 1987 and 1988 would cost $117567218 in lost salary alone. Additional costs would be incurred by the considerable sums spent on medical care and support from social and mental health services as well as informal care from family and friends. Cost to employers of lost working time could be considerable. In a survey of 61 AIDS clinic patients in San Francisco, Greenblatt and her colleagues (1989) found that about half of the subjects had to stop working within three years of experiencing symptoms of HIV although 87% had worked before the onset of symptoms.

AN OVERVIEW OF AIDS AND HIV

AIDS stands for Acquired Immune Deficiency Syndrome. HIV stands for Human Immunodeficiency Virus, understood to be the cause of AIDS. The virus is especially sinister in that it damages the very system designed to protect the body from attacks by viruses, bacteria and other organisms. It integrates into the proteins at the core of human immune system cells. Once inside the cell the virus is invisible to the body's defence system. Most people infected with the virus will become ill with AIDS eventually though some may remain healthy indefinitely. Although there is no cure, doctors are becoming expert at treating and preventing AIDS-related infections, thus prolonging life and improving the quality of existence for AIDS sufferers.

Infection is generally believed to be caused by the HIV virus entering the bloodstream. This occurs through sexual intercourse without a condom (or if it leaks or is used wrongly), the introduction of infected blood or blood products through transfusion, the use of infected injecting equipment, or if infected body fluids such as blood or semen enter the bloodstream through a break in the skin.

It is difficult to become infected: people exposed to blood through their occupation such as accidentally pricking themselves with needles just used on HIV infected persons, very rarely become infected themselves. Rastrelli and his colleagues (1989), studying accidental exposure to HIV among 102 health care personnel found no cases of HIV infection. Nevertheless, staff exposed in this way experience high levels of distress following the injury (Marrie *et al.*, 1989). There have been a few cases of transmission through occupational exposure (CDS, 1987) but the majority of cases of HIV among health care staff have arisen from their own sexual or drug using behaviour. It should not need to be emphasized therefore that casual encounters with HIV positive persons in terms of hugs, kisses or handshakes, or touching things they have used such as towels or cups, represent no danger to others. Dealing with blood spills can be done safely if the simple precaution is taken of wearing gloves and wiping with a 10:1 water to bleach solution. A refusal or inability to believe this information has led to distressing consequences for HIV infected people.

After exposure to the virus it can take up to three months, sometimes longer, for the body's immune system to produce a response in the form of antibodies to the virus. Although these antibodies are ineffective in terms of neutralizing the virus, they can be detected by means of tests on blood samples. It is these antibody tests which are used to determine whether or not someone has been infected with HIV and if this is the case, the test is positive and the person is often described as being HIV positive. Before the antibodies are produced it is possible to be infected with HIV but produce a negative test result. The period between infection and the production of detectable antibodies, is called the window period. About one-third of those who become HIV positive, experience a brief flu-like illness at the time when antibody is produced.

The virus usually remains inactive for several years. The average length of time between becoming infected with HIV and developing AIDS is about eight years, though some people become ill far sooner while others may remain well indefinitely. During this time some symptoms may appear, for example profuse night sweating, thrush, and persistently swollen glands. Some infections not regarded as AIDS related are nevertheless more common among people with HIV, e.g. tuberculosis.

Before being diagnosed as having AIDS, patients must fulfil certain criteria. They must suffer from at least one of a list of defined opportunistic infections and, usually, in addition show laboratory evidence of HIV infection (e.g. an HIV antibody positive test). Opportunistic infections are those which become established when the immune system is damaged. They could be fought off easily by the immune system of a healthy person. It is possible to die from opportunistic infections and the consequences of having a damaged immune system before full blown AIDS is diagnosed. There are over 40 different infections which are recognized as being AIDS related. The most common are specific forms of skin cancer and pneumonia which in other circumstances would be considered extremely rare. Other infections are caused by organisms which affect the gut, the eyes, the brain and most other parts of the body.

Before full blown AIDS is diagnosed but after HIV has become active and symptoms have appeared, patients are described as having AIDS Related Complex (ARC). Although doctors now use more precise categories to describe various stages in the development of AIDS, patients and lay people find it useful to continue to use this term.

The complexity of AIDS-related complaints makes it very difficult for patients to understand what is happening to them. AIDS-like symptoms are so common in other contexts that everyday illnesses which affect HIV positive people as often as they do everybody else, might be interpreted as something far more serious by the sufferer. Even anxiety has many symptoms in common with those of HIV, which if misinterpreted can become even worse!

THE PSYCHOSOCIAL IMPACT OF AIDS AND HIV

The psychological and social effects of HIV manifest themselves in many different areas. Ironically, the level of psychological distress experienced by people with HIV might directly influence the outcome of the illness. The reverse is also true. The HIV positive diagnosis and signs of progress to illness can damage significantly psychosocial adjustment. The picture is further complicated by the possibility that the groups with a high prevalence of HIV infection also have a high prevalence of psychological disorders. Distress appears in a variety of forms, the most common being anxiety and depression which will be discussed below.

Lifestyle may influence the course of illness. Behaviour which is detrimental to health is thought to increase the chance of progressing to AIDS. Patients are encouraged to give up smoking, drinking and drug taking. There is no direct evidence to support these views except that intravenous drug use appears to be related to faster onset of AIDS-related symptoms among intravenous drug users (Hubbard *et al.*, 1988). Positive changes in behaviour are believed to increase the chances of maintaining good health. Exercise, eating healthy food, avoiding late nights and reducing stress are all related to improved immune functioning. Whether or not these lifestyle changes will limit the progress of HIV and prolong life is as yet unknown. There is evidence that stressful events and psychological distress are related to the development of HIV-related illness among previously well HIV positive men (Kessler *et al.*, 1989).

The tragedy of HIV infection is that it seldom affects those with few other burdens to bear. On the contrary, those with HIV infection are often already in circumstances conducive to psychological distress and social isolation. Although the infection is becoming more widespread it is still more prevalent among homosexuals, drug abusers and haemophiliacs. Where this is not the case, such as in urban communities in Central Africa, it is more commonly found where there is poverty, malnutrition and a high prevalence of other communicable diseases. Even within the already stigmatized groups of HIV positive drug users in the United States, HIV is more common among black and Hispanic drug users.

Homosexual men have additional burdens placed upon them, which heterosexual men do not suffer. Stigma, a failure by others to tolerate their expression of sexuality and the lack of a social structure which allows the development and recognition of gay relationships all contribute to this burden.

Most drug users experience problems related to addiction. Obtaining drugs and the means by which they can be administered can become a full-time occupation usually involving criminal activities—theft, drug dealing and prostitution. Many come from poor backgrounds, may have little schooling and poor personal resources with which they can rebuild their lifestyle once they attempt to give up drugs. The physical effects of the drug can mask other ordinary physical complaints, which, when drugs are no longer used, can frighten the HIV positive user. The former drug user can have special difficulties adjusting to the routine of legal employment.

Haemophiliacs have a chronic life threatening debilitating illness to cope with, even before receiving a diagnosis of HIV positive. It is not surprising that research findings indicate that individuals in these groups are likely to suffer from high levels of psychological distress and social isolation even without HIV. It is easy to imagine the devastation the diagnosis can cause to these already vulnerable groups.

The additional vulnerability of the groups discussed above has been examined by some research workers. HIV positive homosexual men appear to suffer from higher levels of psychological distress than HIV positive drug users (Seidle and Goebel, 1987). A sample of gay men at various stages of HIV infection who were attending a medical outpatient clinic was studied (Atkinson *et al.*, 1988). The sample included HIV negative gay men and heterosexual controls. All of the gay men including those who were HIV negative experienced higher levels of psychiatric disturbance than the heterosexuals.

Drug users too are more likely to suffer from higher levels of psychological distress than people who do not use drugs. The suicide rate among heroin addicts, for example, was found to be between five and seventeen times higher than among the population in general (Emery, Steer and Beck, 1981). The drug abuser may be using the drug as a means of coping with stress (Wills and Shiffman, 1985).

Examining psychiatric history in a mixed group of HIV positive individuals and comparing them with HIV negative individuals at risk and heterosexual controls, Gala and his colleagues (1989), found that the HIV positive subjects and those at risk of infection were more likely to have had a previous psychiatric history than the controls. This supports the view that these groups are predisposed to psychological difficulty. However, there is mixed evidence that levels of distress appear to be greater among those who are positive, especially as they progress to illness. In one study which compared people with HIV but without symptoms with ARC and AIDS patients, it was found that the first group did not have an especially high rate of psychological distress. It was only with progress of illness that the difficulties emerged (Kelly and St. Lawrence, 1988). Not all research supports this view. For example the study cited above by Atkinson *et al.* found that although all the gay groups were more distressed than heterosexuals, the HIV positive subjects had a higher rate of recent psychiatric disturbance than HIV negative controls. This could be in reaction to the heightened uncertainty related to this condition (Miller, Weber and Green, 1986) as well as the impact of a life threatening disease. Indeed any life threatening illness is accompanied by higher than normal levels of psychological problems. Of patients suffering from terminal illness, 25% were found to be depressed (Brown *et al.*, 1986).

It appears therefore that a number of different factors contribute to the distress suffered by HIV positive people. Firstly, they are often predisposed to psychological problems because of previous life circumstances. Secondly, the diagnosis of HIV seems to cause additional levels of distress. Finally, progress to ARC and AIDS appears to cause further distress, partly in relation to the nature of the illness and partly as a result of expected reactions to news of a terminal illness.

So far no discussion has taken place regarding the form in which psychological distress manifests itself. This is summarized by Miller and Brown (1988) as follows:

- Shock
- Fear and anxiety
- Depression
- Anger and frustration
- Guilt
- Preoccupation with health

The first of these manifestations, shock, is discussed below in the context of HIV testing. Anxiety is characterized by three groups of problems. The first come under the category of physical symptoms. These are related to natural physiological reactions to potentially threatening situations and can be diverse and very dramatic. They include breathing difficulties, heart palpitations, muscular tension, headaches, dizzy spells, panic attacks, digestive problems and general aches and pains. These symptoms can be alarming and may be interpreted as symptoms of HIV. The second area of anxiety involves problems in thinking. Although a diagnosis of HIV is a frightening prospect, it can be made worse by thinking about it in a catastrophic manner. The client may believe that illness will ensue immediately and be of a horrible nature, that everyone around him or her can see or guess that he or she has the virus, or that relatives or friends will reject him or her if they knew about the diagnosis. Sometimes the worries can be unrelated to the diagnosis but because of this additional burden, they become overwhelming. Finally, anxiety manifests itself in terms of unhelpful behaviour such as avoiding going to places which are reminders of the HIV. Such avoidance behaviour often serves to exacerbate the problem.

One client described these problems:

> I felt so alone . . . I thought that everyone would guess about the virus and that I would lose all my friends. I thought they couldn't handle it. They would notice my physical shape. I thought that they knew but didn't want to say anything. I started to avoid going to work. I'd phone in sick and then got sick lines from the doctor. Soon I found myself making excuses not to go out at night. I became so preoccupied with myself I suppose I must have become boring.

Depression is not just feeling blue and low. Of course HIV will cause periods of feeling down. Depression describes a condition which is more prolonged and goes beyond the expected reactions of grief and loss on diagnosis. Often depressed people suffer from poor sleep, poor appetite, periods of inexplicable weepiness, a feeling of being slowed down, of not functioning well. Patients often complain of poor concentration and memory (this sometimes triggers fears of AIDS-related dementia). Suicidal thoughts often appear and these should always be taken seriously. Thinking often centres around a feeling of low self-esteem—'Who would want to have anything to do with me now that I've got this disease'. People with depression often experience hopelessness about the future, not believing that the situation can improve. They often feel that things around them are going wrong—'Nothing works out for me'.

People with HIV can experience feelings of anger and frustration. Sometimes this is focused on anger with the person who may have passed the virus to them. At other times it is related to feeling frustrated because so little can be done to overcome the virus. Anger with oneself for having caught the virus is closely tied to feelings of guilt. Having caught a sexually transmitted disease, having used drugs or feeling that being homosexual is wrong, may contribute to such feelings, even extending to the belief that somehow the virus is a punishment for this behaviour.

Preoccupation with health is sometimes related to HIV diagnosis and often centres round checking for signs of illness or constantly seeking reassurance that everything is going well. Although it is quite normal for someone who is HIV positive to worry about his or her health, the preoccupation with health can become very handicapping as the checking can take over much of a person's day. Sometimes it occurs in ritual form, checking over the entire body for blemishes and spots. The moment the check is completed more doubts flood into the mind—'Did I check for that, did I really make sure there were no marks on my leg? What about that little mark on my cheek? I'd better take another look'. And so on and on.

Anxiety and depression are relatively commonplace and we all suffer from these, usually to a minor degree from time to time. All workplaces will experience workers performing badly or requiring time off work because of emotional disorders and, as previously discussed, HIV positive workers are no exception. Supportive and understanding colleagues can help to reduce the impact of these problems.

HIV AT WORK

The effect of HIV in the workplace is determined to a great extent by the attitudes and fears within society and individuals. These have been described above. There are more specific ways in which workers' performance and career development are affected both by the psychological and physical consequences of their infection and by the attitudes of their colleagues and employers.

The quality of relationships with colleagues for someone who is HIV positive will have an important impact on subsequent adjustment and ability to remain at work. Fellow workers who have little understanding about HIV and AIDS may fear that they themselves will be infected merely by working alongside someone with HIV. Any accidents involving blood spills may cause panic among those who are not aware of safe cleaning procedures.

At a broader level prejudice associated not only with HIV but with homosexuality and drug abuse may also affect the level to which a person with HIV will be accepted at work. The social isolation and stigma mentioned above apply with greater force at work where the HIV positive person may experience them on a repeated and personal basis. Even those suspected of being gay or of having a history of drug use may experience fearful and negative reactions from their colleagues in relation to HIV.

At a personal level HIV can affect performance at work in a number of ways. The psychological impact of the virus on the individual has been discussed in detail above and any of these psychological problems may arise. Workers with HIV may find that their mood limits concentration, tolerance of pressure and energy levels in the same way that emotional problems would affect others, occasionally requiring days off work. Of course, many HIV positive people are well adjusted and do not experience any deterioration in their work. The effect of their diagnosis may lead them to throw themselves into their work with renewed vigour.

Some people with HIV experience neurological problems because of direct effects of the virus on the brain or infections in the brain which are related to impaired immunity. These problems may influence performance, especially in jobs requiring high levels of concentration. Some respond to drug treatment. Neurological problems are usually associated with a more general physical decline and it would be unusual if they were diagnosed in someone who is working. It is far more likely that poor memory and concentration at work are related to problems with mood.

Physical health also affects performance at work. Even in a healthy individual, days off may be required for routine medical checks. If he or she becomes ill, more prolonged periods may be necessary though periods of good health between bouts of illness are likely.

Career prospects for someone who is positive can be damaged by the attitude of the employer who may fear that he or she will not be able to cope with additional responsibilities. It should be borne in mind that the period between becoming infected and becoming ill can be very long and that the employee may never become ill. It is not only the employer who determines career prospects. The person with HIV may review future plans and concentrate on domestic or leisure activities rather than career.

Many people with HIV choose not to discuss their status with their employer because of the problems outlined above. It is only when information leaks out or colleagues start to guess what is going on, that the issue is raised, often in the context of a crisis. If no preparations have been made, the reaction may be enough to drive the worker away for good. Employers should think in advance how they would deal with such an issue both in terms of individual counselling for the employee and training for his or her colleagues. Individual counselling is discussed below. Staff training should address the following issues:

(1) The minimal risk of infection through casual contact.
(2) Safety procedures, especially those for cleaning up blood spills which should be adopted in all cases, not only among those known to be positive, since many may not know or wish to reveal to others that they have HIV. Any spill of body fluid should be cleaned if possible by the person himself or by others using rubber gloves and dilute bleach. Cuts or sores should be kept covered. Local health advisers should be

consulted about the best procedure for dealing with accidental exposure to body fluids.

Certain groups of workers most at risk of occupational exposure to blood or other body fluids need special training, for example, first aid staff, nurses, doctors, hospital laboratory staff, fire fighters, ambulance workers, refuse collectors and home helps. Suitable equipment should be easily available to staff. These guidelines could be included among general guidelines on other aspects of safety at work. Counselling should be available to those who may have been exposed accidentally to blood or other body fluids.

(3) As workers are far more likely to become infected as a result of their sexual or drug using behaviour, it would also be useful to include information on safer sex and the risks of intravenous drug abuse. It might be worth considering installing condom vending machines especially in the work social club or bar.

(4) Workers should have an opportunity to discuss their fears and attitudes regarding HIV in an effort to reduce the effects of prejudice and fear. These discussions should also include issues on attitudes towards gay people and drug users.

A sympathetic employer could retain valuable workers with HIV by responding to their need for time to receive medical treatment or counselling as well as understanding that the employee may go through periods of psychological distress. The counselling issues described below are not those which an employer would be expected to explore but are included so that the employer can understand the various difficulties encountered by the HIV positive worker.

COUNSELLING ISSUES

Testing

There is no consensus on whether or not testing should occur in the workplace. Employers are concerned about the potential cost of employing someone with HIV. There are many other physical complaints more common than HIV for which compulsory assessment is not required (e.g. breast cancer) and which may prove as costly. There are also concerns about ways in which the virus may affect neurological functioning and the worker's ability to perform complex mental tasks. Again, there are other causes of neurological damage which are not always assessed (e.g. alcoholism) and functional tests of mental abilities and work-related skills would be more useful. Finally, as previously discussed, the test is not conclusive—employees who had been recently infected may have a negative test result. There might be some justification for testing those who, if HIV positive, might present a real risk to others, for example surgeons, but medical staff are trained to avoid passing on infection to patients and in general there seems little justification for the expense and cost of counselling and testing all employees.

In the context of the workplace, the issue of testing takes on special difficulties. Confidentiality is important. Employees will feel unwilling to let their employer know that testing is taking place. Counselling organized through the workplace may not be acceptable unless the client feels certain that no intimate personal details will go beyond the counsellor. Understandably the employee will fear that a positive result will lead to loss of work. Where testing is compulsory as part of employment contracts (for example, to work in Saudi Arabia), testing is done on a routine basis with little worry that the result will be positive. Thus those receiving a test for these reasons may not be adequately prepared for a positive result. Failure to provide skilled counselling would also result in the loss of a valuable opportunity for education about the virus at a time when the client is likely to be especially receptive.

Many people wishing to be tested believe they have been at risk of exposure to HIV. Many have not thought through the implications of the test. It is unlike most other diagnostic tests because there is no cure for the virus. The role of the counsellor in discussing these issues with the client is to elicit his or her motives for being tested, to assess risk to provide information and to prepare him or her for a possible positive result.

Motives for testing range from visa requirements through the need to reassure oneself about a relatively low risk episode, to a confirmation of a new certain positive result. The first job for the counsellor is to examine the assumptions behind such motives. Many drug users feel certain that they are positive and wish to know their result because they believe they would have access to more comprehensive drug treatment services. It is often necessary to reassure them that though the risk is high, it is by no means certain that infection has indeed occurred—some drug users have taken extraordinary risks yet remained free of HIV! Many heterosexual individuals with a one-off sexual encounter with an unknown partner may feel confident that the result will be negative. The counsellor's role in this case is to acknowledge that the risk is not very high but that, nevertheless, the client should prepare himself or herself for the possibility that the result may be positive. More and more so-called low risk individuals are discovering that they are in fact HIV positive. By contrast some people are unreasonably convinced of a positive result and having engaged in fairly low risk activity are certain that they have been infected. The counsellor in all these cases needs to give appropriate feedback about the real risk of being positive and counsel accordingly.

To offer appropriate advice to clients, risk behaviour must be assessed. Belonging to a 'risk group' is not as relevant as actual behaviour. A gay man who has been monogamous with a monogamous partner is no more at risk than a monogamous heterosexual couple whatever the sexual activity. A heterosexual person with very many partners is much more at risk. More and more cases of heterosexuals with only one or two fairly steady partners being infected with HIV have been reported. Nobody can be complacent about the chances of catching the virus, nor are those who have caught the virus necessarily members of a high risk group. Whatever the reason for testing, it should never be assumed that the client will be HIV negative and he or she should be prepared accordingly.

Assessing risk leads to the most intimate level of questioning, which should be conducted in a way that ensures minimal embarrassment and maximum confidence in the counsellor. Confidentiality must be ensured.

Once the initial preparation has been done in terms of assessing motives for testing and potential risk, information regarding the virus is delivered. This includes the three-month or more window period discussed above, the length of time one is likely to remain well, risk to others, ways to protect oneself, and possible medical treatments. As little information can be absorbed after the shock of a positive result, information about the virus, the ways in which it can or cannot be transmitted and treatments available need to be communicated prior to testing. Misinformation which is often difficult to shift at that time is the belief that one will die very soon, or that one is very infectious to others even through casual contact. Such information is not wasted on those receiving a negative result—the counselling session is a valuable educative measure.

Clients often assume that those around them will cope badly with the news and feel unable to tell relatives or lovers. Sometimes they tell inappropriate individuals who are poor at dealing with the information. Prior to the test it is worth exploring who could be told and how these friends or relatives could be helped. Then comes the final and difficult task of looking at the costs and benefits of actually going ahead with the test.

One paradoxical question raised during testing is 'What is good about knowing one is positive?' At first glance, nothing at all. On further consideration, positive aspects of having such knowledge can be explored. It can motivate the client to alter his or her behaviour to protect him or herself and others in a way that thinking one *might* be positive can never do. Preparation can be made for the future, from arranging appropriate housing, to writing a will. Greater efforts can be made to restore or maintain family contact. At a planning level, a more accurate picture of numbers of HIV positive patients helps to provide for the future. As has been seen, positive changes in lifestyle—taking exercise, eating well and cutting down on drinking and drug taking can positively enhance immunity and knowledge of one's result can provide the catalyst for such positive changes. It will also enable the counsellor to introduce the client to a support network for those with the virus. There are groups who could put one in touch with supporters, and help with practical problems. Most important of all, knowing one's HIV status at an early stage enables regular medical follow-up to take place and treatment to be made available as soon as it is appropriate.

The other side of the coin is the need to examine the bad things about knowing that one is positive. Does the client have the resources to cope with this information? Once the result is told the information cannot be taken back. One client described his feelings this way:

> I can't bear the uncertainty—I feel as if a sword were hanging over me and any minute it will fall. Sometimes I wish I had AIDS and the whole thing were over with.

The uncertainty of outcome, the endless fight against the illness and the problems those around might have in coping with one's diagnosis may be intolerable. Many people who find they are positive have to give up work or find their ability to work seriously affected by the psychological and social consequences of the diagnosis. For some, it is better to remain ignorant. A decision to avoid testing should always include the decision to avoid placing others at risk in future in case one is positive.

Becoming Positive

Some of the psychosocial consequences of a positive diagnosis have been discussed above. The counsellor's role at this time is to help the client throughout the initial stages following diagnosis, aiming at helping to provide a satisfactory system for coping with the diagnosis in the long term. The main problem at an early stage is the client's reaction of shock. The little grain of hope for a negative test result is crushed, and suddenly the consequences of the diagnosis begin to be understood.

There are no right or wrong methods of coping, though some are associated with better outcome. Active coping, trying to fight the virus, thinking positively and discussing one's status with others appears to predict better outcome than passive acceptance (Leiberich *et al.*, 1989; Kelly and St Lawrence, 1988). However, for each individual, coping will take on a different style which may change over time.

At early stages there are three issues to deal with. The first is coping within oneself. It is important to retain a sense of oneself as a valued person despite the diagnosis, as well as grasping all the complex information required to understand the infection. Coping strategies need to be developed to remain calm and rational in the face of disaster. The second hurdle is dealing with others. Breaking news to others, selecting recipients of the news and being prepared for their reaction are all difficult hurdles to overcome. The counsellor often has as great a task helping those close to the client come to terms with the diagnosis as the client himself. At work it is sometimes advisable to tell a sympathetic employer who will be more understanding subsequently if the client has low days or requires time off work to attend clinics. Thirdly, practical problems will arise regarding finance, future career, housing, insurance and so on. Obviously these are all tied together. A supportive partner or family member will help in the coping process.

Interventions to help HIV positive people to cope can be divided into several groups of strategies (Kelly and St Lawrence, 1988) of which two, social support and stress coping, will be discussed.

The provision of social support can help people with HIV. These supports can be informal, by friends or colleagues providing support, or formal, through the client joining an organized support group. Gay men who are able to disclose their positive status to a supportive group tend to have a better adjustment than those who do not do so. The process of disclosure appears to lessen emotional distress, perhaps because the burden of the knowledge can be shared with others. Only anecdotal evidence supports these suggestions (Kelly and St Lawrence, 1988).

The use of various stress coping techniques is thought to reduce the impact of the diagnosis. One example of such an approach can be seen in a coping training package offered by McKusick, Conant and Coates (1985). They provided relaxation training and cognitive coping training. The clients were taught to re-appraise anxious or depressive thinking. More general information and health education were also offered.

Other strategies commonly adopted largely fit into the two categories already described. For example the use of alternative medicines, which is very popular among people with HIV, seems to help in the management of stress and in a development of control over one's health. The use of self-empowerment strategies allows the client to take control and provides much needed social support in an atmosphere of self-disclosure which is believed to be beneficial. One example of such a strategy is the body positive movement, in which groups of HIV positive people attempt to deal with their HIV status in a positive way.

Although coping can be assisted in a number of ways, individuals have great personal resources, often surprising themselves with their own strength in dealing with the issues as they arise. It should be borne in mind that although one talks about general 'coping', which strategy is used depends very much on specific situations. For example the issue of having children is important. For some clients with mixed feelings about having children, the thought of not being able to have them can be dealt with by emphasizing the positive aspects of not having children (more resources, more freedom, less responsibility). For those who would have liked children, the role of aunt or good neighbour can be developed, the client taking on baby sitting for others or cultivating a closer relationship with their nieces and nephews. Those who choose to keep their diagnosis a secret must then learn how to cope with the mother who keeps asking why there are no grandchildren, the flatmate who wants to know more about the visits to hospital, or the employer who wonders why so many sick days are taken. Coping takes place at a detailed day-to-day level, and over time, coping systems may change. It is important never to be critical of the strategy the client is using but to attempt to direct him or her to alternatives.

Becoming Ill

The next crisis in the process of coping with HIV is the stage of becoming ill. It is at this point that confidentiality becomes much more difficult to maintain. Treatment usually takes place in an infectious diseases unit or other clearly identifiable setting where visitors and relatives can begin to piece information together. The course of illness among AIDS patients is quite different from other terminal illnesses which are usually accompanied by a steady decline (with perhaps one or two periods of remission). HIV illness can be followed by complete recovery and maintenance of good health for months or even years. As each illness appears, the outcome of that particular episode is not known. The client could recover completely, or die. For some patients this new kind of uncertainty is intolerable.

Women

Although at present the majority of HIV positive people are men, women are affected and have different problems to face. Most HIV positive women in this country acquired the virus through intravenous drug use but a substantial minority became infected sexually. As well as coping with the problems outlined above, women have special problems in the area of child rearing and pregnancy. The issues surrounding whether or not to conceive or to continue with a pregnancy when there is a risk that the baby could be infected are complex and difficult. For women with HIV, whether or not their children are infected, there is the problem of caring for the child if the parents are ill or dead.

Women are often affected indirectly. Although men care for people with AIDS it is more often women who have to make alterations in working life to care for AIDS patients. It would be a mistake to assume that female employees will be unaffected by HIV.

CONCLUSIONS

Clearly HIV and AIDS will have an increasing role in the workplace in future, with enormous financial and human cost. It is likely that many people with the virus will suffer from psychological distress.

The distress experienced by people with HIV can be alleviated if counselling and guidance are available from an early stage. Counselling at the time of testing is especially important as it provides a useful educational tool for those who are negative while giving essential information and preparation to those who are found to have the virus.

Their ability to cope and contribute at work could be greatly influenced by the attitude and level of understanding shown by employers and colleagues. Education and appropriate training would do much to prepare workers to accept a colleague with HIV without fearing that they will catch the virus. A carefully drafted workplace policy on HIV would ensure that appropriate action can be taken if someone with HIV experiences difficulties in terms of physical illness, psychological distress and adverse reactions from colleagues or customers.

REFERENCES

Anon. (1988). Ten percent of US firms have workers with AIDS, *Personnel Management*, 9 May.

Atkinson, J.H., Grant, I., Kennedy, C.J., Richman, D.D., Spector, S.A. and McCutchen, J.A. (1988). Prevalence of Psychiatric Disorders Among Men Infected with Human Immunodeficiency Virus, *Archives of General Psychiatry*, **45**, 859–64.

Becker, M.H. and Joseph, J.G. (1988). AIDS and behavioural change to reduce risks: a review, *The American Journal of Public Health*, **78**(4), 394–410.

Brown, J.H., Henteleff, P., Barakat, S. and Rowe, C.J. (1986). Is it normal for terminally ill patients to desire death? *American Journal of Psychiatry*, **143**(2), 208–11.

Carwein, V. and Ray, C. (1989). Labor productivity losses to Nevada's and the American economy resulting from premature death due to AIDS, Paper presented at the Fifth International Conference on AIDS, 8 June, Montreal.

Communicable Diseases (Scotland) Unit (1987). Update: Human immunodeficiency virus infections in health care workers exposed to blood of infected patients—USA, *AIDS News Supplement*, CDS Weekly Report, number 25.

Communicable Diseases (Scotland) Unit (1989a). Acquired immune deficiency syndrome (AIDS)—United Kingdom, *AIDS News Supplement*, CDS Weekly Report, 8 April.

Communicable Diseases (Scotland) Unit (1989b). Human immunodeficiency virus (HIV) infection United Kingdom, to 31 March 1989, *AIDS News Supplement*, CDS Weekly Report, 29 April.

Communicable Diseases (Scotland) Unit (1989c). WHO estimates of AIDS/HIV by the year 2000: Major increase in HIV/AIDS expected, *AIDS News Supplement*, CDS Weekly Report, 27 May 1989.

Emery, G.D., Steer, R.A. and Beck, A.T. (1981). Depression, hopelessness and suicidal intent among heroin addicts, *The International Journal of the Addictions*, **16**(3), 425–9.

Gala, C., Martini, S., Pergami, A., Rossini, M., Russo, R. and Lazzarin, A. (1989). Psychiatric history among homosexuals and drug addicts infected with human immunodeficiency virus, Paper presented at the Fifth International Conference on AIDS, 7 June, Montreal.

Greenblatt, R.M., Yelin, E., Hollander, H., McMaster, E., Kidd, J. and Filson, M. (1989). Work disability among AIDS clinic patients, Paper presented at the Fifth International Conference on AIDS, 6 June, Montreal.

Hubbard, R.L., Marsden, M.E., Cavanaugh, E., Rachel, J.V. and Ginzburg, H.M. (1988). Role of drug-abuse treatment in limiting the spread of AIDS, *Reviews of Infectious Diseases*, **10**(2), 377–84.

Kelly, J.A. and St Lawrence, J.S. (1988). AIDS prevention and treatment: Psychology's role in the health crisis, *Clinical Psychology Review* **8**, 255–84.

Kessler, R., Joseph, J., Ostrow, D., Phair, J., Chmiel, J. and Rusk, C. (1989). Psychosocial co-factors in illness onset among HIV positive men, Paper presented at the Fifth International Conference on AIDS, 6 June, Montreal.

Leiberich, P., Engeter, M., Hermann, C., Harrer, T., Olbrich, E. and Kalden, J. (1989). Coping of HIV infected persons and AIDS patients, Paper presented at the Fifth International Conference on AIDS, 6 June, Montreal.

Marrie, T., MacIntosh, N., Streight, R. and Sclech, W. (1989). The emotional impact of needlestick injuries on health care workers, Paper presented at the Fifth International Conference on AIDS, 4–9 June, Montreal.

McKusick, L., Conant, M. and Coates, T. (1985), The AIDS epidemic; a model for developing intervention strategies for reducing high risk behaviour in gay men, *Sexually Transmitted Diseases*, **12**, 229–33.

Miller, D. and Brown, B. (1988). Developing the role of clinical psychology in the context of AIDS, *The Psychologist: Bulletin of the British Psychological Society*, **2**, 63–6.

Miller, D., Weber, J. and Green, J. (1986). *The Management of AIDS Patients*, Macmillan, London.

Perroni, L., Albertoni, P. and Soscia, F. (1989). Transmissions of HIV infection in heterosexual partners of HIV+ drug addicts, Paper presented at the Fifth International Conference on AIDS, 6 June, Montreal.

Pittman-Lindeman, M., Miller, D. and Sowa, P.E. (1989). Assessing the cost of AIDS to both patients and the health care institution, Paper presented at the Fifth International Conference on AIDS, 6 June, Montreal.

Plansringarm, K., Akarasewi, P., Wright, N. and Choopanya, K. (1989). Second seroprevalence survey among Bangkok's intravenous drug addicts (IVDA'S), Paper presented at the Fifth International Conference on AIDS, 6 June, Montreal.

Rastrelli, M., Ferrazzi, D., Vigo, B. and Gianelli, F. (1989). Risk of HIV transmission to health care workers and comparison with viral hepatitides, Paper presented at the Fifth International Conference on AIDS, 4–9 June, Montreal.

Robertson, J.R., Bucknall, A.B.V., Welsby, P.D., Roberts, J.J., Inglis, J.M., Peutherer, J.F. and Brettle, R.P. (1986). Epidemic of AIDS related virus (HTLV-III/LAV) infection among intravenous drug abusers, *British Medical Journal*, **292**, 527–9.

Seidle, O. and Goebel, F. (1987). Somatic reactions of homosexuals and drug addicts to the knowledge of possible HIV test result, AIDS-Forschung, **4**, 181–7. (Cited in Kelly, J.A. and St Lawrence, J.S. (1988). AIDS prevention and treatment: Psychology's role in the health crisis, *Clinical Psychology Review*, **8**, 255–84.)

Shilts, R. (1987). *And the Band Played On*, Penguin, London.

Wills, A.T. and Shiffman, S. (1985). Coping and substance use: a conceptual framework. In S. Shiffman and A.T. Wills (eds) *Coping and Substance Use*, pp. 3–24, Academic Press, London.

Chapter 5.2

AIDS Sufferers at Work and the Law

Brian W. Napier, Queen Mary and Westfield College, London

INTRODUCTION

The issues raised in any AIDS-related problem are so wide ranging that any approach which hopes to go beyond the superficial must begin by narrowing down the field of enquiry. Here we are looking at AIDS in the employment context, and for reasons of space we begin by excluding several possible aspects of this phenomenon. In employment law we shall not consider general questions relating to the consequences of illness, even incapacitating fatal illness, since these are matters addressed in Chapter 5.1. In passing, however, it can be said that because AIDS is no more than a disease, albeit a particularly feared and dangerous one, some of the conclusions reached here about the state of the law may apply to other contagious diseases affecting people at work. Also excluded from the present discussion are questions of legal liability which raise general questions of health and safety in the working environment. Neither shall we here be concerned with the implications of the transmission of AIDS by an employee to a third party, nor with general questions of tortious or criminal liability associated with AIDS arising out of the employment relationship. The significance of AIDS in relation to duties of confidentiality within the employment relationship is only briefly touched upon, and there is no consideration of the significance of AIDS testing of employees from the point of view of civil liberties. Several of these excluded issues have been discussed in other studies which have focused on AIDS and employment (Southam and Howard, 1988; Social Services Committee, 1987).

It has to be said that this study deals only with the significance of AIDS in British employment law, although the problems transcend national boundaries. It is instructive to contrast and compare the response of different legal systems, especially those (such as the United States) where there is specific legislation which attempts to curb discrimination on health grounds

Vulnerable Workers: Psychosocial and Legal Issues. Edited by M. J. Davidson and J. Earnshaw

(Widdows, 1988). AIDS may also be considered as a phenomenon which raises important questions relating to basic human rights (Sieghart, 1989), and to incidental matters associated with the protection of privacy. For example, the recording of medical data on computers should be in accordance with specific international standards (Council of Europe, 1989).

Having begun by clearing away a number of issues, it should be said that the discussion will be broadened in one important respect. It will rarely be possible—and definitely not useful in the context of employment law—to separate discussion of the disease itself from discussion of the response of the non-infected to it. It has been well said that 'HIV/AIDS is predominantly a social phenomenon with serious medical sequelae'. This means, in the employment context, that we must consider not only action taken against those who carry or are suspected of carrying the disease, but also the significance of behaviour by colleagues of these persons, or third parties such as customers, which manifests the hostility and fear associated with the disease. Indeed, it is the prejudice and fear which uninfected persons have about the disease which arguably makes it such a serious danger to society.

A useful beginning is to identify what it is about AIDS that makes it special, in the sense of setting it apart from other diseases. One important point to note at the outset is that our present scientific knowledge about AIDS—how it is transmitted, and other information relating to the incidents of the disease—is still developing. Or, to put it less positively, we cannot yet be confident that our actual knowledge of the aetiology of the disease is accurate or complete. In the words of Rose J in a recent case dealing with the confidentiality attaching to the identity of AIDS suffers (X v. Y [1988] 2 All ER 648, 652), 'The way in which the virus spreads is not fully understood although much is known.' It seems established, however, that AIDS (strictly speaking, HIV infection) can be transmitted between adults in only one of two ways: (a) sexual intercourse, and (b) intimate contact (including transfusion) with infected blood, blood products, semen or cervical secretions. Additionally, AIDS may be contracted perinatally by a child born to an infected mother. There is no evidence to support the view that AIDS may be spread by insect bites, droplet inflection, use of communal eating or drinking vessels, contact with common external objects (such as toilet seats), or any form of non-intimate social contact.

What is it that makes AIDS so different from other diseases? Obviously, there is much which AIDS has in common with other virus-born diseases like hepatatis B, in terms of risk of infection, frequently fatal consequences, and popular disapproval towards the lifestyles of those affected. Thus the special status of AIDS may be said to lie more in the particular combination of characteristics associated with it, rather than in any feature or features unique to it. Such a combination is likely to include the following four considerations:

(1) The fear of contracting an incurable disease, with high mortality rate.
(2) The rapidly changing state of scientific opinion about the disease and how it is transmitted, together with awareness that currently expressed scientific advice may well be imperfect.
(3) The fear that numbers likely to be affected by the disease will grow to epidemic proportions, causing major social problems in the medium to long term.
(4) The critical perceptions many people have about the lifestyles of most who are carriers of the AIDS virus

There is now no shortage of sources of advice about what AIDS is and what precautions should be taken against it. But, at a practical level there is a need to distinguish between advice which tells us how good, responsible and reasonable citizens should respond to the risks associated with AIDS, and that which predicts the likely response of the courts and tribunals to the employment-related problems likely to be encountered as a consequence of the disease. The likelihood of any one document accurately combining what may be called these medically/socially prescriptive and legally descriptive functions is small. In most of the literature on AIDS-related problems there is certainly inadequate differentiation between the 'is' and the 'ought' in relation to the legal position. Although usually prompted by creditable libertarian philosophies of tolerance and understanding on the part of authors (not to mention those whose concern is for the promotion of 'good' industrial relations), such a mixing of issues does not in the long run assist in spreading the understanding which society must have if it is to combat effectively the AIDS phenomenon.

THE LEGAL FRAMEWORK

Several attempts have been made to provide a framework for discussion of the topic in English law (Fagan and Newell, 1987; *Industrial Relations Legal Information Bulletin*, 1988); there exists also a detailed study of the relevant law in the United States (Leonard, 1987). The issue has been considered from the point of view of human rights law as well as the domestic law of the United Kingdom, and it has been pointed out that the refusal of employment on arbitrary grounds may well constitute an infringement of the 'right to work' in the sense in which that term is used in international law (Sieghart, 1989, pp. 54–8). The World Health Organization and the International Labour Organization, in a jointly published document

(WHO/ILO, 1988) have given an important lead in stating that HIV infection should not, by itself, constitute either grounds for generalized pre-employment screening, discrimination in employment conditions or termination of employment. But it would be naive to suppose that such statements will by themselves prevent discrimination in practice, and it is necessary to go on to consider what specific legal protections are available in domestic law. For the purposes of this analysis we shall organize the issues into three categories following an obvious chronological sequence: (a) recruitment, (b) conditions of employment and (c) dismissal.

Recruitment

English statute law imposes no limitations on a refusal to employ a person, except where the refusal is on grounds of sex or race, or time-expired criminal conviction under the Rehabilitation of Offenders Act 1974. As and when the Employment Bill of 1990 (currently before Parliament) becomes law, this list will be extended to include refusal to employ on grounds related to trade union membership. The common law in England does not recognize such refusal as amounting to an actionable wrong. And so it follows that unless selection procedures designed to eliminate possible carriers impinge upon such standards, the unsuccessful job seeker is left without remedy. There is no equivalent to the principle of good faith (*Treu und Glauben*) which, in the jurisprudence of the Federal Republic of Germany, has been interpreted to impose limitations on the types of question which may be asked in a pre-contractual relationship, and which limits, in particular, enquiries which violate the constitutionally protected right of privacy. Neither do we find in English law any willingness to elevate AIDS-related discrimination to a common law tort, as has occurred in the jurisprudence of certain US states. We might thus expect this legal situation to be clearly stated in official documents about AIDS, however regrettable the decision of a prospective employer to refuse employment to someone who is thought to be at risk from infection. But the main official statement on the subject (Department of Employment, 1988) is less than clear on this point. It states (para. 8)

> Employers are free in law to decide whom they wish to employ but they must not discriminate either directly or indirectly on grounds of sex or race. In almost all occupations there is no risk of an infected person passing the virus on to others, and this would not therefore generally be a reason for treating them any differently from other job applicants.

This is a good example of how an official document unsatisfactorily combines prescription and description, for the quoted passage carries the implication, to all but the trained lawyer, that refusal of employment may amount to the kind of discrimination which is unlawful.

In point of fact, however, neither sex nor race discrimination is obviously involved where there is refusal to employ because of actual or suspected AIDS, or an associated reason (such as AIDS-related illnesses). The explanation is simple; the essence of discrimination is that like cases are treated differently on specifically prohibited grounds of sex or race, whereas where rejection occurs the prospective employer would no doubt treat all suspected AIDS carriers in the same way, whatever their sex or race. This is sufficient to defeat any argument based on *direct* discrimination. But could there be any argument on the basis of *indirect* discrimination? Unlike direct discrimination, the concept of indirect discrimination depends not on the application of sexually explicit criteria, but on the application of apparently neutral rules or conditions which in fact affect disproportionately different categories of persons. (Where an apparently neutral criterion is applied with the intention of excluding persons of a particular sex or racial group, it is uncertain whether this is direct or indirect discrimination (cf. *James* v. *Eastleigh Borough Council* [1990] IRLR 288, HL).) Since the statistical evidence demonstrates that, to date, AIDS disproportionately affects men (because of the strong link with forms of male homosexual contact), could it be said that refusal to employ might amount to indirect sex discrimination against men, within the meaning of the Sex Discrimination Act 1975, s.1(1)(b)? The relevant part of the Act provides:

> (1) A person discriminates against a woman in any circumstances relevant for the purposes of any provision of this Act if ... (b) he applies to her a requirement or condition which he applies or would apply equally to a man but (i) which is such that the proportion of women who can comply with it is considerably smaller than the proportion of men who can comply with it, and (ii) which he cannot show to be justifiable irrespective of the sex of the person to whom it is applied, and (iii) which is to her detriment because she cannot comply with it.

There are several arguments which could be mustered against the conclusion that discrimination against AIDS sufferers is indirect discrimination against men. First, the proportion of AIDS infected persons who are male will vary according to geographical region. While the association with male homosexual behaviour may be high in certain regions of Britain, in others (e.g. Edinburgh) it may be significantly different, because the disease is primarily spread by the sharing of needles among drug abusers. What is more, the classification of AIDS as primarily a disease affecting male homosexuals may prove to be inaccurate over time, as we know it can be transmitted by heterosexual sexual contact as well as in certain non-sexual ways. Indeed, AIDS in Africa is such a terrifying problem precisely because it is spread by heterosexual relations. It is therefore not necessarily true that discrimination against AIDS sufferers amounts to indirect sexual discrimination against males. Secondly, even if the link between AIDS and males *is* accepted as established (at least for most regions of Britain at the present time), then the conclusion that such a practice amounts to indirect discrimination does not necessarily follow in all cases. It would be a simple matter for an employer to seek to justify his or her refusal to employ on the ground that he or she did not wish to employ persons of homosexual tendencies. However regrettable and narrow minded such an attitude may be, it has never been contrary to any law in the United Kingdom to refuse employment on these grounds; the courts are unlikely to make it so on the ground that in addition to being homosexual the individual concerned is or is suspected of being, HIV positive. The third basis for arguing that penalizing AIDS sufferers is not unlawful indirect discrimination against men raises more fundamental questions. Under the Sex Discrimination Act 1975 (s.1(a)(b)(ii)), the person who imposes a requirement or condition that is allegedly unlawful because of its unequal effect has a successful defence if he or she can prove that the requirement or condition imposed, which was to the detriment of the person complaining, was none the less, in the circumstances, 'justified'. The question of knowing how and when justification is made out is one of the most difficult and controversial areas of discrimination law. Could an employer who refuses employment to a man who is HIV positive, 'justify' the imposition of such a criterion? The answer to this lies in the case law governing the interpretation of the term. Recent dicta of the House of Lords have suggested that the word should be construed in the same manner as s.1(3) of the Equal Pay Act 1970, the provision which allows for a 'material factor' defence to a claim made for equal pay. As a consequence, one possible line of argument could focus on the possible economic costs to the employer should an employee develop the symptoms of the disease. In the situation where an employer operated a benefit scheme for his or her disabled ex-employees, the point might be made that the burden of supporting someone requiring expensive medical treatment for AIDS could be disproportionately large. Perhaps for this reason an otherwise indirectly discriminatory refusal to recruit might be seen as justified.

The case law dealing with s.1(3) shows, however, that the employer is not restricted to a narrow economic justification by way of excuse for an apparently discriminatory act. The employer can also rely on other reasons, such as administrative efficiency, or external market forces. None the less, he or she would in all these situations have to show that the requirement or condition was 'reasonably necessary' to obtain the desired result. The decisions in several cases (e.g. *Jenkins* v. *Kingsgate (Clothing Productions)*

Ltd [1981] IRLR 388, EAT per Browne-Wilkinson J at 394; *Bilka-Kaufhaus GmbH* v. *Weber von Hartz* [1986] IRLR 317, ECJ) point to the same conclusion.

There is also, however, an older body of authority derived from the law of racial discrimination (where the statutory provisions are in this respect identical) which suggests that justifiability means no more than that the employer must show reasons for his or her action which would be 'acceptable to right-thinking people as sound and tolerable reasons for so doing'. This was the phrase used by Eveleigh LJ in the well-known decision of *Ojutiku and Oburoni* v. *Manpower Services Commission* [1982] IRLR 418, CA. Whether such persons would be seen as harbouring fear and hostility to those suspected of AIDS is a moot point, but the possibility cannot be ruled out. This analysis has, however, become less pressing in the light of a recent important decision of the Court of Appeal in 1989 (*Hampson* v. *Department of Education and Science* [1989] IRLR 69) which proposes a revised and more restricted interpretation of the meaning of 'justified'. While not expressly overruling the *Ojutiku* decision, the court said that to decide whether a requirement or condition is 'justified' requires an objective balance to be struck between the discriminatory effect of the requirements or condition and the reasonable needs of the person who applies it. Even under this new and (for the complainant) more favourable approach, however, a question remains as to how 'reasonable needs' are to be defined. The Court of Appeal in *Hampson* did make it clear that it would be inadequate merely for the employer to show that in his or her opinion justification existed, but to what extent should public policy be brought into the matter? (The House of Lords ([1990] IRLR 302) has reversed the decision of the Court of Appeal, but on grounds unconnected with the matter in hand.)

A refusal to employ an HIV-positive person because of the opposition and disruption the recruitment of such an individual would be likely to cause among existing staff and customers might be defended on either the earlier or later interpretation of the meaning of 'justified'. It would certainly be more difficult under the later *Hampson* decision, since the *Ojutiku* test posits a decision which simply reflects common standards of behaviour among employers. Of course, the argument so far assumes that there are no special circumstances attending the refusal of employment. It would be much easier to justify a refusal to employ someone HIV-positive in a health care job where it is recognized that there is a risk (albeit small) of infection to patients (BMA, 1987), though in the *X* v. *Y* decision (above) it was said that the risk of AIDS-infected doctors passing on the disease to those they were treating was only 'slightly more than negligible'.

All things considered, the adverse treatment, whether in relation to recruitment, terms of employment or dismissal, of persons HIV-positive (or thought to be) seems unlikely to pose much danger, from an employer's point of view, of liability for indirect sex discrimination under the Sex Discrimination Act 1975. Perhaps a more interesting question is whether there might be liability for indirect racial discrimination if an employer were, for example, to refuse to recruit any person emanating from Uganda or Zaire, or other country where the disease was rife. Any outright ban on the recruitment of persons of particular nationalities would amount to direct discrimination on racial grounds, a concept which is defined so as to include nationality or national origins. Unlike indirect discrimination, direct discrimination cannot be 'justified' within the meaning of the Act. A slightly more subtle approach might be to refuse to employ all persons who had, perhaps during the years of prime sexual activity, lived on a permanent basis in countries where the incidence of AIDS was high. Or such individuals might be required to undergo screening to confirm HIV status as a precondition of employment. The imposition of such a criterion would certainly be capable of amounting to indirect discrimination on the assumption that some detriment to the individual in question could be shown; whether an employer might be able to 'justify' this would depend on the approach taken in interpreting this term, as discussed above.

Before leaving the area of discrimination it is necessary to say a word about the enquiry conducted by the Equal Opportunities Commission into the recruitment policies of the airline Dan-Air (EOC, 1987). (See also Chapter 8.2.)

As is well known, the company had for many years a policy of not employing men as temporary cabin staff. This policy long antedated awareness of AIDS, and indeed was originally defended by the company on the basis of customer preference. But when the company was finally formally challenged about its practices by the Equal Opportunities Commission, it sought to defend its position by introducing a specious argument based on: (a) the prevalence of homosexuality among male cabin staff and (b) the danger to passengers from AIDS following accidental work injuries involving blood. Independent medical evidence found the company's claims 'unsubstantiated and groundless', and the EOC proceeded to issue a non-discrimination notice against the company, under s.67 of the Sex Discrimination Act 1975. The whole affair provides an interesting example of how the public fear of AIDS can be exploited, but it does not address the central question mentioned above, which is whether measures taken to exclude from employment certain categories of high-risk individuals of one sex (typically male homosexuals) will amount to unlawful discrimination against men as a whole.

Conditions of Employment

Once we move from the process of recruitment to the treatment of existing employees, we move into a different legal context. While the prohibition against discrimination on grounds of race or sex continues once employment is under way, these controls are supplemented by other standards. Most importantly (and obviously) employees have a contractual relationship with their employer, the content of which is fixed not just by what is expressly agreed between them, but also by what is implied as a matter of law or fact. Furthermore, there is a range of extra-contractual duties imposed on the relationship, most importantly the duty under s.2 of the Health and Safety at Work Act 1974 which obliges the employer to ensure, so far as is reasonably practicable, the health, safety and welfare at work of all his or her employees. This statutory duty overlaps to a considerable extent with the implied duty under the contract of employment by which an employer is bound to take reasonable care for his or her employee's safety, and also with the general duty of care imposed on the employer by the tort of negligence. A recent decision of the Court of Appeal expresses the relevant principle thus: '[t]he law...requires the master to use all reasonable care to diminish any danger, if he cannot eliminate it...and, if he cannot effectively eliminate it so that significant risk remains, he may be required to give to the servant such information which he has to help the servant to evaluate properly the benefit of the job against the risk' (*Reid* v. *Rush and Tompkins Group plc* [1989] IRLR 265, CA per Gibson LJ at 270).

From the employer's point of view, AIDS-related issues affecting persons in employment may arise in several different ways. Once the disease has been diagnosed then there will be questions regarding entitlement to sick pay, duration of sick pay, and in time it may be important to know whether after long incapacity the contract of employment has become frustrated. These are questions which can arise with any serious illness, and for that reason they are not considered here. The employer may, however, seek to take specific steps which involve changes in working conditions, and these will be directly related to AIDS infection, or the fear of it.

The employer may wish to introduce precautionary measures intended to assist in the limitation or diagnosis of the disease. This could involve changes in working practices, or requirements that employees be tested or screened in order to discover the existence of infection. Secondly (and much more rarely), the employer may be faced with an allegation by an employee who has become infected with AIDS that he or she, the employer, bears some responsibility in law for the transmission of the disease. The two situations raise very different legal issues. The first, dealing with the contractual rights of the parties, is, in a sense, highly artificial. Except where the outcome is the ending of the employment relationship, an action for damages for breach of the contract of employment will not usually be seen as a worthwhile exercise, for the damages are likely to be small in most situations, and there will be no recovery for any injury to feelings caused by breach.

Litigation is of course much more probable when the contract comes to an end and the aggrieved party has nothing further to lose in his or her dealings with the ex-employer. The question whether there has been breach of contract will not decide whether the dismissal is judged fair or unfair under the statutory law of *unfair* dismissal, although it will be crucial in any claim of *wrongful* dismissal, i.e. dismissal which is in breach of the terms of the contract of employment. But the number of such wrongful dismissal claims is small, and they usually arise only when a dismissal without notice or with short notice has taken place. Unfair dismissal, on the other hand, is relatively common, and there is one particular situation in which the question of breach of contract may arise. Before the substance of the fairness of a dismissal can be considered, it has to be established that a dismissal has indeed taken place. The definition of dismissal in the employment legislation includes the situation where the employee terminates the contract in circumstances where he or she was entitled to do so without notice because of the employer's conduct. (Employment Protection (Consolidation) Act 1978, s.55(2)(c)). If a resignation takes place on the part of an employee who declines to have anything to do with changes in working practices or procedures which the employer says he or she is going to introduce, will this amount to a 'constructive' dismissal for the purposes of claiming that dismissal was unfair?

The test of constructive dismissal is, broadly, whether the employee has left in response to a breach of a fundamental term of the contract or in response to a renunciation of the contract as a whole; a constructive dismissal will generally (but not always) lead to a finding that a dismissal is unfair. Constructive dismissal is for the employee to prove.

In the present context, the answer to the question asked above depends essentially on what are the rights and duties of an employer in respect of an employee who is found to be, or suspected to be, a carrier of the AIDS virus. Problems arise because of the need to balance the range of duties owed to the affected individual with those owed to other members of staff and to third parties. The difficulty of deciding what is the contractual position is likely to be especially acute in the absence of express terms dealing with such issues in the contract itself. From a practical point of view, the advice to give to the employer who wishes to maximize his or her contractual rights to test or transfer employees is simple—he or she should make provision for this in the terms of employment on which staff are engaged. But for existing staff without such terms the position is likely to be complicated by the existence of competing (and to some extent conflicting) implied terms. The role of implied terms in fixing the terms of employment relationship is well established and a complex subject in its own right. The following implied terms may be regarded as particularly relevant here:

- The obligation on the employer to take reasonable care for the employee's safety, including the provision of a proper working environment (*Matthews* v. *Kuwait Bechtel Corporation* [1959] 2 QB 57, CA; *Graham Oxley Tool Steels Ltd.* v. *Firth* [1980] IRLR 135).
- The obligation on the employer to act reasonably in dealing with matters of safety or complaints about lack of safety drawn to his or her attention by an employee (*British Aircraft Corporation Ltd* v. *Austin* [1978] IRLR 332).
- The obligation of the employer to maintain the employee's trust and confidence within the relationship. (*Woods* v. *W.M. Car Services (Peterborough) Ltd* [1981] IRLR 347, CA).
- The obligation of the employer to provide reasonable support to an unpopular employee subjected to harassment by fellow employees (*Wigan Borough Council* v. *Davies* [1979] IRLR 127).

In addition to these implied terms, which are likely to form part of every contract of employment, a court or tribunal may find other implied terms on the basis of the usual contractual tests of 'officious bystander' or 'business efficacy'. Traditionally the device of the implied terms has given great power to judges to shape the employment relationship. But recently the Court of Appeal has insisted that a term was only to be implied into a contract of employment where it could be shown that it was necessary and had been omitted because it was so obvious that there was no need to make it explicit (*Stubbes* v. *Trower, Still & Keeling* [1987] IRLR 321, CA).

In certain 'high-risk' jobs involving the provision of health services it is acknowledged that there is a small risk that the virus may be communicated otherwise than by sexual contact. In such a situation, an employer who failed to take reasonable steps to prevent such transmission might be seen as negligent. In such cases the courts might well accept, by way of an implied term of the contract of employment, that an employer was entitled to transfer to different types of work, or even suspend, someone HIV-positive who was in a position to place others at risk. Such a power to transfer or change conditions of employment would be additional to the residual right to direct how and where work is to be done, which any employer enjoys over his or her workforce by virtue of the doctrine of managerial prerogative.

It is unlikely that an implied term giving the employer the right to require testing for AIDS among staff would ever be recognized by a court. Certainly such a term would not be generally implied, and indeed any attempt to insist on testing could well amount to a fundamental breach of contract, on the basis that such an act by the employer was destructive of mutual confidence in the relationship.

In the 'high-risk' jobs referred to above, however, the arguments for the implication of such a term in the contract are much stronger, given the public interest in minimizing the risks of infection and the employer's need to be able to take steps to limit his or her own potential liability in tort. The question is (or should be) largely hypothetical, however, since the employers of health care staff are alerted to the dangers and can be expected to have amended their terms of employment to give them such powers of testing they require. But what of other staff who would be expected to work alongside a person who is thought to be infected? There is a good chance that other members of staff may refuse to work alongside such persons. Whether such disobedience would give their employer grounds for a fair dismissal is a separate question which is considered below. As far as contractual terms are considered, however, it seems unlikely that fear of infection would be justification for refusal to obey an instruction, otherwise lawful, which would require an employee to work alongside a possible carrier of the virus. To put the matter another way, a direction to work alongside an AIDS (or suspected AIDS) carrier would not be so unreasonable as to fall outside the employer's general powers of direction under the contract.

Employer's liability for AIDS transmission

It is not possible to be categorical about the position of an employer should there be transmission of AIDS to one of his or her employees as a result of an accident at work. The chance of this occurring (and the victim being able to prove it has happened) are, according to the available evidence, very small. None the less, the potential consequences for the employer are so serious that it is worthwhile briefly sketching the possible legal position.

The employer does not by law guarantee the safety of his or her employees; he or she merely is under a duty, in contract as well as in tort, to take reasonable care to ensure that safety is not endangered. What amounts to 'reasonable care' will, of course, vary according not only to the circumstances of the risk, but also of the relevant employer and employee. In deciding whether negligence is established, the courts will distinguish between risks which are 'real' and risks which are no more than ' a mere possibility which would never influence the mind of a reasonable man' (*Charlton* v. *The Forrest Printing. Ink Co. Ltd* [1980] IRLR 331, CA).

A failure by an employer to observe the precautions recommended in currently authoritative sources of advice about how to deal with AIDS might well be seen as behaviour falling below the behaviour expected of 'the reasonable man'; indeed, it might even be seen as amounting to a situation in which no reasonable employer would expect an employee to work. The significance of the situation being so classified is, of course, that quite apart from any liability arising out of negligence, it could amount to a fundamental breach of contract by the employer, entitling the employee to resign and successfully maintain constructive dismissal, as discussed above.

This possibility leads on to the final aspect of substantive law to be considered.

Dismissal

Will it ever be fair to dismiss an employee who has (or is suspected of having) AIDS? What if fellow employees refuse to work alongside their colleague? And what of the dismissal of employees who refuse to work alongside such a fellow employee? Could there be any reduction in the award of compensation for an unfair dismissal where the reason for dismissal was AIDS infection, but the employee had contracted the disease by drug abuse or sexual activity? These are key questions, to which, unfortunately, it is simply not possible to give categorical answers at the present time, because of the lack of guidance given by decided cases.

In the law of unfair dismissal, the discretion of the industrial tribunal to decide on the question of 'reasonableness' arising under s.57(3) of the Employment Protection (Consolidation) Act 1978 is all important, and in most cases the categorization of the dismissal will turn on this issue. It is true that, before considering s.57(3), a tribunal will have to be shown by an employer that there existed a fair reason for the dismissal, and the range of such reasons is strictly limited by statutory definition. But the reasons include not only the 'capability' of the employee to do his or her job, but also (under s.57(1)(b)) the concept of 'some other substantial reason of a kind such as to justify the dismissal of an employee holding the position which that employee held', and this may be wide enough to cover the opposition shown to continued employment of a suspected carrier by fellow workers, or by customers or suppliers. AIDS (or suspected AIDS) would probably not, by itself, constitute a fair reason for dismissal, for it has been held that 'other substantial reason' excludes dismissal for a 'trivial or unworthy reason' (*Kent County Council* v. *Gilham* [1985] IRLR 18, CA).

In a decision which is discussed also in Chapter 8.2, the Employment Appeal Tribunal accepted that 'homosexual tendencies' could amount to 'some other substantial reason, (*Saunders* v. *Scottish National Camps Association* [1980] IRLR 174). On the other hand, in the recent industrial tribunal decision of *Buck* v. *The Letchworth Palace Ltd* IT 36488/86, 3.4.87, the view was expressed that a dismissal on grounds of homosexuality or the antagonism of fellow employees to homosexuality would render a dismissal unfair.

But it would be an unimaginative employer who made his or her defence rely solely on the proposition that he or she was dismissing for homosexuality (or AIDS infection) alone. The point is made above that it will often be possible for an employer to fasten upon some associated 'conduct' of the employee who is homosexual, and to rely on this as the basis for the decision to dismiss.

Assuming the employer has been able to put forward a fair reason for the dismissal, the next question is whether in the circumstances he or she has acted reasonably in relying upon this reason as justifying the dismissal (Employment Protection (Consolidation) Act 1978, s.57(3)). The determination of 'reasonableness' depends so much on the individual circumstances of the case that it is not possible to predict with any confidence how an AIDS-related dismissal might be assessed. As is well known, an industrial tribunal, in reaching its decision, is not supposed to 'second guess' the employer's judgement and substitute its own views on how it would have dealt with the case. It should rather ask whether the decision to dismiss falls within the 'band of reasonable responses' open to a reasonable employer in the circumstances (*British Leyland (UK) Ltd* v. *Swift* [1981] IRLR 91, CA). Its decision is subject to correction on appeal only if it can be shown that in reaching it there was an error of law, or if the tribunal's approach was so wrong that it could be described by the words, 'My goodness, that was certainly wrong' (*County Council of Hereford and Worcester* v. *Neale* [1986] IRLR 168, CA). These are the general rules which apply to this crucial deliberation. In addition, some specific principles established over the years may be mentioned.

First, the question of reasonableness has always to be seen in the context of the particular employer. It is not a question to be determined at large, by reference to general values current in society, but by reference to the standards of the employer who has dismissed (Thomson, 1982). This means that it will be necessary to take into account the nature of the job and the previous experiences of the employer in applying the 'band of reasonable responses' test.

Secondly, s.57(3) requires an assessment to be made of the reasonableness of the employer's conduct, not the justice (or lack of justice) as far as the employee is concerned. This principle of fundamental importance emerges from the wording of the statute, and is confirmed by the decision of the House of Lords in *Polkey* v. *A.E. Dayton Services Ltd* [1987] IRLR 503, HL. That decision also emphasizes the importance, for the purpose of deciding the reasonableness issue, of seeing whether the employer has followed proper procedures before dismissing. In the context of an AIDS-related dismissal, this could well mean that an employer should follow the advice given in official publications, such as the Department of Employment/Health and Safety Executive Booklet, and make sure that all the workforce were acquainted with the relevant facts.

Thirdly, in a case where the dismissal is carried out because the employer is faced with a hostile and frightened workforce, there is the question of what weight, if any, should attach to the pressure which is brought to bear upon him or her. There are no authorities directly in point, but in the past the courts have accepted that, for example, the opposition of an important customer to the continued employment of a particular worker can be relevant in deciding upon the reasonableness issue, although it will not by itself be conclusive of the outcome (*Scott Packaging & Warehousing Co. Ltd* v. *Paterson* [1978] IRLR 166; *Grootcon (UK) Ltd* v. *Keld* [1984] IRLR 302). In the one reported tribunal decision on an AIDS-related dismissal (*Buck* v. *The Letchworth Palace Ltd* (above)), pressure from hostile fellow workers was accepted as a factor in the decision that the dismissal was fair. It can be strongly argued that, as a matter of public policy, the law should not countenance such a view. In the United States, for example, it has been established as a general rule that co-worker or customer preference is not a sufficient defence for an employer who commits a discriminatory act against his employee (Leonard, 1987, p.116). But there is no such equivalent legislation in Britain, and there is no real support for this point of view in the cases dealing with unfair dismissal. One statutory provision which could have significance is s.63 of the Employment Protection (Consolidation) Act 1978, which states that, for the purpose of deciding the reason for dismissal or the reasonableness issue, no account is to be taken of any pressure which, by calling, organizing, procuring or financing a strike or other industrial action, or threatening to do so, was exercised on the employer to dismiss the employee. It is uncertain, however, how far this provision would be brought into operation in the event of pressure being brought to induce a dismissal, since it is probably necessary for the action to be associated with bargaining before it will trigger s.63 (*Faust* v. *Power Packing Casemakers Ltd* [1983] IRLR 117, CA).

CONCLUSIONS

As one commentator has observed (Orr, 1988) 'the law should have no truck with the unsubstantiated fears which the virus can all too readily summon. Instead, the law must move forward as scientific and medical knowledge of the disease develops, never exceeding what is known of the AIDS virus.' Translating this noble aspiration into practice is, however, not an easy matter. It has been recognized in the English courts that there is a public interest in encouraging actual or potential AIDS sufferers to go to seek medical care without having to fear identification. But there is still a long way to go. This chapter has shown that, at present, the response of employment law to the AIDS phenomenon is far from settled. We lack authoritative guidance from the judges on how the law of unfair dismissal, tortious liability and contractual obligations will adapt to the particular problems posed by the disease, and with few exceptions we can only speculate as to how principles will evolve.

Perhaps the major question—which emerges most clearly in the law of unfair dismissal—is the extent to which the law should be 'norm reflecting' as opposed to 'norm setting' (Elias, 1981). Should the law require standards of behaviour no higher than those found in society at large (excluding only the most extreme forms of unreason and prejudice) or should it go further and demand responses which show a higher level of compassion and understanding than is commonly found among business-minded employers? It is, perhaps, too easy to say that the latter is the right approach. In deciding which answer is correct, it should not be forgotten that the law of unfair dismissal does not operate in the abstract, but within the values and choices available in a free market (and increasingly deregulated) economy. It would be naive to imagine that, apart from the physical and mental suffering it engenders, AIDS does not also have an important economic significance in our society. This is not just to be measured in the costs of caring for those who suffer from the disease, or the lost productivity of those who fall ill. Who will want to eat at the restaurant where the staff are believed to be HIV-positive? Or be treated by the doctor who is so afflicted? Only those with an unusually strong social conscience will disregard the nagging but powerful fears that urge us to distance ourselves from the disease by the exercise of choice, especially where this is easily available. The answer to this particular problem is only partly to be found in taking steps to promote proper confidentiality and discretion among those who know of the identity of AIDS sufferers, necessary though such steps are (cf. *X* v. *Y*, above). It also has to be accepted that the employers of (and others associated with) AIDS victims will encounter financial loss because of the unallayed fears ordinary members of the public have and will continue to have towards the disease. There is a serious question to be answered about who—the employer or society at large—should bear these costs.

In this context it is interesting to note that it is in the public sector, where commercial considerations are not so prominent, that we have seen the most active and determined steps to implement effective anti-AIDS employment policies.

It must be doubted whether industrial tribunals and courts are ready to force the pace towards a 'norm-setting' attitude in employment law, particularly that concerned with unfair dismissal. But we might look with greater expectations towards legislation. There already exist statutory provisions which make the dismissal of a woman because of pregnancy (or reason related thereto) automatically unfair, and, as previously mentioned, the government in its current Employment Bill is in the process of enacting legislation which will give rights to individuals refused employment because of a reason associated with trade union membership. If there is serious concern about the plight of AIDS sufferers it would be a relatively simple matter for a similar approach to be taken towards AIDS. In the United States, as already noted, there exist various instances of state legislation which prohibit AIDS testing as a means of determining suitability for employment, and s.504 of the 1973 Vocational Rehabilitation Act (which covers workers in federal employment) provides that no otherwise qualified handicapped individual shall be subjected to discrimination in employment solely by reason of his or her handicap. Whether AIDS and other infectious diseases are properly designated as 'handicaps' is a matter of controversy under US law. But there is no reason in principle why legislation prohibiting discrimination against AIDs sufferers, actual and suspected, should not be enacted for Britain. It is, of course, highly unlikely that any such development will take place. Partly this is because the enactment of such a measure would cut across the tenet of faith which has motivated government thinking over the last decade—that there should, so far as possible, be deregulation of the employment relationship in the interests of securing the flexibility we are told is needed for employment growth. But there is another reason too. It is very unlikely that any reform would be countenanced which, by securing special protection for one particular group of disadvantaged employees and job seekers, would draw attention to the plight of the disabled, the handicapped and the old. Workers in these categories are also vulnerable, and suffer badly from public prejudice and discrimination when they look for work and in the terms of their employment. Unless and until we have general effective provision made in statute law for the protection of the disadvantaged, it is naive to expect special measures to deal with the employment dimension of AIDS.

REFERENCES

BMA (1987). Third statement on AIDS, p. 16.

Council of Europe (1989). Recommendations No. R. (89) 2 of the Committee of Ministers to Member States on the Protection of Personal Data Used for Employment Purposes.

Department of Employment/Health and Safety Executive Guide to AIDS in the workplace (1988).

Elias, P. (1981). Fairness in unfair dismissal: trends and tensions, 10 *ILJ* **201**, 213.

EOC (1987). Equal Opportunities Commission, Formal Investigation Report: Dan-Air, January 1987.

Fagan, N. and Newell, D. (1987). Aids and employment law, *New Law Journal*, **137**, 752.

Industrial Relations Legal Information Bulletin, **354**, 1 June 1988.

Leonard, Arthur, S. (1987). Aids in the workplace. In H.D. Alton *et al.* (eds) *AIDS and the Law*, Yale University Press.

Orr, Alistair, (1988). AIDS: Adapting the law, *New Law Journal*, **138**, 388.

Sieghart, P. (1989). *AIDS and Human Rights: A UK Perspective*, British Medical Association Foundation for AIDS.

Social Services Committee (1987). Third Report from the Social Services Committee, Session 1986-87, Problems Associated with AIDS.

Southam, C. and Howard, G. (1988). *AIDS and Employment Law*, Financial Training Publications Ltd, London.

Thomson, J. (1982). Crime, morality and unfair dismissal, *Law Quarterly Review*, **98** 423, 445.

WHO/ILO (1988). *Statement from the Consultation on AIDS and the Workplace*.

Widdows, K. (1988). AIDS and the workplace: Some approaches at the national level *International Journal of Comparative Labour Law and Industrial Relations*, **4**, 140.

PART III

Vulnerable Workers in Terms of Victimization

Chapter 6

Violence and Vulnerability in the Workplace: Psychosocial and Legal Implications

Kate Painter, Middlesex Polytechnic, Enfield, UK

INTRODUCTION

Concern about the extent and nature of violence at work has increased throughout the 1980s. The aim of this chapter is to summarise what is currently known about violence in the workplace—its extent, causes and impact upon employees—in addition to describing some of the legal and social policies being adopted to prevent it. The main focus will be upon violence which occurs in the public sector with a more detailed discussion of the impact of violence on working women.

DEFINING VIOLENCE AND VULNERABILITY

There is no widely accepted definition of violence at work, not least because the global use of the term 'violence' encompasses incidents varying greatly in nature and severity, across a wide range of employment settings. To some extent the lack of a nationally agreed definition has been overcome by a number of recent publications which have attempted to define the nature of violence with reference to the particular context of the workplace and the nature of the service being provided.

The first real attempt to get to grips with the issue was a Health and Safety Executive publication (Poyner and Warne, 1986). Here, violence was not so much defined as described. It ranged from the most serious aspects of physical violence (death and serious injury) to non-physical violence, including verbal abuse and threatening behaviour. This broad spectrum of behaviours was clarified further by the Health Services Advisory Committee (HSAC) in a survey which examined violence in the National Health Service

Vulnerable Workers: Psychosocial and Legal Issues. Edited by M. J. Davidson and J. Earnshaw

(1987). Violent incidents were allocated to one of four categories: major injuries requiring medical assistance/hospitalisation; minor injuries, requiring basic first aid; incidents involving threats with a weapon (no injury); and, finally, incidents of verbal abuse.

The most recent and specific contribution is contained in the DHSS Advisory Committee on Violence to Staff (1988). In the areas of DHSS concern, 'violence' means:

> The application of force, severe threat or serious abuse, by members of the public towards people arising out of the course of their work whether or not they are on duty; and it includes severe verbal abuse or threat where this is judged likely to turn into actual violence; serious or persistent harassment (including racial or sexual harassment); threat with a weapon; major or minor injury; fatalities.

Certainly, the common theme to emerge from the flurry of publications on public sector services is that violence must be defined according to wide criteria.

VULNERABILITY: RELATING THE OBJECTIVE TO THE SUBJECTIVE

Any attempt to estimate the objective incidence of violence at work and relate this to its impact on individuals must take into account the subjective aspect of the problem—human evaluation. In an article entitled 'It's part of the job' (Painter, 1987), it was emphasised that an individual's perception of a violent incident will be influenced by the relative social and physical vulnerability of the employee and assailant. Physical aspects of vulnerability refer to physical powerlessness to defend oneself from attack and the physical and emotional consequences of violent abuse. Social vulnerability will be influenced by an individual's social characteristics: gender, race, age, social class, health, temperament and appearance. It will also be affected by frequent exposure to the threat of violence and the context and culture of the service being provided.

Violence at work is a subjectively experienced relationship and we are not all equally vulnerable or resilient. The meaning assigned to an incident will differ depending on the people and circumstances involved. For example, an objective approach to the problem of violence at work would be one that constructed the problem as a continuum of discrete incidents ranging from serious assault at one end, to foulmouthed 'verbals' at the other. While paying lip service to the effects of the latter the emphasis tends to be on the former. Statistics are then compiled on the basis of quasi-legal definitions of serious or actual bodily harm, which involve serious or minor injury, major or minor medical assistance and so on. The empirical evidence assembled would then reveal how serious and trivial incidents were evenly or unevenly distributed across a particular occupational grouping. This might also be followed with caveats to be taken into account when reading the tables, such as how important it is to put the incidence of attack in the context of its rarity within the service as a whole.

To some extent this 'objective' approach is discernible in recent attempts to define violence at work. The problem with it is that the incidence and impact of 'non-physical' violence is trivialised and the subjective component, essential in any definition of violence, is obscured. Within the employment context, there is no such thing as an 'objective' punch, bite or threat simply because, 'the "same" punch can mean totally different things in different circumstances'. (Young, 1988). Thus, a physical assault by an elderly, female, geriatric patient in an acute surgical ward upon a young, physically robust, male staff nurse is not the same as a random, unprovoked, physical attack by a young, male, outpatient in accident and emergency, upon a middle-aged, female nurse. The statistics may show that two assaults have taken place but give no indication as to their relative seriousness as defined by the victim.

Violence and unequal vulnerability are two sides of the same coin. Attempts to define and measure violence at work must take into account the victim's perception of the seriousness of the incident. Violence at work involves a social, as well as an employment, relationship. Violence is perceived differently by different people and its impact is dependent on the social and material circumstances within which it occurs.

This is not to suggest that there is no consensus over what constitutes serious violence. Obviously, it is worse to be killed, maimed or physically injured at work than it is to be threatened or intimidated by aggressive members of the public. But, as I will argue later, the impact of non-physical violence upon women employees can be as great as physical assault. Any definition of violence, must take into account the objective and subjective components of the violent act and it is the privilege of different employees, who may well have varying tolerance levels, to define for themselves and their employers what is, and is not, acceptable behaviour in the workplace.

THE EXTENT OF THE PROBLEM

Though violence at work appears to be on the increase, firm empirical evidence is harder to come by. In 1982 and 1987, the TUC held conferences for union representatives of members exposed to assault and abuse from the public. The magnitude of the problem was indicated by the wide range of occupations at risk: public transport workers, social workers, teachers, nurses, postmen and postwomen, housing officers and DHSS officials, to name but a few. A recent Labour Research Department survey of 210 workplaces, found that 67% of workplaces believed that violence against employees had increased over the past five years and that 72% of employees had suffered threats of violence. So just how much violence is there?

Recent surveys have attempted to establish the incidence and distribution of violence towards staff. Though widespread, it is clear that violence is a misfortune suffered unevenly throughout the public sector. It is also evident that many incidents of physical assault, threats and verbal abuse are massively under-reported.

A survey of social workers revealed that one in ten social workers is assaulted at work each year; the figure rises to one in four in inner city areas. Even within the profession, risks were greater for some than for others. Residential social workers are more at risk of violence than their community colleagues but even in the community there were high risk situations where the potential for violence is inevitably greater, for example, taking children into care and sectioning mentally ill patients. However, it was also estimated that there was a huge discrepancy between officially reported and self-reported incidents. Only 1 out of 259 social workers who had been assaulted in the previous five-year period had reported this to their line manager. The extent of under-reporting was put at 1 in 20 (Rowett, 1986).

Violence in the public sector is focused geographically in certain areas and socially upon particular employees. One of the most comprehensive surveys undertaken by HSAC into violence to health service personnel found that out of 3000 respondents, 1 in 200 had been assaulted; 1 in 10 had suffered minor injuries requiring medical treatment; 1 in 21 had been threatened with a weapon and 1 in 6 had experienced verbal abuse within the previous 12-month period. The rates of assault rose to 1 in 4 on staff in psychiatric units and to 1 in 5 for those in geriatric hospitals, mental handicap units and accident and emergency wards.

Certain grades of staff were also more vulnerable to attack. As Table 1 shows, 36% of student nurses experienced minor assault; 40% had been threatened with violence. Ambulance staff also encountered increased risks: 42% of this group had been threatened with violence.

Table 1. *Violent incidents classified by occupational group*

Though disturbing, the figures mask the incidence of multiple victimisation and the compounding of violence on specific individuals. Let us take, for example, student nurses. At first glance, if one aggregates the incidence of violence, then it appears that approximately 92% of this group have been victimised within the previous 12 months. But such global figures are misleading since they conceal the reality that some individuals will have been assaulted *and* threatened and for some, both violations may have

Table 6.1 Violent incidents classified by occupational group

	Major	Minor	Weapon	Threat
Hospital doctors	0.5	5.9	3.0	19.3
GPs	0.5	0.5	5.0	24.9
Student nurse	1.6	36.4	13.6	40.2
Staff nurse	0	20.2	7.3	33.7
Charge nurse	1.6	17.2	8.6	24.2
Ambulance staff	1.7	17.4	17.4	42.1
Catering	0	1.1	1.1	1.1
Laundry	0	2.0	0	5.9
Domestic	0.6	3.0	3.0	4.2
Porters	0	8.1	3.2	21.0

Taken from *Violence to Staff in the Health Services* (HSAC, 1987, p.3). Reproduced with the permission of the Controller of HMSO.

occurred on a number of occasions. The effect of multiple violence is further compounded by the fact that this group comprises one of the lowest paid grades in the health service. They are young; the majority are women; they work unsocial hours and hence are more likely to experience the vagaries and risks associated with using public transport at off peak time or the unwelcome prospect of a walk home in the dark. In short, those who are most likely to be the victims of violence at work, are also most likely to experience other social problems and inequalities which further compound the injustice of violent and abusive behaviour in the workplace.

There are no national statistics on violence at work, and until these exist it is not possible to present a national assessment of the problem. Unfortunately, this has not stopped some bodies aggregating the data and coming out with overall risk rates which show, for example, that men are more at risk from violence than women. Any statement to this effect is inaccurate not only because of the twin problems of under-recording and reporting but also because current statistics are skewed in favour of those groups who have actually implemented a comprehensive monitoring and recording system for reporting incidens. For example, 80% of all reported work-related violence involves public transport staff. This does not necessarily mean that this group of workers (the majority are men) are at the greatest risk of violence, though the risk rate is high. It is estimated that four or five out of every 100 staff in London are assaulted each year (a rate identical to that of inner city teachers and social workers). Rather, the prominence of transport staff in the aggregated statistics on violence at work is a reflection of the efficient recording procedures adopted by public transport employers as a result of union pressure.

There is a need for more in-depth research into the nature and distribution of the violence in the workplace. The HSAC survey is to be welcomed since it reveals, to some extent, the focusing of violence on vulnerable workers. However, large-scale postal questionnaires are not the most effective means of eliciting information on violence of any sort. They also suffer the disadvantage of a low response rate. The HSAC survey had an overall non-response rate of 40% and one cannot assume that the level of violence among those who did not respond is equal to that of those who did. It may be the case that the violence rate of the 66% of those who *did not* respond from the hospital sector was higher than the 33% who replied.

To summarise: inaccurate statistics have a crucial bearing on policies designed to prevent violence to staff. Estimation of any social problem is a comparative process and one has to have valid and reliable methods and procedures to assess fully whether it is worse in some places rather than others and whether it is focused on particular individuals. Without accurate information it is unlikely that effective preventive policies will be developed.

THE IMPACT OF VIOLENCE ON VICTIMS AND SERVICES

The impact of violence and threatened violence has short-term and long-term effects both for the individual and the organisation. Injury is not just physical but emotional and psychological and threats can be equally as severe in impact as assault, depending on an individual's vulnerability. Physical reactions include headaches, nausea, shingles, digestive problems, fear, trembling and disrupted sleep patterns which can result in frequent absence from work. Violence also has psychological effects. Victims report: being in a constant state of alert to the possibility of attack, a lack of trust in people, irritability, depression, fear of meeting the same situation again, feelings of anger, guilt, shame and a loss of confidence resulting from switching from coper to victim (Dunham 1977; The Guardian, 1987). The symptoms not only affect morale in the workplace but also affect relationships at home. In extreme cases these symptoms lead to a condition which has been labelled 'post traumatic stress disorder'.

The intensity of impact will be influenced by an individual's social characteristics but it will also be compounded or assuaged by the context and culture of the workplace, i.e. the attitudes, values and beliefs which affect the way individuals make sense of their role and working environment. If assaulted or continually threatened with violence, the individual is likely to question the values and meaning attached to their occupation since their work is often in providing care, concern or a public service. It can be a dehumanising experience, which will be compounded if others make moral judgements about their competence. Rowett's (1986) study indicated that the majority of social workers, including those who had been assaulted, believed that social workers who were attacked were more overbearing, aggressive, incompetent and inexperienced than those who had not been victimised.

Research indicates that teachers, nurses and social workers are reluctant to report incidents of violence because it will be seen as a sign of professional incompetence and personal failure. This creates an atmosphere of mistrust and insecurity which can fragment a staff group. Much depends on managerial attitudes and professional ethos. For example, it is part of the ethos of being a teacher, social worker or policeman, that one is able to deal with any situation that arises. This can expose employees to more danger because individuals may remain in potentially dangerous situations if the organisation or profession expects it of them whereas their instincts may be urging them to withdraw.

If victims of violence are left unsupported at work then they will feel exploited, devalued and resentful. This will inevitably affect the quality of service being provided. Individuals resign or informally withdraw their services, avoiding potentially violent people or situations. For example, general practitioners and health visitors are increasingly refusing to venture into areas where violence has occurred. There is little doubt than when there is a conflict between the safety and care of the client or the security of the worker, many public servants are adopting a safety first policy and looking after themselves (London Weekend Television 1987). And it is the most vulnerable members of our community who will suffer as a result: abused children, battered women, the mentally ill, the unemployed, the homeless. So what can be done to protect those carers whose job it is to protect the weaker members of our society?

PREVENTIVE POLICIES

Just as there is no single cause of occupational violence, so there is no simple solution. There is increasing recognition that the most effective preventive strategies are those which are locally based and specifically geared to the type of workplace and employee most at risk. It is not possible to give a detailed account of the range of initiatives which have been adopted. Consequently, the following section briefly reviews some of the current literature and common themes to emerge from it.

Recording and Reporting Procedures

The lack of accurate reporting is at the heart of the problem. What is required is an immediate government directive to implement a standardised national reporting system. At present, the majority of violent incidents remain outside the schedules of notifiable offences. Under The Reporting of Injuries, Diseases and Dangerous Occurrences Regulations 1985, employers are only under an obligation to report to the Health and Safety Executive those assaults which cause death, or injury involving absence from work for three days. There is no obligation to report as a 'dangerous occurrence' assaults which do not involve more than incapacitation for three days. Nor is there any obligation to report threats or verbal abuse.

Reporting violent incidents should be a mandatory requirement of all staff. Staff should be positively encouraged to report any abusive behaviour which frightens or upsets them. Incident forms should be publicised and easily available; within the organisation someone should be allocated the responsibility for keeping the records of violent incidents separate from reports of accidental injury.

Once implemented it is essential that procedures are monitored in order that lessons can be learned. Without systematic collation of data the problem of violence will continue to be regarded as an isolated problem which impinges upon a minority of individuals rather than as an occupational hazard. It is equally important not to exaggerate the risks but at present they are minimised. There is a striking indifference to the constant exhortations of the TUC for improved reporting and monitoring procedures. Following the death of three social workers in a two-year period, a survey was undertaken by the British Association of Social Workers (1987). It found that few social work departments had issued guidance to staff on how to report or avoid violent incidents. A similar picture emerged from the survey carried out by the Labour Research Department, which revealed that less than half of the organisations where assaults had occurred had implemented a system for monitoring violence.

Training

Some employers, for example Birmingham City Council, Ashford Borough Council, Strathclyde, Haringay, South Glamorgan social service departments have taken the problem seriously and introduced training programmes which teach staff how to diffuse and contain violence (See for example, Strathclyde Regional Council, 1986). The courses are designed to improve interpersonal skills, teach staff how to recognise impending signs of violence and how to cope with it. Some go as far as teaching the basic techniques of self-defence, though the general consensus is that self-defence may be of little practical use in real-life situations and may increase the risk of injury to the victim or assailant. The Suzy Lamplugh Trust, set up in memory of the London estate agent who disappeared in 1986, has done more than most to heighten awareness of violence at work. The trust has run a number of seminars and training courses and has developed a training pack and video designed to give employers advice, guidance and materials to set up their own courses.

Adequate training is a vital component of any package of preventive measures and, arguably, employers have a duty under the Health and Safety at Work Act to protect staff by providing such training. But some caveats need to be sounded. Skills training is not a 'cure all' for violence. It may be tempting for employers faced with a sense of urgency to be seen to be doing something, to introduce a short course for all staff and expect them to become instant experts in the area. Earlier, reference was made for the need for more research to identify the nature and extent of occupational violence. It is reiterated here because in the search for instant, cheap solutions, this phase is easily dispensed with. But cures cannot be found for ailments which are not fully diagnosed. Furthermore, training is of little use unless it is reinforced by the employer and that raises an additional problem. Because of increasing pressures to cut public sector costs, employers are faced with a dilemma; if more resources are devoted to protecting employees it means that there is less available for the clientele they are there to assist.

Situational and Social Prevention

Other employers, most notably housing departments in local authorities and DHSS offices, are adopting practical security measures to prevent violence. Counter grills, protective screens, self-locking doors, bolts, personal alarms and panic buttons are increasingly being erected in public offices. These measures are intended to create a safer workplace by altering the design of the situation/environment without reference to the underlying causes of violence or the motivation of the assailant. The major objection to such measures is that they create a barrier which adversely affects the quality of relationship between staff and the public. Indeed, some housing departments have withdrawn security measures because they have actually heightened aggression towards staff. Yet, realistically, certain employees do require practical protection of this type. As the father of Isobel Schwarz, the social worker murdered by her client, put it:

> If society feels that the life and happiness of a sick and disadvantaged individual is more valuable than a social worker, nurse or policeman then you should be against any devices which protect such staff. But, if you equate their lives and values to society then a social worker, policeman, nurse kept alive is more use to the clientele than one who is dead or permanently injured, physically or emotionally.
>
> (File on Four 8.12.87)

Nevertheless, the long-term consequences of such measures can lead to a fortress society and may even displace violence. When banks increased their counter security, robbery was displaced to transit carriers of cash. When these targets were hardened, robbery increased in building societies and post offices. If one merely replaces violence at work by violence outside it or on softer targets, violence is not being prevented. Thus, the Health and Safety Executive recommends more long-term social preventive measures through increased education in schools. The Suzy Lamplugh Trust has made videos to inculcate the importance of handling situations in a non-violent manner and to make children aware of health and safety issues as part of the core curriculum. Meanwhile, it is important to remember that situational and social preventive measures are not mutually exclusive options and should be pursued in tandem.

Victim Support and The Voluntary Sector

Measures to combat violence to staff must be tackled before, during and after its occurrence. Whatever measures are implemented it is unlikely that violence at work can ever be totally eliminated and much can be done within the organisation to support those who are subjected to it. Within the organisation sensitive debriefing not only indicates managerial support for staff, it also facilitates a vital source of information about the cause, nature, time and place of the incident which is invaluable if similarly patterned events are to be prevented in the future. Sometimes this will be sufficient. For those more seriously affected emotionally and physically, counselling services may well be required. At a time of economic stringency, it is unrealistic to expect all employers to appoint a full-time counsellor. Moreover, given the ethos, culture and climate of some organisational settings, this would not necessarily be the best measure to adopt because of the stigmatisation which can result from referral.

Within the community there are resources which can be utilised to support victims of violence at work. In 1979 the National Association of Victim Support Schemes was set up and by 1986 there were 293 schemes operating throughout the country. Though they differ in quantity and quality between regions, they do offer short-term, practical and emotional help to all victims of crime. The services are offered on a vuluntary basis, not as a cost cutting exercise but as a means of giving 'a clear message that fellow citizens do care' (NAVSS, 1981). The majority of referrals to the schemes are through the police, though self-referral is also possible. There is a need to develop closer official links between the workplace and community if the needs of victims are to be met at a time when public sector budgets are being cut. As an annual report of NAVSS (1982) put it:

> No single existing agency could provide all the knowledge and skills needed but spread throughout our community all the necessary resources already exist. (Mawby and Gill, 1987, p. 92.)

Criminal and Civil Justice: The State Response to Occupational Violence

As with any case of assault, employees may involve the police in order to bring a criminal prosecution against the assailant. At present the decision to involve the police is left with the employee and many do not take this option either because they are afraid of reprisals or because they fear that police involvement may harm future relationships with the client. The view taken here is that all reported assaults should automatically involve the police and that the prosecution should be brought by the employer not by the employee. Where known violence is a recurring problem, public notices to the effect that assaults on staff will lead to immediate police involvement should be prominently displayed. In the meantime some employers provide legal assistance to staff who wish to bring a prosecution following assault at work. In relation to criminal proceedings, the court can make orders for compensation against individuals convicted ot a criminal offence.

COMPENSATION AND INSURANCE

Victims of physical injury at work can claim financial redress through the Criminal Injuries Compensation Board (CICB). The Board has been criticised by trade unions for the derisory amounts awarded to victims in this respect. Others have pointed to general problems of access. As with criminal prosecution, the onus is on the victim to claim compensation from the Board and many who are entitled to claim do not know of its existence. Neither do victims qualify for legal aid to pursue a claim. The assumption is that legal representation is unnecessary (as with Industrial Tribunals), but where victims have been legally represented before the CICB their chances of gaining compensation were twice those of victims who went unrepresented. As Mawby and Gill comment,

> ...full access to the benefits of the system is prevented by lack of knowledge of its existence and, among those ending in a personal hearing, by a lack of legal advice.
>
> (Mawby and Gill, 1987)

In recognition of the lack of state compensation for employees injured at work, some employers have extended their insurance schemes to include 'personal accident and assault' which compensates employees for any damage sustained to their personal property, as well as taking into account compensation for distress caused by violence.

HEALTH AND SAFETY AND EMPLOYMENT PROTECTION LAW

Three possible legal responses to violence at work emerge from employment law. These concern the employer's common law obligation to take reasonable care of an employee, the statutory duties placed on employers by the Health and Safety at Work Act and the law relating to employment protection, particularly the claims of unfair dismissal and discrimination at work.

Common Law Duties

Theoretically, a victim of violence is entitled to pursue an action in tort in the civil courts in order to recover damages for personal injury. These actions may be taken against the assailant on the basis of an intentional assault, or be mounted against the employer alleging a breach of his implied contractual duty to provide a safe system of work.

In practice, a number of difficulties surround this form of action. As is often the case, the assailant is considered a 'man of straw' and does not possess the resources out of which to pay any damages award. In the context of an action against the employer, quite aside from the expense and delay which pervades the civil process, there is the difficult task of proving a breach of the duty of reasonable care on the employer's part. While there are no comprehensive data about the number of successful claims against employers brought by injured employees, there are three cases recorded in the law reports, all involving attacks on employees by robbers, and all resulting in unsuccessful claims (see *Williams* v. *Grimshaw* III KIR 610; *Houghton* v. *Hackney Borough Council* III KIR 615; *Charlton* v. *Forrest Ink Co Ltd* [1980] IRLR 363).

The Health and Safety At Work, etc., Act 1974

Under s.2(1) of the Act, employers have a duty to ensure, *so far as is reasonably practicable*, the health, safety and welfare of their employees and criminal penalties ensue when this duty is broken. Consequently, it is possible for safety representatives to argue that this provision is wide enough to require employers taking measures to prevent incidents of violence at work. However, it is also possible for employers to invoke the qualifying phrase 'reasonably practicable' to limit the action they are obliged to take, arguing that the costs of instituting training programmes and providing a more secure workplace far outstrip the risks of violence at work.

The nature of the employer's duty in this sphere was discussed in *West Bromwich Building Society* v. *Townsend* [1983] IRLR 147. In this case, the High Court allowed the building society's appeal against the serving of an improvement notice requiring it to fit anti-bandit screens. The Court held that, in determining whether a failure to adopt a particular precaution amounts to a contravention of s.2(1), it was not sufficient to show that it was *physically practical* to take that precaution; it was also relevant to consider whether in the circumstances it would have been *reasonable* to do so. The Court was of the view that the employer had behaved reasonably because there was evidence that the fitting of screens had been considered but, on advice from insurers and other authorities, had been rejected. The informed view was that, if threatened with violence, staff should not offer resistance.

Employment Protection

Apart from the law relating to health and safety, there may be some limited support for the victims of violence from the provisions of statutory employment protection enacted in the mid-1970s.

Victims, or threatened victims, of assault who feel that their employer has not taken adequate steps to protect their safety could resign and claim that their employer's conduct amounted to constructive and unfair dismissal. It should be stressed, however, that this legal remedy must be seen as a last resort given that the employee must terminate the employment in order to claim and is unlikely to be reinstated if successful.

Moreover, those few employees who have tried the constructive dismissal avenue as a means of gaining some legal recompense for violence, and fear of violence, to which they have been exposed have experienced mixed fortunes.

In *Keys* v. *Shoefayre* [1978] IRLR 476, an Industrial Tribunal held that Mrs Keys was entitled to treat her employer's failure to take steps to improve security at their shop in Peckham, following an armed robbery, as conduct entitling her to resign and claim constructive dismissal. The tribunal considered that it was a fundamental term of the contract that the employer should take reasonable steps to operate a safe system of work. Given that in the instant case the shop was in an area where crime was rife, it was held that any reasonable manager would have taken precautions to protect the staff. The employer's argument that employers with similar shops in the area had also done nothing to protect their staff was regarded as no excuse.

In the more recent case of *Dutton & Clark Ltd* v. *Daly* [1985] IRLR 363, the applicant was not successful in her claim for constructive dismissal. Certain statements in the EAT judgement, if widely adopted, would make the chances of a successful claim by an employee who fared for his or her safety extremely slim. Mrs Daly had resigned from her job as a clerk/cashier in a building society, following two armed robberies. In deciding that the employers, in the circumstances of the case, were not in breach of their duty to take reasonable care for their employee's safety, Sir Ralph Kilner-Brown ruled that the industrial tribunal had misdirected themselves in finding that the employee had been constructively dismissed without themselves assessing whether the action was outside the band of reasonableness to be expected of a reasonable employer. He reasoned that:

> . . . . if it is possible that some reasonable employer might have done no more and no less than this employer did, then there was not a fundamental breach of contract and the lady was not entitled to say she was forced to resign.

Since it was developed by the courts, the 'range of reasonable responses' test to the question of the fairness of the dismissal has made it much more difficult for employees to succeed in unfair dismissal claims. The extension of the test to the question of whether there has been a constructive dismissal is unsupported by authority. If adopted, it would allow employers to employ the very argument that failed in the *Keys* case, viz. that their omission adequately to protect employees was excusable because other 'reasonable' employers, in similar circumstances, were equally inactive. Such an approach would completely undermine the already limited protection the unfair dismissal action may provide to the employee exposed to the risk of violence.

Other parts of the structure of statutory employment protection have promised, at least initially, to be of more use to employees exposed to particular forms of violence. It has been held by the Court of Appeal and the Scottish Court of Session that, in appropriate circumstances, sexual harassment and racial abuse will amount to unlawful discriminatory behaviour by the employer or other of his or her employees (see *De Souza* v. *Automobile Association* [1986] IRLR 103; *Strathclyde Regional Council* v. *Porcelli* [1986] IRLR 134). These are valuable decisions, not least because, in contrast to constructive dismissal, the employee does not have to resign in order to make a claim. The obvious limitation is that they cannot be used as form of protection against this type of abuse by members of the public.

Two recent appeal decisions, however, appear much less encouraging for victims of sexual and racial harassment. In *Snowball* v. *Gardner Merchant Ltd* [1987] IRLR 397, the vital issue was the extent to which evidence as to a woman's attitude to sexual matters is to be regarded as admissible in order to determine the degree of detriment and injury to feelings she suffered following sexual harassment. The EAT held that the evidence was admissible because it was 'pertinent to enquire whether the complainant is... unlikely to be very upset by a degree of familiarity with a sexual connotation'. Why a woman's *consensual* sexual behaviour should be relevant in order to determine the degree of emotional trauma she has experienced as a result of *unsolicited* and *unwelcome* sexual advances beggars belief. It places the woman victim in a horrifying double jeopardy: the victim of sexual abuse and yet aware that if she does take legal action the whole spectrum of her sexual attitudes and experiences may become a matter of public record.

In *Balgobin and Francis* v. *London Borough of Tower Hamlets* [1987] IRLR 401, the EAT supported an Industrial Tribunal finding that the employers were not liable for proven sexual harassment of the two women applicants by a male fellow worker because the employers could rely on a defence under s.41(3) of the Sex Discrimination Act by showing that they 'took such steps as were reasonably practicable' to prevent the employee doing the acts complained of. They did not know what was going on; they were generally providing proper and adequate supervision of their staff and they had made known their policy on equal opportunities. In short, according to the EAT, it was 'very difficult to see what steps in practical terms could reasonably have been taken to prevent that which occurred from occurring'. This view was sustained even though there was no evidence that any employees had been given training or guidance on the operation of the equal opportunity policy or told that sexual harassment was unlawful under the Act.

These decisions put real obstacles in the path of those seeking protection from sexual and racial harassment through the courts and tribunals, with the *Snowball* case providing a positive disincentive to bringing a claim. (For a detailed discussion on the legal issues and series of proposals as to how employers should respond to the problem of sexual harassment see Vivienne Gay's account in Chapter 7.2.)

THE CAUSES OF VIOLENCE

Individual versus Social

For some (often of a conservative frame of mind) the cause of violence can be located at the level of the individual personality. From this perspective, people are regarded as innately aggressive or violent as a result of an undisciplined and disorderly family background. These inadequate, social misfits are dependent on state benefits and the increase in violence is no more than their inept response to resist the aim of government to withdraw benefits for the undeserving. Physical and verbal aggression are a means of asserting their rights and resisting the intention of government to make people independent of the state. Such attitudes were inculcated during the permissive, liberal era of the 1960s and 1970s with its emphasis on consumerism and demand for benefits; a demand which is so often seen as incommensurate with effort. From this viewpoint violence at work is conceptualised as purely voluntaristic activity. Individuals are aggressive for purely instrumental reasons. They see violence as a way of forcing the welfare system to be more generous to them more quickly.

For others (often of liberal persuasion) the cause of violence is determined by social circumstances which pressure people into behaving violently. Here the emphasis is put on financial cuts which have brought public services to breaking point because of reductions in staff, benefits and housing stock. The increasing pressures that are put on the system and those dependent upon it for the basic necessities of life, have caused the increase in violence and have led to a situation where public sector staff are now seen as aggressors who withhold benefits rather than individuals who are there to provide a service.

Increases in physical and verbal aggression cause rapid staff turnover which exacerbates the problem as new, inexperienced staff are left to cope with an irate public who identify them as part of an inefficient and bureaucratic system which imposes sanctions upon the public. Changes in government policy (e.g. the Social Fund which replaced supplementary benefit with discretionary loans; community care policies which decant the mentally ill and disturbed into the community without sufficient resources to cope; and the 'right to buy' policy which has decimated the public housing stock) are major contributory factors to the increase in violence in the public sector.

Alternative explanations as to the causes of violence lead to opposing preventive policies. For the conservative the answer is to deter and prevent violent acts through harsher penalties and/or target hardening techniques. For the liberal it is the system and government policy that need to change.

The view taken here is that because the nature of violence in the public sector is so diverse, simple dichotomous explanations are inadequate. For the most part, violence at work is voluntaristic but it occurs in the most determined circumstances. The nature and causes of violence differ across various occupational groupings and if preventative action is to be effective each incident must be analysed within the social and material circumstances within which it occurs.

Nor is it possible to say with certainty that the increase in violence at work is symptomatic of an increasingly violent society. The complexion of violence may well be changing because two things are occurring simultaneously. Firstly, there is a deterioration in the standards of behaviour in some sections of the population and, secondly, others are becoming more sensitive to (and intolerant of) violence in all its forms. Ironically the perceived increase in violence at work may reflect that we are living in a more civilised society which finds violent, insulting and abusive behaviour, increasingly intolerable.

VIOLENCE AND WORKING WOMEN

None of the literature offers a gender-specific analysis of the problem violence poses for working women. In the absence of research in this area I will focus on women employees as victims by drawing together the factors already discussed. Violence at work is not focused exclusively on women but when it occurs its impact is greater because the perceived seriousness of any incident is a function of five related factors: risk of victimisation; the culture and values of different social groups; compounding social problems; differential vulnerability; and unequal social relationships. Each of these interrelated aspects of violence will be discussed in turn.

Risk of Victimisation

Current statistics conceal risk rates for men and women for reasons outlined in an earlier section. However, it is plausible to argue that the objective risks women face are at least equal to, if not greater than, those of men because a high proportion of women are employed in public sector services where the incidence of violence appears to be on the increase (nursing, teaching, social work and to a lesser extent policing). The 1988 British Crime Survey included questions on crime at work. Interviews were carried out with a 'core' sample of 10 392 individuals in England and Wales and it was found that a quarter of all violence to workers occurred because of the nature of the work they did and 50% of all threats against women were job-related. It also confirmed the findings of more localised surveys, that welfare workers and nurses faced above-average risks of violence (Mayhew, Elliott and Dowds, 1988).

Social Inequality and Cultural Difference

Women are more vulnerable to violence not simply because they are physically at a disadvantage but because they are more sensitive to violence and within the labour market they are frequently located in the highest risk, lowest paid occupations and placed in the front line. At any one time in the inner city, the streets are being 'manned' by women police officers, the casualty units by female nurses and cases which fall betwixt and between are, more often than not, covered by social workers, the majority of whom are female. Women in all these occupations suffer discrimination in promotion, a process which distances those at the top from face-to-face contact with the public. The fact that women are at the sharp end, where the propensity for violence is greatest and economic inequality most striking, makes them more unequal victims than men. But this is not just a question of different experiential reality, it is also a question of different values and culture. As Young (1988) so eloquently puts it in a wider context:

> It is easy to see how crime has had a greater impact on women as well as at the same time, women are more sensitive to violence. For in the last analysis many women react to the adversity of the world by creating a culture which is opposed to violence, whilst men frequently react to adversity by creating a culture of machismo which is insensitive to violence and, indeed, in some groups glorifies it.

Compounding Social Problems and Violence as a Social Relationship

In addition to experiencing physical and non-physical violence as officially defined, women experience sexual harassment and incivilities that men seldom encounter. These experiences are very real problems in themselves, as well as compounding the effects of more serious incidents. They occur at work, at home and in the street and create a very different reality for women. Consequently, the gravity of violence at work cannot be understood fully without linking it to the everyday abuses women experience in every facet of their lives. Violence to working women occurs in an unequal social, physical and economic relationship and though not totally gender based, the particular problem has to be analysed in the context of women's experience in relation to the structure of their lives as a whole. It is a grave injustice that women who are so seldom violent, are so frequently the victims of violence in our society.

CONCLUSION

A significant proportion of employees in the public sector are exposed to violence, though the limited amount of research undertaken indicates that risks of victimisation are unevenly distributed. Any attempt to estimate the full extent of the problem is hampered by a lack of clear definition, by an absence of standardised reporting, recording and monitoring procedures and by employee reluctance to report all but the most serious incidents that occur. These shortcomings are interrelated, but until they are overcome, the true picture will remain blurred.

Violence in the workplace poses particular problems for women because of their sensitivity, culture, vulnerability and powerlessness. There is scant legal protection for victims, though much can be done within the workplace to minimise risk and support those victimised and greater use could be made of existing support networks in the local community. Nevertheless, policies designed to prevent violence will have little long-term impact until the underlying causes of violence at work are addressed. These lie outside the workplace in an economic and social structure which is increasingly divisive, unjust and unequal; in central government policies which undermine public sector services, promote privatisation and emphasise the individual at the expense of the community; in the values at the heart of the system, namely, individualism, greed, survival of the fittest and cut-throat competition. It is a striking paradox that the values which are seen as essential for economic and individual success are identical to those which can be used to explain the behaviour of violent people in and out of the workplace.

Of course it can be argued that values, culture, economic and social deprivation do not *cause* violence in the workplace any more than they cause it in the street or in the home but they must have something to do with it. Essentially, if violence at work is to be prevented it must first of all be understood in relation to a wider political and economic climate. The last decade has not only seen an upward spiral in recorded and perceived risks of violence within the workplace, it has also been a time in which chaotic labour market practices and government policies have economically and socially marginalised whole sections of the population while simultaneously reducing the rights of those in work. In this context violence at work is simply one manifestation of discontent in a society which is increasingly characterised by unfettered competition, individualistic ideology and demoralised social and industrial relations.

REFERENCES

DHSS (1988). Violence to staff, *Report of the DHSS Advisory Committee on Violence to Staff*, HMSO, London.

Dunham, J. (1977). The effects of disruptive behaviour on teachers. In *Education Review*, **29**.

File on Four (8.12.1987). Violence at work, BBC, Radio Four.

HSIB (1988). Preventing violence to staff, *Health and Safety Information Bulletin*, **154**, 4 October.

Health Service Advisory Committee (1987). *Violence to Staff in the Health Services*, HMSO, London.

London Weekend Television (15.5.1987). Violence to Social Workers.

Mayhew P., Elliott D. and Dowds, L. (1989). *The British Crime Survey*, HMSO, London.
Mawby, R. and Gill, M. (1987). *Crime Victims: Needs, Services and the Voluntary Sector*, Tavistock, London.
NAVSS (1981). *First Annual Report.* NAVSS, London.
NAVSS (1982). *Second Annual Report*. NAVSS, London.
Painter, K. (1987). 'It's part of the job': Violence at work. In *Vulnerable Workers in the UK Labour Market : Some Challenges for Labour Law, Employee Relations*. Vol. 9, No. 5, MCB Univ. Press Ltd., Bradford.
Poyner, B. and Warne C. (1986). *Violence to Staff : A Basis for Assessment & Prevention*, Health and Safety Executive. HMSO. London.
Rowett, C. (1986). *Violence in the Context of Local Authority Social Work*, Institute of Criminology, London.
Strathclyde Regional Council (1986). Violence to staff.
The Guardian (8.4.1987). Taking a beating.
Trades Union Congress (1987). *Preventing Violence to Staff : Progress Report*.
Young, J. (1988). Risk of crime and fear of crime : a realist critique of survey based assumptions. In M. Maguire and J. Pointing (eds) *Victims of Crime : A New Deal*, OUP, Milton Keynes.

Chapter 7.1

Sexual Harassment at Work: The Psychosocial Issues

David E. Terpstra, University of Mississippi, USA and
Douglas D. Baker, Washington State University, USA

INTRODUCTION

In recent years it has become apparent that sexual harassment presents both a pervasive and a serious problem for women in the workplace. Estimates of the actual extent of harassment vary widely due to the differing definitions employed and the types of individuals surveyed. However, one study of over 20 000 US federal government employees reported that 42% of the women surveyed had been sexually harassed in the previous 24 months (US Merit Systems Protection Board, 1988). Working men experience sexual harassment as well, but the reported frequency of occurrence is much lower. The study mentioned above reported that only 14% of the men surveyed had been sexually harassed over the same time period.

The seriousness of the problem of sexual harassment should not be underestimated. As we will demonstrate later in this chapter, the individual victims of sexual harassment experience a wide range of negative psychological and physiological outcomes. The victims' relationships with others, both at work and at home, can also suffer as a result of sexual harassment. Furthermore, sexual harassment frequently leads to negative job-related outcomes for the victims. The organization in which the sexual harassment takes place also pays a high price for such behavior. The US Merit Systems Protection Board (1988) estimated that sexual harassment cost the federal government $267 million over a two-year period. That figure represented the cost of reduced productivity ($204.5 million), paying sick leave to employees who missed work ($26.1 million), and replacing employees who left their jobs ($36.7 million). Litigation resulting from sexual harassment can also be quite costly to an organization. Individuals who have been harassed seem increasingly willing to seek redress by filing suits in the

Vulnerable Workers: Psychosocial and Legal Issues. Edited by M. J. Davidson and J. Earnshaw

federal court system or by lodging complaints with equal opportunity or fair employment agencies (*New York Times*, 1986). A number of circumstantial factors affect the outcomes of sexual harassment charges, but the potential costs can be substantial.

In light of the pervasiveness and seriousness of the problem of sexual harassment, it is not surprising to witness a significant increase in the number of published articles dealing with the issue. The purpose of this chapter is to review a portion of the published literature regarding sexual harassment. (The review is limited primarily to US literature; thus, it should be noted that an American perspective is being presented throughout this chapter.) The primary focus will be on the negative outcomes experienced by the victims of sexual harassment. However, to provide a more complete understanding of those negative outcomes, we will first examine the events and processes leading up to them.

Figure 1 presents a simplified model of the events and processes that precede the negative outcomes experienced by victims of sexual harassment.

The remainder of this chapter will be loosely structured around the model presented in Figure 1. First, the antecedents and causal factors underlying the occurrence of sexual harassment will be examined. Second, we will examine the various forms of harassment that occur. Next, we will address the importance of individuals' perceptions of those forms of harassment that are experienced. Then, we will examine individuals' immediate reactions upon being sexually harassed. Finally, we will examine the longer term negative outcomes experienced by the victims of sexual harassment. Following our examination of these topics, we will briefly discuss some implications and recommended actions for both individuals and organizations.

ANTECEDENTS OF SEXUAL HARASSMENT

As the labor force participation rate for women continues to increase, so too does the potential for socio-sexual problems between men and women at work. Several explanations have been set forth to account for the occurrence of sexual harassment. For the purposes of the present discussion,

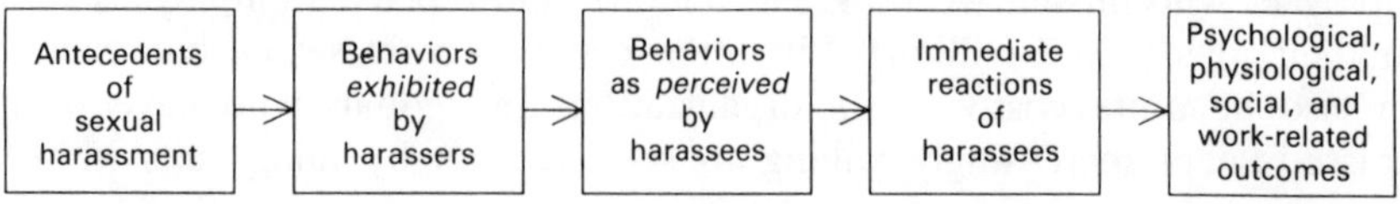

Figure 7.1 A model for the study of sexual harassment

the existing explanations will be classified into four general categories: biological, sex-role conditioning, intentional/instrumental, and organizational.

The most simplistic explanation contends that sexual harassment is merely the result of biological forces or physical attraction (Tangri, Burt and Johnson, 1982; Terpstra and Baker, 1986a). The fact that men are more apt to harass members of the opposite sex than are women would be explained either by claiming that men have stronger sex drives than women, or (if one were to assume equivalent sex drives) that men are biologically more aggressive than women and thus more apt to engage in sexual harassment. While some research suggests the existence of sex-related differences in personality and behavior, these differences typically account for no more than 1% to 5% of the population variance (Caplan, McPherson and Tobin, 1985; Eagly and Carli, 1981; Hyde, 1981). Furthermore, there is controversy over the extent to which such differences are due to biological factors or sex-role conditioning.

A second explanation for the occurrence of sexual harassment centers on the role of learning or conditioning (Terpstra and Baker, 1986a). It is argued that men and women have been exposed to different socialization pressures and have been conditioned to behave in a way that is consistent with existing sex-role definitions (Barry, Bacon and Child, 1957; Weitzman, 1979). Men's sex roles encourage them to be dominant, aggressive and forceful. It is the man who is expected to initiate sexual activity with the woman. Women, on the other hand, are encouraged to be submissive, passive and receptive to the demands of men (Henley and Freeman, 1975). Viewed in this light, sexual harassment is simply the exhibition of conditioned behaviors that are in accord with male sex roles.

The explanations reviewed above have assumed that sexual harassment is a natural by-product of either a man's biological urges or his conditioning history. The role of the conscious intentions of the harasser was not explicitly recognized. Some, however, have argued that men may intentionally harass women in order to maintain their position of economic privilege or their position of greater power or status (Farley, 1978; Rich, 1976). According to this view, sexual harassment is a means by which men can maintain dominance over women in the workplace and in society in general. Sexual harassment thus serves an instrumental function for men.

The final class of explanations relates to organizational characteristics that may contribute to the occurrence of sexual harassment. It has been suggested, for example, that formal status and power differentials between men and women in organizations may set the stage for sexual harassment (Tangri, Burt and Johnson, 1982). Since women still are more likely to be employed in positions subordinate to men, it is argued that men have more opportunities to use their position of authority, legitimate power, or reward power to make sexual demands of their women subordinates. The sex ratio of an organization or work group may also stimulate the occurrence of sexual harassment (Gutek, 1985; Gutek and Morasch, 1982; Kanter, 1977). Societal sex-role attitudes and behaviors are hypothesized to be more likely to carry over into the workplace when women are in the minority in an organization. This, in turn, may contribute to a higher rate of sexual harassment for such women. A recent survey of organizations seems to support this hypothesis, as it was found that formal sexual harassment complaint rates for organizations varied in accordance with the percentage of males in those organizations' workforces. The highest complaint rates were found in firms where the workforce was at least 75% male (Fritz, 1989).

Each of the above explanations (with the possible exception of the biological explanation) bears some degree of validity. Socialization pressures and sex-role conditioning may lead some men to view sexual harassment as an acceptable socio-sexual behavior. Furthermore, these views may be reinforced to the extent that sexual harassment is seen as being instrumental in the preservation of men's position of greater status, power and economic well-being. Finally, certain organizational characteristics and contexts may contribute to higher rates of harassment.

BEHAVIORS EXHIBITED BY HARASSERS

Having briefly discussed the antecedents of sexual harassment, we will now examine the forms of sexual harassment exhibited by the harassers. There is a good deal of difficulty in determining the boundaries of sexual harassment. In other words, which behaviors constitute sexual harassment and which do not? In the United States, the Equal Employment Opportunity Commission (1980) has defined sexual harassment as:

> Unwelcome sexual advances, requests for sexual favors and other verbal or physical conduct of a sexual nature when submission to such conduct is made either explicitly or implicitly a term or condition of an individual's employment; submission to or rejection of such conduct by an individual is used as the basis for employment decisions affecting the individual; or such conduct has the purpose or effect of unreasonably interfering with an individual's work performance or creating an intimidating, or hostile working environment. (p. 25024)

The ambiguity of the above definition has allowed the US courts considerable discretion in ruling upon the legality of various forms of socio-sexual behavior. Generally, the courts have ruled that socio-sexual behaviors that lead to adverse employment-related consequences for the victims constitute illegal sexual harassment. But, until recently, there was some question as to whether socio-sexual behaviors that were not linked to tangible adverse employment-related consequences constituted illegal sexual harassment. (See Chapter 3 for details on recent US court rulings regarding the legality of such behaviors.)

A wide range of behaviors can be viewed as falling within the legally defined boundaries of sexual harassment. Some indication of the types and frequencies of behaviors actually experienced by the victims of sexual harassment has been provided by the previously mentioned survey of government employees (US Merit Systems Protection Board, 1988). The survey asked the women respondents which of seven forms of harassment they had experienced over the past 24 months. The most frequently reported forms of harassment were unwanted sexual teasing, jokes, remarks, or questions (35%); unwanted sexual looks or gestures (28%); and unwanted deliberate touching, leaning over, cornering, or pinching (26%). Less frequently reported forms included unwanted pressure for dates (15%); unwanted letters, telephone calls, or materials of a sexual nature (12%); unwanted pressure for sexual favors (9%); and actual or attempted rape or sexual assault (0.8%).

Additional information regarding the forms of harassment encountered by women comes from a study by Gutek (1985). She asked 827 working women whether they had ever experienced any of eight types of harassment at work. The types of harassment most frequently mentioned were nonsexual touching (74%), sexual comments meant to be complimentary (68%), looks and gestures meant to be complimentary (67%) and sexual touching (33%). Relatively fewer women reported having experienced sexual comments meant to be insulting (23%), looks and gestures meant to be insulting (20%), socializing or dating as a requirement of the job (12%) and sex as a requirement of the job (8%).

A somewhat different (and perhaps less representative) approach for assessing the nature and frequency of sexual harassment behaviors experienced by women was taken by Terpstra and Cook (1985). They examined the 81 sexual harassment charges filed with a state equal employment agency over a two-year period. Unwanted physical contact (36%), offensive language or remarks (29%), sexual propositions unlinked to job conditions (22%) and requests for socialization or dates (20%) emerged as the harassment behaviors most commonly reported by the complainants. Such behaviors as sexual propositions linked to threats of negative job consequences (12%), sexual assault or rape (8%), sexual propositions linked to promises of positive job consequences (7%) and unwanted nonverbal attention (5%) were reported less often by the complainants.

The studies reviewed above document the pervasiveness of the problem and provide more detail regarding the specific forms of harassment actually encountered by women in the workplace. The behaviors exhibited by harassers range from sexual looks and comments to sexual assault and propositions linked to threats of negative job-related consequences. The severity of the forms of harassment seems to be inversely related to the frequency of their occurrence; yet, even the less severe behaviors may be seen by some individuals as constituting an intimidating, hostile or offensive working environment.

Some mention of those individuals responsible for sexual harassment might also be made. Regarding organizational status, it would appear that co-workers and peers are the most common harassers of working women. The US Merit Systems Protection Board study (1988) found that 69% of the harassers of women were co-workers or peers, while 31% were superiors. Similarly, Gutek's (1985) survey found that supervisors (44%) were less likely than nonsupervisors (56%) to be the initiators of sexual harassment. Regarding personal characteristics, the data indicate that approximately two-thirds of the harassers of women are married (Gutek, 1985; US Merit Systems Protection Board, 1981). Also, the harassers of women are usually older than their victims. A 1981 survey conducted by the US Merit Systems Protection Board found that the harasser was older than the victim in 68% of the incidents reported.

BEHAVIORS AS PERCEIVED BY THE HARASSEES

In accordance with the model of sexual harassment (Figure 1) presented earlier, we will now turn our attention to the recipients of sexual harassment. Who are the victims of sexual harassment, and how do they perceive the various forms of sexual harassment that they experience?

Research indicates that women are far more apt to be the victims of sexual harassment than are men. Furthermore, these women tend to be younger (under 35) than the general population. Women who are single, divorced, or separated are also more likely to experience harassment than women who are married. The data also indicate that women with college degrees or higher are more apt to report having been sexually harassed than women with less education (Gutek, 1985; Terpstra and Cook, 1985; US Merit Systems Protection Board, 1981, 1988). The findings regarding educational status should be interpreted with caution, however. It is possible that well-educated women perceive more types of socio-sexual behaviors to be sexual harassment, and are less tolerant of such behaviors than are less educated women. In summary, it would appear that the 'typical' victims of sexual harassment tend to be young, well-educated, unmarried women.

Among those individuals who have been harassed, there are wide differences in how various forms of sexual harassment are personally perceived. An incident of harassment that is considered mildly offensive by one individual might be seen as serious enough to warrant a formal complaint by another individual. At an even more basic level, there is considerable disagreement as to which types of socio-sexual behaviors actually constitute sexual harassment. Sexual harassment is, after all, a matter of individual perception.

Several studies have investigated individuals' perceptions of various forms of socio-sexual behaviors. For example, the US Merit Systems Protection Board (1988) surveyed federal employees regarding their perceptions of six different forms of harassment. The forms of harassment and the corresponding percentages of women who felt the behaviors constituted sexual harassment were as follows: uninvited pressure for sexual favors (99%); uninvited and deliberate touching, leaning over, cornering, or pinching (95%); uninvited letters, telephone calls, or materials of a sexual nature (90%); uninvited pressure for dates (87%); uninvited sexually suggestive looks or gestures (81%); and uninvited sexual teasing, jokes, remarks, or questions (72%).

Gutek (1985) also surveyed a large sample of working women with regard to their perceptions of eight categories of socio-sexual behaviors. The behaviors and associated percentages of women who thought that the behaviors were sexual harassment were: sex as a requirement of the job (98%); socializing or dating as a requirement of the job (96%); sexual comments meant to be insulting (86%); sexual touching (84%); looks and gestures meant to be insulting (80%); sexual comments meant to be complimentary (34%); looks and gestures meant to be complimentary (29%); and nonsexual touching (7%).

Finally, a study by Terpstra and Baker (1988a) gauged the perceptions of working women with respect to a somewhat wider range of socio-sexual behaviors. The 18 forms of behaviors and the percentages of working women who perceived the behaviors to be sexual harassment were: sexual propositions linked to the threat of negative employment-related consequences (100%); sexual propositions linked to promises of positive employment-related consequences (98%); sexual touching (96%); actual or attempted sexual assault or rape (94%); sexual propositions unlinked to employment-related consequences (91%); arm around the individual (89%); obscene, sexually oriented gestures directed toward the individual (88%); remarks about the individual's sexual characteristics or sexual potential (85%); sexual propositions stated as a game or joke (85%); obscene, sexually oriented graffiti directed toward the individual (77%); wolf-whistle (48%); squeeze on the shoulder (47%); staring at or looking the individual over (44%); off-color, sexually oriented jokes not directed toward the individual (39%); repeated requests for dates or socializing (38%); coarse, sexually oriented language not directed toward the individual (30%); obscene, sexually oriented graffiti not directed toward the individual (25%); and obscene, sexually oriented gestures not directed toward the individual (13%).

The studies reviewed above indicate that some forms of socio-sexual behaviors are rather consistently perceived to be sexual harassment. For example, such behaviors as sexual assault, sexual propositions (whether linked or unlinked to employment-related consequences), physical contact of a sexual nature, and sexually offensive remarks or gestures directed toward the individual seem to be generally perceived as sexual harassment. Less perceptual consensus emerges, however, with respect to such behaviors as complimentary sexual comments, coarse, sexually oriented language or jokes not directed toward the individual, sexual looks and gestures, and touching that is not overtly sexual. While some individuals see these behaviors as contributing to a sexually offensive working environment, others do not.

Differences in individuals' perceptions of various socio-sexual behaviors seem to be influenced by both personal and situational variables. The personal variable that is most frequently cited as an influence upon individuals' perceptions is sex or gender. Research indicates that women perceive a wider range of socio-sexual behaviors to be sexual harassment than do men (Gutek, 1985; Gutek, Morasch and Cohen, 1983; Konrad and Gutek, 1986; US Merit Systems Protection Board, 1988). One's level of education may also influence perceptions of sexual harassment. Women with more education seem to be less tolerant of various forms of sexual harassment than less educated women (Gutek, 1985; US Merit Systems Protection Board, 1981; Terpstra and Cook 1985). In other research, Terpstra and Baker (1986b) assessed the influence of several psychological and demographic variables upon individuals' perceptions of sexual harassment. They found that perceptions of sexual harassment were rather complicated functions of the interactions of such variables as sex, attitudes toward women, religiosity, locus of control and self-esteem. Still other research has suggested that such variables as sex-role identity (one's concept of being masculine or feminine) (Powell, 1988), ethnicity and marital status (Gutek, 1985) and managerial level (Collins and Blodgett, 1981) may influence individuals' perceptions of sexual harassment.

The research reviewed above indicates that perceptions of sexual harassment are not simple linear functions of one or two underlying variables. Rather, sexual harassment perceptions appear to be a function of a more complex set of interacting factors related to the person and the situation. For example, Terpstra and Baker (1986b) have developed a model in which perceptions of sexual harassment are viewed as being determined by a continuous and multi-directional interaction between personal variables (e.g. values, attitudes, psychological characteristics and demographic characteristics) and situational variables (e.g. organizational factors and variables associated with the harasser or offender). The reasons for individuals' varying perceptions of sexual harassment are not yet fully understood. However, it is clear that those perceptions may influence both the type of reactions exhibited and the types of outcomes experienced by the victims of sexual harassment.

IMMEDIATE REACTIONS OF THE HARASSEES

We will now examine the types of immediate reactions exhibited by harassees in response to sexual harassment, as well as the frequency of occurrence of those reactions. We will also briefly discuss the relative effectiveness of various types of reactions, and the influence of situational and personal variables upon the individual's choice of reactions.

In an attempt to identify the range of potential reactions to sexual harassment, Terpstra and Baker (1989a) asked working women and college student women and men how they would react to each of 18 forms of sexual harassment. The resulting 4356 written reactions were content analyzed and systematically sorted into the following 10 classes of reactions: leave the field (quit job, transfer); external report (report to Equal Employment Opportunity Commission, state or local agency, contact police, take legal action); internal report (report to supervisor, manager, or other company official); physical reaction (slap or hit, kick, shove away, remove hand, physically resist, physically retaliate); alteration (change self [behavior, clothes], change or alter environment); negative verbal confrontation (verbally attack or abuse, threaten, embarrass, ridicule, curse, scream); positive verbal confrontation (ask or tell to stop, talk or discuss, explain why behavior is bothersome); avoidance (avoid person, avoid area); ignore/do nothing (no action, ignore, stay cool); and other reactions (be flattered or complimented, tell others/enlist help, visual/gestural action, indirect action, give in, opportunistic view). As to the relative frequency of employment of the 10 classes of reactions, three dominant reactions emerged: positive verbal confrontation (24%), internal report (20%) and ignore/do nothing (15%). Each of the remaining classes of reactions exhibited employment rates of 7% or less. No significant differences in the use of reaction types were found for working women versus women students. With respect to sex differences in the employment of reaction types, only two significant differences emerged. The results indicated that men were more likely to leave the field than women. Also, men were more apt to employ physical reactions in response to sexual harassment than were women. The results also suggested that the types of reactions employed varied substantially as a function of the form of sexual harassment behavior experienced.

The types of reactions to sexual harassment were also examined by the US Merit Systems Protection Board (1981, 1988). In the 1988 study, for example, the Board asked those employees who had experienced sexual harassment which of nine types of reactions they had employed in dealing with the harassment. Although the classes or types of reactions were not empirically or systematically derived, the results gave some indication of the relative frequency of employment of various reaction types. The nine categories of reactions and associated percentages of employment for women and men were: ignored behavior or did nothing (women—52%, men—42%); avoided the person (women—43%, men—31%); asked/told the person to stop (women—44%, men—25%); made a joke of the behavior (women—20%, men—20%); threatened to tell or told others (women—14%, men—8%); reported the behavior to supervisor or other official (women—15%, men—7%); went along with the behavior (women—4%, men—7%); transferred, disciplined, or gave poor performance rating to the harasser (women—2%, men—3%); and did something other than the reactions listed above (women—10%, men—6%). The two most frequently employed reactions were to either ignore the behavior or to avoid the harasser. The above figures also indicated that women employed six of the nine categories of reactions more often than did men. A summation of the percentages associated with the reaction categories suggested that women were more likely than men to employ multiple reactions in response to an incident of sexual harassment.

One other finding reported by the US Merit Systems Protection Board (1988) involved the relative use of formal versus informal reactions. The Board found that only 5% of both female and male victims reported that they took formal action in response to sexual harassment. Formal actions were defined here as filing a grievance or adverse action appeal, filing a discrimination complaint, or requesting an investigation by their agencies. Thus, the Board concluded that the victims were much more likely to take informal than formal actions in response to sexual harassment. It might be noted, however, that this survey did not report the relative employment of reaction types by specific form of sexual harassment behavior. It may be the case that formal reactions are the dominant response to more severe forms of sexual harassment. Since the more severe forms of sexual harassment occur much less frequently than less severe forms of harassment, one might expect the frequency of employment of formal reactions to be quite low.

Other researchers have provided data that support the US Merit Systems Protection Board's (1988) finding that, in general, victims tend to employ more informal methods of coping with sexual harassment. For example, Benson and Thomson (1982) reported that the tactic of avoidance was the most common response to sexual harassment in their survey of harassment victims. Similarly, a survey conduccted by Loy and Stewart (1984) found that the most common response strategies for all types of harassment combined were informal responses: women tended to either ignore the harassment or verbally deal with the harasser. A recent survey of human resource executives of large business organizations conducted by *Working*

Woman magazine revealed that the organizations received only 1.4 formal sexual harassment complaints per 1000 women employees (Sandroff, 1988). Gutek (1985) also reported that few victims in her survey reported incidents of sexual harassment to authorities. Gutek suggested that many victims thought that reporting the incident would lead to trouble and involve too much time and effort. This view was echoed by the US Merit Systems Protection Board (1988), which concluded that most victims did not believe that the benefits of formal action outweighed the possible consequences.

Little information is available regarding the relative effectiveness of different reaction types in curtailing sexual harassment and reducing the negative outcomes associated with such behavior. The individuals in the US Merit Systems Protection Board (1988) survey were asked whether their reactions to sexual harassment 'made things better'. The reaction classes and percentages of women and men who felt that the reaction 'made things better' were: asked/told person to stop (women—61%, men—66%); avoided the person (women—45%, men—55%); threatened to tell or told others (women—55%, men—24%); reported behavior to supervisor or official (women—49%, men—35%); transferred, disciplined, or gave poor performance rating to harasser (women—48%, men—22%); made a joke of the behavior (women—40%, men—38%); ignored behavior/did nothing (women—29%, men—37%); went along with the behavior (women—16%, men—19%); and did something other than the actions listed above (women—77%, men—39%). The results indicated that for both men and women, asking or telling the person to stop was seen as the most 'effective' reaction listed in the survey. The results also suggested the existence of significant sex differences in the perceived effectiveness of the various classes of reactions.

While the above findings are of definite interest and utility, the survey failed to report relative effectiveness data by specific form of harassment. One would think that the effectiveness of various reactions would vary by specific form of sexual harassment. Additionally, more specific criteria relating to psychological, physiological, social and job-related outcomes might have been more useful than such a general criterion as 'made things better'. Clearly, more research is needed in this area.

As was the case with perceptions of sexual harassment, differences in individuals' choice of reaction types are apparently influenced by several situational and personal variables. One of the most important situational variables influencing the selection of reaction type is the severity of the harassment behavior. For example, Baker and Terpstra (1988) found that for more severe forms of sexual harassment, the most frequent reactions were: internally or externally report the incident; leave the field (quit or transfer); and physically react. For the less severe forms of harassment, the most common reactions were: ignore/do nothing; positive or negative verbal confrontation; avoidance; and alteration (self or environment). Loy and Stewart (1984) and Terpstra and Baker (1989a) also provided data that indicate that the type of reaction is significantly influenced by the severity of the harassment behavior. The status of the harasser *vis-à-vis* the victim has also been shown to be an important determinant of reactions. Livingston (1982) performed a secondary analysis on the sexual harassment data collected in the 1981 US Merit Systems Protection Board survey. Her results indicated that women were more likely to use more assertive reactions when the harasser was of higher job status. Furthermore, the use of formal reactions tended to be restricted to cases of severe harassment where the harasser was the victim's superior.

The personal variable that appears to exert the strongest influence upon one's choice of reactions is sex or gender. Several studies have suggested that sex plays an important role in one's choice of reactions; however, the findings regarding sex have not been consistent (Livingston, 1982; Terpstra and Baker, 1989a; US Merit Systems Protection Board, 1988). In some instances, women appear to react more passively than men; in other instances women appear to choose more assertive reactions than men. The key to these puzzling findings seems to be the type of harassment confronting the individual. For example, Baker and Terpstra (1988) found that women were more apt than men to react assertively in response to more severe forms of harassment. Conversely, women responded less assertively than men when confronted with less severe forms of harassment. Thus, women seem to have a wider repertoire of reactions than men in response to various forms of sexual harassment. This many be due to women's greater experience and familiarity with harassment.

Personality characteristics also seem to moderate individuals' reactions to sexual harassment. Baker and Terpstra (1988) and Gruber and Bjorn (1986) have found that one's level of self-esteem may be an important determinant of reactions to sexual harassment. Individuals with low self-esteem tend to respond more passively to sexual harassment than individuals with higher self-esteem. Individuals with low self-esteem may simply lack confidence in their ability to effect change via their actions. Or perhaps such individuals feel that they have somehow brought the incidents of harassment upon themselves. For example, Jensen and Gutek (1982) found that victims who endorsed behavioral self-blame statements were less likely to have taken more assertive responses. Additional research has suggested that such variables as life satisfaction (Gruber and Bjorn, 1986), locus of control, religiosity and attitudes toward women (Baker and Terpstra, 1988) may also influence individuals' reactions. Once again, it would appear that several variables combine to influence one's choice of reactions to sexual harassment.

As our review indicates, a wide range of reactions to sexual harassment is possible. The individual's choice of reaction types appears to depend upon both personal and situational variables. In general, however, many victims of sexual harassment choose to either ignore the incident or avoid the harasser. Reactions other than these may be more effective at stopping the harassment and reducing the negative outcomes associated with it.

OUTCOMES OF SEXUAL HARASSMENT

The final component of the model of sexual harassment presented in Figure 1 deals with the negative outcomes experienced by the victims. The occurrence of sexual harassment can lead to a wide range of negative personal and professional outcomes for its victims. Admittedly, it is rather difficult to categorize the various outcomes of sexual harassment, as many of these outcomes are interrelated. However, for the purpose of the present discussion, the outcomes of sexual harassment will be classified into four categories of outcomes: psychological and emotional, physiological and medical, social and interpersonal, and work related.

Several studies have documented the negative psychological and emotional consequences that often result from the experience of sexual harassment. One of the first such studies was conducted by the Working Women United Institute, who surveyed a small sample of women attending a meeting on sexual harassment (Silverman, 1976). Those women in attendance who had been sexually harassed were asked whether the experience had resulted in any emotional effects: 78% answered affirmatively. Of those women who reported emotional outcomes, 78% reported feeling angry, 48% reported feeling upset, 27% reported feeling alienated, alone, or heipless, 23% reported being frightened, and 7% reported feeling indifferent.

Additional information on the potential negative psychological and emotional outcomes associated with sexual harassment comes from a study by Crull (1982). Crull gathered data from women who had been harassed and had sought assistance or counseling from the Working Women's Institute: 90% of Crull's sample reported that the sexual harassment incident had produced psychological stress symptoms. The outcomes most frequently mentioned were general tension and nervousness. Additionally, the experience of sexual harassment often resulted in persistent anger and fear.

The two pioneering studies mentioned above provided some extremely valuable information regarding the potential negative psychological and emotional outcomes associated with sexual harassment. However, both studies employed nonrepresentative samples of women (women who chose to attend a meeting on sexual harassment, and women who sought assistance or counseling in regard to sexual harassment). A somêwhat more representative study of the psychological and emotional outcomes of sexual harassment was conducted by Loy and Stewart (1984). They conducted a telephone survey of approximately 500 individuals which included several questions related to sexual harassment. Those individuals who had been sexually harassed were then asked what negative emotional consequences they had experienced as a result of the harassment. Three-fourths of the individuals who have been harassed said that they had experienced some form of distress due to their harassment. The most frequently experienced distress outcomes were nervousness (26%), irritability (20%) and uncontrolled anger (19%). Furthermore, the data indicated that, in general, the more severe the type of harassment, the greater the likelihood of emotional distress.

A similar survey was conducted by Gutek (Gutek, 1985; Jensen and Gutek, 1982). The women in this survey who had been harassed were asked how they felt after the incident. More than 40% of the women reported that they felt disgust after the incident. And approximately one-third said that they experienced anger as a result of the incident. Additional outcomes reported by the victims in this survey were feelings of anxiety or hurt (less than 15%), and feelings of depression, sadness, or guilt (less than 10%).

In light of the results presented above, it is clear that sexual harassment takes a tremendous psychological and emotional toll on its victims. The outcomes of sexual harassment include tension and anxiety, uncontrolled and persistent anger, feelings of fear, alienation, and helplessness, sadness and depression, and unwarranted feelings of guilt or self-blame.

Not surprisingly, the negative psychological and emotional outcomes reported by the victims of sexual harassment are frequently accompanied by complaints of physiological and medical problems. Numerous studies point to a significant link between psychological or emotional stress and physiological changes in the individual. In fact, it is estimated that from 50% to 70% of physical illnesses may be attributable to stress-related origins (Ivancevich and Matteson, 1980). Some of the physiological and health effects thought to result from stress include diseases of the heart and blood vessels, kidney diseases, certain forms of arthritis, diabetes mellitus, ulcers and stomach disorders, skin disorders, chest and back pains, headaches and migraines, insomnia, tiredness and loss of sexual interest (Cox, 1978; Selye, 1976).

While relatively few studies have systematically investigated the physiological and medical outcomes associated with sexual harassment, there is some evidence of a general nature to support the link. In the previously mentioned study by Crull (1982), 63% of the victims who had sought assistance from the Working Women's Institute reported physical symptoms that they thought had been brought on by the incident of sexual harassment. The most frequently mentioned physical outcomes were nausea, headaches and tiredness.

The more representative studies conducted by Loy and Stewart (1984) and Gutek (1985) also produced evidence of the negative health effects associated with sexual harassment. Gutek found that 15% of the women victims of sexual harassment reported that their health was adversely affected. Similarly, Loy and Stewart found that some of the victims had experienced physical distress of a result of sexual harassment. Insomnia, stomach problems and weight loss were among the outcomes reported by the victims in their survey.

The large survey of government employees conducted by the US Merit Systems Protection Board (1981) also asked those who had been harassed if their emotional or physical condition had been affected by the harassment: 33% of the women and 21% of the men said that their emotional or physical condition became worse as a result of their experience. However, it is not known what portions of the above percentage figures are attributable to physical problems and what portions are attributable to emotional problems.

More empirical data relating to the specific physiological and medical outcomes attributable to sexual harassment would be desirable. Yet, enough evidence exists to support the link between the experience of sexual harassment and serious physical and health-related outcomes.

The victims of sexual harassment also experience a range of negative social and interpersonal outcomes. The negative psychological and emotional effects of sexual harassment, such as uncontrollable anger, anxiety, irritability, fear and depression, spill over and affect the victims' relationships with others outside of the workplace. Additionally, the physiological and medical outcomes experienced by the victims of sexual harassment (e.g. tiredness, insomnia, headaches, nausea and stomach problems) quite likely limit the individuals' desire and ability to interact with others. Thus, it is not surprising to find evidence documenting the adverse social and interpersonal effects suffered by the victims of sexual harassment.

Gutek (1985) surveyed over 800 women and found that 15% of those who had experienced sexual harassment reported that the incident had affected their relationships with other men. Hamilton *et al.* (1987) also provide support for the above finding, and suggested that some victims may displace the negative emotions and feelings associated with the harasser on to other males with whom the victim interacts. The husbands or lovers of sexual harassment victims may be particularly susceptible to the effects of such displacement. Reports of divorce, marital strain and sexual problems as a result of an incident of sexual harassment are not uncommon (Crull, 1984; Dunwoody-Miller and Gutek, 1985; MacKinnon, 1979). Hamilton *et al.* (1987) also cite data which suggest that the victims' relationships with other family members may also be negatively affected. They report cases in which the victims' relationships with sons, daughters and mothers have been strained as a result of sexual harassment. The experience of sexual harassment clearly constrains and changes some victims' relationships with others in the personal arena.

There is evidence that the victims of sexual harassment also report negative social and interpersonal outcomes at work as a result of their experience. For example, in Gutek's (1985) survey of women workers, 28% of those who had experienced harassment reported that the incident affected how they related to other people at work. Similarly, Tangri, Burt and Johnson (1982) analyzed the survey data collected by the US Merit Systems Protection Board (1981) and found that 15% of the victims of harassment reported that the experience had worsened their ability to work with others. Schneider (1982) has also reported that sexual harassment appears to limit the victims' potential for forming friendships or alliances with co-workers.

The reasons for victims' social and interpersonal difficulties with others at work can likely be attributed to both the actions and attitudes of the victims, and the actions and attitudes of the co-workers of the victims. The emotional and psychological trauma experienced by the victim of harassment may render that person less willing and able to interact with others at work. Studies by Crull (1982) and Benson and Thomson (1982) provide some support for this contention, as they found that some victims tended to avoid other co-workers following an incident of sexual harassment. Even if the victims of harassment do not socially withdraw, the victims may indirectly keep co-workers at a distance. Individuals undergoing psychological or emotional distress may be perceived by some as 'not fun to be around'.

Co-workers' actions and attitudes also seem to contribute to the negative social and interpersonal outcomes experienced by the victims of harassment. Loy and Stewart (1984), for example, produced findings which suggest that co-workers are apt to ignore individuals who have been sexually harassed. Some victims of sexual harassment may be perceived by co-workers as 'trouble-makers' after the harassment incident (MacKinnon, 1979). Additionally, some co-workers may distance themselves from victims of sexual harassment to avoid any possible repercussions related to being viewed by management as associating with a 'trouble-maker'.

The social and interpersonal consequences of sexual harassment may often be overlooked by individuals unfamiliar with the problem. Yet, as the foregoing discussion indicates, these negative outcomes are, indeed, serious. Furthermore, the negative social and interpersonal outcomes experienced by the victims of sexual harassment exert a strong influence upon the victims' work-related attitudes and outcomes.

Many of the psychological/emotional, physiological/medical and social/interpersonal outcomes are intertwined and may also manifest themselves in negative work-related outcomes for the victims of sexual harassment. For example, there is evidence that individuals' general attitudes toward work suffer as a result of sexual harassment. The survey of US government employees found that 36% of the women who had been harassed reported worsened feelings about work (Tangri, Burt and Johnson, 1982; US Merit Systems Protection Board, 1981). Similarly, Gutek's survey of women workers found that 38% of those who had been harassed reported that the incident had negatively affected their feelings about their jobs (Gutek, 1985). Additional research has attempted to identify some of the more specific components of such negative attitudes toward work. Such research has found evidence of lowered job satisfaction (Gutek, 1985), dread of work (Jensen and Gutek, 1982), decreased motivation (Crull, 1982; Gutek, 1985; Jensen and Gutek, 1982), lowered organizational commitment (Gutek, 1985), feelings of distraction (Jensen and Gutek, 1982), less ability to concentrate (Crull, 1982) and decreased confidence in one's job skills and competence (Benson and Thomson, 1982; Crull, 1982).

The individuals' level of job performance and productivity may also be negatively affected by the experience of sexual harassment. Crull's (1982) nonrepresentative survey of women who had sought assistance as a result of sexual harassment found that 75% of the women victims said that their job performance had suffered. The more representative surveys conducted by the US Merit Systems Protection Board (1981, 1988) reported less substantial decreases in performance. For example, the 1981 survey found that approximately 10% of both women and men victims reported declines in both the quantity and quality of their individual performance.

In addition to negatively impacting the victims' work-related attitudes and performance levels, sexual harassment may also result in the deterioration or loss of more concrete, tangible employment benefits. One of the most serious tangible work-related outcomes is the loss of one's job as a result of sexual harassment. For example, Terpstra and Cook's (1985) study of individuals who had filed formal sexual harassment charges with a state Equal Employment Opportunity (EEO) agency found that 66% of the cases involved job discharge. An additional 16% of the complainants had quit their jobs in response to the sexual harassment incident. Crull's (1982) survey of women who had sought assistance in regard to sexual harassment reported equally staggering job loss outcomes. More than 25% of the victims in Crull's study had been fired or laid off, and an additional 42% had quit their jobs due to sexual harassment. The more representative surveys of sexual harassment conducted by Gutek (1985), Loy and Stewart (1984), and the US Merit Systems Protection Board (1981) have found that between 2% and 7% of the victims have been fired, and between 7% and 15% have quit their jobs as a result of sexual harassment.

Less serious, tangible work-related outcomes that have been found to be associated with the incidence of sexual harassment include transfers, demotions, lowered performance evaluations, unfair wages, denied promotions, decreased training opportunities, not being hired, and poor job references (Crull, 1982; Gutek, 1985; Loy and Stewart, 1984; Terpstra and Cook 1985; US Merit Systems Protection Board, 1981, 1988).

The work-related outcomes reviewed above are, perhaps, the most visible of all the negative outcomes experienced by the victims of sexual harassment. The severity and extent of the negative work-related outcomes experienced by women victims may be seen by some as lending credence to the contention that sexual harassment is a means by which men can protect their jobs and their position of economic privilege (e.g. Farley, 1978; MacKinnon, 1979). Regardless of the validity of such a contention, the fact remains that sexual harassment operates to restrict severely the careers and work-life experiences of many women.

In summary, the evidence reviewed in this section indicates that the negative outcomes that result from the experience of sexual harassment are serious and extensive. The psychological and emotional trauma, the potential health-related problems, the social and interpersonal difficulties, and the adverse work-related consequences caused by sexual harassment combine to paint a rather depressing picture of the problem. If more of the perpetrators of sexual harassment were cognizant of such outcomes, it is possible that some might be less inclined to engage in sexually harassing behavior.

RECOMMENDED ACTIONS

The primary purpose of this chapter was to examine the nature of sexual harassment and identify and review the negative outcomes experienced by the victims. Thus, our focus was directed more toward problem identification than problem resolution. Any discussion of sexual harassment, however, would seem to be incomplete without some mention of recommendations aimed at reducing the negative effects of such behavior.

Stronger sexual harassment legislation may be one possible means of controlling the problem. Additionally, the focus of future legislation might be directed more toward the prevention of sexual harassment. For example, some states in the United States have recently passed bills that make it an unlawful employment practice to fail to take reasonable steps to prevent sexual harassment from occurring (Gutek, 1985). Similarly, regulatory agencies might adopt stronger stances toward sexual harassment, and more vigorously enforce compliance with sexual harassment laws and guidelines. Furthermore, the guidelines on sexual harassment issued by regulatory agencies might be modified in the interest of greater clarity and specificity.

In addition to stronger and more specific legislation, there are some organizational and individual actions that might be taken to lessen the problem. For organizations to take any type of action to curb sexual harassment, they must first be convinced of the need to address the problem seriously. This might be achieved by making top management aware of the serious and extensive human costs of sexual harassment (the negative psychological/emotional, physiological/medical, and social/interpersonal costs). It might also be achieved by making top management aware of the high organizational costs associated with sexual harassment (e.g. litigation costs, reduced productivity, and turnover and replacement costs). Once organizations recognize the need to initiate and support efforts to arrest sexual harassment, several actions are possible.

It may be possible to control the problem partially at the point of entry into the organization. Selection and screening procedures for new employees might be modified to include thorough reference and background checks designed to uncover previous sexual harassment behaviors on the part of job applicants.

Orientation sessions for new employees and training sessions for existing employees have also been recommended as a means of fostering a greater awareness of the problem of sexual harassment. Interestingly, the 1988 US Merit Systems Protection Board evaluated the sexual harassment training programs of 22 government agencies and found no correlation between an agency's estimate of the amount of training provided to employees and the reported rate of harassment within an agency. It was concluded that training had no effect upon the problem of sexual harassment. The Board suggested that the training programs might have been more effective had they been more carefully tailored to meet the needs of each particular agency. It is also possible that training alone may not be sufficient to change behaviors which are firmly rooted in individuals' belief systems. For example, Jensen and Gutek (1982) have suggested that it may be necessary to change workers' fundamental sex-role attitudes in order to eliminate sexual harassment.

It has also been recommended that organizations develop forceful, formal sexual harassment policies that clearly specify the types of behaviors that are forbidden and the penalties associated with each type of sexual harassment behavior. The severity of the penalty should vary in accordance with the severity of the type of behavior. Serious penalties (e.g. dismissal for more serious forms of sexual harassment) should increase the motivation of potential harassers to refrain from engaging in sexual harassment. The sexual harassment policies and penalties should be adequately communicated to new and existing employees. The establishment and communication of formal complaint and investigation procedures would also seem to be an important element of an organization's sexual harassment system. Special complaint channels that allow the victim to bypass the immediate supervisor (who may be the harasser) should also be specified. Once a sexual harassment complaint is lodged, it should be investigated quickly and thoroughly. If evidence of harassment is found, the organization should take immediate action to penalize the perpetrator, thereby reinforcing the credibility of the system in the eyes of other employees.

Managers and supervisors might also be encouraged to look actively for personnel problems that might suggest potential sexual harassment. Changes in employees' behavior or work habits might be indicative of underlying sexual harassment problems. High turnover or absenteeism figures for women in specific organizational units might also signal a potential problem related to sexual harassment. Periodic satisfaction or organizational climate surveys might also yield information on possible harassment problems. It may also be advisable for management to review carefully all major personnel decisions (performance appraisals, promotions, demotions, disciplinary actions and discharges) for evidence of bias due to sexual harassment. Formal procedures might be developed that provide for multi-level reviews of all major personnel decisions.

If an incident of sexual harassment is uncovered or brought to the attention of management, the organization might consider providing counseling for the victim. Such supportive action on the part of management might help to alleviate the potential negative psychological/emotional, physiological/medical, social/interpersonal and work-related outcomes experienced by the victim. Consideration might also be given to providing counseling for those with whom the victim interacts closely (both at work and at home). Finally, if the harasser has not been fired, the organization might require mandatory counseling for the individual as part of the action taken against him or her. This may stop the harasser from engaging in such behavior in the future. In many instances, harassers who are fired simply move on to harass individuals in other organizations. Thus, sexual harassment, in its totality, has not been lessened; it has merely been redistributed among other organizations that do not carefully screen applicants for such behavior.

There are several actions on the part of the individual victim that might also serve to curtail sexual harassment. As the studies reviewed earlier indicate, many individuals seem reluctant to deal assertively with the occurence of sexual harassment. Many individuals react to sexual harassment by ignoring the harasser or doing nothing. And relatively few victims report the incident to management or invoke formal complaint mechanisms. However, as the findings from the US Merit Systems Protection Board (1981, 1988) suggest, there may be more effective reactions. For example, simply asking or telling the harasser to stop may work in some cases. A more assertive form of confronting the harasser is suggested by Rowe (1981). She suggests that the victim write a detailed letter to the harasser that describes the behavior, the circumstances and the emotions involved. Further, the letter should state what needs to be done to rectify the situation. The letter should then be delivered in person to the harasser, with a witness present. Rowe states that when such action is taken, there is typically no response from the harasser and the sexual harassment stops.

If confronting the harasser fails to stop the behavior, the victim should consider a formal complaint to management. If the organization has a progressive stance toward sexual harassment and adequate policies and procedures for dealing with sexual harassment, this action may be effective. Failing organizational action, the victim might consider formal legal action. Research conducted in the United States by Terpstra and Baker (1988b, 1989b) has shown that complainants are much more likely to win their cases if the sexual harassment was of a serious nature (sexual assault, unwanted physical contact, or sexual propositions accompanied by threats or promises of a change in one's job status), if they had witnesses or documents to support their cases, and if they notified management of the harassment and no action was taken. In such instances, individuals in the United States have a good chance of winning their cases.

Individuals might also be encouraged to take steps to lessen the negative psychological/emotional, physiological/medical and social/interpersonal outcomes which frequently follow the experience of sexual harassment. If the organization does not offer or provide supportive services, the victim might seek out such services on her or his own. Sexual harassment is a problem that should not be ignored.

REFERENCES

Baker, D.D. and Terpstra, D.E. (1988). Determinants of reactions to sexual harassment, Paper presented at the 48th Annual Meeting of the Academy of Management, Anaheim, California, August.

Barry, H., Bacon, M.K. and Child, I.L. (1957). A cross-cultural survey of some sex differences in socialization, *Journal of Abnormal and Social Psychology*, **55**, 327–32.

Benson, D. J. and Thomson, G. E. (1982). Sexual harassment on a university campus: The confluence of authority relations, sexual interest, and gender stratification, *Social Problems*, **29**, 236–51.

Caplan, P.J., MacPherson, G.M. and Tobin, P. (1985). Do sex-related differences in spatial abilities exist? *American Psychologist*, **40**, 786–99.

Collins, E.G.C. and Blodgett, T.B. (1981). Sexual harassment: some see it . . . some won't, *Harvard Business Review*, **59**(2), 76–95.

Cox, T. (1978). *Stress*, University Park Press, Baltimore.

Crull, P. (1982). Stress effects of sexual harassment on the job: Implications for counseling, *American Journal of Orthopsychiatry*, **52**, 539–44.

Crull, P. (1984). Sexual harassment and women's health. In W. Chavkin (ed.) *Double Exposure*, Monthly Review Press.

Dunwoody-Miller, V. and Gutek, B.A. (1985). Sexual harassment in the state workforce: Results of a survey, Report to the California Commission on the Status of Women—SHE Project.

Eagly, A.H. and Carli, L.L. (1981). Sex of Researchers and sex-typed communications

as determinants of sex differences in influenceability: A meta-analysis of social influence studies, *Psychological Bulletin*, **90**, 1–20.
Equal Employment Opportunity Commission (1980). Interpretive guidelines on sexual harassment, *Federal Register*, **45**, 25024–5.
Farley, L. (1978). *Sexual Shakedown: The Sexual Harassment of Women on the Job*, McGraw-Hill, New York.
Fritz, N.R. (1989). Sexual harassment and the working woman, *Personnel*, 4–8, February.
Gruber, J.E. and Bjorn, L. (1986). Women's responses to sexual harassment: an analysis of sociocultural, organizational and personal resource models, *Social Science Quarterly*, **67**, 814–26.
Gutek, B.A. (1985). Sex and the Workplace, Jossey-Bass, San Francisco.
Gutek, B.A. and Morasch, B. (1982). Sex-ratios, Sex-role spillover, and sexual harassment at work, *Journal of Scoial Issues*, **38**(4), 55–74.
Gutek, B.A., Morasch, B. and Cohen, A.G. (1983). Interpreting social–sexual behavior in a work setting, *Journal of Vocational Behavior*, **22**(1), 30–48.
Hamilton, J.A., Alagna, S.W., King, L.S. and Lloyd, C. (1987). The emotional consequences of gender-based abuse in the workplace: New counseling programs for sex-discrimination, *Women and Therapy*, **6**, 155–82.
Henley, N. and Freeman, J. (1975). The sexual politics of interpersonal behavior. In J. Freeman (ed.) *Women: A Feminist Perspective*, Mayfield, Palo Alto.
Hyde, J. S. (1981). How large are cognitive gender differences? *American Psychologist*, **36**, 892–901.
Ivancevich, J.M. and Matteson, M.T. (1980). *Stress and Work: A Managerial Perspective*. Scott-Foresman, Glenview, IL.
Jensen, I. and Gutek, B.A. (1982). Attributions and assignment of responsibility in sexual harassment, *Journal of Social Issues*, 38(4), 121–36.
Kanter, R.M. (1977). *Men and Women of the Corporation*, Basic Books, New York.
Konrad, A.M. and Gutek, B.A. (1986). Impact of work experiences on attitudes toward sexual harassment, *Administrative Science Quarterly*, **31**, 422–38.
Livingston, J.A. (1982). Responses to sexual harassment on the job: Legal, organizational and individual actions, *Journal of Social Issues*, **38**(4), 5–22.
Loy, P.H. and Stewart, L.P. (1984). The extent and effects of the sexual harassment of working women, *Sociological Focus*, **17**(1), 31–43.
MacKinnon, C. (1979). *Sexual Harrassment of Working Women: A Case of Sex Discrimination*, Yale University Press, New Haven, CT.
New York Times (1986). A grueling struggle for equality, 9 November, 12–13.
Powell, G.N. (1988). *Women and Men in Management*, Sage, Newbury Park, CA.
Rich, A. (1976). Of Women Born, Norton, New York.
Rowe, M.P. (1981). Dealing with sexual harassment, *Harvard Business Review*, **59**(3), 42–6.
Sandroff, R. (1988). Sexual harassment in the Fortune 500, *Working Woman*, December, 69–73.
Schneider, B. (1982). Consciousess about sexual harassment among heterosexual and lesbian women workers, *Journal of Social Issues*, **38**(4), 75–97.
Selye, H. (1976). *The Stress of Life*, McGraw-Hill, New York.
Silverman, D. (1976). Sexual harassment: Working women's dilemma, *Quest: A Feminist Quarterly*, 3(3), 15–24.
Tangri, S., Burt, M.R. and Johnson, L.B. (1982). 'Sexual harassment at work: Three explanatory models, *Journal of Social Issues*, **38**(4), 55–74.
Terpstra, D.E. and Baker, D.D. (1986a), A framework for the study of sexual

harassment, *Basic and Applied Social Psychology*, **7**(1), 17–34.

Terpstra, D.E. and Baker, D.D. (1986b). Psychological and demographic correlates of perceptions of sexual harassment, *Journal of Psychology Monographs*, **112**(4), 459–78.

Terpstra, D.E. and Baker, D.D. (1988a). A hierarchy of sexual harassment, *The Journal of Psychology*, **121**(6), 599–607.

Terpstra, D.E. and Baker, D.D. (1988b). The outcomes of sexual harrassment charges, *The Academy of Management Journal*, **31**(1), 185–94.

Terpstra, D.E. and Baker, D.D. (1989a). The identification and classification of reactions to sexual harassment, *Journal of Organizational Behavior*, **10**(1), 1–14.

Terpstra, D.E. and Baker, D.D. (1989b). The influence of Supreme Court decisions and selected case variables upon sexual harassment outcomes, Paper presented at the 49th annual Meeting of the Academy of Management, Washington, DC, August.

Terpstra, D.E. and Cook, S.E. (1985). Complainant characteristics and reported behaviors and consequences associated with formal sexual harassment charges, *Personnel Psychology*, **38**(3), 559–74.

US Merit Systems Protection Board (1981). *Sexual Harassment in the Federal Workplace: Is It a Problem?* US Government Printing Office, Washington DC.

US Merit Systems Protection Board (1988). *Sexual Harassment in the Federal Government: An Update*, US Government Printing Office, Washington DC.

Weitzman, L.J. (1979). *Sex-Role Socialization: A Focus on Women*, Mayfield, Palo Alto.

Chapter 7.2

Sexual Harassment: Legal Issues, Past and Future Developments

Vivienne Gay, Barrister, London, UK

INTRODUCTION

Until recently the phrase 'sexual harassment' had not been heard in the courts or tribunals of the United Kingdom. It had no meaning in statute or case law. Then various organizations (e.g. trade unions, the Equal Opportunities Commission, the National Council for Civil Liberties, Women Against Sexual Harassment) began to create or adopt working definitions in order to move the debate and public consciousness along. It was generally felt that the definition should be wide enough to include both physical and verbal harassment, covering offensive words, lewd gestures, uninvited and unwanted touching and requests for sexual favours as well as sexual assaults ranging from the relatively minor right through to rape or forced acts of participation. The role of pin-up photographs or the display of pornographic pictures in the workplace is something which is also receiving attention from concerned groups.

The lack of a name and definition perhaps explains why sexual harassment has not emerged very obviously as a wrong for which the courts or tribunals could give a remedy. No legislation specifically renders sexual harassment unlawful and no remedies have been crafted to assist those who are affected. None the less, some early signs of judicial awareness of the existence of sexual harassment may be identified, arising initially from the overlap of the tort of assault and battery with the crime of assault (in all its varying degrees of severity).

First, for a long time the Criminal Injuries Compensation Board has given compensation to victims of rape or sexual assault who come within the criteria of its scheme. The Criminal Injuries Compensation Board is a governmental organisation which was recently established on a statutory basis. Senior barristers with experience of personal injury work are appointed

Vulnerable Workers: Psychosocial and Legal Issues. Edited by M. J. Davidson and J. Earnshaw

to the Board and make individual decisions about the disbursement of funds to the victims of crimes, usually based upon a consideration of the case papers (statements to police, witness statements and brief medical reports). If a case is particularly serious or if a victim seeks more money than has initially been offered, the case will come for an oral hearing before three members of the Board. There is no detailed system for publishing awards of the Board, although those representing victims sometimes send short reports of what they see as particularly good awards to legal publications. It could well be that some of the claims made to the Board arose out of incidents of sexual assault at work.

Second, the ordinary civil courts (County Court and High Court in England and Wales; Sheriff's Court and Court of Sessions in Scotland) have recently been used by victims of rape or sexual assault as a means of claiming compensation from the perpetrators, see, for example, *W* v. *Meah* [1986] 1 All ER 935. Claims have to be made out to the ordinary civil standard ('on the balance of probabilities'). It is not necessary that the defendant in the civil case should have been convicted in the criminal courts, but if there has been a conviction it will effectively determine the issue of liability in favour of the victim because the criminal courts operate to a higher standard of proof. Where the perpetrator has money or means (for example is still in employment or owns his own home) there is usually some hope that he will be able both to satisfy the judgment and to pay the costs of the case. Claims are now being made in this way by women who have been sexually assaulted at work. The remedy which the courts can award is financial compensation for physical or psychological injury and for loss of earnings and other out of pocket expenses or future loss.

Third, and more specifically work related, is the recognition in the Court of Appeal in 1978 that unwanted amorous advances by an employer to a female employee could constitute conduct amounting to constructive dismissal so as to entitle the employee to resign and claim to have been unfairly dismissed, see Lawton LJ in *Western Excavating Ltd* v. *Sharp* [1978] ICR 221, 229.

Since Britain became a member of the European Community in 1972, Community law (Articles of the relevant Treaties, Directives, Resolutions and decisions of the European Court of Justice) has also been very relevant to our jurisprudence. In some cases the legislative provisions of the European Community are directly effective in Britain without the need for them to be incorporated into an Act of Parliament. This is true *inter alia* of Article 119 of the European Economic Community, which establishes the right to equal pay for men and women, and to some extent of Directive 76/207 which extends and elaborates Article 119, asserting that it includes the right to equal treatment without discrimination on the grounds of sex. Arguably, this is sufficient to cover sexual harassment. The Directive can be relied upon by individuals in the United Kingdom where their employer is an organ of the state, for example a health authority or local council. In practice, no sexual harassment claim has been brought under these provisions and it seems unlikely that a UK applicant would be assisted by them, in view of the developing jurisprudence under domestic legislation. There is a proposal to produce a Directive on sexual harassment (Rubenstein, 1988). However, as mentioned in Chapter 2, at present the European Parliament has only instructed the European Commission to draw up a code of practice on the issue, with a view to monitoring its adoption and effect. This is perhaps a form of benign cold storage.

The most recent development is the use of the Sex Discrimination Act 1975 to make employers liable for their own acts and for the acts of their employees, when a woman is subjected to conduct ot the type described above on the basis that such conduct constitutes unlawful sex discrimination. It is this last development which it is intended to examine in greater depth below.

THE SEX DISCRIMINATION ACT 1975

Relevant Provisions

The Act starts by defining sex discrimination in s. 1 as less favourable treatment of a woman than a man (or vice versa) on the grounds of sex. Section 6 makes it unlawful for an employer to discriminate against a woman in various ways related to employment, namely:

(1) in the arrangements made for determining who should be offered employment;
(2) in the terms on which employment is offered;
(3) by refusing to offer employment;
(4) in the way access is offered or refused to opportunities for promotion, transfer, training and the like;
(5) by dismissing the woman or 'subjecting her to any other detriment'.

It is often meaningless to say that an employer is liable for the things he does when the employer is a company, partnership or any unit other than an individual. To overcome this the Act incorporates the principle of vicarious liability which is already well established in UK law: s. 41(1) provides that anything done by a person in the course of his employment shall be treated for the purposes of the Act as done by his employer as well as by him, whether or not it was done with the employer's knowledge or approval. Matters could have been left there, but Parliament chose to ameliorate the employer's position by providing in s. 41(3) that it would be a defence for an employer to prove that he took such steps as were reasonably practicable to prevent the employee from doing the act complained of, or from doing in the course of his employment acts of that description. A person who knowingly aids an employer to do an act made unlawful by the Act shall, by s. 42, be treated as himself doing an unlawful act. In other words, an employee may be personally liable under the Act for acts of sex discrimination.

Complaints of sex discrimination in the employment field 'may be presented to an Industrial Tribunal', (see s. 63 of the Act). The remedies which an Industrial Tribunal may give are set out in s. 65. They consist of a declaration as to the rights of the parties, an order for compensation and a recommendation that the employer should within a specified period take certain action in order to obviate or reduce the adverse effect on the complainant of any act of discrimination to which the complaint relates. Compensation is to be assessed in the same manner as any other claim in tort, subject to the limit imposed on Industrial Tribunals by s. 75 of the Employment Protection (Consolidation) Act 1978, which is presently £8925. Financial compensation may include a sum for injury to feelings.

Does the Sex Discrimination Act Outlaw Sexual Harassment?

The issue here was whether sexual harassment constitutes discrimination on the grounds of sex or whether it is actually caused by something more than a mere difference in gender, such as physical attraction. This type of conundrum was first considered by Industrial Tribunals in relation to discrimination against pregnant women and women with young children, see *Turley* v. *Allders Department Stores Ltd* [1980] ICR 66; *Hayes* v. *Malleable Working Men's Club* [1985] ICR 703; and *Hurley* v. *Mustoe* [1981] ICR 490. Mr Mustoe ran a bistro at which he had a policy of not employing as waitresses women with young children. He had no corresponding policy in relation to men. On this basis the Employment Appeal Tribunal came in its judgment, rapidly and without discussion of the arguments once it had established the policy on the facts, that Mr Mustoe's policy directly discriminated against women. In English jurisprudence, therefore, nothing lay in the way of a sex discrimination claim which showed that an employer treated certain women less favourably than he would treat a man. The fact that the employer operated a 'gender-plus' policy (e.g. female gender plus pregnancy or female gender plus children) as the basis for less favourable treatment did not prevent that treatment from being discrimination on the grounds of sex within the meaning of the Act.

Just what the UK tribunals would make of a sexual harassment claim was a matter of conjecture and academic discussion during the late 1970s and early 1980s. The debate was vigorously resolved in the mid-1980s by the Employment Appeal Tribunal, Scotland, in the case of *Porcelli* v. *Strathclyde Regional Council* [1985] ICR 177. Mrs Porcelli worked as a science laboratory technician. In late 1982 two male laboratory technicians were appointed to work with her. They pursued a course of conduct towards Mrs Porcelli which appeared to be calculated to get rid of her. Part of what they did was simply malicious, for example, destroying or removing Mrs Porcelli's belongings: the rest of their conduct had sexual overtones, comprising suggestive remarks and deliberate, unnecessary physical contact. Mrs Porcelli's evidence included the following:

> Mr Coles would, for example, pick up a screw nail and ask me if I would like a screw. Another example was when he picked up a glass rod holder—which is shaped like a penis—and asked if I had any use for it. On several occasions he opened the *Daily Record* at page 3 and commented on my physical appearance in comparison with that of the nude female depicted in the newspaper.

Against this background the Industrial Tribunal had concluded that the men had treated Mrs Porcelli as they did because they obviously disliked her. They would have treated a man whom they disliked just as unfavourably as they treated Mrs Porcelli, even though the specific nature of the unpleasantness might well have been different. The Employment Appeal Tribunal held that the Industrial Tribunal had fallen into error. The conduct of the men which had sexual overtones could have had no relevance in their conduct towards a male employee whom they disliked. The male lab technicians subjected Mrs Porcelli to a campaign of sexual harassment which they would not have directed against a man. In that sense their treatment of her was different and less favourable. The detriment which Mrs Porcelli suffered was that she felt obliged to seek transfer from their joint place of work to another school. Although she had applied for the transfer, it was not a voluntary request: 'it was clearly forced upon her'.

The Scottish Court of Session (Court of Appeal) upheld the Employment Appeal Tribunal's decision (see [1986] ICR 564), saying that if the form of unfavourable treatment or any material part of it which is meted out included a significant element of a sexual character to which a man would not be vulnerable, the treatment is on the grounds of the woman's sex within the meaning of the Act. In the present case, the treatment of Mrs Porcelli, which was in the nature of sexual harassment, was adopted because she was a woman. The weapon used was based upon the sex of the victim. Since this form of treatment would not have been used against an equally disliked man, the treatment was different in a material respect from that which would have been inflicted upon a male colleague. That the treatment which would have been accorded to an equally disliked man would have been equally unpleasant or even more cruel did not answer the question posed by the Act. Upon a proper application of the Act, it was impossible to say other than that Mrs Porcelli had been treated less favourably on the ground of her sex than a man with whom her position fell to be compared would have been treated. Lord Emslie said, 'Sexual harassment is a particularly degrading and unacceptable form of treatment which it must be taken to have been the intention of Parliament to restrain.'

This decision while not strictly binding on English courts would be regarded as a very persuasive authority at all levels up to and including the Court of Appeal.

Industrial Tribunal Decisions on Sexual Harassment

There is now a fairly substantial body of cases which have involved Industrial Tribunals in making decisions about sexual harassment issues. Two of these cases were decided before the Employment Appeal Tribunal decision in *Porcelli*. They dealt with the issues briefly, deciding in each case that the reason for the woman's dismissal was because of her adverse reaction to or rejection of the male's sexual advances. It was, therefore, a reason clearly related to her sex and was unlawful discrimination. The first of the cases, *Walsh* v. *William Rutter* (unreported, Case No. 38432/82), achieved some notoriety because the female employee was dismissed after she poured a glass of lager over the head of the accountant, who was also a friend of the respondent's managing director, because he had made suggestive remarks and grabbed at her arm and neck at a farewell party for a fellow employee.

In many of the succeeding cases the tribunals have had to make a decision as to whether they believed the individual employee, who was making the complaint of sexual advances or verbal sexual abuse, as against the male employee or boss who was denying it. Frequently tribunals have found themselves able to prefer the evidence of the woman. In a case where a junior administrative officer put up with verbal and physical harassment for a period of about $2\frac{1}{2}$ years, the tribunal recognised that this was because she felt too vulnerable to complain until after she had discovered that other women were also being harassed and after she had been confirmed in her post. This lapse of time did not prevent her from complaining of continuous sex discrimination or constructive dismissal, see *Fall* v. *Lothian CRC* (unreported, Case No. S/107/86).

The facts are occasionally discussed at great length in these tribunal decisions: the law is usually more shortly put, tribunals being generally content to say that they are following the law as set out in the Act and in *Porcelli*. On the whole, it does appear that the 'industrial jury', which is what an Industrial Tribunal is said to be, can cope with the issues of what might be called straightfoward sexual harassment cases. I turn now to cases which for one reason or another have proceeded beyond the Industrial Tribunal, which have thrown up difficulties or shortcomings in the use of the Act against harassment and which have not always made good law.

Difficulties in the Use of the Law

What constitutes less favourable treatment on the grounds of sex?

The Race Relations Act 1976 contains the provisions relating to discrimination on the grounds of race, which are equivalent to those in relation to sex in the Sex Discrimination Act, and race cases thus provide useful analogies. In *De Souza* v. *The Automobile Association* [1986] ICR 514, Mrs De Souza (described in the report as 'a coloured woman') complained that she had been discriminated against on grounds of her race after she overheard one of the respondent's managers tell another, with respect to her, to get his typing done by 'the wog'. An Industrial Tribunal found that these words had been spoken but that Mrs De Souza had not been unlawfully discriminated against. She lost her appeal to the Employment Appeal Tribunal and the case was taken to the Court of Appeal. Giving the judgment with which the other two members of the Court agreed, Lord Justice May said that Mrs De Souza had not been treated less favourably by anyone:

> . . . . even though the use of the insulting word in respect of the appellant may have meant that she was being considered less favourably, whether generally or in an employment context, than others, I for my part do not think that she can properly be said to have been 'treated' less favourably by whomsoever used the word, unless he intended her to overhear the conversation in which it was used, or knew or ought reasonably to have anticipated that the person he was talking to would pass the insult on or that the appellant would become aware of it in some other way.

On this approach, referring to a woman as a 'slag' or a 'slut' would not be held to be treating her less favourably unless it was said to her or known or reasonably anticipated that she would hear of it. There seems, in principle, to be no need for this restriction upon the meaning of the words of the statute: it is hard to think of some equivalent insult which could be used of a man (or, as the case may be, a white man) and such treatment will usually have a felt effect even if it is not done directly to the person concerned.

In March 1990 an Industrial Tribunal in Scotland held that lewd behaviour in the form of conversation and songs amongst male factory workers (including the singing of a verse with the immortal line 'Put your gums on my plums' and unsavoury references to menstruation) could constitute 'treatment' of a woman within earshot to which she, as a woman, was vulnerable in a way which a man was not. The employers argued that the incidents had not been directed at the woman and that in a factory setting the words used were not exceptional. The Tribunal rejected both arguments and made a finding of unlawful sex discrimination, see *Johnstone* v. *Fenton Barnes (Scotland) Ltd*, Unreported Case No. S/1688/89.

The other aspect of the requirement for less favourable treatment which has given cause for concern is the need to have a man, real or hypothetical, with whose treatment that of the woman can be compared. In cases where the harassment consists of direct physical assault, sexual invitation or verbal abuse it will be relatively easy for a tribunal to assume, as was done for example in the *Porcelli* case, that no man would have been treated in the same way. But what about the cases where a woman reacts to harassment in a certain way and is then dismissed because of that reaction? It would have been possible for the industrial tribunal in the *Walsh* case (above) to say that although she was originally harassed by the accountant, she was dismissed for pouring lager over his head, as would any man have been who had reacted to a displeasing or upsetting conversation in the same way. In consequence, it could be argued, although the dismissal was unfair, it was not on the grounds of sex. This argument did not appeal to the Manchester Tribunal which decided Mrs Walsh's case. The Tribunal said:

> If the applicant had been unable to attend the party and a male employee had driven the other three girls to Bredbury Hall and formed one of the group in the bar where Mr Devine had appeared on the scene, it is most unlikely, to say the least, that he would have received the treatment at the hands of Mr Devine that she received. There would have been no report to [the managing director] and no question of any dismissal would have arisen. In the most unlikely event of such male employee receiving similar treatment from Mr Devine to that which the applicant was obliged to suffer that night, it is most improbable, in our view, that he would have been dismissed for resisting such treatment. In our judgment the respondents did discriminate against the applicant by dismissing her and we find her complaint to be well founded.

This was a necessary finding because the applicant did not have sufficient length of service to make a claim for unfair dismissal. Its success depends upon the tribunal taking the necessary step and assuming that it was 'most improbable' that a man would have been dismissed for reacting as did Mrs Walsh. It will usually be impossible to prove this matter by direct evidence, because any employer who is asked (in chief or in cross-examination) would be likely to say that he would treat a man the same as he treated the applicant. The *Walsh* Tribunal apparently felt that there was no break in the line of sex-based treatment from the moment the harassment began until the time of the dismissal. This is a robust and acceptable solution to the dilemma.

Compare the Employment Appeal Tribunal's more recent approach. In *Balgobin and Francis* v. *London Borough of Tower Hamlets* [1987] ICR 829, two female employees complained to their employers that they were being sexually harassed by a probationary chef with whom they worked. The chef was suspended and enquiries were held which were inconclusive, in part because the chef created enormous disturbances by accusing the women of theft from their employers. After the enquiries were concluded, the women were required to continue working alongside the male chef. It was argued that this constituted less favourable treatment of the women that would have been given to a man, in that they were exposed to the anticipated risk of further sexual harassment. That risk arose because of their sex. In consequence of the less favourable treatment, they suffered the detriment of having to work in intolerable conditions. The Employment Appeal Tribunal held that the situation was intolerable and that it had a sexual context, but that the reason that the women were exposed to it was not because they were women but because they were employees who were required to work with the chef. They were not required to work with him because they were women. In consequence, the employers did not treat the women less favourably on the grounds of their sex. Further, if they were compared to a man to whom homosexual advances had been made, they would not have been treated less favourably than him.

There is a double flaw in this argument. First, the Act is not concerned with the reason or motive for which treatment is meted out, see *R* v. *Birmingham City Council, ex p. E.O.C.* [1989]2 WLR 520 and *James* v. *Eastleigh Borough Council* [1990]2 All E.R. 607, both in the House of Lords. The legal test is that of effective cause: 'but for' their sex the women would not have suffered a continuing detriment. The effect on the women of having to work alongside the perpetrator of the harassment was clearly less favourable than it would have been had they been men. Second, if the chef had made homosexual advances to a man, and that man had then been required to work alongside him, the treatment of that man would also have been less favourable treatment on the grounds of his sex. There would have been a sexual component that was directly related to his gender. The fact that a homosexual man might also have been put back into the same situation by the employer does not mean that the treatment was not less favourable to the women on the grounds of their sex: if anything, it reinforces that it was.

The treatment must be to the woman's detriment

The respondents in the *Porcelli* case conceded in the Court of Session that if Mrs Porcelli was discriminated against within the meaning of s. 1 of the Act she could complain that she was subjected to a detriment within the meaning of s. 6 of the Act. This was against a background in which the Employment Appeal Tribunal had set out that the detriment suffered was that Mrs Porcelli had had to seek a transfer to another school. Lord Emslie in the Court of Session said that the appellants were well advised to make that concession because detriment simply means disadvantage in its statutory context. Lord Justice May in the *De Souza* case (above) held that a racial insult which was not directly or indirectly addressed to the relevant employee is not enough by itself to constitute a detriment within the meaning of the Race Relations Act, even if it caused the employee distress. However, he went on to indicate that there was no need for the sexual or racial discrimination to consist of a dismissal or other disciplinary action by the employer, or of some action by the employee such as leaving the employment or seeking transfer to another place of work, in order for a detriment to be proved. Provided that the

> putative reasonable employee could justifiably complain about his or her working conditions or environment, then whether or not these were so bad as to be able to amount to constructive dismissal, or even if the employee was prepared to work on and put up with the harassment

that too could constitute a detriment. He then held that in the circumstances of the *De Souza* case it had not been shown both that she was, and that the reasonable coloured secretary in like situation would or might be, disadvantaged, 'that is placed at a disadvantage in the circumstances and condition in which they were working in the way I have indicated'.

This sets the test in relation to detriment as both a subjective and an objective one. First, the employee must show that she was disadvantaged in relation to her employment conditions. Second, she must show that a reasonable employee similarly circumstanced would also have felt disadvantaged. The applicant in any case can give evidence as to how she felt. The decision as to the reasonableness or otherwise of her response will presumably be made by the judges or tribunal members deciding the case, most of whom are white and male with no training or particular aptitude in understanding the effects of discrimination.

In *Wileman* v. *Minilec Engineering Ltd* [1988] ICR 318 the Employment Appeal Tribunal held that in deciding whether the harassment to which a woman was subjected constituted a detriment, an Industrial Tribunal was entitled to take into account the fact that on occasions the applicant wore clothes to work which were scanty and provocative. This was a case in which over a period of about four years the applicant was sexually harassed by a director of the respondents who made salacious remarks, rubbed up against her when she was at work, fondled her hands, lent her 'saucy' books, asked her to go out with him and talked about pornographic videos. Ms Wileman's evidence was to the effect that she did not wear scanty clothes. The perpetrator of the harassment said that he did not notice her clothes much, although she did wear rather outlandish clothes. A couple of other witnesses for the respondents said that Ms Wileman wore scanty clothes on occasion. The Employment Appeal Tribunal found that there was therefore material upon which the Industrial Tribunal could say that on occasion Ms Wileman's clothes were scanty and provocative. They went on:

> We think that the Industrial Tribunal were entitled to take into account as an element—not a decisive element but an element—in deciding whether the harassment to which she was subjected really did constitute a detriment. Leaving aside this case, if a girl on the shop floor goes around wearing provocative clothes and flaunting herself, it is not unlikely that other people—particularly the men—will make remarks about it; it is an inevitable part of working life on the shop floor. If she then complains that she suffered a detriment, the tribunal is entitled to look at the circumstances in which the remarks are made which are said to constitute that detriment. That is all the Industrial Tribunal were saying. In our judgment, they were perfectly entitled to say so.

The Tribunal awarded only £50 compensation for injury to feelings and the Employment Appeal Tribunal upheld this. While in principle there may be little wrong with the ideas expressed by the Industrial Tribunal and the Employment Appeal Tribunal, in fact they were not logically applied. The harassment of which complaint was made and the detriment alleged did not arise out of the wearing of any particular clothes. This was confirmed beyond peradventure by the evidence of the perpetrator. The fact that a woman wears scanty clothes may provoke comments about her clothes, but it does not invite physical contact, requests for dates or talk about pornographic videos. Nor can it indicate that when those matters occur, the applicant has not suffered a detriment.

In the *Wileman* case there was a preliminary issue before the Employment Appeal Tribunal, as to whether the employers could call fresh evidence. They wanted to put before the Tribunal the fact that after the hearing Ms Wileman had posed for a national newspaper in a flimsy costume. Their argument was that it was relevant both as to whether she did in fact suffer any detriment and as to whether if she suffered any detriment it was of such minimal amount that the compensation for injury to feelings should be reduced. The Employment Appeal Tribunal rejected the application, on the basis that the evidence was unlikely to be relevant and was of little if any probative value. The Employment Appeal Tribunal said:

> Quite clearly, the picture itself cannot affect, in any way, the question of physical harassment. Secondly, its probative value in relation to the comments made by the director seem to us to be almost minimal. A person may be quite happy to accept the remarks of A. or B. in a sexual context, and wholly upset by similar remarks made by C; the fact that she was upset to the extent that the tribunal have found by the remarks made by the director is not in our judgment vitiated in any way by the fact that she was perfectly willing to pose for the national newspaper. That she may have been upset by the remarks about going topless, and then appears in a national newspaper in the way that she did, are not necessarily inconsistent.

This reasoning must be correct. It contrasts favourably with the view of the Employment Appeal Tribunal the year before in Mrs Snowball's case, see below.

Is the perpetrator of the harassment acting 'in the course of his employment'?

There is an enormous amount of case law in the United Kingdom about the issue of whether an employee is acting 'in the course of his employment' at the time when he commits some wrong for which it is sought to make the employer liable. The law was authoritatively summarised most recently in two Court of Appeal cases, see *Aldred* v. *Nacanco* [1987] IRLR 292 and *Irving* v. *The Post Office* [1987] IRLR 289, the latter being a racial harassment case and therefore of direct relevance to any discussion on sex discrimination/sexual harassment.

Mr and Mrs Irving, who are black and of Jamaican origin, lived next door to a Mr Edwards with whom they did not get on well. Mr Edwards was a postman whose duties included sorting mail. He was authorised to write on letters for the purpose of ensuring that they were properly dealt with. While sorting mail, he saw an envelope addressed to the Irvings. On the back he wrote 'Go back to Jamaica Sambo' along with a cartoon of a smiling mouth and eyes. The letter was delivered to the Irvings who were greatly upset by it and who sued the Post Office. In the Court of Appeal the one issue in dispute was whether the Post Office was vicariously liable for Mr Edwards's action in drawing and writing on the envelope. The Court of Appeal rehearsed the finding of the County Court to the effect that Mr Edwards was not authorised to do what he did and that he knew perfectly well that what he did was wrong. His act was wholly improper. Lord Justice Fox stated that since he was dealing with an act which was unauthorised by the employer, it was necessary to decide whether what was done was merely an unauthorised or prohibited mode of doing an authorised act or whether it was wholly outside the sphere of the employment so that the employers were not liable. He said:

> The doctrine of vicarious liability is necessary for the reasonable protection of innocent third parties. But out of fairness to employers, limits have to be set to it. That is perhaps more particularly evident in a case such as the present where the Post Office is sought to be made liable for the wilful wrongdoing of Edwards, which the Post Office in no way authorised. . . . the act of writing on the envelope was not part of the manner in which Edwards performed his duties, and does not become so merely because he did it quickly while on duty sorting mail. Save that it was done in working hours, it was unrelated to his duties.

The Court had cited to it two cases in which it had been said that judges should not divide the task which an employee was doing into separate component activities, but most look at the matter in the round, see *Rose* v. *Plenty* [1976] 1 WLR 141 and *Ilkiw* v. *Samuels* [1963] 1 WLR 991. It was urged on the Irvings' behalf that the job upon which Mr Edwards was engaged at the time that he wrote on the envelope was within the scope of that employment. The Court of Appeal rejected that argument, Mr Justice Sheldon saying that if it were to succeed it would establish a principle which other cases had expressly said to be wrong, namely that something was in the course of employment if the employment simply gave the opportunity for it to be done.

Against the background that the incident occurred during working hours, while Mr Edwards was engaged on his employer's behalf in sorting mail and that he was, for some purposes, permitted to write on envelopes, this is a decision which could very easily have gone the other way. It is regrettable that the Court of Appeal in dismissing the appeal used such strong language, because much of what they said could prevent any allegation of sexual harassment ever being held to be committed by an employee in the course of his employment. It shines through the judgments that the Court of Appeal was critical of the Irvings for not having been satisfied with disciplinary action that had been taken against Mr Edwards by the Post Office.

Fortunately the negative nature of the *Irving* decision may be mitigated by the decision of the Employment Appeal Tribunal in the recent case of *Bracebridge Engineering Limited* v. *Darby* [1990] IRLR 3. Mrs Darby left her place of employment to go and wash her hands prior to leaving work. She was permitted to do this some 10 minutes before the end of the official day. Her chargehand and the works manager saw her going, told her that it was too early for her to leave and picked her up bodily, carrying her into the chargehand's office where she was assaulted by having her legs placed around the body of one of them. At some stage the door was shut and the other groped under her skirt and made some obscene comment. Mrs Darby got free, left the office and complained to two women whom she saw before she left the premises. At the start of work the next day she complained to the general manager who made what the Industrial Tribunal subsequently found to be an insufficient investigation and effectively exonerated the two men. Mrs Darby gave a week's notice and left her employment, feeling that she was not prepared to stay in the circumsntaces. The Industrial Tribunal found that she had suffered sexual harassment amounting to sex discrimination for which the employers were liable and that she was unfairly dismissed. On appeal, there were two main arguments. The first was to the effect that since there was only one act of harassment of which complaint was made, it could not be sexual harassment because the verb 'to harass' implies a concept of repeated actions. The Employment Appeal Tribunal dismissed this argument. What is required is less favourable treatment: it does not matter whether that treatment fits some other definition or category.

The second argument was that the chargehand and supervisor had not been acting in the course of their employment at the time of the assault but had been on a frolic of their own. The Employment Appeal Tribunal was not impressed by this argument. The men had purported to be disciplining the applicant in connection with misconduct by her at her place of employment. They were clothed with the authority to carry out disciplinary action by the respondents. The whole event was part of an unauthorised mode by which they carried out their authorised functions. The Employment Appeal Tribunal was not prepared to analyse whether the men were authorised to pick Mrs Darby up, authorised to carry her into the room and so on. This decision may be seen as a victory for common sense and as indicating that sexual harassment claims can be sustained against employers even when based on the actions of fellow employees, at least where the activity is carried on by a supervisor or someone in a position of power in relation to the female employee (as is, of course, often the situation).

Has the employer taken 'such steps as were reasonably practicable' to prevent the discriminatory treatment (harassment)?

It must be that Parliament intended that employers should have the burden of establishing that they took some real steps to prevent acts of sexual harassment in order to escape liability by using this defence. Where, for example, a complaint is made but the harassment continues thereafter, it should be very difficult for an employer to show that he had taken reasonable steps to prevent it. What about cases where the employer simply does not know that the harassment is going on until the female employee leaves work or brings a claim in the Industrial Tribunal? Cynics will suggest that there is nothing that an employer can do in such circumstances. Experience from American cases teaches that this is not so. Employers can have and expound an equal opportunities policy. They should make it clear both in the equal opportunities policy and in disciplinary and grievance codes that sexual harassment will not be tolerated and that it will be regarded as serious misconduct. Of itself, this is insufficient. It is apparent that women are slow to complain of sexual harassment. They must be encouraged to do so in order to prevent the spread of such harassment and its disruptive effect. Employers should set up and promulgate some system whereby a woman will know to whom she can complain if harassment commences. It will not generally be appropriate to rely upon the usual system of line management complaints, because all too frequently harassment will come from the person directly responsible for a female employee. There should be every attempt to have a female employee out of the direct reporting line to whom employees can complain. They should know that their complaints will be taken seriously and that they will be followed up. Employers should liaise with trade unions as to how to deal with complaints. Managers must be encouraged to recognise sexual harassment. Above all, employers must be seen to deal with harassers. It is not appropriate, as happens all too frequently, that the woman who is making complaint should be moved from her job. In *Balgobin and Francis* v. *London Borough of Tower Hamlets* (above) when the women canteen workers who were being sexually harassed eventually complained to a female superior, she answered to the effect that the man also did the same to her! The women brought a claim in the Industrial Tribunal complaining in part that by virtue of the harassment they had had to work in an insalubrious environment. The Industrial Tribunal found the complaints of sexual harassment were true, but concluded that:

> No-one in authority knew what was going on prior to 24/10/85. Prior to that time the Respondents were running the hostel with proper and adequate supervision insofar as the staff were concerned. They had made known their policy of equal opportunities. We do not think that there were any other practicable steps which they could have taken to foresee or prevent the acts complained of.

In consequence the respondents made out the defence. On appeal the Employment Appeal Tribunal by a majority upheld the decision of the Industrial Tribunal, saying that it was very difficult to see what steps in practical terms the employers could reasonably have taken to prevent that which occurred from occurring. This is an answer which effectively makes a nonsense of the defence in the Act. In the event, there was demonstrably lax supervision and the Employment Appeal Tribunal conceded that it may well be that ‘the supervision could have been improved’.

Taken at face value the decision in *Balgobin and Francis* would drive a coach and horses through the Act. In practice, it may be hoped that as time passes and employers can be expected to become more aware of the dangers of sexual harassment, so tribunals will expect more of them.

Problems of Procedure

Privacy/publicity

Industrial Tribunal proceedings are heard in public and may be freely reported in newspapers, on television, etc. The governing regulations (SI 1985/16, Reg. 7) provide for a tribunal to sit in private where one of four criteria is satisfied, namely:

(1) Interests of national security require privacy.
(2) Evidence will involve the disclosure of information which it is prohibited by statute to disclose.
(3) Evidence will require the giving of information which was given to the witness in confidence.
(4) Evidence may consist of material the disclosure of which could cause substantial injury to the employer's business.

None of these encompasses the embarrassment/distress of a woman required to talk publicly of the details of a sexual assault and such cases are heard in public (unless, as on at least one occasion, the employer has sought a private hearing in order to avoid potential harm to his business!).

Although other Regulations give tribunals fairly wide procedural powers, none can be said to extend Regulation 7. The Contempt of Court Act 1981 provides for some restrictions on reporting of cases, but it is crafted primarily to suit criminal cases and is not an apt instrument for use in tribunal proceedings. In consequence cases of sexual harassment are likely to be heard in open tribunal and once the media knows of them, to receive extensive publicity.

One recent development is that where an allegation of rape is made, s. 4 of the Sexual Offences (Amendment) Act 1976, as amended by the Criminal Justice Act 1988, will serve to protect the anonymity of the victim/applicant. In essence, neither the woman's name or address nor any picture of her may be published in any way likely to identify her as a rape victim. Looking to the future, it is arguable that pursuant to Regulation 8 (1) (general discretion to conduct the proceedings as appears most suitable for their 'just handling') a tribunal could request witnesses and the media not to identify the victim of a sexual assault, or to use only an initial, at least until the case is concluded.

The widespread adherence in the United Kingdom to the principle of open justice is generally seen to be a laudable matter. It may not be appropriate to seek to depart from this principle in tribunal sexual harassment cases, but the corollary of this must be that there should be no trawling through a woman's sexual past in cross-examination.

Cross-examination

Mrs Snowball, a catering manager, alleged that she had been sexually harassed by her district manager in that he had asked her to make love on the office table, had sent her suggestive underwear and sex magazines and had pestered her with telephone calls. The manager denied the allegations. During Mrs Snowball's evidence she was cross-examined about her sexual attitudes in an attempt to show that, if the harassment had occurred, she had not suffered any injury to her feelings as a result. It was suggested that she had talked to fellow employees about her bed as a 'playpen' and about her black satin sheets. She denied this. The employers then wished to call evidence to establish the truth of the allegations which had been put in cross-examination. Mrs Snowball's Counsel objected but the Industrial Tribunal Chairman ruled that such evidence was admissible. On appeal, the Employment Appeal Tribunal held that the Industrial Tribunal was entitled to rule that evidence as to Mrs Snowball's attitude to matters of sexual behaviour was relevant and admissible. The basic principle of admissibility of evidence is that all evidence which is relevant is admissible. Compensation for sexual harassment must relate to the degree of detriment and, in that context, there has to be an assessment of the injury to the woman's feelings, which must be looked at both objectively with reference to what any ordinary reasonable female employee would feel and subjectively with reference to her as an individual. The evidence was relevant both for the purpose of determining whether whe was unlikely to be very upset by a degree of familiarity with a sexual connotation so as to challenge the detriment which she claimed to have suffered and any hurt feelings, and for the purpose of testing her credibility in relation to her denials in cross-examination.

What is wrong with this argument is that it assumes that a woman who may enjoy saucy talk in certain situations will not be upset or offended by advances from someone whom she does not like or in whom she is not interested. It is now recognised in criminal courts in the United Kingdom and it was also recognised in the case of *Wileman* (above) that consensual intimacy with A is no indication of consent to intimacy with B. In such circumstances, evidence of previous voluntary licentious behaviour cannot be evidence of a lack of detriment when participation is not voluntary. The *Wileman* case came later than Mrs Snowball's case and may be regarded as impliedly overruling what was said there.

Remedies

The effective remedy with which we are here concerned is the award of compensation, that is damages for injury to feelings, any resulting ill-health and repayment of financial losses such as wages. Concerning injury to feelings, tribunals have made awards varying from a nominal £50, to Ms Wileman, to £3000 to Mrs Fall, (decision of a Scottish tribunal, discussed above, in which the applicant suffered some 2½ years of unwanted amorous advances, including fondling and kissing) and most recently £6235 to Mrs Whittington in *Whittington* v. *Morris and Greenwich Health Authority* (unreported, Case No. 17846/89/LS), for some 14 months of harassment followed by a year in which she regularly met the perpetrator at work and was therefore distressed and upset. The award was made against the employers and the perpetrator of the harassment both of whom were sued in the Industrial Tribunal.

It may be that as people presenting claims become more used to sexual harassment cases, evidence will be martialled in such a way as to produce higher awards. Doctor's reports and expert psychiatric evidence will be seen to be appropriate, just as in any other personal injury action.

The Court of Appeal in *Alexander* v. *The Home Office* [1988] ICR 685 established that aggravated damages are available to the victims of racial discrimination, that is, additional damages to compensate for the hurt and humiliation suffered in all the circumstances. *Alexander* was brought under provisions of the Race Relations Act not relating to employment, but the aptness of aggravated damages in employment cases was accepted by an Industrial Tribunal when making an award under this head of £2000 in 1988 and it was not challenged by the employers when the case went on appeal, see *City of Bradford Metropolitan Council* v. *Arora* [1989] IRLR 442.

In *Alexander* an award of exemplary damages was also made, that is, the plaintiff was awarded a sum which was intended to punish the defendants for arbitrary and oppressive misuse of their public power. The Industrial Tribunal in *Arora* also awarded £1000 by way of exemplary damages for unlawful race and sex discrimination. On appeal this part of the decision was reversed on the basis that the facts (discriminatory interviewing and failure to shortlist) did not fall within the category of oppressive, arbitrary or unconstitutional acts, so that exemplary damages were not available. It was further suggested that had Parliament intended to introduce a punitive element into damages for discrimination it would have done so expressly.

To sum up: it seems probable that most acts of sexual harassment could give rise to a proper claim for aggravated damages, but that exemplary damages are unlikely to be obtainable.

The other remedies available pursuant to the Act are that tribunals may also make declarations as to the rights of the parties involved (unlikely to assist the victim of sexual harassment), and that they can make a recommendation as to the future conduct of the respondents. This is a vastly under-used power, but it is also one which is unlikely to benefit many applicants in sexual harassment cases. At best, if some clear grievance procedure and/or awareness training were to be recommended, those still in employment might hope to gain an improved environment, but only a tiny minority of the victims of harassment are still in the same employment at the date when their cases are decided. One such was Mrs Whittington (above) and the Tribunal in her case made a recommendation, upon which the employers acted, that the perpetrator should be moved to a post in which he would no longer meet the applicant at work.

Where the victim of sexual harassment has been dismissed (as in *Walsh* (above) or has resigned (as in *Bracebridge Engineering* v. *Darby* (above)) in circumstances which constitute constructive dismissal, relatively substantial damages for loss of earnings may be recovered, subject to the tribunal's statutory maximum (i.e. £8925, plus a set basic award assessed by age and length of service if unfair dismissal is also proved).

SUMMARY AND CONCLUSIONS

The Sex Discrimination Act 1975 was not designed to render sexual harassment unlawful but can usefully be interpreted so to do. There will frequently be difficulties relating to proof in cases that almost invariably arise from conduct committed while victim and perpetrator were alone together. None the less, tribunals have shown themselves prepared to believe women's complaints and to disbelieve their harasser's denials. Problems in relation to establishing the vicarious liability of the employer will persist: one way to deal with this is to join the harasser as a co-respondent, relying on the provisions of s. 42 ('aiding unlawful acts'). Levels of damages have not been high but may be expected to increase. Bringing a case is always likely to be a trying or distressing experience for the applicant: the support of friends and the presence of a concerned advocate (whether lawyer, friend or union representative) are invaluable. Subject to these caveats, there is now a clear, well-established legal route to a remedy for the employee who has suffered sexual harassment at work.

REFERENCE

Rubenstein, M. (1988). *Report on the Dignity of Women at Work*, EEC (available from HMSO).

Chapter 8.1

Lesbians and Gay Men in the Workplace: Psychosocial issues

Celia Kitzinger, Polytechnic of East London, UK

INTRODUCTION

In the office lunch hour, three women share sandwiches and gossip about their weekend. The first talks about her new boyfriend and the film they saw together; the second complains about her husband who spends Saturday night with his mates and refuses to help with the children or housework; the third, Sally, is silent and oddly evasive. The other two are accustomed to her reticence. Sometimes they tease her about it, sometimes they offer to introduce her to suitable men, and sometimes they wonder about her personal life, imagining an unrequited passion, or a secret affair with a married man. Nobody has guessed the truth; Sally has lived for the last eight years with her lesbian partner. Like most lesbians and gay men, she conceals her homosexuality in the workplace. Like most lesbians and gay men, she finds this concealment painful, a constant cause of stress and anxiety. Like most lesbians and gay men, she has heard too many anti-lesbian and anti-gay comments at work to risk coming out as lesbian herself.

This chapter explores the psychological, social and personal/political issues related to being gay or lesbian at work. What are the problems for people who, like Sally, conceal their homosexuality? What is involved in coming out as gay at work? How do heterosexuals react to such disclosures? And how can we all work to combat heterosexism in the workplace?

GAY INVISIBILITY AND THE HETEROSEXUAL ASSUMPTION

Most lesbians and gay men are in paid employment outside the home: like other people they have to support themselves. The overwhelming majority have their work choices primarily influenced by factors other than their

Vulnerable Workers: Psychosocial and Legal Issues. Edited by M. J. Davidson and J. Earnshaw

homosexuality—in particular, social class, race and gender. Unless they clearly indicate their sexual identity when applying for jobs (and few do), sexism, racism and classism are far more powerfully influential than heterosexism in determining employment opportunities, and gender is the single most significant determinant of an individual's location within the labour market. The majority of male workers are employed in jobs where the workforce is at least 90% male, while most female workers are in jobs which are at least 70% female (Phillips and Taylor, 1980). This is true for lesbians and gay men too: most gay men work in traditionally 'male' jobs, and most lesbians in traditionally 'female' jobs. Employed in such posts they are typically invisible as gays or lesbians.

Gay men's and lesbians' invisibility in the workplace is partly a function of the heterosexual assumption, whereby everyone is assumed to be heterosexual until proved otherwise. Heterosexuality is generally overtly displayed in the workplace—engagement and wedding rings, photographs of spouses or children on the desk. Casual conversations about weekend activities and new boyfriends or girlfriends, impending weddings, and flirtations between colleagues, all serve to confirm the workers' heterosexuality, and are often seen as ways of humanising an alienating workplace—'Just a bit of fun'. Heterosexual relationships are formed in the workplace: a survey of 645 readers of the magazine *Wedding Day* found that a quarter had met their marriage partner at work (cited in Hearn, 1985). Heterosexual relationships are reinforced when colleagues enquire after husbands or wives, or support each other through difficult experiences—a birth or death in the family, a divorce or remarriage. Other (to some, less acceptable) manifestations of heterosexuality in the workplace include bragging about (hetero)sexual conquests, anti-gay and anti-lesbian jokes, sexual harassment and pornographic displays (calendars, pin-ups) in men's canteens and offices. Women's presumed heterosexuality is on display in some jobs as part of the value of the commodity or labour power itself: some secretaries, receptionists, boutique assistants, airline hostesses are required to present themselves as attractively feminine, subservient and heterosexual (Hochschild, 1983): and the 'oldest profession' for women revolves around heterosexuality. In the overwhelming majority of workplaces heterosexuality is assumed as the natural and normal way to be. Heterosexual behaviour, mannerisms and clothing are openly exhibited and serve as a continual focus of conversation. In the face of this pervasive presentation of heterosexuality in the workplace, the traditional liberal attempt to impose a division between the 'private' and the 'public' domains cannot be sustained. Contrary to the common assertion that sexuality belongs in the 'private' domain and work in the 'public', it seems that heterosexuality has established a virtually unchallenged monopoly of the public arena (Hearn, 1985; Kitzinger, 1987a).

DECEPTION AND SUBTERFUGE

While the heterosexual men and women who construct and act to perpetuate it are typically unaware of this pervasive heterosexual consensus, lesbians and gay men in the workplace are usually acutely conscious of the heterosexual assumption, and experience themselves as 'outsiders' or 'aliens'. Most attempt to fit in by assuming a heterosexual front. Even among those lesbians and gay men who are sufficiently open about their homosexuality to risk taking part as subjects in research, it is consistently found that about three-quarters engage in various forms of subterfuge to conceal their homosexuality in the workplace (Hedblom, 1972; Moses, 1978; Hedblom and Hartman, 1980; Friend, 1980; Levine and Leonard, 1984; Schneider, 1984). Such subterfuges may include careful conformity with gender-role stereotypes (skirts, long hair and make-up for women, and a macho demeanour for men), introducing lovers or partners as 'friends', avoiding casual conversations about home life, changing pronouns, inventing—or even acquiring—suitably remote financé(e)s or spouses, passing appreciating remarks about the opposite sex, and inviting a gay person of the other gender to social functions. Interviews carried out by the author with 10 gay men and 14 lesbians in the course of preparing this chapter (all unattributed quotations come from these interviews) reveal that such subterfuge is commonplace: 'I do on occasion set out to deceive them,' admitted one secondary school teacher in her forties. 'I talk about heterosexual relationships, or about a boyfriend of mine, because I can, because I've had them, and it's not a lie. It's just not heartfelt, it's not *essentially* true.' A gay man described how he dressed for committee meetings: 'I can do it quite well. I've got a set of clothes in my wardrobe I call my "hetty outfit" and I slick down my hair and paste a parting in it and I wear my tie and I can look very straight.'

DISCRIMINATION AGAINST GAYS AND LESBIANS

Concealment of homosexuality is rooted in fear of ostracism, taunts, violence, discrimination, harassment and the loss of jobs. The infamous s. 28 (Chapter 8.2) prevents school teachers from presenting 'positive images' of homosexuality in the classroom, and a recent survey found that fewer than one in three British people thought it acceptable for homosexuals to be employed as schoolteachers, while 70% believed homosexual relationships to be always or mostly wrong (Jowell, Witherspoon and Brook, 1986). Because most people believe that children should be socialised into heterosexuality at home and at school, and because anti-gay attitudes are used to reinforce traditional gender-role stereotypes (Kitzinger and Kitzinger,

1989), homosexuals who work with children are particularly likely to bear the brunt of anti-gay discrimination and prejudice. Heterosexual employers often subscribe to a 'corruption theory' of homosexuality, believing that other employees or vulnerable client groups (children, the mentally ill) will succumb to homosexual pressure or temptation, and the gay person is seen as rampantly sexual, driven by indiscriminate sexual desire. Many also adhere to oppressive notions that lesbians and gay men are 'sick' or 'perverted', or that they suffer from character defects such as instability or untrustworthiness. Although there is no support for such views in the psychological literatures (e.g. Freedman, 1975; Kitzinger, 1987a), many people still believe them, and this has negative consequences for homosexuals. Three-fifths of the women interviewed in one study predicted discrimination if they were discovered to be lesbian, often citing examples of discrimination against other gay people as evidence: 'I would not come out to my supervisor because there was a woman who did and she went through hell! My supervisor mocked her and abused her and eventually fired her. I know I would be too', or 'I know I would be fired. There is a lot of gay-baiting in my office as well as anti-gay remarks and jokes. One gay man was already fired' (Levine and Leonard, 1984). These fears seem to have some foundation in reality: a quarter of lesbians in this study reported actual instances of job discrimination (Levine and Leonard, 1984). In another study, 12% said that they were asked to resign, were fired, or were given warnings when their homosexuality became known to their employers (Saghir and Robins, 1973), and about one-fifth of Bell and Weinberg's (1978) respondents said that their homosexuality had had a harmful effect on their careers, with 21% of the white homosexual males saying that they lost or almost lost their jobs because of it. The respondents I interviewed reported similar fears:

> I would like to be out at work but, you know, you can lose jobs just on the sheer fact of being lesbian. And now with Clause 28 teachers are particularly vulnerable. I mean, I work with five- and six-year-olds and they're all very affectionate and there's lots of physical contact. I don't know how that would be viewed differently if they knew I was a lesbian.

> I'm not out at work because I'm a paid worker in a voluntary organisation and they rely on people donating large sums of money, and it would only take one of them to take exception to the fact that there's a lesbian on the pay role and it would make life very difficult—for the organisation, and for me.

> I think if the committee as a whole knew they had two homosexual men working with children they'd be horrified, because of course we all know that all homosexuals pervert children! And with Clause 28 you only have to have a nosy neighbour stick a head around the door . . . So I live knowing that if

> someone wants to do the dirty on us, they could, and we'd probably lose our jobs.

Because of fears like these, many gay people monitor their mannerisms, clothing and appearance in order to become 'just like everyone else, only more so'. For most this is experienced as leading a double life; their self-presentation at work is 'a façade', 'a mask', 'an act', 'a total sham'.

ALIENATION AT WORK: STRESS AT HOME

The psychological, sociological and sexological literature on homosexuality vividly describes the resulting sense of alienation. Gay men and lesbians in the workplace have, in Goffman's (1963) terms, a 'discreditable identity'—an identity which, if it became known, could lead to persecution. According to Schneider (1984) 'closeted lesbians suffer from a sense of powerlessness and significant strain and anxiety at work . . . and 39 per cent felt that the anxiety about being found out was paralysing'. A gay man, quoted in Bell and Weinberg (1978), describes how 'you have to be on your guard . . . like when straight guys would discuss their sex exploits, I had to keep quiet and felt uncomfortable', and another feels 'chronic, severe anxiety—to the point of being incapacitated on the job . . . It's the loneliness, the feelings of guilt, fear of rejection.' A gay man, who works as an engineer with British Telecom told me:

> It's virtually all male and there's a lot of swearing, and they're very macho and loud and into cars and women and football . . . When I first started it was very very difficult and I didn't enjoy it at all. They kept prying and asking 'what did you do last night?', and because they realised I was single they tried to fix me up with women.

A lesbian in her forties whose jobs have included nursing, librarianship, gardening and secretarial work said:

> I've always felt marginalised at work, on the edge, never felt like one of the gang. In the past, apprehension about how people might treat me negatively affected my self-confidence. There were years when there was nobody, nothing, to say 'no, you needn't be stuck on the margin'. It was a precarious existence . . . It's affected my career and my ability to stay in jobs. I was always changing my career, hoping to find somewhere I would feel at home.

Among closeted gay men and lesbians, a constant self-consciousness is commonplace, along with anxious self-questioning, 'Have they guessed?' and 'What would they do if they knew?'

The feeling of marginalisation derives in part from the fact that one's most important relationships and experiences are uncommunicable: 'the tensions that come when people are talking about their home life and you realise that your home life is unmentionable—the subject of continual little lies, constant small evasions'. A lesbian who feels 'cut off' from other people describes how women at work 'come in all red eyed and weeping saying, "The bastard's left me and ain't it awful, darling" ... but you can't come in red eyed and weeping and say, "My girl-friend has played me up". So this is why I say up to a point you are cut off' (quoted in Ettorre, 1980, p.33). Lesbians and gay men who decide not to interrupt heterosexual assumptions cannot share experiences like these, cannot casually talk about their lover, or show 'excessive' concern when their 'flatmate' moves out or when their 'friend' is ill. If they do, they are often seen as 'flaunting their sexuality', or become the objects of voyeuristic interest. 'I am so struck by the difference between my divorce from Mary and my breakup with John,' said a young accountant who has worked with the same firm for four years. 'When I was going through the divorce, everyone was supportive and nice, asked me how I was feeling, sympathised, and shared their own experiences with me. Now John and I are separating after two years (exactly the same time I was with Mary) and nobody wants to talk about it. In fact, I think some of them see it as a good thing, and hope that I'll go back to women again.'

Gay people are deprived, too, of public celebration of positive events in their lives. Jenny, who works in catering, describes what happened after her lover had a baby (conceived by artificial insemination) three years ago: 'I was so excited and hyped up, I rushed into work and told everyone, "Laura's had a girl, eight pounds, and this is how the labour went . . .", and they were just embarrassed and didn't know what to say, because I'm not the child's father and I'm not the child's mother, and they don't know how to place me. And then all those conversations about teething and toilet-training and first words—other mothers with kids the same age seem to think I'm an interloper.' Steven contrasted, with some resentment, the public celebrations of his workmates' engagements, weddings and anniversaries, with his own imposed silence about his 25-year relationship with another man.

Employment occupies a large proportion of most people's lives, and colleagues are a significant source of support and shared information about relationships, which can be especially important during crisis periods—a divorce or remarriage, death of a partner, birth of a child. Lesbians and gay men lack this support for their identities and relationships, and the absence of any kind of validation can have serious consequences for those relationships. 'It's like wearing armour at work,' one man explained, 'and it's difficult to shed that armour when I get home — not to feel tense, alert for danger, defensive, when I want to be open and trusting with Mike'. A woman told me 'I don't like Kate to ring me at work, and if we meet after work I walk round the corner and she picks me up out of sight. The problem is that Kate doesn't appreciate the need for secrecy. She resents it that I have to keep her existence a secret, she feels as though I must be ashamed of her. She doesn't seem to understand that caution is essential in my job—we argue about it a lot.'

The imposed rift between the 'private' (lesbian/gay) self and the 'public' employee with the heterosexual persona, can be a source of strain, tension and considerable conflict. There are added worries, too, when legal issues discriminate against gay relationships—when a pension does not cover the partner, when relocation expenses are for one person plus legally defined 'spouse' only, when free education or crèche facilities cover the children only of employee and 'spouse', and not those of the gay person's partner. These anomalies are not just expensive and unfair: they also cause stress, frustration and anxiety, particularly for lesbians whose salaries, like those of women generally, are low anyway and for whom the additional financial worry contributes to the overall lack of validation of gay relationships. The Weinberg–Collins research, published in the mid-1970s, documented different attitudes of homosexuals as compared with general samples of the population. Of the homosexual research sample, 34% felt that 'no one cares what happens to you' (compared with a 23% response from the general population), and when asked if most people could be trusted, 53% of the gay group answered 'no', compared with less than half that percentage of heterosexuals (cited in Ehrlich, 1981). It is easy to see how the stresses and conflicts of the workplace can contribute to this negative view of life.

Some 'gay affirmative' psychologists, concerned about the image of furtive and tortured secrecy that surrounds the homsexual's life, have suggested that there may be positive pay-offs. Gay people in hiding may, says Freedman (1975), become quite sophisticated about the masks people wear, about the relationship between identity and role, and they may also engage in 'creative' (i.e. subterfuge) opposition to the *status quo*. The trauma of coming to terms with being homosexual is also supposed to give a gay person 'crisis competence': 'it may provide a perspective on major life crises and a sense of competence that buffers the person against later crises' (Kimmel, 1978). These alleged psychological 'benefits' are, like the financial savvy of the Jew, or black althleticism, a legacy of oppression.

WORKING IN GAY OR LESBIAN ENVIRONMENTS

Very few gay men and lesbians are able to avoid the stresses involved in working in heterosexual environments. Certain jobs (e.g. for men, hairdressing, interior design, dancing or theatre) have a reputation for being 'safe' for homosexuals, and gay people may curtail their career choices accordingly.

Michael left his job as a builder because of the rampant heterosexism he encountered:

> Having to prove you're a he-man all the bloody time is a pain in the neck. So much of being a he-man is about bragging about the women you're screwing. I wish these men could hear themselves sometimes—they seem to be driven by a pathological need to prove they're not gay. I've got gay friends who are accountants, things like that. They also work mostly with men, but maybe it's not quite so difficult in that sort of set-up just because posh men aren't so upfront about sex and women. (Quoted in Greater London Council, 1985, p.61)

He now works instead as a hairdresser:

> I wanted to work somewhere where I could be free to be who I am. In hairdressing, particularly at the top, you can be as unconventional as you like. I chose this work because I couldn't bear stupid bigots any more, and because I knew there were plenty of people like me in hairdressing. I wanted to be free, and I wanted to be amongst my own kind. (Quoted in Greater London Council, 1985, p.62)

Self-employment and employment in lesbian or gay businesses provide other attractive alternatives for a privileged minority of gay people. A lesbian car mechanic who worked in a garage run by two lesbians, with nine other lesbian employees, described how 'you could go in and when you're sitting around having lunch you could talk about your family, you could talk about your lover, you could talk about what you did last night. It's real nice to get that out and share that.' Lovers were welcomed into the shop during business hours: 'There's nothing like walking into a women's business and being able to walk right up to my lover and kiss her and have lunch with her and have my kids behind me, our kids. But you can't do that in the straight world, you know? It was a real valuable place to be' (Weston and Rofel, 1984). Working with other gay people means that homosexuality is taken for granted and does not have to be concealed, explained, or propogandised: there is a shared set of meanings and understandings about relationships and sexuality.

Listening to lesbians and gay men talking about work in these 'protected' environments makes clear how difficult and painful work in heterosexual environments can be by contrast—and it is these heterosexual, and heterosexist, workplaces with which most must contend. One way of coping is to deny that pain. In fact, many homosexuals draw on the discourse of 'private' and 'public' domains to justify their partial concealment: 'I don't talk about my sexuality at work, no. I think that's absurd, even if you're normal. I just sort of switch off my personal concerns and get on with the job in hand'; 'I keep myself to myself, and don't discuss my private life—it's none of their concern what I do in my own time, as long as I do what

I'm supposed to at work.' Gay people who make such assertions have then to deny the extent to which heterosexuality occupies the public domain, and in particular the workplace.

COMING OUT

Coming out at work is sometimes a direct response to the insistent and blatant heterosexuality of the workplace—an end-of-tether reaction to intolerable pressures, rather than a carefully weighed decision. Veronica Clare was a supply teacher for Buckinghamshire County Council: 'during my fifteen months there I was pushed, sworn at, told I had AIDS . . . I finally blew my top and admitted to a class that I was a lesbian and that I was sick of being treated so badly'. She was forced to leave her job (*Lesbian Information Service Newsletter*, 1987). Another woman 'walked out of a job because there had been lots of anti-gay comments in the office and I finally said, "stop this—I'm gay", and then I rushed off and handed in my notice because I couldn't cope with what I'd done. I didn't know how they were going to take it, and I didn't want to hang around to find out.' Tony was 'fed up with the continual racism at work and I finally exploded, and said "look, if you want to be really offensive, why don't you pick on me for being gay as well as black—I'm homosexual too, you know". So of course, they did. And I had to leave.'

'Coming out' at work is rarely a one-off event: there are always new colleagues, new clients, new students. For most gay people, not prone to explosive revelations, the gruelling reality is that coming out is never finished. Lesbians and gay men are forced to make daily decisions about whether or not to say, whether or not to interrupt the assumptions being made about their presumed heterosexuality, weighing up the risks and possible repercussions of each and every situation. Because coming out has to be continually redone, many gay people are neither 'in' nor 'out' at work, but in some intermediate situation: some people know or suspect they are lesbian or gay, others do not. Many told me that they had never actually *said* they were gay but that 'people must know'; they have refused to assume a heterosexual front, but have also avoided explicit statement of their homosexuality. A 52-year-old senior tutor in a nurse training school told me: 'I think most people would probably know what my leanings are, because I lived with someone for 25 years and was obviously very fond of her, you know. But you just didn't talk about these things.' A social worker says: 'I presume I'm out at work, because I've written things with my name on, and I put a motion forward at a trade union meeting, in my name, for the gay rights issue, so I presume that people at work know I'm a lesbian, because I've never hidden the fact—although no one has ever discussed it with me.' A woman who works as a secretary in the same university department as her lover, a research assistant, said: 'I'm not blatantly out at work, but because Rachel works in the same department, and she's very uncompromisingly out, I'm assuming that people do know. I'm letting it ride on assumptions and gossip. I mean, Rachel is seen to be who I live with. I'm not totally comfortable with that, but, you know, anything for a quiet life.' While many gay people do find that this partial openness is congenial—they neither lie, nor do they challenge heterosexual assumptions with unpalatable truths about their lives—it too has its costs, particularly in the uncertainty it creates about who knows what, and the nasty surprises that can result. 'I thought everyone at work knew I was gay,' a banking clerk said, 'I'd never said I was, but I'd never tried to hide it either. But then when I finally made it explicit, saying I was going on a gay rights march one weekend, everyone reacted with horror and outrage. I was shocked at the reaction—it seemed as though it was okay to *be* gay as long as I never talked about it.' As Hodges and Hutter (1974) point out, 'to share the knowledge of one's homosexuality with non-gay people, but never to speak of it, is to tacitly agree that, like bad breath, homosexuality is something embarrassing, best left unmentioned.' To believe this is itself another legacy of oppression.

Attempting to avoid this uncertainty and silence, Rachel comments that 'it is much easier to go up to people and say "hello, I'm Rachel and I'm a lesbian", which is what I do now, instead of looking for the so-called "right time", because there never *is* a "right" time'. But coming out in so uncompromising a fashion does not solve all these problems—in fact, it often creates new ones. Even if they are not sacked, forced to resign, denied promotion, physically attacked or verbally abused—and many are—there are subtler forms of discrimination which are also painful and can have far-reaching effects. 'I've felt *terrible* when I've lied about myself,' confesses Barbara, 'and in my last job I did lie a lot, and I felt so vulnerable and such a traitor to myself, and I'd come home and think, "if I can't speak the truth it means this relationship isn't as important as someone else's marriage". So now I do tell, and each time I've spent at least two hours calming them down, answering the same questions and dealing with the same stereotypes, and I'm beginning to wonder, is it worth telling someone when you have to explain yourself so much?' A nurse who works with mentally handicapped children came out as gay a few months ago. Since then he has never been left alone with the boys, and 'people have weird ideas about AIDS so that nobody will drink out of a mug I've used'. His relationship with his partner of eight years has become rocky: 'It's as though I'm saying to Kevin, "okay, prove to me that you're worth all this hassle I'm going through at work", and that doesn't make for a good relationship.' Wendy describes similar problems: 'Telling people I work with that I wasn't willing to listen to the "queer" jokes any more was the beginning of my coming out to them. It was also the worst time for sex in my life. Somehow being so vulnerable to my co-workers made it impossible for me to be close to Trish. Almost like I could only stand so much openness' (quoted in Loulan, 1984, pp.124–5).

When only one of the partners in a gay relationship decides to come out at work, this may create real difficulties for the couple. 'I feel Claire is pressuring me to be more public,' one woman said, 'and I am forced into a situation where everyone knows about me because they know about Claire. In a sense she's taken away my right to make my own decision about that, and I resent it.' These problems may be particularly acute when the members of the couple are of a different status, or subject to different oppressions. According to Mark, 'My lover says, "if you really loved me you wouldn't care what your co-workers thought—you'd come out at work like I have": the difference for me is that my co-workers are part of my community as a black person, and in a racist society I *need* that community in a way he doesn't understand.' Rachel's lover, Eve, says, 'every time Rachel kisses me at work I look round to see who she's doing it for. It's always a political statement.'

Coming out does not obviate the need for identity management around sexuality—it only changes its form. Identity management for the closeted gay person is designed to project an image of heterosexuality: identity management for the out lesbian or gay man is designed to project an image of homosexuality that will 'correct' whatever stereotypes or misconceptions the gay person's colleagues are seen as holding. This form of identity management can be, in many ways, as problematic as passing for straight. For example, gay men who try to conceal their homosexuality may be especially concerned to avoid looking 'feminine' (long hair, earrings, or brightly coloured clothes), just as closeted lesbians often try to avoid any hint of 'masculinity' (short hair, trousers), lest their apparent failure to conform with traditional gender-role expectations be seen as a clue to their sexual identity. Ironically, this concern about appropriate gender-role behaviour may be exacerbated by lesbians and gay men who are out at work: 'There's this stereotype that all lesbians are big tough butch women in trousers and crew cuts,' said a librarian whose colleagues know she is lesbian, 'so I make a special effort to do my hair nicely, and wear quite feminine clothing, skirts and make-up, just to sort of say, "look, we're not all like that"'. Another woman worries about the butch femme stereotype: 'My lover and I aren't into roles at all—they're rubbish', she says, 'but because I have short hair and a boyish figure and my lover is more conventionally feminine than I am, I feel people at work see us that way, and I hate it. So I keep dropping comments about how she fixed the car at the weekend while I was cooking dinner—things like that, designed to undermine their stereotypes.' A nurse never mentions any conflicts or problems in her relationship with her lover, 'because I want heterosexual women to realise that life with women is *better*'. 'Everybody thinks gay men are promiscuous,' said a schoolteacher in a long-term relationship, 'so I go out of my way to talk about my cosy home life, but sometimes I feel I'm presenting a totally unrealistic rosy picture of married gay bliss'. Other gay people choose to conform precisely with the conventional stereotypes as a way of reassurring heterosexuals that they are predictable, safe 'deviants': 'I camp it up rather, the limp wrist and all, because then they think they know where they are with me. And they can reassure themselves that they are stiff-wristed heterosexuals.'

TOUCH

Physical contact in the workplace—as part of giving comfort, or instruction, as horseplay or help, as well as flirtation—is very common, and is often part of the job itself—caring for the sick or physically handicapped, working with children or old people. Heterosexual women may cuddle and hug, heterosexual men may indulge in horseplay, but gay people are usually more cautious and may feel very uneasy about touching people at work. 'I never join in the horseplay with the others,' one man told me, 'because whereas for them it's just seen as "messing about", if I did it, they might see it in sexual terms.' Val Carpenter, a youth worker, describes how:

> It's not unusual on girls' weekends or at women workers' conferences for them to be demonstrative with each other, or with the young women, while we remain caught in the straight-jacket of frigidity while we are in the public eye. It remains perfectly acceptable for heterosexual women to enjoy the benefits of relaxing in an all-women atmosphere, even kissing and hugging with other women, while dropping Tom, Dick or Harry into conversation as convenient. But as soon as any lesbians stand 'too close' to each other, or to them, they get jumpy. (Carpenter, 1988, p.179)

'I've never touched a woman in public since I was 14,' said another lesbian, talking about the uneasiness she felt at being asked to guide a blind colleague in an unfamiliar environment: 'I felt totally exposed'. When a heterosexual colleague's baby died, Hannah wanted to hold and comfort her as she wept, but worried about whether the touch would be misinterpreted as a sexual advance and envied the other women's easy confidence when they hugged her. Alison is 'very careful about how I touch women. I don't want people to get the wrong idea, and heterosexual colleagues get jumpy when ever I stand too close.' On the other hand, Barbara's experience is also quite common: 'there's this woman at work who touches me a lot—

she's overfriendly. It's sort of over-compensation, a self-conscious display of tolerance; she's proving she knows lesbianism isn't infectious!'

SEXUAL HARASSMENT

While many lesbians avoid physical contact with women at work, they are often subjected to it from men. They are sexually harassed not just as women, but also specifically as lesbians. One study found that 82% of lesbians had been sexually propositioned, pinched, grabbed, or experienced other sexual approaches (Schneider, 1984). One woman described to me how she was 'pinioned up against the wall by the head chef—I was the second chef—because he thought he was God's gift to women, and because I resisted his advances he had the hump'. Another, reflecting on the prevalence of pseudo-lesbian images in pornography, described how 'this guy, who was considerably senior to me, and who I didn't want to be rude to, told me how he'd always wanted to go to bed with two lesbians, and did I have a partner? I felt so humiliated.' Because of the sexualisation of black women, black lesbians are particularly vulnerable to this kind of abuse. Other lesbians are approached by men anxious to prove that 'you just haven't met the right man yet'.

Gay men, too may be subjected to physical abuse and harassment. Sometimes this comes from men who identify as heterosexual. Talking about his boss, one man told me 'he uses sexual gestures and innuendoes to put me down, to make me feel inferior to him, in a "feminine" role. He's straight, and I don't think it's a sexual thing, so much as a power trip. He's using my sexuality to assert his own power.' Some gay men talked with me about their experience of sexual harassment from women who smile seductively and say things like, 'what a pity you're gay, you're so attractive,' or who imagine that they simply haven't met the 'right woman' yet. While gay men undoubtedly find these advances unpleasant and embarrassing, the experience of sexual harassment is generally much less threatening for men. As one gay man told me, 'I can say, "do you want me to knock your block off", because I can do that—I can hold my own in a real physical sense. I think we men have an advantage there.'

COMBATING HETEROSEXISM AT WORK

Most people who have come out at work feel torn between two extreme responses. Many feel trapped by their colleagues' perception of them into being *nothing but* 'a homosexual', with everything they say and do filtered through that label, with no appreciation at all of their other interests and involvements as human beings. Eve described how 'when people know it colours their whole perception of you. For example, someone from another department phoned up and when I answered she asked, "Is that Gay Smith", and I said, "This is *Eve* Smith", and she realised what she'd said and was very embarrassed and apologised profusely.' Or, equally problematic, the gay person is reassured that 'it doesn't make any difference', and colleagues immediately 'forget' or gloss over the new information, never raising the matter again—as though it were of no importance, as though the people we love and the relationships we have (as hetero- or homosexuals) don't fundamentally affect who we are as human beings. One woman told her boss she was lesbian, and was immediately reassured 'She said, "don't worry, it doesn't make any difference", and I said to her "you don't understand—I'm telling you because I *want* it to make a difference". Of course she didn't have a clue what I meant.'

No one hides his or her homosexuality for 10, 20, 40 years, without this concealment, this fear of discovery and rejection, manifesting itself in each and every aspect of a person's life. No one comes out as gay in a world which denies or condemns their existence, without the stereotypes and prejudices, the curiosity, hostility, voyeurism, and disgust colouring their whole life and permeating all their relationships.

Those heterosexuals who express their concern about anti-gay discrimination frequently do so in the form of advice to gays about how they should behave. 'If only,' say the liberals, 'you behaved with more discretion and dignity instead of shouting your sexuality from the rooftops—what you do in bed is nobody's business but your own'. 'If only,' say the radicals, 'you would *all* come out of hiding—if people realised how many of you there were, people they liked and respected, you could combat the stereotypes'.

But it is not the behaviour of homosexuals, who are oppressed whether in or out of the closet, that is the problem. The problem is the behaviour of heterosexuals. Combating heterosexism in (and beyond) the workplace is the responsibility of each and every person in this country. Based on the material and arguments presented in this chapter and elsewhere (e.g. Goodman *et al.*, 1983; Greater London Council, 1985; Kitzinger, 1987b), the following recommendations are proposed.

At the level of individual attitudes, everyone in the workplace should be aware of heterosexism as a potential problem and take steps to tackle it. It is especially important to recognise that heterosexism in the workplace affects *everyone*. The fear of being accused of homosexuality affects anyone who might be tempted to step outside conventional gender-role stereotypes. A heterosexual man who supported women's objections to pornographic calendars in the office was accused of being a 'poufter'; and women who express strong feminist or anti-sexist views may be accused of being 'man-hating lesbians'. Being lesbian/gay is *good*: nothing short of that will suffice for an answer.

Tackling heterosexism means facing up to the fact that open lesbians and gay men may be assaulted, abused, ridiculed or ostracised, and speaking out against such behaviour, and it involves challenging anti-gay or anti-lesbian jokes and derogatory comments in the same way that racist or sexist jokes should be challenged. One secondary school visited by the author had a prominent display of spoof election posters the children had made, including one illustrated with a caricature of an effeminate gay man, reading, 'If you want pansies, vote for the Ecology Party'. This is offensive and demeaning to gay people; the fact that it was publically displayed in a school entry hall illustrates the degree of acceptability anti-gay attitudes have today. Sometimes it is the assumptions as well as anti-gay statements which need challenging—such as the assumption that divided sleeping arrangements between females and males rules out the possibility of sexual interaction, an assumption which supports the invisibility of gay people. Challenging heterosexism in the workplace means questioning the heterosexual assumption, and understanding that there may always be closeted gay people within earshot, wondering how safe the environment is for them. The responsibility for objecting to heterosexist behaviour should not always rest with gay people and if heterosexuals who challenge anti-gay comments are then assumed to be gay themselves, they should not rush to correct that assumption. In general, heterosexuals should be aware of the privilege they rely on when they signal their heterosexuality (e.g. references to husband or wife, engaging in public physical affection). It is also important that heterosexuals should never force someone they think may be gay to come out, nor demand that gay people confide in them about their personal lives.

More positively, lesbians and gay men often speak with great warmth about those heterosexuals who are willing to offer non-judgemental support and comfort to gay people who need it, and who are willing to celebrate lesbian and gay achievements and relationships. It is not always obvious to heterosexuals in what ways they can be helpful to gay people: they may give offence unintentionally simply because few heterosexuals are fully aware of the depth and range of oppression lesbians and gay men suffer. The best solution is to *ask*! A lesbian mother told me of the gratitude she felt for her son's primary school teacher, a young heterosexual woman:

> All his class were asked to draw a plan of their house and label the rooms, 'kitchen', 'bathroom', 'my bedroom', 'baby sister's bedroom' and so on. Patrick had done this, and one of the rooms was down as 'Lucy and Mum's bedroom'. Apparently the other kids wanted to know who Lucy was and why she didn't sleep in the 'spare room'. His teacher sent me a note the next day apologising for having set the children this task, as it had upset Patrick. She hadn't realised, she said, how intrusive it was, and she asked us how we would like

> to handle anything similar in future. We realised that trying to hide it from the school wasn't going to be much good, so Lucy and I went in and had a talk with her, and she was great. The problem is that I had a custody case pending, so we couldn't afford to be too explicit about our lesbianism, and she understood that but was supportive too.

One gay psychiatric nurse described how, when he left his job to move in with his lover in another town: 'my workmates organised a leaving party which was a touching celebration of the relationship between Keith and myself. About thirty of us gathered in a hotel... they toasted Keith and me [Keith had come up for the day to join in] and bought us a slow cooker for our new home. I wept buckets, but it wasn't until later that I realised what had happened. These people—ordinary working-class folk like me—had come together to celebrate a gay relationship and to wish it success and happiness (Sanderson, 1988, p.93)

However, heterosexism is not simply a result of individual attitudes. Like sexism and racism, heterosexism is institutional. It is deeply ingrained in our society and its institutions and challenging individual attitudes alone will not remove the way that employment practices and methods discriminate against lesbians and gay men. People with responsibility for organisational policies and personnel issues can address institutionalised heterosexism by checking the recruitment and promotion procedures, and the conditions of service and contractual agreements with employees. Most jobs are advertised in the classified columns of the local press. Given the prejudice against lesbians and gays which is often found in such newspapers, many gay people, not surprisingly, do not read them. Most application forms ask potential employees to state their marital status, which causes many lesbians and gay men (particularly older ones, as an 'unmarried' status becomes increasingly unusual with age) to feel wary. Anti-gay clauses in contracts or conditions of service are very common, for example pension schemes or relocation allowances that exclude a same-sex partner, or denial of crèche, sports or canteen facilities to a same-sex partner. Paternity leave, and leave to accompany a pregnant woman to antenatal care, is granted by some employers to fathers, but not to the lesbian co-mother; and compassionate leave (special leave for death or illness) is often limited to the spouse and blood relatives of the employee. When the staff of one large voluntary organisation went through the written conditions of service to look for examples of heterosexist discrimination, they found 11 regulations which clearly excluded lesbians and gays from their provisions (Greater London Council, 1985). Because conditions of service vary considerably from one employer to another, heterosexism in this area can only be eradicated by ensuring that all conditions of service agreements are written down and each paragraph checked to ensure that it applies to all employees—heterosexual, gay, and lesbian alike.

As long as anti-homosexuality in the workplace goes unchallenged, gay men and lesbians will continue to be 'vulnerable workers'—vulnerable to threats, abuse, discrimination and assault. And heterosexuals, too, are placed in a 'vulnerable' position in which their privilege is bought at the cost of other people's oppression, which only their ignorance and the silence of their colleagues prevents them from seeing. It is not just Sally, the lesbian secretary whose story began this chapter, who is suffering because of heterosexism in the workplace, but also her heterosexual co-workers who are denied access to the truths of her life and experience as a lesbian. It is in the interests of *everyone*, gay and straight, to challenge heterosexism in and beyond the workplace, so that we all can make freer and better informed choices about our lives.

ACKNOWLEDGEMENTS

I would like to thank Peter Kent-Baguley, Harriette Marshall and Kate Gleeson for their help in locating interviewees, and for some stimulating discussions on this topic. Naturally, responsibility for the arguments of this chapter is, however, mine alone.

REFERENCES

Bell, A.P. and Weinberg, M.S. (1978). *Homosexualities: A Study of Diversity Among Men and Women*, Mitchell Beazley, London.

Carpenter, V. (1988). Amnesia and antagonism: Anti-lesbianism in the youth service. In B. Cant and S. Hemmings (eds) *Radical Records: Thirty Years of Lesbian and Gay History*, Routledge, London.

Ehrlich, L.G. (1981). The pathogenic secret. In J.W. Chesebro (ed.) *Gay Speak*, Pilgrim Press, New York.

Ettorre, B. (1980). *Lesbians, Women and Society*, Routledge and Kegan Paul, London.

Freedman, M. (1975). Homosexuals may be healthier than straights, *Psychology Today*, **8**, 28–32.

Friend, R. (1980). GAYging: Adjustment and the older gay male, *Alternative Lifestyles*, **3**(2), 231–48.

Goffman, E. (1963). *Stigma: Notes on the Management of Spoiled Identity*, Penguin, London.

Goodman, G., Lakey, G., Lashof, J. and Thorne, E. (1983). *No Turning Back: Lesbian and Gay Liberation for the '80s*, New Society Publishers, Philadelphia.

Greater London Council (1985). *Danger! Heterosexism at Work: A Handbook on Equal Opportunities in the Workplace for Lesbians and Gay Men*, Greater London Council, London.

Hearn, J. (1985). Men's sexuality at work, In A. Metcalf and M. Humphries (eds) *The Sexuality of Men*, Pluto Press, London.

Hedblom, J.H. (1972). The female homosexual: Social and attitudinal dimensions.

In J.A. McCaffrey (ed.) *The Homosexual Dialectic*, Prentice Hall, Englewood Cliffs, NJ.

Hedblom, J.H. and Hartman, J.J. (1980). Research on lesbianism: Selected effects of time, geographic location, and data collection technique, *Archives of Sexual Behaviour*, **9**, 217–34.

Hochschild, A.R. (1983). *The Managed Heart*, University of California Press, Berkeley.

Hodges, A. and Hutter, D. (1974). *With Downcast Gays: Aspects of Homosexual Self-Oppression*, Pink Triangle Press, Toronto.

Jowell, R., Witherspoon, S. and Brook, L. (1986). *British Social Attitudes*, Gower, London.

Kimmel, D.C. (1978). Adult development and aging: A gay perspective, *Journal of Social Issues*, **34**, 113–30.

Kitzinger, C. (1987a). *The Social Construction of Lesbianism*, Sage, London.

Kitzinger, C. (1987b). Heterosexism in Schools, *Values*, **2**, 40–1.

Kitzinger, S. and Kitzinger, C. (1989). *Talking With Children About Things that Matter*, Pandora, London.

Levine, M.P. and Leonard, R. (1984). Discrimination against lesbians in the work force, *Signs*, **9**(4), 700–10.

Loulan, J. (1984). *Lesbian Sex*, Spinsters Ink, San Francisco.

Moses, A.E. (1978). *Identity Management in Lesbian Women*, Praeger, New York.

Phillips, A. and Taylor, B. (1980). Sex and skill: Notes towards a feminist economics, *Feminist Review*, **6**.

Saghir, M.T. and Robins, E. (1973). *Male and Female Homosexuality*, Williams and Wilkins, Baltimore.

Sanderson, T. (1988). Faltering from the closet. In B. Cant and S. Hemmings (eds) *Radical Records: Thirty Years of Lesbian and Gay History*, Routledge and Kegan Paul, London.

Schneider, B. (1984). 'Lesbians at work' in Stimpson, C. and Person, E.S. *Women: Sex and Sexuality*. University of Chicago Press, Chicago.

Weston, K.M. and Rofel, L.B. (1984). Sexuality, class and conflict in a lesbian workplace, *Signs*, **9**(4), 623–45.

Chapter 8.2

Homosexuals and Transsexuals at Work: Legal Issues

Jill Earnshaw University of Manchester, Institute of Science and Technology, UK and *Peter Pace Manchester Polytechnic, UK*

INTRODUCTION

While it is true that in some walks of life a person's sexual orientation will not be a bar to a successful career, as is evidenced by, for example, the affecting autobiography of the transsexual writer Jan Morris (*Conundrum*, first published in 1974) and the exposure given to the transsexual model Tula in the July 1982 issue of *Cosmopolitan*, or the self-confessed homosexuality of some show business people, it is likely that for most working people such 'abnormal' sexuality is a hindrance in the pursuit of a successful working life. Thus, for example, a recent survey commissioned by a financial recruitment agency discovered that some employees left their jobs in the fields of accountancy and personnel management because they wished to adopt a different sexual identity and wanted to avoid the embarrassment and possible prejudice which might accompany their return to work in their new sexual identity.

Although this chapter considers the legal issues affecting both transsexuals and homosexuals at work, there are two initial caveats to be borne in mind. First, it may be misleading to regard transsexualism and homosexuality in the same way because the prejudice which both may engender is, perhaps, more understandable in the case of the latter than the former. This is so because of the criminal consequences of male homosexuality, some of which were mitigated by the Sexual Offences Act of 1967. Secondly, the general thrust of English law in relation to the legal effect of transsexualism has been in relation to the law of marriage. Indeed, it is from the marriage perspective that the human rights dimension of transsexualism has been addressed. In *Rees* v. *United Kingdom* [1986] 9 EHRR 56 the European

Vulnerable Workers: Psychosocial and Legal Issues. Edited by M. J. Davidson and J. Earnshaw

Court of Human Rights, upholding an appeal by the UK government, held that there had been no breach of Articles 8 (the right to privacy) and 12 (the right to marry and found a family) of the European Convention for the Protection of Human Rights and Fundamental Freedoms when a post-operative transsexual was refused permission to have his birth certificate altered to indicate that he was a male. A consequence of this would seem to be that the lack of recognition afforded to the change of sex would prohibit a marriage between a person of the same biological sex. However, in *C* v. *United Kingdom* (1989, *Guardian*, 11 August) the European Commission of Human Rights held that there had been a violation of Article 12 when English law refused to recognise a marriage between a post-operative male to female and a biological male. Rees was distinguished on the somewhat disingenuous ground that in that case there was no willing marriage partner.

DISTINGUISHING BETWEEN TRANSSEXUALS AND HOMOSEXUALS

The sex of an employee might be regarded as the most easily recognisable characteristic of that person. However, it is by no means uncommon for a person to be biologically of one sex yet psychologically to identify with the opposite sex. This gender identity, or gender dysphoria, may lead a person to take irreversible steps to adopt the desired sexual identity. Such persons are commonly known as 'transsexuals'.

In view of popular prejudice, it is important to distinguish transsexualism from homosexuality and transvestism. The homosexual is sexually attracted to a person believed to be of the same biological sex, whereas the transsexual regards such a person as being of the opposite sex. The transvestite obtains sexual arousal from wearing clothes of persons of the opposite sex, whereas the transsexual wears such clothes in order to identify with the chosen sex.

Various theories have been proposed as to the cause of gender dysphoria. It has been suggested that it may be caused by hormonal influences on the developing brain of the foetus, by the lack of a satisfactory father figure during the early years of a male transsexual's upbringing or by psychological influences. Notwithstanding these attempts to explain the origin of transsexualism, the truth obstinately refuses to be revealed.

The social and mental stresses involved in the recognition by an individual that he or she is imprisoned in the body of a person of the 'wrong' sex often lead to sex hormone therapy and eventual surgery. In this way some degree of conformity between a person's chosen gender and anatomical appearance is achieved. Gender reassignment procedures for male (to female) transsexuals involve treatment with the female hormone, oestrogen, surgical removal of the penis and testes and the creation of an artificial vulva and vagina. Those for female (to male) transsexuals involve treatment with the male hormones, testosterone and androgen, mastectomy, hysterectomy, closure of the vagina and construction of an artificial penis and scrotum. It is self-evident that only a person with an invincible belief in the 'wrongness' of his or her biological sex would voluntarily undergo such daunting procedures. It also provides convincing evidence that the psyche may have a more powerful influence on an individual than biology, an influence which the law disregards at its peril.

LEGAL STATUS OF TRANSSEXUALS

The starting point for an investigation of the legal status of a post-operative transsexual is the decision of the High Court in the notorious April Ashley case (see *Corbett* v. *Corbett* [1970] 2 AIIER 33). April Ashley was born as a biological male and Arthur Corbett had married her in the knowledge that she was a male-to-female transsexual who had undergone a 'sex-change' operation. He now sought a decree that the marriage was void on the basis that there could not be a valid marriage between two biological men (since marriage had been defined as the 'voluntary union for life of one man and one woman to the exclusion of all others' in *Hyde* v. *Hyde* [1866] LR 1P & D 130).

The judge identified five criteria relevant to the legal basis of sex determination. These were (i) chromosomal; (ii) gonadal (i.e. the testis or ovary); (iii) genital; (iv) hormonal; and (v) psychological. Because the judge thought that the marital relationship was 'essentially heterosexual in character' the criteria to be adopted must be biological (i.e. (i) to (iii)) so as to identify ' a person who is naturally capable of performing the essential role of a woman in marriage'—whatever that may mean. On this basis April Ashley was a male, and male she must remain.

This decision has attracted considerable criticism (Bates, 1977) and has not been followed in other jurisdictions. Thus in the New Jersey case of *M.T.* v. *J.T.* (355 A 3 d 104 [1976]) the court was prepared to give significant weight to the psychological criterion provided that a sex-change operation had resulted in a person who was able to function sexually as a person of the chosen sex.

In addition, the judge in Corbett was at pains to limit his own decision by stressing that he was not concerned to determine 'legal sex' for all purposes. Disappointingly, it has nevertheless been applied to a wide range of situations which have nothing whatever to do with marital capacity. Thus, it has been applied to the alteration of birth certificates, the determination of the minimum age for retirement, a prosecution for living on the earnings of prostitution, and, as will be seen later, in claims of sex discrimination and unfair dismissal. Yet it provides a recipe for inconsistency in its implicit acceptance of the fact that an individual may have a sexual identity for one purpose (e.g. marriage) yet have a different sexual identity for another purpose:

> It [sex] is relevant . . . to some aspects of the law regulating conditions of employment, and to various State-run schemes such as national insurance, or to . . . fiscal matters. It is not an essential determinant of the relationship in these cases . . . the authorities, if they think fit, can agree with the individual that he shall be treated as a man or a woman, as the case may be. (at p.48).

Thus, for example, a male-to-female transsexual can be treated as a woman for national insurance purposes, and will be able to obtain a passport in her new female name. The Inland Revenue, however will treat her as a man! This relative approach to sexual identity is undesirable and no doubt the cause of much distress. An individual's legal status is a matter which should not be subject to the whim of judicial decision.

EMPLOYMENT OF HOMOSEXUALS AND TRANSSEXUALS

It is a surprising and perhaps disturbing fact that no law in this country specifically prohibits employers from selecting their workforce on the basis of capricious flights of fancy or bigoted and prejudiced views, unless that selection process contravenes the Sex Discrimination Act 1975, the Race Relations Act 1976 or the Rehabilitation of Offenders Act 1974. There is no legislation which outlaws religious discrimination (though see Fair Employment (NI) Act 1989 in Northern Ireland) or discrimination on grounds of age or sexual orientation, nor until the Employment Act 1990, to protect trade union activists against a refusal to employ them. In this the United Kingdom falls behind the North American example despite parallel developments in the law on sex discrimination and sexual harassment. Both Canadian and American federal law forbid age discrimination and a number of American state laws prohibit discrimination on such criteria as arrest record, sexual orientation and even personal appearance. (Equal Opportunities Review, 1989).

It may be argued that such far-reaching legislation is unnecessary or that intervention by law is only appropriate where employers find it easy to discriminate because the criterion on which they do so is clearly apparent. Thus it should be necessary to prohibit discrimination on grounds of sex, or race, or age, because these factors will be made obvious simply by the completion of an application form, or through an interview, or both (but see the counter-argument in Chapter 3). However, the same argument cannot be canvassed on behalf of those whose only fear of disadvantageous treatment is that they are not of heterosexual orientation. It is clearly a fallacy, though a view held by some, that a person's homosexuality is instantly identifiable, that all lesbians are 'butch' or that all gays are effeminate. Even post-operative transsexuals would not normally betray their biological origins.

If this be the case, then why should employers become aware of the sexuality of potential recruits, and what evidence is there to suggest that this would in any case reduce their chances of a job?

In regard to the latter question, examination of dismissal cases discussed later in the chapter will illustrate only too well attitudes to the employment of known homosexuals and transsexuals. In particular it appears to be a widely held view that gays and lesbians are unsuitable for any job involving contact with children (see Chapter 7.2). Additionally there is now the fear that employing homosexuals brings the risk of AIDS and its consequent problems of co-worker and client reactions, into the workplace (see Chapters 4.1 and 4.2). And although only indirectly related to the employment of homosexuals, a recent piece of legislation may well have halted the acceptance of homosexuality in society, and indeed would be seen by many as a retrograde step. This is the notorious Clause 28 (now s. 28) of the Local Government Act 1988. In strict theory Clause 28 simply outlaws the 'promotion' of homosexuality by local authorities, but its consequences in changing attitudes may well be more widespread. Opposing the passing of the bill, Lord Willis described the clause as 'the first breath of a chilly wind of intolerance and the first page of a charter for bigots'. (*Guardian*, 2 February 1988).

Revelation of a Person's Homosexuality or Transsexualism on Recruitment

The majority of people applying for jobs are unlikely to announce, uninvited, that they are not of heterosexual inclination. They may naturally and reasonably fear that such declaration will cost them the job, or they may feel as a matter of principle that such information should not be relevant. In a survey of gay men in the London area, 78% of those who answered the questionnaire said they did not admit to their homosexuality on the last occasion of applying for a job though the same percentage indicated they would like to be open about their homosexuality when interviewed (Greasley, 1986). There are, however, several ways in which a person's sexual orientation may become known to a prospective employer.

First, though homosexual acts between consenting men over the age of 21 and in private were decriminalised by the Sexual Offences Act 1967, there remain certain criminal offences which may be committed by gay men and which have no heterosexual equivalent. A job application form which requires the disclosure of criminal convictions could therefore clearly reveal a person's homosexuality. The most commonly charged of these offences are those of importuning and gross indecency. In the case of importuning the offence is committed only if the defendant persistently importunes or solicits in a public place for an immoral purpose; gross indecency involves sexual activity in a public place. However, the vast majority of these offences involve consensual acts which hardly amount to what may be conjectured by such emotive phrases as 'immoral purpose' or 'gross indecency', and in many instances are obtained by somewhat doubtful police tactics. It is doubtless also the case that many defendants plead guilty in the Magistrates' Court rather than exercise their right to jury trial with its attendant publicity.

Once convictions are 'spent' (any sentence of less than 30 months' imprisonment becomes 'spent' at the end of the rehabilitation period appropriate to the sentence) under the Rehabilitation of Offenders Act 1974 it is unlawful for them to be used as a basis for rejection of a job applicant; indeed it would be unlawful to ask a rehabilitated person about spent convictions. Nevertheless, the protection of the Act is somewhat illusory, for it provides no enforcement machinery, and ignorance and confusion surround its complex provisions; furthermore, subsequent legislation has exempted many occupations and professions from its ambit (Earnshaw, 1990).

Application forms are not the only source of information on potential recruits. References from previous employers may disclose past convictions, indicate known sexual orientation or simply hint perhaps that this candidate 'may be thought to be an AIDS risk'. Furthermore, in an increasing number of instances, the police may disclose criminal records to employers especially where the job in question involves working with children. In fact, where the work involves children and the employer is a statutory body such as a local authority or education authority, two further sources of information exist in order to check the suitability of potential employees. The first is known as 'List 99', and is a list drawn up by the Department of Education and Science, of people who may not be employed as teachers or any other workers in the field of education. Not only criminal convictions, but also substantiated allegations of 'misconduct' may form the basis of a listing. The second is a DHSS consultancy service which gathers information from police records, reports by local authorities and voluntary organisations and 'List 99'. The information is then used to draw up a register of people deemed unsuitable for employment in the childcare field. While it is right and proper that the welfare of children should be safeguarded, there is clearly a danger that a conviction for a sexual offence, or a revelation of homosexuality, will act as an automatic bar without further enquiry. Even the medical profession appears to make such tacit assumptions of unsuitability; in 1978, for example, a candidate for teacher training was refused medical clearance on the sole ground of his being gay (Beer, Jeffery and Munyard, 1981).

Some employers require birth certificates to be produced on applying for a job. While this poses no problem for the vast majority of the population, it will be a cause for great concern to transsexuals. As previously stated, in the United Kingdom there is no provision whereby transsexuals, even post-operative transsexuals, can apply for a revision of their birth certificate to accord with the desired gender. To require production of a birth certificate therefore means that a transsexual's history will be revealed, and his or her attempts to live without reminders of the hated biological sex will be thwarted.

As in the Rees case mentioned earlier, a similar prohibition against revision of birth certificates in Belgium resulted in an application to the Court of Human Rights. The application was disallowed on the basis that the applicant had not exhausted fully his domestic remedies, but the European Commission of Human Rights did comment sympathetically that

> he would in fact be exposed to having to reveal to anyone information relating to his private life and subsequently to being excluded from certain employments, activities and relationships on account of the explanations about his position which he had improperly been required to give. (See *Van Oosterwijck* v. *Belgium*, 3 EHRR 577.)

DOES THE SEX DISCRIMINATION ACT 1975 PROVIDE A REMEDY AGAINST NON-RECRUITMENT?

If the sexuality or transsexualism of a potential employee is used by employers as a basis for rejection, then to what extent is legal redress available? As already indicated, there is no legislation which specifically prevents discrimination against homosexuals or transsexuals, but attempts have been made, both in practice and by academic writers (Pannick, 1983), to argue that the Sex Discrimination Act may provide a possible route. In theory at least, there are various ways in which its provisions could be utilised.

Initially it is necessary to describe what the Act defines as discrimination. 'Direct' discrimination occurs where the employer treats a woman less favourably than he or she would treat a man (or vice versa) on the grounds of her sex. Section 5(3) adds the rider that in making the comparison in treatment one must ensure that 'the relevant circumstances in the one case are the same, or not materially different, in the other'. Thus if an employer were to refuse jobs to gay men but not to lesbian women, or to promote lesbians but not gays, then arguably direct discrimination has occurred. (The latter example gave rise to a claim under the US Title VII of the Civil Rights Act in *Valdes* v. *Lumberman's Mutual Casualty Co.*, 26 F.E.P. Cases 252 [1980].)

Similarly, a claim under the Act should succeed if employers refuse to employ *any* members of one sex because they are prejudiced against a proportion of that sex on the grounds of their sexual orientation. This situation arose at Dan Air where for many years a policy had existed of excluding men from cabin staff posts. Following investigation by the Equal Opportunities Commission (EOC) in 1984, the company asserted its unwillingness to change the policy until more information was available on the diagnosis and treatment of AIDS. In its view the risks attached to AIDS were such as to justify the exclusion of male staff, on the basis that AIDS mainly affected homosexuals and that cabin staff, a large proportion of whom were generally homosexual, were sexually promiscuous. It is widely accepted, however, that one's motive for discriminating directly is irrelevant, and the EOC proceeded to issue a non-discrimination notice in October 1986 requiring extensive changes to Dan Air's recruitment policy (EOC, 1987) (see also Chapter 5.2).

However, it is more likely that an employer would be willing to take on men in general, but objects to homosexuals and therefore rejects a particular applicant on this ground. Is the rejected candidate able to allege sex discrimination on the basis that the employer, though not objecting to males in general, nevertheless treats *some* males less favourably? This so-called 'sex plus' factor has proved an acceptable basis for a claim in other contexts. In *Hurley* v. *Mustoe* [1981] ICR 490, where a married woman with children was dismissed when her family circumstances became known, because the employer believed that working mothers as a class were unreliable, a claim of direct discrimination succeeded. Similarly cases of sexual harassment have been won despite the fact that the harasser turned his attentions only to particular women and not to the female workforce in general (see Chapter 7.2).

The weakness in this argument is to ignore s. 5(3), namely that the 'relevant' circumstances must be the same in both cases. In order to compare like with like, employers can therefore point out that the relevant circumstances are that this particular person is attracted to members of the same sex, and that they would not have recruited a woman similarly inclined. There has therefore been no less favourable treatment. In reply, one could only contend that a person's sexuality should not be considered as a 'relevant circumstance'.

Despite the force of the academic arguments, to date the writers are unaware of any successful cases brought under the Sex Discrimination Act.

In America, on whose Title VII of the Civil Rights Act 1964 the UK legislation has been modelled, such attempts have been firmly rejected. In the casc of *DeSantis* v. *Pacific Telephones and Telegraph Co. Inc.*, the court commented that 'whether dealing with men or women the employer is using the same criterion: it will not hire or promote a person who prefers sexual partners of the same sex...', and in the Californian case of *Gay Law Students Association* v. *Pacific Telephone and Telegraph Co.*, the conclusion of the court was that the legislation did not contemplate discrimination against homosexuals (cited in Pannick, 1983).

Transsexuals attempting the same route have fared little better, and have been met by similar reasoning. In 1986 a male transsexual who was proposing to have a sex change operation applied for a job as electronic test technician (*Calvin* v. *Standard Telephone and Cables plc*, London (North) Tribunal, 16.12.86 (CO IT 1835/37)). No deceit was practised upon the company; the applicant applied in a female name and indicated that he would be living and working as a woman for one year prior to the operation. The company did not make an offer of employment, and as a result, a claim of sex discrimination was made. Although by the time of the hearing the operation had been performed, the tribunal took the view that at all relevant times the applicant was male. It reasoned that less favourable treatment had not occurred if under s. 5(3) one made a comparison where the 'relevant' circumstances were the same, namely a person born female who dressed as, and proposed to become a man. Such a person would similarly not be offered employment. The argument that 'relevant circumstances' should not include a person's transsexualism unless it had an impact on the ability to do the job, was rejected.

A tribunal in the earlier dismissal case of *E.A. White* v. *British Sugar Corporation Ltd* [1977] IRLR 121 took the same view. In that case the applicant was born a female but for many years had lived and dressed as a man; she was taken on as an electrician's mate in a project involving work on Sundays. However, the applicant was later confronted by management following rumours in the factory, and subsequently dismissed. The tribunal rejected her claim on two grounds: first that the applicant (whom they regarded as a woman) could not complain of less favourable treatment on the grounds of sex since the company would also have dismissed a man holding himself out as a woman; secondly, the applicant had deceived her employers as to her true status—had they known she was a woman they would have been entitled to refuse to employ her because of the prohibition on Sunday working for women (under the Factories Act) at that time. It is clear from the tribunal report however that such practical considerations as the use of the appropriate toilet were as much at the forefront of management's minds as any other matters.

DISMISSAL: WOULD A CLAIM OF UNFAIR DISMISSAL SUCCEED?

Why should a man be dismissed merely because it is revealed that he is gay, or a woman is revealed to be a lesbian, or a person of either sex because of revealed transsexualism? Surely, the enlightened and logical observer would say, one's sexual orientation cannot possibly have any bearing upon one's ability to do the job, and therefore should never form the basis of a dismissal. This may be so, but not everyone is enlightened and logical; there is widespread ignorance and prejudice surrounding homosexuality and transsexualism which affects not only the personal attitudes of employers but also their concerns about workplace relations and the reactions of clients and customers. Transsexuals may be regarded as freaks, voyeurs who wish to use the toilet facilities of the 'opposite' sex; lesbians are thought to be unsuited to working with girls, and gays with young boys; they are seen as sexual predators, promiscuous and potentially spreading AIDS among the heterosexual workforce by no more than the sharing of a cup. None of these beliefs is borne out by scientific evidence; children are at least as likely to be at risk from heterosexual men as from lesbians or gays, lesbians are less of an AIDS risk than any other section of the population, and it defies logic to regard as sexual predators those who in many cases go to great lengths to conceal their sexuality (Munyard, 1988).

Nevertheless, industrial tribunal cases reveal not only that dismissal because of sexual orientation occurs, but that unfair dismissal claims have a low chance of success. In the LAGER survey (Greasley, 1986), 12 respondents out of the 200 questioned said they had been sacked for being gay. However, the likelihood would be that only a minority of those 12 would even initiate an unfair dismissal claim. The reasons are not difficult to fathom. First, unfair dismissal is available as a remedy only to those who have worked for two years for their employer (unlike sex discrimination claims where no qualifying period exists, but the burden is on the applicant to prove sex discrimination). Secondly, tribunal hearings are conducted in public, so that for the individual concerned the matter is likely to be exacerbated by the potential publicity resulting from a tribunal hearing or media reporting (see Chapter 7.2). Thirdly, although reinstatement is theoretically available as a remedy, in practice compensation is usually awarded and it would no doubt be considered particularly inappropriate to order reinstatement in such cases. Success therefore means a modest financial award, publicity and no job.

Some determined individuals do seek legal redress however. In any unfair dismissal case, it is for the employer to prove that the dismissal was for a potentially fair reason as laid down in s. 57 Employment Protection (Consolidation) Act 1978. Where dismissal is on account of sexual orientation or its implications, the reason chosen is generally 'conduct' or the catch-all 'some other substantial reason of a kind to justify dismissal'. The tribunal must then assess whether the employer acted reasonably in the circumstances including such considerations as whether a fair procedure was followed. However, where in particular the job in question involves working with children, tribunals appear to equate a 'reasonable' employer with the 'average' employer who may well hold prejudiced views personally or be swayed by the prejudices of others. Three examples serve to illustrate the point.

In 1978 Mr Bowly, a schoolteacher of almost 30 years' standing pleaded guilty to an offence of gross indecency with a man in a public lavatory, and was dismissed as a result. The decision of the tribunal was that the dismissal was unfair, on the basis that '. . . there was no satisfactory evidence of any incident suggesting a risk to pupils'.

However, the Education Committee appealed to the Employment Appeal Tribunal (EAT) and the appeal was allowed (see *Nottinghamshire County Council* v. *Bowly* [1978] IRLR 252). The EAT pointed out that the function of the tribunal was not to decide what *they* would have done in the circumstances, but to decide whether or not the Disciplinary Sub-Committee had acted reasonably in dismissing. In their view, this was not a situation where dismissal should automatically follow, nor where it would be automatically unfair, and hence 'the facts of this case lie within that grey or intermediate area where, provided they approach the matter fairly and properly and direct themselves correctly, the Disciplinary Sub-Committee cannot be faulted in doing what in *their judgement* . . . is the just and proper thing to do' (italics supplied).

Did the Sub-Committee act fairly and properly? The Industrial Tribunal clearly thought not, in that there was no evidence of a risk to pupils, but the EAT disagreed. They said, 'it would surely be difficult to say that with his [Bowly's] inclinations and past history it had been established that there was no risk'. The Sub-Committee's view that to employ Mr Bowly would be an unjustifiable risk in the future once it was known that he had even once, 'given in to a temptation of this sort', was not therefore unreasonable.

A similar line of reasoning was applied in the case of *Wiseman* v. *Salford City Council* [1981] IRLR 203. Mr Wiseman was employed as a lecturer in drama and drama therapy at Salford College of Technology, working mainly with mature students and a number in the 16- to 19-year-old age group. His work in the department over a period of four years had attracted considerable admiration, and no criticism had ever been made of his professional conduct. Like Mr Bowly, he was dismissed as a result of a conviction for gross indecency, the principal reason being the potential risk of continuing to employ him in work involving close contact with young people. His argument that his private life and personal life did not impinge upon his professional one was rejected. In confirming the decision of the Industrial Tribunal that the dismissal was fair, the EAT considered the question: 'Is it a self-evident proposition that someone who has done what Mr Wiseman ... had done ... cannot be a risk to teenage boys in his charge?'

In their view it was not self-evident even though 'there may well be a respectable body of opinion which supports it'.

Clearly a man dismissed for homosexual activities will find it a great deal more difficult to challenge his dismissal if tribunals consider the crucial question to be the sufficiency of evidence pointing to *lack* of risk rather than positive evidence indicating that a risk exists. One may feel that many heterosexual men whose heterosexual activities are not in doubt would find a similar difficulty in *proving* that young girls in their care were not at risk. In addition, in both these cases it was felt that the individuals had fallen below the required standards; that they were expected to set an example to their pupils. But, are teachers and lecturers dismissed for adulterous relationships, for drunken behaviour, or for committing criminal offences for which the sentence, as in Mr Bowly's case, was a fine of £25? The suspicion creeps in that double standards might be at work.

The case of *Saunders* v. *Scottish National Camps Association Ltd* [1980] IRLR 174 is arguably even more open to criticism. Mr Saunders was employed at a children's camp, but simply as a maintenance handyman, a position which did not require him to be in contact with camp residents in performing his duties. He was dismissed because it was discovered that he 'indulged in homosexuality', and that parents of the children might object to his being employed there. His contention was that he was able to keep his private life completely separate and was not, in any event, interested in children or young people; a psychiatrist called by Mr Saunders gave evidence in support to the effect that his tendencies did not create a danger to such persons. Nevertheless the tribunal found that a considerable proportion of employers would take the view (regarded by the psychiatrist as lacking scientific basis) that the employment of a homosexual should be restricted, particularly when required to work in proximity and contact with children. The EAT, referring to Bowly's case reaffirmed that provided the employer acts fairly and properly, he cannot be faulted for doing what in his judgment, is just and proper. Yet in each of these cases there seems to be very little examination of just how fair the employer has been. The arguments seem to centre on number, namely, that if a considerable number of employers would take a particular view, then it must be reasonable to hold it. Comparison with sex and race discrimination cases would surely question such an assumption. No doubt there are many employers who, faced with the choice of making redundant a man or a woman, would be tempted to retain the man as being the breadwinner of the family—but such prejudicial views would not justify the dismissal of the woman (see cases cited by

Earnshaw, 1986). It is not uncommon for employers to be reluctant to promote a black employee rather than a white employee for fear of backlash from colleagues or unions, yet to refuse to do so on those grounds would constitute unlawful racial discrimination. The criticism is perhaps best summed up by Mr Bernard Levin who wrote in a much-cited article in *The Times*

> . . . the case of Mr Saunders is an instance of injustice by people who ought to have known better and reinforced by people whose job it was to put it right . . . it [has] been judicially established that a citizen who is wholly blameless may be punished because some people believe that *other* people, might, in certain circumstances, behave wrongly.

It would appear therefore that practising homosexuals who work with children are seriously at risk of being fairly dismissed should their homosexuality become known. But homosexuality of itself will not justify dismissal in every instance. The tribunal in the case of *Bell* v. *The Devon and Cornwall Police Authority* [1978] IRLR 283 conceded that the fact that a man was a homosexual did not render him unfit to be employed as a cook since it had no connection with the capabilities of the job. And in the more recent case of *Buck* v. *The Letchworth Palace Ltd* (IT 36488/88, 3.4.87) the tribunal commented that

> . . . if they had dismissed the applicant merely because he was a homosexual and because his fellow employees object to homosexuals, we feel that there would be little doubt that the dismissal would have been unfair.

The problem is that it would seem relatively easy for tribunals to determine the existence of some additional factor other than mere homosexuality, lesbianism or transsexualism. In 1977 Louise Boychuk was sacked for wearing lesbian badges at work. The tribunal were at pains to point out that she was not dismissed for being a lesbian, she was being dismissed for 'conduct' at work in insisting on wearing a 'sign or symbol' which the employer reasonably felt could cause offence to fellow employees and customers (see *Boychuk* v. *H.J. Symons Holding Ltd* [1977] IRLR 395).

Furthermore, despite the tribunal's own comment in Buck's case (above and see Chapter 5.2), they upheld his dismissal as a cinema projectionist following a conviction for gross indecency, principally because other relief projectionists refused to work with him. It appears this was acceptable because the refusal was based on a fear of AIDS rather than what the tribunal termed 'unreasonable prejudices'. This may seem surprising in view of the fact that relief projectionists did not work with Mr Buck; they worked when he was not there, and the tribunal itself accepted that these employees had over-reacted to the situation. Two other factors were mentioned: first, management's concern about the number of children who visited the cinema;

and, secondly, that Mr Buck was not just a homosexual but '. . . that he was the sort of homosexual who frequented Oxford Circus Underground Station lavatory . . .'. The relevance of such 'factors', in particular in relation to employment as a cinema projectionist, appears extremely dubious.

One ray of hope may exist in relation to procedural aspects. The tribunal in Bell's case were highly critical of the Police Authority's decision to dismiss based simply upon statements couched in very similar terms taken from persons using the canteen, and without further investigation of the substance of the statements. It was also considered unsatisfactory to fail to show those statements to Mr Bell so as to give him the opportunity to comment on them. In Buck's case, the tribunal said 'The respondents did not deal with this matter well . . .' and they criticised the lack of discussion which had taken place prior to dismissal. Since the House of Lords ruling in *Polkey* v. *A.E. Dayton Services Ltd* [1987] IRLR 503 procedural aspects have taken on a much greater significance in assessing the reasonableness of an employer's conduct, and it is certainly no longer permissible to say, as did the tribunal in the case of Mr Buck, that had the employer dealt with the matter properly, the result would in all probability have been the same.

CONCLUSIONS AND PROPOSALS FOR REFORM

The cases discussed present a clear picture of discrimination against homosexuals and transsexuals in the workplace, coupled with an almost complete lack of legal protection against such disadvantageous treatment. While the law can never of itself change people's fundamental attitudes and prejudices, it could at least prevent those who can so fundamentally affect a person's livelihood from making employment decisions based overtly on their prejudices.

In the case of transsexuals the law could additionally make it harder for employers to discriminate by allowing revision of birth certificates, and in the case of post-operative transsexuals, to permit them legal 're-assignment' to the desired sex. However, it is evident that in concerning a person's legal status such re-assignment would be inextricably bound up with public policy. Just as the Church of England was concerned with the reform of the divorce law proposed in the late 1960s, so too it is not inconceivable that it, along with other pressure groups, would have strong views on any legislative proposal which would, for example, permit post-operative transsexuals to contract valid marriages with persons of the same biological sex. One can readily imagine the popular denunciation, albeit mistaken, of 'homosexual marriages'.

If legal recognition of a post-operative transsexual's new sexual identity were to be enacted, it is likely that, following the lead given by some of the Canadian Provinces in relation to the revision of transsexual's birth certificates, an administrative machinery would need to be established in order to control the sex reassignment procedure. The procedure is likely to require pre-surgery counselling, hormone treatment, 'sex change' surgery and certification by an appropriately constituted board. Certification may be dependent upon medical evidence of the success of the operation, success in the sense of the individual's ability to function in society in the chosen gender. In relation to the revision of birth certificates, it is not uncommon for legislation to require that a candidate for re-assignment must, if married, obtain a dissolution of his or her marriage before re-assignment. An alternative approach would be for the certification of re-assignment automatically to dissolve any existing marriage.

Despite the concomitant difficulties of policy, administrative machinery and potential consequences to existing marriages, such problems are evidently not insuperable. At the present time, some nine other European countries including Denmark, Holland, Sweden and Switzerland officially recognise a transsexual's altered state; in addition Norway, Poland and Portugal, while having no mechanism for legal recognition, in fact allow individuals to be assigned to the post-operative sex.

Sex re-assignment and revision of birth certificate would facilitate life in general for post-operative transsexuals, but would not in themselves protect against, for example a refusal to employ where a transsexual's history was known or in some way revealed. For employers would still be able to shield behind the argument discussed earlier in the chapter, namely that they would not have recruited someone of the opposite sex who had a history of transsexualism. What is necessary therefore is legislation along the lines of the Sex Discrimination Act and the Race Relations Act which specifically outlaws discrimination on grounds of sexual orientation or transsexualism. In particular, this would be important because in any event sex re-assignment procedures apply only to post-operative transsexuals and the m ajor surgery involved in sex-change operations may not be appropriate in every case. Furthermore, transsexuals who desire a sex change would normally be expected to demonstrate their ability to function as a member of the chosen sex for at least a year prior to the operation and therefore success in holding down a job would be crucial.

It is also important that the issue should become a matter for the unions and for employers' equal opportunity policies, both of which can attempt to enlighten and educate the attitudes of the workforce in general. Somewhat surprisingly perhaps three government departments now have such policies; the Department of Transport and the Department of the Environment Document warns that

> Staff at all levels must guard against the more subtle and unconscious varieties of discrimination (e.g. on grounds of sexual orientation) which can result from pre-conceived ideas about capabilities or characteristics of particular groups.

And the Department of Education and Science in its Staff Handbook and Personnel Management Statement points out that

> The department wishes to affirm that discrimination on grounds of sexual orientation is not acceptable and that any harassment arising from such a cause will be considered a disciplinary offence ...

A recent example of the effectiveness of union involvement was recounted to the writers during preparation of this chapter. A pre-operative male-to-female transsexual worked for the Passport Office as a casual, but in May 1989 applied on two occasions for permanent status and was refused. On requesting the reason for the refusal she was informed that it was because of her pre-operative status which would potentially lead to time off for clinic visits and surgery. She contacted her union, the Civil and Public Services Association, who followed up the issue through the Chief Welfare Officer, the Equal Opportunities representative and the women's section at the London Home Office Department. Four months later, after pressure from the union, she was finally given a permanent position.

The present lack of legal protection for homosexuals and transsexuals cannot be justified. In terms of numbers they may not be significant groups compared, for example, with women or ethnic minority workers, yet the degree of prejudice and hence discrimination against them is likely to be greater. Furthermore, being a homosexual or transsexual potentially carries an additional problem; the problem of concealment. As Kitzinger points out in Chapter 8.1, such people may work in constant fear of being 'found out' with the attendant and very real risk of the loss of their job. The European Community Social Charter in its preamble stresses the importance of combating every form of social exclusion and discrimination. Let us hope that UK legislators will not be the last to act in this field.

ACKNOWLEDGEMENT

The authors would like to thank Steven Whittle for his help in the preparation of parts of this chapter.

REFERENCES

Bates, F. (1977). *Enforcement of Marriage Revisited*, 6 A-A.L.R. 172.

Beer, C., Jeffery, R. and Munyard, T. (1981). *Gay Workers: Trade Unions and the Law*, NCCL.

Earnshaw, J. (1986). Sex discrimination and dismissal: A review of recent case law, Occasional Paper No. 8505. UMIST.
Earnshaw, J. (1990). Criminal convictions: A bar to equality of employment, *Employee Relations*, **12** (3) .
Equal Opportunities Commission (1987). *Formal Investigation: Dan Air.*
Equal Opportunities Review (1989). Equal opportunity horizons: 1 American state laws, *EOR*, **25** 23.
Greasley, P. (1986). Gay men at work, *Lesbian and Gay Employment Rights*.
Munyard, T. (1988). Homophobia at work and how to manage it, *Personnel Management*, June.
Pannick, D. (1983). Homosexuals, transsexuals and the Sex Discrimination Act, *Public Law*, 279.

PART IV

Vulnerable Workers: 'Major' Minorities

Chapter 9.1

Part-time Workers: Current Contradictions and Future Opportunities

Sonia Liff, Loughborough University, UK

INTRODUCTION

At a time when part-time work is *the* major area of job growth, and employers are being encouraged to develop more flexible ways of organising work for all employees as a response to demographic trends and skill shortages, it may seem strange to be talking about part-time workers as a disadvantaged section of the labour force. Since around a quarter of the workforce currently work 30 hours or less per week (the usual definition of part-time work for statistical purposes) it is also difficult to characterise it as a marginal way of working. In fact for certain sections of the workforce, most notably married women with dependent children, it is the most common basis on which to undertake waged labour.

Despite these facts this chapter will argue that part-time workers are disadvantaged in a number of significant ways. The discussion will deal primarily with women part-timers who, in Britain, make up around 80% of all those working in this way, (Department of Employment, 1989, Table 1.1). This is not to suggest that male part-time workers do not suffer disadvantages that would warrant discussion within such a book. Rather they would be difficult to integrate for two main reasons.

Male Part-time Workers

First, the majority of male part-timers are either past retirement age or are doing part-time work as a second job (or to supplement a student grant). Many of the remainder will give up part-time work as soon as the opportunity to work full time presents itself. This contrasts strongly with the position of most female part-time workers. Many women begin working part time fairly

Vulnerable Workers: Psychosocial and Legal Issues. Edited by M. J. Davidson and J. Earnshaw

early in their working lives and continue for long periods of time. They are likely to live in a household with other wage earners but their income from part-time work is likely to represent their sole independent income. The extent to which the decision to work part time represents a positive choice will be returned to. What does seem clear is that *few* part-time women workers are actively seeking full-time work (Dex, 1988). Thus the extent of the discrepancy between the type of men and women undertaking part-time work makes it difficult to discuss both within the same framework.

Gendered Work

The second point is that analyses of women workers have stressed the extent to which their areas of work, situations and concerns have been under-represented in mainstream industrial psychology and sociology. From this has developed a range of analyses of women's work, women workers and gender relations within the workplacc. These have stressed that it is not enough simply to carry out more studies which include women but rather that one needs a different form of analysis which treats gender as a central theme in understanding developments in the labour force and labour market (for reviews and discussions of this work see Beechey, 1983; Liff, 1987; and Wajcman, 1983). Consequently, this chapter will argue, in line with this approach, that the situation of women part-time workers cannot be understood without a gendered analysis of both the construction of jobs and employee relations.

An important gendered analysis of men undertaking a form of work characterised as typically female needs to be written about men working part time. Unfortunately the lack of available research material makes this beyond the scope of this review. Nevertheless an understanding of ways of working as typically female (as well as the more familiar application of this approach to types of work) will be central to this analysis and may thus throw some light on the position of male part-timers.

This chapter will therefore concentrate on analysing part-time workers as women workers. Furthermore, the analysis will focus on married women who, because of social security restrictions, are the majority of part-time women workers. The chapter focuses on workers in the formal economy where data are available, although it should be noted that many women part-timers probably work outside this.

PART-TIME WORK OR PROPER WORK

There seems to be no intrinsic reason why part-time work should be regarded differently from full-time work. Yet many of the ways part-time work is talked about suggest that it lacks the legitimacy accorded to full-time jobs. For example, many of the arguments which have occurred between Conservative and Labour politicians in recent years about levels of job creation centre on just this ambiguity. Conservatives claim that the economy is booming and that well over 1 million jobs have been created since 1983. Such claims are met with hoots of derision from the opposition. These are not proper jobs, they say, they are part-time jobs for women!

It is true to say that substituting two part-timers for every full-timer would not represent a massive upsurge in the economy (not that this appears to be the source of the majority of new part-time jobs). Furthermore, one could argue that these new jobs do not often match the skills and geographical location of unemployed men. However, something more seems to be at stake.

Part of the unwillingness to see part-time service sector jobs as suitable for displaced manual workers seems to derive from a notion of what is appropriate work for men and women. When it is implied that the new jobs are not 'proper jobs' because they are part-time women's jobs, what is being said is that the two categories are mutually exclusive. An underlying implication is that certain things are unacceptable for men to do. The vehemence with such suggestions are rejected implies that to hold up such work as a possible solution to male unemployment is to add insult to injury. Huws (1985) provides an illuminating discussion of the way in which these views become translated into the left's 'alternative' views about how work should be restructured. Cockburn (1983) sensitively analyses the reactions of male print workers when technical change transforms their jobs into something suspiciously close to 'women's work'.

It is not only the type of work that is a problem. As accounts of male unemployment (Campbell, 1984; Miles 1984) have shown, doing a 'proper job' is very important to male self-identity. Earning a wage sufficient to support a family is still of enormous symbolic importance even though the number of households solely dependent on such a wage is declining rapidly. Home is a woman's place and so for a man to be there, even if only for part of the day, can be felt as an affront to his masculinity.

What is Proper Work?

To try to highlight the thinking behind these ideas and to provide a framework for the following discussion we can consider some mock definitions:

- 'Proper work' is usually found within the manufacturing sector and requires the application of physical and/or intellectual skills.

- 'A proper job' is something which is undertaken for around 40 hours per weeks, 5 days a week, 48 weeks a year, and 45 years of one's life.
- 'A proper worker' is someone who can do 'a proper job'.
- 'A proper wage' (paid to a proper worker for doing a proper job) is one sufficient to support the worker and preferably also to support his dependants.
- 'A proper rest' (what a proper worker deserves after doing a proper job) involves relaxing in a tidy home, not being bothered by demanding children, being able to go out when one feels like it (and many other things!).

One can see from these definitions that it is very difficult for women to ever be accepted as proper workers doing proper jobs. This is not to say that men are invariably doing proper work and so on. Rather that it is far more likely that men rather than women will be doing this type of work on these terms, and that it represents the *image* that comes into our minds when we think about male workers. The mock definitions of proper jobs and so on present a very (male) gendered view of the world of work under apparently gender-neutral language. That is, they suggest that really to be accepted as a worker one needs to work on jobs and terms which are seen as appropriate for or have suited men.

Concepts of part-time work and part-time workers provide a mirror image of proper work and proper workers as a way of understanding employees and employment. That is they provide a (female) gendered analysis of the world of work. Again this should not be taken to imply that all women work in this way; rather that it is our image of how women work. Part-time workers and their jobs in general diverge more from the characteristics of 'proper' workers and their jobs than do women workers as a whole. Thinking about the difference between what is appropriate for proper workers and part-time workers masks other thoughts about men and women workers.

In stressing these connections between part-time work and women's work in general it is not intended to deny the specificity of part-time working. The intention is rather to provide a framework for the account that follows which alerts us to some of the issues that might lie behind arguments about the problems with, and possibilities for, part-time work. In particular it is easy to move from a discussion of the problems part-timers face in making progress at work, or changing the division of labour in the home, to the suggestion that such problems would disappear if proper resources were available to allow them to work full time. If, however, we recognise that part of the views about what part-timers are entitled to, or capable of, comes from underlying views about them as women workers then we might be more wary of drawing too rapid conclusions about appropriate solutions. Conversely, if we recognise that the problems facing part-time workers mask more general underlying views about women workers, then this shows the need for all those concerned with equal opportunites to treat opportunites for part-time workers as a central issue.

The following discussion will focus on two broad aspects of part-time work. First, on the interdependence of part-time working and domestic commitments. Domestic commitments are generally held to be one of the main reasons why so many women work part time. Here it will also be argued that the continuing differences between men's and women's hours of work undermine attempts to reconstitute the domestic division of labour on a more equal footing. Second, the extent to which part-timers are able to gain 'equal opportunities' will be examined. It will be argued that the limited availability of part-time work plays a key role in perpetuating occupational segregation by sex, itself one of the main reasons why women workers' situation is inferior that that of men's. Particular attention will be paid to justifications based on notions of proper jobs and proper workers. Finally, we will look at suggestions that demographic trends will force employers to re-appraise part-time work, including the provision of greater benefits and opportunities. It will be suggested that while some positive developments are occurring they are not available across the board to part-time workers, nor are they likely to do much to break down occupational segregation.

REASONS FOR UNDERTAKING PART-TIME WORK

Returning to Work after Childbirth

In the absence of longitudinal studies, research which has asked women to describe their work histories provides the best source of data on the reasons for undertaking part-time work at particular times. Two sources, the National Training Survey (Elias and Main, 1982) and the Women and Employment Survey (Martin and Roberts, 1984) provide this opportunity. Elias and Main analyse the period 1965–75 and conclude that part-time 'employment is usually undertaken after a period out of the labour force associated with family formation and upon the return to paid employment' (p. 109). Martin and Roberts are able to cover a much longer time period. They found that around 14% of women in their sample had returned to work within six months of having their first baby (a much smaller proportion returned this quickly after subsequent births). Women returning at this time were most likely to take up full-time jobs, presumably ones that had been held open to them as a result of a maternity leave agreement. Women taking more than a year to return to work were more likely to return to part-time work and the proportion making this choice increased the longer women were out of the labour force. Most interestingly they found that women currently having children were returning to the labour force much sooner than had women of an earlier generation. They say, 'half of all the women who had their first baby between 1975–1979 had returned to work for at least a time within four years of the birth while it was almost ten years before a comparable proportion of women with first births in 1950–54 had returned to work. *These changes were almost entirely attributable to increasing proportions of women returning initially to part-time work*' (Martin and Roberts, 1984, p. 137, author's italics).

Working While Children are Young

Surveys which provide a picture of working patterns at one particular point in time support this association between part-time working and the age of the woman's youngest child. For example, the General Household Survey shows that in 1984 just over half of wives with husbands in employment and children aged under five were not employed. Those who were employed were more than four times as likely to be working part time as full time. When the youngest child was aged between 5 and 9 more wives were employed than not, however they were still much more likely to be working part time than full time (Equal Opportunites Commission, 1987). Overall, of all women with dependent children who are in waged work almost 70% of them work part time (EOC, 1987). As one survey comments drily, 'The responsibility for childcare continues to shape the pattern of women's working lives. Approximately four out of ten of the male workforce have dependent children but this has no discernible effect on their working lives beyond the tendency for fathers of dependent children to work longer hours' (Mintel, 1988, p. 95).

The author's research (Liff, 1981a) carried out in a food factory with three part-time shifts (morning, afternoon and evening) and a full-time day shift again showed a strong association between a woman's decision to work part time and the age of her children. In addition it showed that the age of the youngest child correlated with the particular shift chosen. Women with pre-school age children were most likely to work on the evening shift whereas those with the oldest were most likely to be on the morning shift or working full time. Discussing these choices with women it was clear that many had chosen part-time work because they were unhappy with the idea of full-time childcare. Once they had made this decision the wages they could earn made the prospect of paying for childcare untenable. They therefore had to find work which would fit in with ability of family members or neighbours to provide care (a solution which in any case was often felt to be preferable to involving unrelated carers). For women with very young children this usually meant husbands caring for children during an early evening shift. Once children started school, care could be managed (at least during term time) by relatively small amounts of help from relatives or neighbours, for example taking or picking up children from school.

Coping with Domestic Work

It is not only childcare that women take primary responsibility for. Figures from the Henley Centre for Forecasting, cited by the EOC (1987), show that full-time housewives spend 76.6 hours per weeks on 'essential activities' (primarily housework and childcare). This compares with 61.3 hours for part-time women workers and 40.8 for full-time women workers. In contrast full-time male workers spend 33.1 hours per week on such activities. Martin and Roberts (1984) found that 13% of wives working full time and 26% of those working part time said that they did all the housework (husbands did not think things were quite so bad!). Even when the situation was not quite so extreme, both husbands and wives agreed that wives did most of the housework. Social and Community Planning Research (again cited in EOC, 1987) asked married couples about a range of household tasks. Of these only one, repairs of household equipment, was done mainly by the man. The only task shared equally in more than half the households was disciplining children. In well over 70% of households washing and ironing, preparation of evening meal, and household cleaning was done mainly by the wife.

In follow-up interviews with some of the women working full and part time in the food factory mentioned above (Liff, 1985) respondents were asked what they felt about this division of labour. Fifty-six of the women interviewed were in the position of having main responsibility for domestic tasks (that is excluding young women living with their parents), and were also living with others capable of doing such work (usually husbands or children aged over 10). Around three-quarters of these women said that they felt the amount done by other household members was 'about right' or 'fair' although it was usually described as 'very little' or 'a bit'. When asked why they felt this way the majority of part-time workers said that they worked fewer hours than their husbands and were therefore able to do more. Some women just said that they had everything done by the time their husband came home, others that it would not be fair to expect him to start again when he had been working all day.

Women claimed they had more time but in fact described working days lasting from early morning until much later than most men finished. This was particularly true for women working on the evening shift who were looking after a young child all day, preparing a meal for their husbands and then going out to work for four hours. In many cases husbands were only prepared to tolerate this arrangement providing the child was fed, clean and ready for bed. They then left their own dinner things in the sink for when the woman came home! These arguments lost even more plausibility when one spoke to women working full time. They justified similarly unequal divisions of labour in other ways; their husband did overtime or shifts, he had a more strenuous or stressful job and so on. Even sticking to the part-time/full-time distinction the Henley Centre research mentioned above (EOC, 1987) shows that adding together the hours spent on either employment and travel or essential activities does not lead to equal outcomes. Full-time male workers spent 78.1 hours per week on these activities, full-time women workers 85.9 and part-time women workers 83.5 hours per week. These are likely to be underestimates since the amount of free time attributed to part-time women workers, the vast majority of whom will have children (for example 6 hours per weekend day), suggests that general responsibility for children is not included in this total.

Making such points is not intended to suggest that these women were deluding themselves in any straightforward sense. It is important to recognise that for most of these women and, in particular, for those who were relatively happy with their situation, the division of domestic work was not something they sought to explain. They were well aware that a husband who did more than the bare minimum was 'one in a million'. As such they could not really see what there was to explain about the situation—things were just done like that. Pushed in an interview situation to consider why things should be done that way their first response was often to try and find ways to justify the situation. The differing hours of work of men and women is very persuasive in this context, because it is at least a half-truth.

INTERACTIONS BETWEEN DOMESTIC AND WAGED WORK

Women who are employed on a part-time basis do have more time for domestic work than men employed full time; although it could be argued that they 'choose' to work part time because they know they will have to do that much whatever hours they are employed for! It is interesting to reflect that the 'dual role' writers of the 1950s and 1960s (Myrdal and Klein, 1956; Klein, 1965), who did not question the appropriateness of an uneven domestic division of labour, advocated part-time work for just this reason. What is important here is that superficial plausibility of arguments about differing hours of work makes it easy for men to justify their limited involvement in domestic work and women to accept it. Once the argument has moved off the general principle of equal responsibility for a certain set of tasks and on to negotiations about balancing out individuals' time and energy, then there is endless scope for debate. Combined with the other problematic aspects of housework about which feminists have written (Kaluzynska, 1980), such as differing standards and methods, it is hardly surprising that these issues remain unresolved.

Mintel (1988) argues that the key factor in explaining uneven participation in household tasks is discrepancies in income levels. While some economic theorists have long argued that differing earning potential explains the allocation of labour inside and outside the home, this assessment derives from a class-based analysis of household practices. They say that the lowest socio-economic groups have the most equitable divisions of labour and that 'broadly speaking, the greater the differential between the woman's and the man's earnings in a given household, the more likely the woman is to accept an unequal division of labour' (Mintel, 1988, p. 155). So the less a woman is able to earn relative to her husband the less he will do around the home and the less she will object to it. Rather than suggesting that this is a rational agreed decision as would human capital theorists, this analysis suggests that the distribution is the outcome of unequal power relations. Mintel optimistically suggest that all this will change as women increasingly earn as much as men and thus become intolerant of such arrangements.

CONSEQUENCES OF CHOOSING PART-TIME WORK

The different earning potential of part-time and full-time workers as well as notional arguments about who has most time may well then also be important. But whatever the causes it is clear that most women have difficulties in being seen to bring home enough of a 'proper wage' or to have done a 'proper job' to justify have a 'proper rest' when they get home. Their solution, undertaking work on a part-time basis has two consequences: first, it reinforces all the arguments which suggest she does not need or is not entitled to a proper rest; second, it relieves to some extent the pressures experienced by a woman in trying to combine waged and unwaged work and thus reduces the likelihood that she is going to argue about it that strongly in the first place. Things may be difficult when children are very young but women can see that that situation is not going to last for too long and may be prepared to put more effort in on the domestic front while their husbands earn more by doing overtime on their proper job.

Does any of this really matter? After all research shows that women are generally happy with domestic arrangements and this does not differ much between full- and part-time workers. Research on stress levels of part-time workers (Martin and Roberts, 1984) shows that they are no worse than those experienced by full-time workers. The author's research (Liff, 1981b) could even be taken as showing that part-timers were under less stress, although it appeared that this was due to differing financial pressures rather than hours *per se*. In any case many would argue that domestic appliances mean that housework is no longer the drudgery that it was, and does not really need to take up the time most people spend on it.

Even if one were to abandon the general issue of equity, these points can be answered in a number of ways. Many of women's comments are based on fatalism about the alternatives. Comparisons of levels of stress and depression-related illness between men and women give a rather different picture. Time budget research shows no evidence of hours spent on housework decreasing over time. Instead, appliances appear to be used primarily to raise standards. There is also some evidence that as appliances and conveniences have been introduced into the home the contribution of other household members has declined (Luxton, 1980).

Effects on Job Opportunities

What must also be taken into account, however, is the consequences of such choices on women's broader opportunities. Both the National Training Survey and the Women and Employment Survey show that the switch from full-time to part-time work is frequently associated with downward occupational mobility with inevitable consequences for women's likely future prospects. Martin and Roberts show that issues such as convenient hours of work score highly in part-timers' sets of priorities for finding a job whereas full-timers rate factors to do with the type of work and terms and conditions much more strongly. They also found that even though very few women working part time were in jobs with opportunites for promotion, the majority of these did not want to be considered for promotion. Part-time workers were three times more likely than full-timers to cite family commitments as a reason for not seeking promotion. So again it is clear that decisions which appear to be simply expedient in the short term are likely to have highly significant consequences in the longer term.

The picture which emerges is one where women's lack of achievement in the workplace appears as an unfortunate consequence of choices and constraints in the domestic sphere. Because women want to spend time with their children and want time to carry out other domestic tasks or because they are unable to exert influence over other household members to do their share and because state provisions for childcare are minimal, women are forced to absent themselves from the proper world of work. This may take the form of periods outside the labour force, disinterest in 'proper' career development, and working on a part-time basis. It could be argued that it is unfortunate, but inevitable, that women making such choices will find a restricted range of work open to them, since only certain work can be done on this basis. Also they cannot expect to be eligible for the full range of opportunities and benefits available to proper workers. This form of argument is a familiar one. Women no longer condemned by their biology are still nevertheless severely restricted by their social roles. One does not have to deny a substantial level of truth to such arguments to question whether the world of work is really so passive in the construction of part-time workers as a disadvantaged group.

THE NECESSITY FOR FULL-TIME WORK

An important issue to disentangle is the reason for the limited availability of part-time work, both within certain occupations and at higher levels in the hierarchy. A number of writers have explored a range of supply side and demand side explanations of the availability and distribution of part-time work. The most recent and thoroughly researched accounts of the situation in Britain are provided by Blanchflower and Cory (1986) and Beechey and Perkins (1987). Blanchflower and Cory's work is based on an analysis of the 1980 Workplace Industrial Relations Survey which provides very broad coverage but limited information about employers' intentions. In contrast, Beechey and Perkins focused on one geographical area but were able to explore in much greater depth employers' reasons for using part-time labour.

What Comes First; Women's Work or Part-Time Work?

Findings from these two studies are to a large extent complementary. They both acknowledge supply side factors but give greater weight to demand factors than is evident from most accounts of women's work. These focus on either characteristics of the production process, for example where the sequence of operations cannot be altered; or on the nature of the demand for a service which requires availability of labour beyond, or concentration of labour within, the proper working day. Such explanations are partly reinforced by the finding that part-time work is unevenly available across industries and services since if the issue was purely a supply side one, an even distribution would be expected. It does, however, raise the question of why employers only consider part-time workers when the nature of their product or service 'demands' it, shunning this form of labour in other circumstances.

Both studies point out that this need for a flexible labour force could be satisifed in a number of different ways. Blanchflower and Cory explore the connections between use of part-time labour and the use of shift working, outworkers and those on short-term contracts. They also note an association between employment of women in a sector and the likely employment of part-time workers. Beechey and Perkins focus more directly on the gendered aspects of different types of flexibility. They are able to pursue this connection more fully through their discussions with employers. They argue that whereas it is usually thought that a woman is employed *because* a job is part time, in fact the *reverse* is true. Employers have a clear idea of the sex of the worker they expect to be doing a certain job. When they then want such work to be done on a flexible basis they adopt a form of labour flexibility appropriate to that sex-typing. Where the job is sex-typed male, flexibility will take the form of overtime or shift working. When the job is considered appropriate for women it will be offered on a part-time basis.

Limited Availability of Part-Time Work

Beechey and Perkins (1987), also explore the reasons why part-time work is not offered more widely. In doing so they return to issues about women's domestic responsibilities. 'The point to emphasise,' they say, 'is that part-time women workers are defined by their domestic responsibilities' (p. 118). Thus in general when employers think about part-time workers they think of women with lots of other commitments and ties, not particularly interested in their work, liable to be taking time off, and so on. Not surprisingly they find this image relatively unattractive and avoid employing them when they can. However, when they have a woman's job which needs to be done on a flexible basis (or occasionally when they experience labour shortages) they recognise the existence of a group of workers from whom part-time work is a preferred choice.

One could add to this type of explanation considerations based on the dominant views from the proper world of work. Simple work not requiring significant levels of skill or discretion could perhaps be done by people who are not 'proper workers'. However, this would not be appropriate for jobs higher up the hierarchy where commitment and single mindedness are the key. In any case since most people work proper hours how could someone with authority and specialist knowledge function effectively on any other basis? This type of thinking is reflected in an otherwise progressive submission from the Institute of Personnel Management on part-time working to the House of Commons Committee on Employment (IPM, 1989). In one paragraph it is argued that good employment conditions are indivisible and must be equally available to all groups of workers. In another it states that it is perfectly reasonable not to consider part-time workers eligible for promotion (unless they want to switch to working full time). Once again we can see the apparently gender-neutral world of proper work effectively disenfranchising part-time women workers.

Putting these factors together we get a picture of part-time work only being offered when a job is already seen as appropriate for women, when it is fairly low level and when flexibility is required. It is obvious that such criteria are going to lead to a fairly limited and unattractive set of jobs. Returning for a moment to the supply side we can see that women wanting jobs on this basis are going to be stuck at the bottom of a very narrow occupational rut! Evidence to support this view can be found in a study by Robinson and Wallace (1984). They looked at the grades of male full-time, female full-time and female part-time employees in 14 establishments. They found the most significant differences arose from occupational segregation between men and all women. Men were much more likely to be found in higher grade jobs. They conclude that this arose from pre-entry segregation based on differential access to qualifications, skills and experience. Post-entry segregation then compounded this by evaluating male skills and job requirements more highly.

Differences between the grades of full-time and part-time women workers were less extreme but nevertheless evident. These arose through the practice of basing promotion on seniority (with full-timers likely to have longer uninterrupted lengths of service) or on the basis of experience of certain types of work more likely to be available to full-timers. They conclude, 'In all establishments involved in the project, occupational segregation operated to the detriment of women in both full-time and part-time employment. But the growing levels of part-time employment should be seen as part of the process of labour-market segmentation resulting in the employment of women in occupations and industries characterised by a minimum of skills, low pay, few opportunities for training or promotion, and little job security.' (Robinson and Wallace, 1984, p. 45).

OCCUPATIONAL SEGREGATION AND PART-TIME WORK

This is the crucial issue. The strength of occupational segregation by sex is evident in both macro (Hakim, 1979) and micro (Martin and Roberts, 1984) level surveys as well as within the many case studies of women workers (e.g. Pollert, 1981; Cavendish, 1982; Westwood, 1984). Many theories have been advanced about the factors creating and sustaining such segregation but there is general agreement about its significance in perpetuating inequality between male and female workers. The issue here is the role part-time working plays in this process. If, as is suggested by Beechey and Perkins's work, occupational segregation determines the availability of part-time work then those who are only willing or able to work on that basis will be unable to break out of segregated occupations regardless of any other factors.

Relationship to Equal Opportunities Policies

Sex discrimination legislation is based on ensuring equal access, for people of both sexes, to occupations and to the terms and conditions they offer. Most equal opportunity initiatives have seen women workers' position improving through increasing access to higher graded jobs. This focus on supply side factors is completely uncritical of the terms on which jobs are offered. Women are granted equal acccess providing they are judged to be equal in their suitability for the job requirements and in their ability to comply with its terms. But if these terms are constructed around male patterns of work then this is equivalent to rigging the race. Men and women arc being judged by one apparently neutral standard, ability to work full time, whereas in fact many women find this an untenable way of working. Women who say they only want to work part time are seen as opting out of the competition rather than having the competition structured against them (Webb and Liff, 1988).

This sort of logic is very hard to fight. While most women would agree that women should be able to take up any job they are capable of doing, many baulk at the suggestion that the job should be altered to make it easier for them to do so. This is often seen as being unfair to men who were perfectly able to undertake the work in the first place. The differential distribution of domestic labour which led to uneven numbers of men and women seeking part-time work is forgotten. In part it is lost in naturalist assumptions about male and female roles in the home, but the apparently gender-neutral proper world of work also plays a part. Proper hours of work can in fact only be managed comfortably by people who have someone else to carry out substantial parts of their domestic labour and childcare.

Part-time Work and Indirect Discrimination

Requiring jobs to be done on a full-time basis when fewer women than men are able to comply with this requirement is at least potentially indirect discrimination under the Sex Discrimination Act (1976). One important test case has been brought on this basis (*Holmes* v. *Home Office*) but this was of a woman already employed on a full-time basis wanting to transfer to part-time work rather than gain access to another job (see Chapter 9.2). In general, views about the requirements for certain jobs to be done on a full- or part-time basis, *because of the nature of the job*, and conversely the perceived inappropriateness of part-time working in other occupations, seem to have inhibited more radical thinking in this area.

NEW OPPORTUNITIES FOR WOMEN?

It could be argued that this is out of date griping. The significance of offering jobs on a part-time basis has been recognised and employers are being encouraged to take these ideas on board in their own interests. The labour market is no longer slack and skill shortages associated with new technology and the demographic trends leading to a decline in school leavers are forcing employers to offer jobs on terms that suit employees rather than themselves. They can no longer afford to turn their noses up at women with young children. Instead they must think about providing not only part-time hours but career breaks and childcare facilities.

These are appealing thoughts but they need to be analysed very carefully. There would seem to be three possible options that are being conflated. The most positive option would be that part-time workers are being considered on an equal basis for all jobs. The second would be that more women's jobs are being offered on a flexible and supportive basis. The third is that improved terms of work are offered to particular women that employers have an interest in retaining.

Unfortunately there is virtually no evidence for the first option. Part-time working continues to be available in sectors dominated by women. For example 4.3% of workers in the mechanical engineering sector work part time compared with 58% of workers in the hotel and catering sector (Department of Employment, 1989, Table 1.4). There is some evidence that at more managerial or professional levels some employers are willing to offer women more flexible packages including career breaks and possibilities for job sharing (IDS, 1989). But many women in a male dominated environment may be reluctant to take these up knowing that their male colleagues, against whom they will have to compete for promotion, will continue to work proper hours. The suggestion that part-time work will be offered in previously male dominated sectors rests on the assumption that employers will be so concerned about shortages that they will abandon any lingering outdated prejudices about whether such work is suitable for women. A gender-based analysis of occupational segregation suggests such views are much more deep seated and less easily removed.

The Persistence of Occupational Segregation

Evidence from the computer industry, supposedly one of the hardest hit by skill shortages, is not encouraging. A Computer Economic Survey (1986) found that while 95% of data preparation staff (effectively a clerical job) were women, they made up only 18% of programmers and 2% of data processing managers. The Information Technology Skills Agency (1987) reports that the number of women in computing is actually falling. A vicious circle appears to persist; while occupations are still rigidly segregated employers are unlikely to think about restructuring the hours of work they offer and their current employees are unlikely to put pressure on them to do so since they are perfectly able to cope with the existing hours. Conversely, while certain occupations or levels within occupations remain available only to those willing to work full time, then this will be one more barrier discouraging women's entry.

Improved Conditions of Employment

So what of occupations within which women are currently concentrated? Are all women being offered more favourable terms or is flexibility only available to some? Most attention has focused on developments within the banks and the health service. Both are major employers of women school leavers. In the past they have been content to recruit and train each year and accept high rates of turnover as women left to have and care for children. The rapid decline in school leavers is making both sectors rethink this strategy. Career breaks, more flexible hours and in some cases childcare are now being offered, most notably within the finance sector, to encourage trained women to stay or, if they leave, to return to the same employer within a relatively short period (e.g. Boyden and Paddison, 1986).

In some cases these benefits are being offered to all women (Cameron, 1987). However, in the banks it seems much more common to offer them only to women who have risen above a certain level in the hierarchy. The concern is primarily about retaining skills not providing benefits for women. In nursing, responses are being accompanied by a restructuring of occupations. Some nurses will receive higher levels of formal training than before and will undoubtedly be offered a range of benefits to help them combine home and work. The more routine work will be carried out by a new grade of support staff. The terms and conditions they will be offered are still unclear.

Future Prospects

What does seem clear is that employers still seem to regard the provision of part-time work and other benefits as a favour to women. It is still a deviation from proper practice, tolerated because it suits the type of work or because it is necessary in certain labour market conditions to gain required staff. While such views persist it is inevitable that seeking part-time hours will condemn women to occupational ghettos and confirm employers' views that they are not serious in their commitment to work. As a consequence women will continue to be passed over for promotion, training and a living wage. What needs to be recognised is that it is not women's choice of hours that disadvantages them but rather a view of proper work and workers that is incompatible with responsibility for a normal amount of domestic labour.

REFERENCES

Beechey, V. (1983). What's So Special About Women's Employment? A review of some recent studies of women's paid work, *Feminist Review*, **15**.
Beechey, V. and Perkins, T. (1987). *A Matter of Hours*, Polity Press.
Blanchflower, D. and Cory B. (1986). Part-time employment in Great Britain: An analysis using establishment data, Research Paper No. 57, Department of Employment.
Boyden, T. and Paddison, L. (1986). Banking on equal opportunities, *Personnel Management*, Sept.
Cameron, I. (1987). Realising the dividends from equal opportunities, *Personnel Management*, Oct.
Campbell, B. (1984). *Wigan Pier Revisited*, Virago Press.
Cavendish, R. (1982). *Women on the Line*, Routledge and Kegan Paul.
Cockburn, C. (1983). *Brothers: Male Dominance and Technological Change*, Pluto Press.
Computer Economic Survey (1986). Quoted in the *Guardian*, 25.2.1988.
Department of Employment, (1989). *Employment Gazette*, Oct.
Dex, S. (1988). *Women's Attitudes Towards Work*, Macmillan.
Elias, P. and Main, B. (1982). *Women's Working Lives: Evidence from the National Training Survey*, Institute for Employment Research, Warwick University.
Equal Opportunities Commission, (1987). *Women and Men in Britain*, HMSO.
Hakim, C. (1981). Occupational segregation, Research paper No. 9, Department of Employment.
Huws, U. (1985). Challenging commoditisation—producing usefulness outside the factory. In Collective Design/Projects (eds), *Very Nice Work If You Can Get It: The Socially Useful Production Debate*, Spokesman.
IDS (1989). *Maternity Leave and Childcare*, IDS Study 425, Jan, IDS Ltd.
Information Technology Skills Agency (1987). Quoted in the *Guardian*, 25.2.1988.
Institute of Personnel Mangement (1989). Part-time working—its role in the labour market and impact on the economy, Comments to the House of Commons Committee on Employment, Institute of Personnel Management.
Kaluzynska, E. (1980). Wiping the floor with theory—A survey of writings on housework, *Feminist Review*, **6**.
Klein, V., (1965). *Britain's Married Women Workers*, Routledge and Kegan Paul.
Liff, S. (1981a). 'Part-time employment among women factory workers, *Employee Relations*, **3**, 1.
Liff, S. (1981b). Mental Health of Women Factory Workers, *Journal of Occupational Behaviour*, 2.

Liff, S. (1985). Occupational sex-typing: Sexual and technical devisions of labour, Unpublished Ph.D. thesis, University of Manchester.

Liff, S. (1987). Gender relations in the construction of jobs. In M. McNeil (ed.) *Gender and Expertise*, Free Association Books.

Luxton, M., (1980). *More Than a Labour of Love*, The Women's Press.

Martin, J. and Roberts, C. (1984). *Women and Employment: A Lifetime Perspective*, HMSO.

Miles, I. (1984). Work well-being and unemployment: A study of men in Brighton. In P. Marstrand (ed.) *New Technology and the Future of Work and Skills*, Francis Pinter.

Mintel (1988). *Women 2000*, Mintel.

Myrdal, A. and Klein, V. (1956). *Women's Two Roles*, Routledge and Kegan Paul.

Pollert, A. (1981). *Girls, Wives, Factory Lives*, Macmillan.

Robinson, O. and Wallace, J. (1984). Part-time employment and sex discrimination legislation in Great Britain Research Paper No. 43., Department of Employment.

Wajcman, J. (1983). Working women, *Capital and Class*, 18.

Webb, J. and Liff, S. (1988). Play the white man: the social construction of fairness and competition in equal opportunity policies, *Sociological Review*, **36**, 3.

Westwood, S. (1984). *All Day, Every Day*, Pluto Press.

Chapter 9.2

The Legal Vulnerability of Part-timers: Is Job Sharing the Solution?

Patricia Leighton, Anglia Higher Education College, UK

INTRODUCTION

The United Kingdom has proportionally the second largest part-time workforce in Europe. It amounts to approximately 18% of recorded economically active workers. Inevitably, any disadvantage such workers suffer in economic and occupational terms is of greater significance for the UK workforce as a whole than elsewhere in Europe. Job sharing can be defined as the voluntary sharing by, usually, two people of the pay and benefits of a full-time post. It is the interface between these two work patterns and the question of whether job sharing can, indeed, provide essential benefits and protections usually denied part-timers which is the subject of this chapter. A popular view of job sharing has been that it has been equal opportunities tokenism but is not a serious work pattern. An air of whimsy has often surrounded it in the public's mind. These issues must also be addressed.

The pace of growth, and the fact that women so dominate the part-time workforce has led to increased interest and research into the characteristics and issues affecting part-timers. Indicators of their more significant role have been the debates surrounding the concept of the flexible workforce—a debate increasingly familiar within the European Community, and a number of research projects such as those prompted by the International Labour Organization (ILO) which have sought to examine the consequences of 'peripherality' in the workforce. The position of part-timers in terms of legal and occupational protections has been examined and some unsurprising conclusions drawn.

Statute and case law reveal that many part-timers have been deliberately excluded from major and minor legal protections. Part-timers have not arrived at a disadvantaged state by accident. Since 1965, and the first major

Vulnerable Workers: Psychosocial and Legal Issues. Edited by M. J. Davidson and J. Earnshaw

protective statute—the Redundancy Payments Act, legislation has developed the tradition of excluding those who work less than 16 hours a week (or eight if they have worked continuously for at least five years). Why was this? There is no obvious or stated answer. There was no debate on the issue nor, indeed, of the decision to establish the two-year period of continuous employment as a qualification for the major employment rights. From the outset, the classic groups of vulnerable workers—temporary, casual, domestic workers, as well as part-timers—were created by legislation.

The legal position of part-timers must be explored in some detail. However, two immediate thoughts arise. First, it is clear that the deliberate statutory policies to downgrade part-timers have been mirrored by managerial ones. These are manifest in relation to occupational benefits, especially practices regarding holiday and sick pay and occupational pensions. At a more humdrum level part-timers are often treated differently regarding health and safety at work arrangements, recruitment and induction, and regarding access to social and fringe benefits. Secondly, and perhaps more importantly, the rationale for the many occupational practices remains obscure. Are part-timers more unreliable, less productive, subject to a higher level of absenteeism and turnover? Most vitally, are the ideas of part-time work and career progression incompatible? And are responsible and senior posts inappropriate for part-time work?

It is these last two questions that will dominate this chapter. It will be necessary to question some of the assumptions regarding full-time work The process of establishing job-share schemes—their essence being part-time work which provides security and opportunities comparable to full-time posts, will inevitably involve such questioning. Job sharing has grown enormously over the last two years, and is beginning to develop widely in the private as well as the public sector. In order to discuss in detail the reasons for growth as well as the issues which arise from job sharing it is necessary to have a clearer view of the situation, both legal and otherwise, of the part-time workforce.

PART-TIMERS AND THE LAW

As previously mentioned, many part-timers have always been disadvantaged in employment law. There was never any intention to see part-timers as proportions of full-time posts and give proportionate rights. Part-time work in legal terms is essentially a different kind of work. However, it must be borne in mind that part-timers who work more than 16 hours (eight if continuously for five years) are subject to the major protections regarding unfair dismissal and redundancy. Part-timers working fewer hours do not qualify for some basic protections, for example, they are not entitled to receive written terms of work as required by s. 1 of the Employment Protection (Consolidation Act 1978 (EPCA). In practice, many part-timers are provided with this information but the availability to employers of the option of establishing a contract merely orally or with very limited information can clearly emphasise second rate status.

Even at a very basic level the lack of written material makes it far more difficult to assert contractual rights. It may be correct in strict legal terms that for most intents and purposes oral terms are as equally valid as written terms but in disputes problems of proof are relatively greater.

Part-timers working less than 16 hours a week do not qualify to receive guaranteed payments when they are laid off by their employer. However, it is the major protections of unfair dismissal and redundancy payments which are usually seen as the main indicators of disadvantage. It has been estimated that less than 50% of part-timers qualify (Hakim, 1989) and there is debate about the extent of deprivation (Disney and Szyszczak, 1989). Sometimes, simple, practical problems intrude. Take the case of the peripatetic photography teacher employed by Surrey County Council for a number of years. She had a series of contracts to teach in different schools. None of the contracts individually added up to 16 hours; aggregated they did. When the teacher was no longer required she claimed a redundancy payment. Her argument was simply that although for technical reasons individual contracts were issued the reality was of an employee making a significant weekly contribution to the LEA, but who happened to work in different establishments. The House of Lords judgment was that the contracts had to be seen singly and her case was lost (*Lewis* v. *Surrey CC* [1988] IRLR 509). The decision has major implications for many part-timers—educational psychologists, health service specialists and the like who will be similarly viewed. The decision illustrates the continuing view of courts and tribunals of looking at part-time work in a narrow way and paying scant attention to its broader contribution.

Similar attitudes emerge in the case law concerned with unfair dismissal. Clearly, an employer is justified in dismissing a part-timer for misconduct or incapability. However, can a workforce reoganisation containing a plan to focus on full-time work constitute lawful grounds for sacking part-timers? It appears that if the employer can show that this was a genuine move designed to improve efficiency dismissals *can* be justified. The technical ground is that of 'some other substantial reason'. This approach has not been without its critics (IDS, 1987), not least because it appears to accept the lesser value of part-timers.

More developed is the case law on redundancy payments. A line of cases suggests that if an employer wants to replace part-time work with full-time work, the dismissal will be justified by redundancy. Dismissals will qualify part-timers for the statutory redundancy payment provided they have been working the minimum number of hours, though the likelihood is that the amount of compensation will be less, not least because the compensation formula is based on weekly earnings.

However, this gloomy situation has to be tempered in the light of other areas of law. The first and by far the most significant is anti-discrimination law, not least because the part-time workforce is overwhelmingly dominated by women. Put succinctly, part-time work generally equals women's work. Hence many forms of disadvantageous treatment have been successfully challenged. Although the law is fiendishly complex and often inconsistent it is arguable that, for example, decisions to declare redundant part-timers before full-timers can be discriminatory, refusals to allow a woman to return to part-time work after maternity leave and even objections to proposals to job share by previous full-timers can give grounds for complaint. It cannot be said that clear judicial policies have emerged, and there are frequent signs that judges intimate that employers should generally be free to insist on full-time work if they wish. There are clear signs of tension in this area of law, which can be illustrated by the recent decision in *Clymo* v. *Wandsworth BC* [1989] IRLR 122. Here a branch librarian became pregnant, but wanted to return to her post on a job-share basis. She proposed to share it with her husband who was a deputy librarian elsewhere in the borough. The employers rejected the proposal and a claim was made that their response was discriminatory. The EAT felt the employers to be justified; not only was such a post inappropriate for part-time work but Mrs Clymo in effect, having decided to have children could not also expect to carry on her career as she wished.

A clearer picture has emerged with regard to occupational benefits, not least through the promptings of the European Community. The Treaty requires both equal pay and equal treatment for women, and throughout Europe part-time women workers, especially in situations where part-time equals female work, have been able to challenge their exclusion or unfavourable treatment in, say, occupational pension schemes. Most important has been the decision in *Rinner-Kühn* v. *FWW Spezial-Gebauderei-nigung* [1989] IRLR 494. German law on occupational sick pay limits the obligation on employers to pay to those employers working over 10 hours per week. This was successfully challenged in the European Court as being discriminatory to women who dominate the part-time workforces in all but one of the EC member states. The decision has enormous potential for challenging not only employers' practices but also state regulations. Indeed, there are encouraging signs not only from case law but from research studies into employers' practices (IDS, 1986) that change is well on its way. This is not to say that part-timers generally are being treated to *pro rata* occupational and fringe benefits but rather that there has been some progress.

WIDER IMPROVEMENTS

Coincidentally with a gradual improvement in occupational benefits (but *not* of legal protections) pressure has been mounting within the European Community for fairer treatment of part-time and temporary workers. The so-called Social Dialogue, the European Social Charter, as well as concerns from the ILO have all urged improved protections. The Draft Directive on Atyical Work requires *pro rata* treatment for workers doing more than eight hours a week. The feeling is that although currently resisted by the UK government, it is only a question of time before it becomes operative. It is to be anticipated that the UK government will continue to resist wider change (DE, 1988) and much will hinge on the political will of the Community in the run-up to 1992 to implement the initiatives.

Already tangible is Directive 356/1986 which has found form in the 1989 Social Security Act. This will by 1993 require equal treatment of men and women regarding 'occupational social security'. Included are sick and injury pay, pensions and retirement arrangements. Given the composition of the part-time workforce in the United Kingdom the implications of this Act will be major. Another area of law which has improved the lot of part-timers is the equal pay legislation. The introduction of the equal value provisions have helped many women—not so much through case law victories but through re-grading traditional 'female' jobs. However, one unanswered question remains. This is the extent to which an employer can claim that the fact that a job is done part time can be legitimately reflected in pay rates. Case law suggests that the onus is on the employer to show in what way(s) the part-timer is of less value, *pro rata*, than a full-timer (*Bilka-Kaufhaus* v. *Weber von Hartz* [1986] IRLR 317).

Although there has been some progress, a central problem remains: the feeling that part-timers are in various ways of less value than full-timers. Research (Leighton and Rayner, 1986; Atkinson and Leighton, 1990) continues to show that many employers hold firmly the view that part-timers are less committed to the workplace, and less worth investing in.

PART-TIMERS AND JOB SEGREGATION

Although accurate statistics are hard to come by it appears that the vast majority of part-time posts are not only relatively poorly paid but are confined to lower grades. While it is perfectly possible to envisage part-time members of 'quangos' the idea of senior hospital managers, a part-time bank manager, personnel manager, headteacher or sales and marketing executive seems to strain credulity. Full-timers are needed, it is argued, to maintain continuity, consistency and commitment. Supervisory and managerial roles cannot be undertaken by part-timers. It follows that few management training courses are open to part-timers and that in so far as training is provided for part-timers, it is largely confined to vocational skills. In addition, most training is on the job or requires attendance at seminars which are often at inconvenient times. This militates against many part-timers who are working part time because of domestic responsibilities. Although there have been developments towards open learning and self-managed courses, their potential for extending training to career orientated part-timers has not been fully explored.

The overall picture is of part-timers concentrated in relatively low skilled jobs, especially in service industries or 'marking time' in professional occupations until they can re-enter full-time employment. Although research indicates that many part-timers are content to mark time, especially those with young children, it would be wrong to assume that all part-timers are merely 'pending' full-timers. A number of groups within the part-time workforce may not or cannot have that intention. Prominent will be those who have retired from one job but who will be financially penalised if they undertake a significant number of hours' work; those who have ongoing domestic responsibilities; the disabled who are physically or psychologically unable to tolerate the demands of full-time work; those who have a second job or a hobby; and those who simply dislike the idea of full-time work. Numbers are hard to quantify but it is likely that in an economic climate where there are increasing numbers and acceptance of dual income families, and of the validity of the choice of part-time work, they will continue to grow.

If part-timers are largely confined to lower and medium grade posts and are not able to participate fully in training which is central to career progression can this be objectively justified?

There are two aspects of this issue: the first concerns the character of part-timers themselves; the second concerns characteristics of some types of jobs. Although there is relatively little work done in developing effective models, or even guidelines on labour costs, many have argued that part-timers are relatively more expensive to employ. For example, they attract slightly higher *pro rata* national insurance contributions than full-timers. When this is added to relatively higher recruitment and personnel management costs cogent arguments seem to emerge to justify lower pay and denial of access to occupational benefits, especially where administrative costs are high. Additionally, there are suspicions that part-timers are subject to higher wastage rates and absenteeism, both of which would add to labour costs.

Research appears not to support these views (IS, 1986). Although there are indeed variations in turnover and absenteeism rates they are associated with levels of work and not with part-timers as such (Wood and Smith, 1989). In general, the higher the post the lower the absence rate, although in some sectors patterns of labour wastage are more closely associated with particular occupations. Detailed inspection of tax and national insurance issues shows that any differences between full-time and part-time work are very marginal. At the same time others suggest that part-timers are relatively more productive than full-timers, which more than offsets any other increased labour costs (Leighton and Winfield, 1988).

However, the image remains that not only is part-time work less beneficial to an organisation, but that posts above certain levels are only suitable for full-timers. Attention must now be turned to the emerging experience of job-share arrangements which have challenged these attitudes.

THE NATURE AND OBJECTIVES OF JOB SHARING

The idea of job sharing is relatively new. It originated in the United States and has been promoted by organisations such as New Ways to Work, which has an active UK offshoot. The objectives of job sharing are simple. A better quality of part-time work (EOC, 1982) is achieved through consciously dividing a full-time post (hopefully a professional or supervisory post) so as to provide adequate legal and occupational benefits for the employees. The typical public sector 35-hour a week post when divided in two will ensure both job sharers have statutory protections and, if properly introduced, will retain accrued occupational rights. Essentially, a job sharer is half a full-timer.

Much of the early impetus came from equal opportunities policies, often backed by public sector trade unions. Schemes arose after careful negotiation or sometimes through the initiative of an individual manager who established an *ad hoc* arrangement. Some organisations developed detailed job-share policies, others had jobs sharers in post but no formal policy. The early 1980s saw a confused picture, with hard data difficult to obtain, but a clear impression of growing popularity. Studies of a regional nature (Leighton and Rayner, 1986) or sectoral based nature (NWW, 1986) provided evidence of managerial and trade union attitudes and of the variety of arrangements. Conferences and training sessions developed. There was growing interest, but continuing reluctance by many employers, especially in the private sector. Job sharing was associated with 'soft' equal opportunites policies and, in the view of many, with the less cost conscious public sector. By the mid-1980s the United Kingdom had perhaps a few thousand job sharers, overwhelmingly women with young children. Typically, they were previous full-timers who had returned to job share their own or similar post after maternity leave. They were librarians, secretaries, planning and housing officers and were increasingly working in the health and education services. Many asserted the view that equal opportunities for women meant rejection of the concept that after maternity leave you returned full time or not at all.

These were pioneering job sharers, who were determined that job sharing would work; that it would not be too confusing, disruptive or inefficient. They worked hard (often beyond their stipulated hours), often used their own time and resources to liaise with their job-share partner and were aware of the overt or covert reservations of their colleagues and managers (Leighton and Buckland, 1985).

By 1986 the climate was changing, especially in the public sector. Skill shortages were forcing employers to divert energies towards retaining key employees. The level of vacancies in central government departments caused one manager to comment, 'Anything's on the agenda now. We can no longer insist on full-time work' (Leighton and Rayner, 1986). Proposals to job share were met with increasingly favourable responses. Many of the apparently deeply held views that certain posts could *only* be done on a full-time basis were rapidly revised. By 1987 statistics were showing that several central government departments were employing considerable numbers of job sharers (Civil Service, 1987). However, research shows that many employers remained sceptical of job sharing and at best saw it as a short-term response for some employees until they returned to full-time (and proper!) work. It is self-evident that job sharing will only overcome some of the handicaps suffered by part-timers if, first, job sharing is widely accepted and, secondly, if job sharing itself provides adequate support and protections for the employees themselves.

In addition, job sharing is attractive only if senior and responsible posts are available to job share. Many potential jobs sharers seek something more than a slightly 'up market' part-time post. They assert the validity of part-time work itself. Job sharing will only thrive if organisations treat it seriously and provide adequate support. Job sharers do not want to be apologised for or marginalised; they do not want to be seen as tokens of an 'equal opportunities employer'. In other words, they want a reality—a worthwhile and rewarding post. Some will want to job share for a short while; others foresee job sharing as a way of working for an indefinite period.

Job sharing is a unique work pattern in that it has been consciously and coherently developed in order to overcome disadvantages. It can be seen as running against tides which have led to increased casualisation, temporary work and freelance arrangements. Job-share arrangements are always negotiated because each job share is unique. The number of options is considerable. Two people can share one job; three people can share two posts; two people can each do 0.6 of a post giving, in effect, six days a week between them. Negotiation may lead to questioning whether the full Monday to Friday period needs to be covered: might it be preferable to leave the post 'uncovered' during quiet periods so as to maximise the time sharers have together?

More usually job-share arrangements involve a week on/week off pattern or one sharer works Monday to Wednesday lunch time and the other works to Friday afternoon. Personal preferences can surface and be accommodated in discussions. Posts which can be shared are varied, but still tend to be concentrated in professional posts within the public sector. The reasons people job share similarly vary, but domestic responsibilities appear still the major one.

Hence, evidence suggests growing interest and experience of job sharing. Early promptings by equal opportunities policies have been supplanted by acute recruitment and retention problems in many occupations, especially in the south of England. Demographic trends—the so-called vanishing school leaver—have put pressure on employers to substitute older women for young workers. Opportunities to job share appear a particular attraction to women who would be tempted to enter or return to the labour market for a satisfying part-time career (IMS, 1989). Despite the increasingly favourable climate the issue remains whether job sharing does offer rewarding and secure work. To return to the original question; does job sharing cure or significiantly ease the disadvantages traditionally associated with 'normal' part-time work? It is now necessary to consider research.

RESEARCH STUDIES

One of the major advantages of job-share research is that the need to articulate the terms of the contract of employment and work out in detail the day-to-day workings of the job share ensures there is usually both extensive written material as well as informed employees to interview. In addition, the high levels of commitment to make a job share work on the part of job sharers themselves necessarily involves much monitoring, evaluation and self-examination. In short, job sharing is a fertile and rewarding area of employment relations research.

Projects have explored the general issues of job sharing and its development in specific sectors of employment such as local government and the NHS (New Ways to Work, 1986; IMS, 1989), and its development in a particular geographical area (Leighton and Rayner, 1986). The experiences and attitudes of job sharers themselves (Leighton and Buckland, 1985) and the impact of job sharing at the workplace more generally (Leighton and Winfield, 1988) have also been examined. All the studies have to be set in the context of both law, and current managerial and trade union policies. Most heavily relied upon will be the last study. This set itself the question 'Does job sharing work?', and took the form of seven in-depth case studies drawn from both the private and public sector. Deliberately, complex and demanding jobs were chosen—two in journalism, one in training, one in a central government department with direct contact with the public and two in senior policy development posts in the public sector. Most job sharers worked in workplaces based on teamwork and all in complex organisations. As well as the job sharers the personnel manager, colleagues, subordinates and clients/customers or other appropriate parties, and trade union officials were interviewed.

THE EXPERIENCE OF JOB SHARING: SOME KEY QUESTIONS

To provide a context for analysis the situation of many part-timers has revealed a number of typical drawbacks. They can be summarised as follows:

- Relatively poor pay levels and other conditions of work.
- Lack of adequate protection from the legal framework.
- Poor support from trade unions.
- Relatively poor levels of access to training, especially management training.
- Lack of availability of promotion and career development to senior posts.
- Lack of integration into the workforce.
- Lack of appreciation from management of the contribution made by part-timers.

Clearly, many of these drawbacks are interrelated, and they also subsume other problems, such as the frequent failure of managements to provide comprehensive information, even on health and safety and the lack of involvement of part-timers in social facilities. Examination of the experience of job sharing will focus on these issues.

Pay and Conditions of Work

This was the first and most obvious aspect given attention by job share promoters and negotiators. Part-timers are traditionally paid on an hourly rate; job sharers' pay is expressed as a proportion of the pay of the full-time post. This will normally be to the advantage of job sharers when looked at overall. Most significantly, job sharing also implies dividing the other full-time conditions—access to sick pay, paid holidays, expenses and allowances and the like. Most job-share arrangements have achieved a satisfactory division, although the fact that bank holidays are predominantly on Mondays has caused some predictable difficulties. The way out has often been to devise a scheme of one sharer 'compensating' the other, or more complex time off *in lieu* arrangements. This flexible approach typifies job sharing and distinguishes it from the more rigid traditions associated with part-time work. The only major problem area, though one which most job-share arrangements have overcome, is that of occupational pensions. All the existing research predates the impact of the so-called portable pension which may well prove an attractive proposition for job sharers who foresee a range of work patterns during their career. The particular problem has been that traditional occupational pensions require contributions based on earnings, and provide pensions related to level of salary at time of retirement. The twin issues of maintaining contributions and getting adequate recompense, especially for a job sharer who job shared just prior to retirement after full-time career (and full-time contributions), have had to be dealt with.

A number of creative schemes have evolved, and in any event the pension climate generally is rapidly changing so as to become more flexible. A system of contribution credits accrued over a period, and a pension based on those credits or an averaging has eased many situations. The overall position is that although it was initially difficult to accommodate the needs of job sharers, particularly where they were previous full-timers, solutions are generally in hand.

Legal Protections

The handicaps faced by part-timers can be overcome by ensuring that each works more than 16 hours a week. The aim outlined a recent White Paper (*Building Businesses . . . not Barriers, 1985*) to raise the threshold to 20 hours has been thwarted. At the same time the 1988 White Paper (*Employment for the 1990s*) has clearly indicated the government's continuing intention not to extend legal protections. Essentially, workplace protections have to be negotiated through contracts—the law will not provide any greater 'floor of rights' (Painter, 1987).

Two main issues emerge. Together they raise the question of whether job sharers have overcome legal vulnerability of part-timers. The first is the issue of continuity of employment; the second that of job security and the workings of unfair dismissal and redundancy provisions.

Important legal rights—maternity rights as well as job security—depend on continuous periods of employment of, usually, two years. A job-share arrangement of, say, a week on/week off nature has been questioned as to whether continuity is preserved. It will be preserved providing the whole relevant period is governed by a contract of employment, or, failing that, the period is a 'temporary cessation of work' (Schedule 13, para 9 EPCA).

Some commentators (IDS, 1987) doubt whether a week on/week off arrangement, where in one week there are no hours worked, preserves continuity. However, it is suggested that this is incorrect as it can be argued that either the week off remains 'governed by a contract' or it is a 'temporary cessation' anticipated by the contract. In other words, it is temporary because the employer clearly anticipates return the following week. The issue remains to be tested but it is unlikely that job-share arrangements are vulnerable in this regard.

Much more serious and an area revealed through research as of considerable anxiety is the issue of job security. A particular problem arises when one of the job sharers leaves and the employer is faced with the dilemma of what to do with the vacancy. Reactions vary, but most employers want to keep alive a range of options. Unless it is carefully negotiated many employers will wish to avoid a situation where they are forced to advertise the remaining 'half'. Early job-share policies, especially those created so as to maximise equal opportunities, contained a requirement that when one sharer left the employer would offer the post on a full-time basis to the remaining sharer or advertise the vacancy. Case studies in the recent analysis of job sharing (Leighton and Winfield, 1988) showed employers less willing to be this flexible. One employer in the voluntary sector reserved the right through contract to 'review the situation', and another (in the public sector) to use 'their best endeavours' to find a replacement. However, in general, out of the seven organisations in the study three had left the situation open and the job sharers we interviewed were fatalistic about the likely outcome. In one case (disabled job sharers in a local authority) they felt the situation was so insecure that each hesitated leaving for to do so would make the remaining partner so vulnerable.

The research also showed that some employers still fail to set out the position in their contract. The only relatively secure groups appear to be civil servants, not so much because their employment documentation provides adequate protections but rather that the occupation already allows for redeployment. The research showed that if a job share was successful, when one of the sharers left the 'half' would be offered to an appropriate person who had indicated an interest in job sharing. It is not unusual for one post to be occupied by up to five individuals over a period of time. In this way job sharing can be kept alive.

It has to be said that the issue of what to do when a sharer leaves reveals one of the central dilemmas of job sharing. Some feel that one of the major purposes of job sharing is to facilitate entry or re-entry to full-time work. They feel that when one sharer leaves the first priority must be to give the sharer the right to occupy the post on a full-time basis. Others argue that this dilutes job sharing; it denies the validity of job sharing as a work pattern by downgrading it to 'pending' full-time work, and that job sharers themselves should be committed to part-time work.

Despite these tensions most job-share arrangements which address the problem aim to leave discretion with the employer and to minimise the options for employees. They may adopt a formula which will seek the views of the remaining sharer but the employer will decide whether to keep the job share alive, or redeploy the sharer into other part-time work, or require the sharer to go full time, or leave.

What are the legal implications for the job sharer? An order redeploying the sharers will be lawful if the contract reserved the right: similarly, a demand that they go full time. However, the second situation may contravene anti-discrimination legislation, at least if the sharer is a woman. Case law suggests that in some circumstances, demanding that a woman works full time will be discriminatory (*Home Office* v. *Holmes* [1984] IRLR 299). Alternatively, a woman may rely on the provisions of European Community law as being discriminatory on grounds of sex. It is impossible to be confident on the area because of the technicalities of anti-discrimination law.

Another scenario which is unpromising for job sharers is where a remaining job sharer is offered a post on a full-time basis, rejects it and is dismissed. If the contract requires her or him to work full time there can be little argument. Where it did not it could be found that such a change constitutes constructive dismissal as being a fundamental breach of contract. However, it is possible that if the employer could show cogent reasons why there was a need for a full-timer, or that the job share arrangement had not proved successful, the dismissal could be fair. As discussed earlier, courts and tribunals still remain sympathetic to an employer's judgement that work had to be carried out full time.

Overall, job sharers cannot rely on job security and research continues to show that this is a major area of concern (Leighton and Winfield, 1988). In principle, the varying needs of employers and employees ought to be capable of articulation, but the fears of many employers that they might be encumbered with job-share arrangements which they see as too inflexible have encouraged the unsatisfactory situation.

Trade Unions and Job Sharing

Although many unions, especially those with a high proportion of women members and those operating in the public sector such as NALGO have become supportive of atypical workers there remain strong traditions of apathy or even hostility towards work patterns such as job sharing. The 1986 study (Leighton and Rayner) set out to determine unions' views from both central union policies, and at branch level. Somewhat surprisingly, many unions (and the TUC) did not have a formal policy on job sharing at that time. This mirrored general attitudes which saw many work patterns as diluting the workforce and undermining the bargaining position of full-time workers. Other trade union reservations centred on the reluctance of job sharers and other groups to join unions. All the research studies, even those dealing in detail with the situation at individual workplaces, reflected these attitudes. Many job sharers felt, whether justified or not, that if it came to a choice in a dispute the interests of job sharers were likely to be sacrificed. They saw a difference between union support for a job-share policy (which was generally forthcoming) and support for individual sharers when they faced opposition or difficulties.

There are recent signs that union attitudes are becoming more supportive, but it has to be recognised that job sharers can cause tensions in individual work units, especially between job sharers and ordinary part-timers, and between sharers and the employee who covers for them when they are not at work. Union officials occasionally have an invidious task to decide whom to support.

Training and Promotion

At this juncture major problems emerge from research. They are inextricably linked with the issue of job segregation. The traditional view has been that as senior posts are inappropriate for part-timers there is relatively little point in training them beyond occupation–specific skills. Management training in particular would not be worth investing in. However, some practical issues of training do exist. As discussed earlier, given that many job sharers work part time due to domestic responsibilities or because they have a second career, the usual structures of training—daily seminars, weekend conference at a set time—may not be for job sharers. Job sharers themselves often feel reluctant to attend courses during their working hours, 'I am reluctant to ask for training when I am only here half a week' (Leighton and Winfield, 1988, p. 33). Even technology training, such as use of word processors and computers, can be difficult to arrange. Health and safety, equal opportunities, customer relations and self-awareness courses will probably be even harder to fit in.

Promotion can also be hard to achieve. A few employers are willing to promote the job sharers as a team, providing each is individually capable of the more senior work. If only one is considered capable and is promoted the employer may well be faced with resentment from the remaining sharer, or the employer will decide not to promote so as to maintain good relations. If one is promoted, all the problems discussed earlier of filling the 'gap' will have to be dealt with. All this inevitably places responsibilities on management to anticipate and develop an effective strategy for dealing with these issues, a task which can be quite demanding.

Job Segregation

Of all issues this one is fundamental. The tradition has been that all senior posts and many types of work require full-timers. Even employers who extensively use shift work allow flexi-hours or other work patterns do not generally question this view. In the 1986 study even employers sympathetic to the needs of part-timers or job sharers were unwilling to let them operate above a certain level. This might be a salary point or grade. They might be barred from posts which had significant managerial or supervisory roles. The views were that jobs need 'continuity' and 'coherence'; some need policy development and others involve contact with third parties such as clients, patients and customers—such people would find job sharing too confusing!

One of the job sharers in the 1988 study summed up the views of many job sharers as follows, 'I have not heard of any job split manager in the . . . Department. I did say I was interested in other work in my last report and I went up to regional office for an interview. I was told it would be difficult to find a partner or part-time job which would interest me. I was to let her know when I wanted to go full time again' (Leighton and Winfield, 1988, p. 33).

However, the case studies clearly showed that job sharing can work in senior and complex posts. Of the seven organisations studied, all the job sharers were in professional posts. In two, the job sharers were journalists, in one case working on a national daily, in the other on a weekly magazine. Another job share was in a particularly stressful area of social work, two had line managerial responsibilities in central government departments and two had senior administrative or managerial posts. In the last two cases the work was creative, policy orientated and involved working in a team. The object of the research had been to explore the impact of job sharing on the efficiency and productivity of the post, on colleagues and subordinates and on people the job share liaised with.

Under close scrutiny and hard and frank interviewing the outcome was that such job shares do require careful planning but that they can be highly successful. Indeed, it is arguable that job sharing in senior posts can be more effective than in more routine, more easily divided posts. The comments, 'Two heads are better than one', they can, 'Play to strengths', and one by a subordinate that, 'I benefit from two perspectives; two levels of input' are typical (Leighton and Winfield, 1988, pp. 37, 24, 44).

A glance at emerging evidence of stress and so-called executive burn-out appears to lend support to the view that some jobs are too demanding for full-timers. Indeed, it is arguable that a new form of vulnerability has begun to attack these full-timers whose jobs become too demanding, especially at senior levels. Informal discussions with managers in the education service have shown that initial responses to suggestions of job sharing headteachers' posts have ranged from incredulity to undisguised mirth. And yet wastage rates of headteachers are high and increasing, as is the complexity of the job itself. It may well be that it is an ideal post to job share, providing there are major attitudinal changes to the idea that demanding posts can only be carried out full time.

Hence, the underlying problem as discussed earlier is that employers are not yet willing to question the so-called advantages of full-time work. In one of the case studies in the 1988 research where the job sharers had been involved in the production of a weekly journal, the line manager was convinced that he needed full-timers. He referred to a job sharer as 'a tourist'. There were enormous pressures from outside (to get to print) and the journalists 'need to build up team spirit and retain momentum' (Leighton and Winfield, 1988, p. 39).

However, managers in an inner city borough where the job sharers headed a policy unit found job sharing an asset. One manager said, 'They take away a particular area of policy and develop it', 'When I ask either one of them to do something, they go back and talk about it and I get the impression they make a greater contribution to what is being said' (Leighton and Winfield, 1988, p. 37).

The overall inference remains that job sharing is gaining acceptance in higher posts but only slowly. This remains a key issue.

Integration and Support at the Workforce

Many of the early job-share arrangements, unsurprisingly, concentrated on severely practical issues of pay and conditions. However, research shows that job sharers have equal concerns about remaining peripheral at the workplace. Some sensed resentment by full-time colleagues, 'They think that we are on a cushy number' (Leighton and Winfield, 1988, p. 25) and few felt they had adequate feedback on job sharing. They thought managers were generally, 'neutrally supportive' or 'passively supportive'. Few sharers felt they had enough information about job sharing and some were worried about how they would get on with their partner. They were sensitive about effective communication both between themselves and others, and job sharers in managerial and supervisory posts were sometimes aware that subordinates could exploit the situation or drive a wedge between the sharers. There were tensions about such basic issues as willingness to be rung at home, and perceived time wasting. One commented, 'If I chat at work it tends to be purely about work. I don't go out for lunch . . . I eat at my desk' (Leighton and Winfield, 1988, p. 37). However, despite these problems, most of which arose because the job share was highly visible in a work unit, the job sharers themselves enjoyed job sharing. The following comments were typical. ' . . . job sharing enhanced my productivity,' 'Work is less of a daily slog . . . now I look forward to work.' 'I gained an enormous amount from working with a partner who was different from me and had different strengths.' Most job sharers recognise that at least they have retained their hold on the career ladder.

Perhaps the most satisfying aspect of job sharing for many is the degree of control they have over the terms and execution of the post. This process can be time consuming and demanding. It requires experimentation, self-evaluation and self-confidence, for example, to admit that your partner is, say, a better administrator or communicator and should thus deal with those aspects of the post.

CONCLUSION

All in all, it cannot be said that job sharing has overcome all the disadvantages of part-time work. Many legal and occupational difficulties remain, but perhaps it is the increased self-respect and degree of responsibility for the way work is carried out (especially in senior posts), the opportunity to challenge assumptions and to have a more balanced work/leisure/home life which constitutes the success of job sharing.

Perhaps also the experience of the research studies demonstrates the deep-seated problems of vulnerability at the workplace. Some are severely practical and, with energy and commitment, can be overcome by individuals. Progress on occupational benefits and the organisation of the workload has been considerable. There are inevitable demands on management who will be called upon to consider issues rarely addressed in relation to full-timers. This can be very exciting and can lead to far more efficiency and satisfaction. Other problems are not within the capability of employers as they concern adjustments to legislation and fiscal policies. Even with the major initiatives to attract women into the workforce, it has to be doubted whether changes in the law will go beyond the minimum of those required by the European Community.

The area which has to be dealt with if job sharing is to be more widely accepted is the assumption of the intrinsic superiority of full-time work. The organisational culture will have to be radically changed though with the impact of demographic changes and skill shortages many organisations are already far down this road.

REFERENCES

Atkinson, J. and Leighton, P. (1990). *Part Time Working in Senior Posts*, Institute of Manpower Studies.
Civil Service (1987). The growth in numbers of part timers and job sharers, Informal Paper, Department of Trade and Industry.
Department of Employment (1988). *Employment for the 1990's*, Cm 540.
Disney, R. and Szyszczak, E. (1989). Part time work: A reply to Catherine Hakim, *Industrial law Journal*, **18**, 223.
EOC (1982). *Job Sharing: A better quality of part time work*, Equal Opportunities Commission.
Hakim, C. (1989). Protective legislation and part time employment in Britain, 19 *Industrial law Journal*, **19**, 69.
IDS (1986). Study 347 *Private Sector and Part Timers*, Income Data Services.
IDS (1987). Employment Law Handbook 39, *Contracts of Employment*, Income Data Services.
IMS (1989). *Job Sharing in the National Health Service*, Report by J. Buchan and N. Meager.
IS (1986). *Absenteeism from Work*, Industrial Society.
Leighton, P. and Buckland, P. (1985). *Job Sharing: Defining the Issues*, Department of Law Research Paper, The Polytechnic of North London.
Leighton, P. and Rayner, C. (1986). *Job Sharing in SE Essex*, Employment Relations Research Centre, Anglia Higher Education College.
Leighton, P. and Winfield, M. (1988). *Does Job Sharing Work*? Industrial Society and Anglia Higher Education College.
NWW (1986). *Job Sharing: Putting Policy into Practice*, New Ways to Work.
Painter, R. (1987). Floor of rights, a clear case of subsidence, *Vulnerability in the UK Labour Law*, special edition of *Employee Relations*, December 1987.
Wood, D. and Smith, P. (1989). Employers labour use of strategies, Department of Employment Research Paper No. 62.

Chapter 10.1

The Experience of Black Workers

Paul Iles, Open University, Milton Keynes, UK and Randhir Auluck, Coventry Polytechnic, UK

INTRODUCTION

Britain is increasingly developing into a multi-cultural and multi-racial society, and one which affords equity and equality for all its citizens—at least, in theory. The extent to which this is manifest in reality is open to debate, and dependent, in part, on individual and collective political and social perspectives. Nevertheless, a wide body of academic analyses and empirical research would suggest that black people (variously labelled as 'ethnic minorities', 'coloured people', 'deprived communities', 'immigrants', and so on) continue to be subject to experiences of inequality, oppression, social injustice and disadvantage in all sectors of society and all aspects of life (see Fryer, 1986; Cashmore and Troyna, 1983; Ben-Tovim, 1978; Miles, 1982; Dominelli, 1988; Alderfer and Thomas, 1988).

The concept of 'race', issues of 'racism' and 'racialism', and the relationship between 'multi-culturalism'/'cultural awareness' and 'multi-racialism'/anti-racism have been widely explored from within various perspectives, e.g. historical, sociological, psychological, political, economic (Banton, 1972; Husband, 1982; Sivanandan, 1985). One specific aspect that remains controversial is that of definition. Disagreement continues about the categorisation of the groups and communites that provide the central focus of such debates. Struggles for specific and appropriate labels have been broad ranging, sometimes confusing and constantly shifting (almost cyclic in some ways). For the purposes of simplicity and clarity we will be using the term 'black' in preference to other forms of categorisation, and this will refer to people of Asian, African and Caribbean descent.

It is acknowledged that oppression and social disadvantage are also experienced by other non-indigenous communities, such as Italians, Greek and Turkish Cypriots, the Chinese, Irish and Jews. However, it has been argued that Asians, Africans and Caribbeans tend to share similar experiences

Vulnerable Workers: Psychosocial and Legal Issues. Edited by M. J. Davidson and J. Earnshaw

of being consistently and systematically subjected to extreme forms of racial oppression as a consequence of their visible difference from indigenous communities—that is, their physiological (and consequently, social and political) 'blackness' (Brown, 1984; BILT, 1987; Katz, 1977). We also use the category 'black' in order to maintain some consistency with the categorisation frequently employed within statistical catalogues and survey reviews. 'White' ethnic minority groups such as Cypriots or Italians frequently remain invisible, embedded within the general 'White European' category.

In this chapter, we will specifically examine issues related to black people and employment. Although British organisations are increasingly demonstrating a general interest in issues of 'equal opportunity', the response from employers, academics and researchers in terms of black people's experiences of employment has tended to be limited. Particular attention needs to be directed towards an analysis of employment patterns and variations in relation to black/white and male/female employees. This chapter will attempt to provide a critical overview of comparative employment experiences, primarily in relation to race, and to a lesser extent in relation to gender. The impact of racial and gender differences in employment will be a thread that will run throughout the discussion. Consideration will also be given to some of the main organisational responses generally developed in response to the perceived constraints experienced by black employees.

BLACK MEN IN THE LABOUR MARKET

The Labour Force Survey, based on interviews with members of around 60 000 households and averaged over the three years 1985–87, provides us with most of our information on ethnic origins and the labour market (Department of Employment, 1988). Around 4.6% of the population of working age, about 1.55 million people, is of African, Afro-Caribbean or Asian origin. Given the age structure of the various groups involved, this proportion is likely to grow in the coming years. Given this growth, and the demographic changes in the 1990s that are likely to lead to severe skill shortages, the successful organisation is likely to be one that manages diversity and equal opportunities effectively.

One of the most notable features is the lower economic activity rate found among young black males aged 16–24: 61% of these, as compared to 84% of the relevant white population, are economically active. In part this is due to the higher proportion of this group in full-time education, particularly those of Asian origin. In addition, unemployment rates are much higher for this group. Unemployment rates are much higher for black workers generally (19% versus 11%), and black people are more likely to be unemployed within every age and sex group. The highest unemployment rates (*c*.30%,

34% for Afro-Caribbean men, compared to a white unemployment rate of c.18%) are for young men between 16 and 24. Indeed, among all age groups black male unemployment is around twice as high as white male unemployment, being particularly high for men of Pakistani/Bangladeshi origin.

The Labour Force Survey also indicates that unemployment rates for black people have declined more rapidly than for white people between 1986 and 1987 (from over 21% to 17.1%, as compared to a fall from 11.5% to 10.5% for the white population). This fall, particularly marked among Afro-Caribbean men, seems to be regarded as evidence of a possible weakening of racial discrimination in employment (Department of Employment 1988). However, in the early 1960s at a time of nearly full employment, black and white unemployment rates were almost equivalent, though not pay or job levels. Much of the recent growth in employment seems to have been in the more peripheral or secondary labour market sectors characterised by part-time, casual and low paid work, such as in hotels, catering and retail. Black workers could be being disproportionately hired in these sectors and still be acting as a secondary labour force (Wrench, 1989).

These higher unemployment rates cannot be attributed to lower qualifications among black workers. Unemployment rates are higher among black people than white people at each level of qualification. The relative disparity between black and white workers is actually more marked for those groups with higher qualifications, especially among the younger age groups. For young black men, unemployment rates are twice as high for the group with qualifications, but only a little higher for those with no qualifications. Possessing qualifications may help black people avoid unemployment, but not as much it seems as they help white people (see Table 1).

Self-employment seems markedly greater for men of Indian and Pakistani/-Bangladeshi origin (26% and 22% as compared to 15% of white men). Black men also appear more likely to be concentrated in distribution, hotels, catering and repairs (26% as compared to 16% of whites) and to be relatively strongly represented in transport, communications and the health services.

Similar proportions of white and black men seem to be in non-manual and manual jobs, and the Labour Force Survey indicates similar proportions in managerial and professional and clerical and related jobs. White manual workers are more likely to be in craft and similar jobs. Substantial variations occur within the black population, with over 55% of men from Indian origins being in non-manual jobs (42% being professional and managerial) as compared with only 25% of Afro-Caribbean men (12% professional and managerial).

To some extent, however, this apparent convergence between black and white men in terms of job levels may be a product of regional concentration. The statistics also give little indication of level *within* categories, so we do

Table 10.1 Unemployment rates by highest qualification level, ethnic origins, age and sex. Average, spring 1985–87 (percentages)

Males	All origins	White	Black	Females	All origins	White	Black
16–64				16–59			
All	11	11	20	All	11	11	18
Higher qualifications	4	3	9	Higher qualifications	5	5	—
Other qualifications	10	9	19	Other qualifications	11	11	22
No qualifications	18	18	25	No qualifications	13	12	19
16–24				16–24			
All	18	18	30	All	16	15	29
Higher qualifications	9	8	—	Higher qualifications	7	6	—
Other qualifications	14	14	28	Other qualifications	13	12	27
No qualifications	32	32	38	No qualifications	30	30	—
25–44				25–44			
All	10	9	16	All	10	10	15
Higher qualifications	3	3	—	Higher qualifications	6	6	—
Other qualifications	8	7	14	Other qualifications	10	10	17
No qualifications	18	18	23	No qualifications	13	13	16
45–64				45–59			
All	9	9	20	All	6	6	—
Higher qualifications	4	3	—	Higher qualifications	3	3	—
Other qualifications	8	8	—	Other qualifications	6	6	—
No qualifications	12	11	24	No qualifications	8	7	—

not know the ethnic distribution between, for example, higher and lower level professional and managerial jobs. Given the over-representation of black people in the London labour market, with its markedly higher proportion of non-manual jobs, it is also necessary to compare black and white workers within the same labour market. Other surveys of black male workers show considerable disparities in pay and working conditions to the disadvantage of black men (Brown, 1984).

BLACK WOMEN IN THE LABOUR MARKET

Before 1984, most surveys of black workers' position in the labour market ignored black women. The first major survey to deliberately attempt to include black women was the 1984 Policy Studies Institute survey (Brown, 1984) which, while reporting substantial earnings differentials between black and white men, reported few differences between black and white women. It seemed as if sexism in employment was so pervasive that it swamped any effect due to racism for women.

However, Breugel (1989) argues that this survey is likely to have underestimated the involvement of Asian women, in particular in home-working, family employment and paid childcare, overestimating black women's pay and job levels. If one takes into account the longer hours worked by black women, their concentration in London where pay is higher, and their better qualified, younger age profile, the racial disparities between women emerge much more strongly. Re-analysing the survey data shows that in full-time jobs black women earn lower hourly rates than white women. Drawing on data from the London Living Standards Surveys, Breugel (1989) also shows that black women in London earn substantially less than white women. Black women graduates earned only 71% of white women graduates, and black women were more likely to work shifts, were less likely to enjoy fringe benefits, and were more likely to work in poorer physical conditions.

Female economic activity rates decline with age for white women but remain steady for black women, with Afro-Caribbean women having the highest activity rates of all women and women of Pakistani/Bangladeshi origins having the lowest activity rates (Department of Employment, 1988). In general, unemployment rates for black women are higher than for white women (18% versus 10% overall, and 29% versus 15% for 16–24-year-olds). Racial differences in unemployment rates between women seem particularly marked in London (Breugel, 1989). Asian women in particular are less likely to be economically active between 16 and 24, in part due to a higher percentage of women of Indian origin being in full-time education and in part due to the greater likelihood of young women of Pakistani/Bangladeshi origin attributing inactivity to domestic or family reasons (Department of Employment, 1988).

The Labour Force Survey also shows that more white women are found in non-manual jobs (66% versus 61%). Similar proportions of all ethnic groups seem to be found in professional and managerial work and in clerical and related work. However, black women seem more likely to be in full-time work than white women (63% versus 51%). This apparently fairly similar occupational profile conceals the very poor *full-time* jobs held by many black women. Widely different kinds of jobs are grouped together in most official surveys, often obscuring differences within job categories, such as those between state enrolled nurses and state registered nurses or between word processors and personal assistants. Black women seem more likely to hold the poorer jobs within categories, less commensurate with their qualifications (Breugel, 1989). The relatively high proportion of black women in non-manual jobs reported in the Labour Force Survey also again appears to be in part a function of their greater concentration in the London labour market. Outside London proportionally fewer black women work in non-manual jobs. In addition, if part-time workers are separated off, racial differences between women seem much starker. Given the lower income per head for black households in each type of household, black households seem much more reliant on black womens' full-time earnings (Breugel, 1989).

RACIAL DISCRIMINATION IN EMPLOYMENT

A series of studies conducted prior to the passage of the 1976 Race Relations Act revealed widespread racial discrimination in employment and elsewhere. Using job applicants matched for gender, age, qualifications and experience but differing in ethnic origin, such surveys showed that discrimination in employment was far more marked for black applicants from Asian and Afro-Caribbean origins than for white ethnic minorities from southern European backgrounds (Smith, 1976).

It might be expected that the passage of the 1976 Race Relations Act, making both direct and indirect discrimination illegal, would make such discrimination considerably less common. In fact, many studies of recruitment and of the position of black workers in various industrial regions throughout the 1970s and 1980s have revealed substantial continuing discrimination in employment. For example, many Asian migrants in particular came in the 1950s and 1960s to northern cities like Bradford (Singh, 1987; Singh and Ram, 1986), and Rochdale (Penn, Scattergood and Martin, 1990). They found poorly paying, low-skilled work in local textile and manufacturing industries at a time of labour shortages and an increasing reluctance of white workers to take on such jobs under such poor conditions. However, many non-skilled jobs in traditional industries have collapsed. For example, between 1971 and 1984 textile employment in Rochdale fell from 16 000 to 3400. This has led to much unemployment in the Asian community, with little evidence that Asian parents or their children have significantly penetrated other sectors of employment and with many indications that their economic position has deteriorated in the 1980s (Penn, Scattergood and Martin, 1990). Similarly in Bradford in the 1980s over twice as many black young people, mainly of Asian origin, remained unemployed (Manpower

Services Commission, 1987; Clough, Drew and Jones, 1988).

It might be hoped that the growth of new service industries such as retailing or catering would compensate for this loss of traditional employment. However, a study of recruitment to a Leicester shopping centre in 1984 showed that a far higher ratio of white applicants to black applicants were successful in obtaining jobs. Employers seemed unable to identify any specific differences in abilities, qualifications or experience which might explain such disparities, and in part such differential recruitment was attributed to internal appointments, informal recruitment from friends and relations, and subjective selective criteria applied by untrained recruiters (Commission for Racial Equality, 1985).

Another study of recruitment into a variety of skilled manual, secretarial, clerical, office junior and sales representatives' jobs also showed substantial racial discrimination. Black applicants matched in gender, experience and qualifications applying by telephone or letter, in London, Birmingham and Manchester were much less likely to be called for interview (Brown and Gay, 1985).

In part such discrimination seems related to pervasive ethnic stereotypes, as shown in a study of recruitment to 40 retailing, manufacturing and public organisations (Jenkins, 1986). Employers often seemed to operate with two major selection criteria: 'aceptability' and 'stability'. 'Acceptability' might be judged from applicant manner, attitude or appearance; 'stability' might be judged by age, family background and employment history. Both criteria operated to the disadvantage of women and black people, and black people were seen both in terms of specific ethnic stereotypes and as likely to cause 'problems' for customers, clients or fellow workers. Word-of-mouth recruitment was often used, favouring the relatives and friends of existing employees. This was in part a conscious stategy designed to reduce uncertainty in selection and foster a positive 'family firm' image and climate. It had the effect of disadvantaging black applicants by excluding them from access to information networks, given a predominantly white workforce. This adverse effect of informal recruitment methods and unsolicited letters has been shown to disadvantage black workers in other studies (Commission for Racial Equality, 1982).

Such informal recruitment methods may particularly disadvantage black workers since many studies have shown that black job applicants seem more reliant on formal recruitment channels such as the careers service or job centres (e.g. Commission for Racial Equality, 1983). Even here, however, they are likely to find themselves at a disadvantage. A study of job centres in 1985 showed that black job seekers, though using job centres more often, needed to make more applications to obtain employment than white job seekers (Manpower Services Commission, 1986).

BLACK GRADUATES

In the 1970s and early–mid-1980s most studies of racial discrimination in the United Kingdom were of recruitment into manual and routine non-manual jobs. Similarly in the United States up to the mid-1970s, most studies of racial discrimination were of industrial jobs (e.g. Purcell and Cavanagh, 1972). However, in the late 1980s attention seems to have switched to black graduates and professional recruitment, just as the mid-1970s saw the beginning of American studies into black managers and professionals.

It might be thought that the possession of educational and professional qualifications would reduce the effects of racial discrimination, given that 'lack of qualifications' is often cited as an explanation for black under-representation. However, the analysis of unemployment rates discussed above shows that discrimination and disadvantage persist at all levels of qualification. Studies of black graduates and of specific professional groups confirm this picture.

For example, a large-scale study of black non-university graduates has highlighted the greater difficulties they face in securing employment and jobs commensurate with their qualifications (Brennan and McGeevor, 1987, 1988). Twelve months after graduation in 1982, 70% of white graduates as compared to 47% of matched black graduates were in full-time employment. Asian graduates were particularly likely to be unemployed, even though they had often graduated in such 'vocational' subjects as science and engineering. Black graduates were also more likely to be found in jobs at levels below their qualifications, and to receive lower salaries. When matched according to course, sex, degree class and institution, black disadvantage was even more marked. Educational qualifications did not seem to eradicate disadvantages related to ethnic origin.

A further study of recent graduates has also demonstrated widespread apparent discrimination against black graduates, many of whom found it more difficult to obtain jobs than similarly qualified white graduates; often securing less satisfying work (Commission for Racial Equality, 1990). Another large-scale survey followed the work histories of black and white graduates (Johnes and Taylor, 1989). Black graduates were less likely to have fathers in professional or managerial occupations and more likely to have fathers in low-skill occupations (the jobs of their mothers were not mentioned). They were also likely to have lower A-level scores. Despite this, no significant differences emerged with regard to degree class. A significantly smaller proportion of black graduates obtained employment and a higher proportion was unemployed six months after graduation. Six years later, black graduates were twice as likely to be unemployed, but no significant differences were noted in salary levels, experience of promotions or post-graduate professional qualifications.

BLACK PROFESSIONALS

Several recent studies show the greater difficulties faced by black people in Britain in obtaining professional employment. Black students seem to face greater difficulties in gaining access to higher education (Lyon, 1988) and may be systematically discriminated against when seeking professional education. For example, St George's Hospital Medical School had discriminated against women and black applicants since at least 1982 (Commission for Racial Equality, 1988a). A computer program had been devised to simulate the decisions of interviewers. It gave lower scores to female and black applicants as compared with similarly qualified white male applicants.

Similarly a study of chartered accountancy training found that white applicants to accountancy firms were much more likely to be successful than black applicants (Commission for Racial Equality, 1987b). All the partners, and 95% of the professional employees of the 14 largest firms were white, and the 'white male public school' image projected in recruitment literature appeared to discourage black and female applicants. In 1986, the overall success rate for white applicants to the largest firms was about four times that of black applicants, and black applicants seemed disproportionately rejected at the pre-selection, first interview, and second interview stages. In part this seemed due to a preference for applicants from the 'best' universities with the 'right' extra-mural interests, and in part due to detrimental stereotypes held by selectors about black applicants (e.g. 'too keen to please', 'too aggressive', 'lacking in sparkle').

Less than 2% of teachers in one study of eight local education authorities in England were black, often concentrated in the lowest grades and in shortage subjects. Equivalent career progress to white teachers seems more likely in schools with significant numbers of black pupils and governors (Commission for Racial Equality, 1988b).

Given an ageing black teaching force and continuing low black recruitment (Searle and Stibbs, 1989), the number of black teachers seems unlikely to grow, and may even decline. This is likely to have severe effects on black children's access to relevant role models and white pupils', parents' and teachers' attitudes to black people.

A small-scale study of 16 Bradford Asian teachers has indicated that headteachers had unrealistically high expectations, that Asian teachers were often exploited in being expected to act as interpreters or translators without reward or recognition, and that such teachers were expected to take the initiative on multi-cultural and anti-racist policies. These teachers also felt marginalised, isolated and trapped in low status positions and under pressure, with few allowances made for mistakes. Racism, both covert and overt, made them wary of recommending a teaching career to young black people. In addition, Asian students saw low pay, low status and racism among pupils and teachers as a disincentive to entering teaching (Singh, 1988).

Studies of the nursing profession have also shown substantial under-representation of black people in senior nursing positions, and in some forms of internal career development training (Commission for Racial Equality, 1987a). Nearly 70% of black staff in this study believed that they had been treated unfairly with respect to race.

Again, a national survey of police employment in 1987 has shown that many police forces fail to reflect the proportion of black people in their areas in their staffing patterns, especially above the role of constable. Most police forces appeared to focus on recruitment, with less concentration on monitoring, career progression or promotion (Oakley, 1987). This contrasts with the situation in many police forces in the United States, where issues of affirmative action, active recruitment of minorities, alternative entry routes, more attention to supervision on field work training, better career planning, and challenges to the allocation of discriminatory work assignments and hostile work climates have often been addressed (e.g. Hunt, 1987). Similarly the recent attention to black under-recruitment in the British armed forces and the publicity given to cases of racial discrimination and racial harassment contrasts with the attention given to race training in the US Army following the racial disturbances in 1969 (Nordlie, 1987).

BLACK MANAGERS

Virtually all the studies we have of black managers are from the United States. The lack of progress of black managers in the United States was originally attributed to cultural background or to a lack of educational qualifications. Black culture was perceived to be inadequate in socialising black people into the necessary entrepreneurial attitude, work ethic or orientation to ambition and initiative necessary to succeed in business (Fernandez, 1975). However, such speculations are contradicted by the evidence that need for achievement and need for power scores of black and white college students do not vary significantly as a function of race (Lefkowitz and Fraser, 1980). Some studies have also shown that black managers and MBA students in the United States seem to be *more* individually oriented and to place a *higher* value on independence than white managers and MBA students (Brenner, Blazini and Greenhaus, 1988). They also seem to place a high value on upward mobility (Fernandez, 1975).

Though white US managers have also tended to see black managers as lacking in qualifications, Fernandez (1975) showed that black managers tended to be over-qualified for the jobs they held. White managers also tended to hold internally contradictory stereotypes. Furthermore, black managers reported racial discrimination in access and in treatment once employed (see also Jones, 1973, 1986; Dickens and Dickens, 1982). Black managers also experienced negative stereotyping, a lack of cooperation from white managers, exclusion from informal networks, and increased visibility and performance pressures. Such managers frequently felt always 'on stage', with their mistakes bringing them extra penalties. They often felt that they had to bridge a credibility gap, usually being sidelined into routine, 'showcase', or 'black jobs' in welfare, personnel, equal opportunity, or in dealing with black staff or customers. Such positions were not on the main career track that typically led to upward advancement, power, influence or status.

Such findings in American studies of black managers resemble those often reported for white women managers in Britain (see, for example, Hammond, 1988; Davidson and Cooper, 1984; Davidson, 1985). Parallel findings have also been reported with regard to mentoring. Successful women in the United States have been reported as even more dependent on the kind of supportive, advisory and sponsorship functions that mentors may give than successful men (McKeen and Burke, 1989). In part this may be due to their exclusion from male informal networks; used by men to give access to information and support. Women, however, may be less likely to obtain satisfactory mentors. Senior male managers and potential mentors may perceive women as lacking in leadership or managerial qualities or as a risk to their own careers. They may exclude women from contacts and access to information, and even in mentoring relationships may be over-protective, allow gender stereotypes to inhibit the personal and career development of their female mentees, forcing them into 'traditional' supportive roles. Potential male mentors may also seek to avoid female mentees due to sensitivity concerning the negative effects of gossip, jealousies and innuendoes surrounding cross-gender relationships. Women's self-confidence and self-efficacy may suffer due to a lack of appropriate role models, and male mentors may be insensitive to such issues as discrimination, stereotyping, tokenism, sexual harassment and home/work conflicts. Female mentors may be unavailable due to their under-representation, their own career difficulties, and over-loading from female potential mentees.

Black managers may experience similar difficulties in finding suitable mentors in white-dominated organisations. Some US studies of white–black mentoring have reported that such relationships tend to reflect the state of consciousness of both parties. Some black managers did seem able to establish supportive relationships with white and black senior managers, finding them useful in dealing with racial barriers and performance demands

(Thomas, 1986; Alderfer and Thomas, 1988; Davis and Watson, 1982). Mentoring relationships across racial and sex boundaries may pose particular difficulties, given the history of race relations involving white male sexual exploitation of black women and controls on the sexuality of white women and black men. Such relationships may be easier to establish between white and black women. These difficulties may make partners in mentoring relationships 'cool' their relationships to preserve only the instrumental aspects, to the detriment of the overall relationship (Thomas, 1989).

Whether such dynamics apply to cross-race/cross-gender relationships in the United Kingdom remains to be investigated.

Other American studies have shown that white, black and other minority managers can have very different views of the state of race relations in their organisation and the best ways forward to improve race relations at work. Black managers have been found to be much more critical of the way they are treated in white corporations than other minority managers, such as Hispanics, Asian Americans and Native Americans (Fernandez, 1981). In another study (Alderfer *et al.*, 1980; Alderfer and Smith, 1982) black managers were found to have very different and more group-based views than white managers.

ORGANISATIONAL RESPONSES

There are numerous initiatives, within the scope of the positive action provisions of the 1976 Race Relations Act, that organisations can take to improve the position of black employees at work, even in the absence of wider political activities.

Recruitment Initiatives

Organisations can seek to recruit more black employees through widening their basis of recruitment and targeting schools, colleges, community centres, employment agencies, magazines and journals likely to be used by black people. They can also advertise in community languages, ensure that vacancies are advertised publicly in formal agencies such as job centres and the careers service, and state in their literature that they are an equal opportunities employer which particularly welcomes applications from black people. Recruitment publicity can also employ photographs and illustrations depicting black and white men and women in a variety of jobs at a variety of levels, and incorporating biographies and pen portraits of both black and white employees. Organisations will also need to review their informal recruitment policies which include such practices as recruiting through word of mouth, given their adverse impact on the recruitment chances of black applicants to predominantly white organisations.

Selection Initiatives

Most attention in Britain seems to have been directed to formalising selection criteria so that they truly reflect the qualities and skills necessary to perform effectively in a job, and not just those thought to lead to effective job performance. This requires a systematic prior job analysis (Iles and Auluck, 1988, 1989). It also requires that selectors are trained in avoiding prejudice and stereotyping.

It has been increasingly recognised that black applicants may be discriminated against at all stages of the selection process, from the job description to the person specification to the selection criteria and procedures used. Criteria not relevant to the job and irrelevant educational or literacy requirements may be included, while such job-relevant experience and skills as familiarity with black community languages, cultures or preferences and aspirations may be excluded. Tests may be used with inappropriate language requirements or cultural biases.

Many organisations have begun to organise recruitment and selection training, which may include information about the 1976 Race Relations Act, the Commission for Racial Equality Code of Practice, and the organisation's equal opportunity policy. It may also include such exercises as using application forms from male and female applicants of different ethnic backgrounds, assessed against a job description and person specification. Focusing attention on possible reasons for unfair discrimination, viewing video tapes of selection interviews to highlight key learning points, and carrying out selection interviews with applicants from different ethnic groups may be included, with feedback on ways interviewer behaviour may have been discriminatory (Toplis, 1983).

From the early 1980s, racism awareness training (RAT, Katz, 1977) has come to be used in the United Kingdom as a major approach to training selectors in awareness of racism, bias and prejudice, especially in local government and the voluntary sector. This approach, originating among white educators in North America following the black urban rebellions in the 1960s, took as its starting point the notion that Britain is a racist society and that racism, embedded in white history, white culture and white psychology is a white problem. However, new white anti-racist consciousness is possible through a structured programme where whites may become more aware both of personal prejudices and stereotypes and of institutional practices that disadvantage black people, and can take action to counteract them.

In Britain such training has been criticised as failing to provide evidence that behavioural or structural changes follow any shifts in attitude (Pumfrey, 1985; Tomkin, 1987). Some radical black activists have also criticised it for sloganising, for personalising racism, for commercialising anti-racism into packages, and for employing a moralistic, accusatory tone that misdirects energies and dissociates racial from class oppression (Gurnah, 1984; Sivanandan, 1985). However more recently such training has included skills training in interviewing and selection and firmer links with organisational outcomes, practices and staffing targets. As well, it has become more popular as one element in a strategy that also needs to include developments in policy, staffing, communication, appraisal and reward. Unlike previous efforts at 'cultural awareness' such training does seem to address directly white racism and avoids pathologising or victimising black cultures as 'the problem'. It appears to point out to white employees that they can sustain institutionally racist structures by colluding in them, remaining silent, or blaming others while avoiding action themselves (Tomkin, 1987).

Recent developments in 'anti racist training' or 'equality training' have sought to build on these pespectives by enabling work teams to identify structural barriers, see the links between racism, sexism and oppressions related to class, disability and sexual orientation, and link such training to organisational outcomes like monitoring changes in workforce composition and to positive action targets (Tomkin, 1987; Alibhai, 1988a, 1988b; Iles and Auluck, 1988, 1989).

Less attention appears to have been directed in the United Kingdom to the development of alternative selection procedures to interviews. Some selection procedures such as biodata, cognitive ability tests and personality inventories seem more valid predictors of job performance than traditional unstructured interviews, but also seem to display potential for adverse impact against black people, other minorities and women (Robertson and Iles, 1988; Iles and Robertson, 1989). More promising techniques include criteria referenced interviews, where job analysis is used to identify the skills and qualities required by job incumbents and interviewers are trained to focus on such criteria. Situational interviews, where job analysis is used to identify hypothetical situations critical to effective job performance and where candidateś responses to their situations are assessed against the responses given by high performers, also seem more valid predictors of job performance and to display less adverse impact against black applicants. Work sample tests, where applicants perform a set of tasks sampled from the normal range of tasks performed by job holders, also seem well regarded by applicants and display less adverse impact (Robertson and Kandola, 1982; Robertson and Iles, 1988).

Perhaps the most promising technique, certainly for the selection of managers and other professional groups, is the assessment centre, involving groups of participants assessed in multiple exercises by groups of trained assessors against a variety of job-relevant criteria determined through job analysis. Such centres have been shown to be perhaps the most valid predictors of managerial successes and performance, and applicable to selection, identification of potential, diagnosis of training and development needs, and organisation and management development (Iles and Robertson, 1989). They have also been shown in US studies to be equally valid predictors of male and female managerial performance (Moses and Boehm, 1975; Ritchie and Moses, 1983). British studies have shown equal numbers of male and female candidates selected for further development in the National Health Service through assessment centres (Alban Metcalfe, 1989a) and assessment centre ratings to be unrelated to gender or appearance (Iles, 1989; Iles and Robertson, 1988).

However, race effects in assessment centres have been less fully investigated, especially in Britain. In one US study, black women received lower ratings on some dimensions than white women, and different dimensions of behaviour had significant relationships with rated job performance (Huck and Bray, 1976). Another study showed that some assessment ratings for black women were significantly related to the number of white males in their assessment group. As the number of white males rose, their ratings on some dimensions declined (Schmitt and Hill, 1977).

These findings show that further examination needs to be made of the various stages involved in the assessment centre process. The sample from which the selection criteria are elicited, the definition of the criteria used, the design and selection of tests and exercises, the composition of the assessors' group, the selection of assessors, the composition of the assessees' group, the publicity and nomination procedures employed, and the pre-screening techniques employed all need to be examined. The kinds of feedback that are given, the personal development plans and actions that result, and the way the centre as a whole is to be evaluated will also need to be monitored (Alban Metcalfe 1989a; Iles, 1989).

Performance Appraisal Initiatives

Race and gender effects in the way job performance is appraised have been most fully examined in the United States, with inconsistent results. Some studies have shown that the sex and race of both ratee and rater influence the level and variance of performance ratings and the confidence with which performance ratings are made. Assessors seem to rate members of their own group with more confidence than members of other groups (Schmitt and Lappin, 1980). A meta-analysis of ratee/race effects by Kraiger and Ford (1985) also showed that raters gave slightly higher ratings to ratees of their own race, especially in field studies where blacks constituted a small percentage of the workforce.

A field study of black and white US managers has also shown that social behaviour factors correlated more with overall job performance measures for black ratees (Cox and Nkomo, 1986). Black and white managers seem to be assessed against differential performance criteria, a finding similar to that obtained by Huck and Bray (1976) with regard to assessment centres. Black American managers seem to be confronted with a more complex set of performance criteria than white managers, with greater emphasis on their ability to fit in with established social norms (see also Fernandez, 1981; Davis and Watson, 1982; Dickens and Dickens, 1982).

Much less work has been done on performance appraisal and race in the United Kingdom. Some studies have shown that ratings of promotability, but not performance, in the Civil Service tend to favour men (Williams, 1989), that women tend to receive less specific and more innocuous feedback (Corby, 1983) and that performance appraisals may disadvantage women managers (Bennett, 1986). Female success on 'male' tasks may also be attributed to luck or task ease rather than to skill or ability (e.g. Deaux, 1976). Similar biases against black people as judged by white norms may also occur, but remain to be investigated. Possible organisational responses may include rater training with an emphasis on racial and cultural differences and identification of raters' biases and stereotyping. In addition, the use of more objective appraisal processes such as behaviourally anchored ratings scales and management by objectives may help, as well as the use of multiple raters, peer evaluations, and committees above the level of the immediate boss. Since the salience of race in affecting ratings seems to decrease with an increasing percentage of black people in a work group (Kraiger and Ford, 1985), increasing the numbers of black people within organisations both vertically and horizontally is likely to make performance appraisals more objective and accurate.

Positive Action Initiatives

Organisations are increasingly developing various initiatives under the banner of positive or affirmative action. These tend to be viewed as strategies of 'empowerment' and a means of addressing some of the constraints experienced by black people in the labour market. **Positive action** is an issue that has been debated and is subect to some confusion. It is, for example, sometimes inappropriately presumed to be interchangeable with the concept of 'reverse' or 'positive discrimination' which is perceived by some to be further perpetuating unfair practice (Glazer, 1975). Rather, positive action is aimed at promoting fairer practice and making more effective use of the potential within the available workforce.

Positive action approaches have been developed in response to those sections of the Race Relations Act (1976) and the Sex Discrimination Act (1975) which allow employers to implement corrective measures where there is under-representation on the basis of race or gender (Commission for Racial Equality, 1985). Positive action is intended to provide a tool to reduce the impact of barriers to equality of opportunity which would still remain if overt discrimination was eliminated. Initiatives within this framework have been developed with respect to recruitment and selection, and staff development and training programmes. Positive action measures can, for example, be targeted at encouraging individuals from specific racial groups to apply for jobs where they are under-represented, or developing training to enable them to become more effective in their particular areas of work.

Positive action and recruitment

Racial origin can be interpreted and applied as a Genuine Occupational Qualification in recruitment, under s. 5 (2)(d) of the Race Relations Act. An individual's racial category can be defined as an essential criterion for selection in cases where, for example, the work concerns the direct provision of services promoting the welfare of people from their specific racial background and when this can best be provided by a person from the same community. Local authority social services and education departments are two obvious types of organisations where use has been made of this provision.

Other forms of positive action within the area of recruitment and selection include, for example, exemption of formal and professional qualifications, accreditation of prior and experimental learning, targeting systems, monitoring of interviews by an independent/'neutral' assessor, race and gender recording. Some organisations do include an equal opportunities representative/equality officer or trade union representative on selection and interviewing panels, either systematically or when specifically requested, as a means of attempting to ensure 'fair play'.

Local authority organisations have used s.11 of the Local Government Act 1966 as a means of securing additional funding to develop posts to respond to the welfare needs of black communities (Cross *et al.*, 1988). Section 11 funding has simultaneously been a way of employing black workers (such as ESL teachers, welfare assistants, interpreters, etc.). However, s.11 funded posts have been surrounded by controversy and criticism (Dominelli, 1988; Cross *et al.*, 1988).

In general, all such positive action strategies do have a number of merits and can serve to enhance black people's experiences within the employment sector, if adequately resourced and supported and if appropriately and effectively implemented and monitored. If such schemes are misapplied and mismanaged, they can precipitate a whole different set of organisational obstacles which obstruct black peoples' entry into and development within organisations.

Positive action and staff development

Numbers are not the only issue. Equality strategies aimed at numerical targets only go so far in promoting access to employment opportunities. Organisations involved in systematic and comprehensive monitoring of employees on the basis of race and gender are now recognising that effective recruitment and selection procedures are only part of the equality equation. Monitoring 'throughput' as well as 'input' has tended to indicate that even in organisations where targets have been met, the level at which black workers are located remains problematic. That is, black workers tend to be located in lower strata of the organisation hierarchy, on lower incomes, with poorer conditions of service.

Some organisations have attempted to address this problem through various staff development and training programmes specifically aimed at responding to the particular needs of black staff. These range from the secondment of unqualified black staff on to professional/accredited courses to training in interpersonal effectiveness, management development and career development. Ealing Borough Council and Birmingham City Council are two organisations that have attempted to implement such programmes systematically. Both these organisations have additionally developed training programmes aimed specifically at black women employees, in recognition of their experience of being 'doubly disadvantaged' on the basis of both their race and gender. Given that black women tend to be located within low-grade and low-paid posts (their representation in managerial levels is nominal or non-existent), such training is aimed at developing the participants through the introduction of black women only management development and career development programmes.

These programmes include, in addition to the standard content around issues of skills, styles, functions and effectiveness, specific focus on interpersonal effectiveness in relation to managing conflict derived from racism and/or sexism (and, indeed, other categories of oppressive practice) within the work context. Attention is also directed towards developing awareness of anti-discrimination legislation and codes of practice, and insight into formal and informal organisational constraints. Opportunity and encouragement are provided for participants to reflect on and to construct appropriate individual and collective strategies for dealing with organisational blocks. Strategies frequently generated through this process include networking, co-counselling, action learning sets and mentor systems.

Certain organisations have provided opportunities, assistance and resources for black workers to establish formally recognised support networks. Although such employees are allowed to meet in work time, the groups may remain autonomous and independent of the organisation to the extent that they can construct their agenda and are not subject to official monitoring. These networks and groups are intended to be a source of personal and professional support, a forum for exchanging information and shared concerns, a vehicle for problem solving, and a self-help mechanism for enabling black workers to realise their potential within the context of their organisation.

The actual impact and effectiveness of such positive action initiatives (including numerical recruitment and staff development targeting) is difficult to assess, either quantitatively or qualitatively, given the range of variables within such a framework. This is an area that requires further, comprehensive and systematic study and research.

Responses to positive action

The extent to which these positive action strategies affect the recruitment, retention, development and progression of black workers remains subject to speculation. The implementation of such approaches clearly requires consistent monitoring and evaluation.

Positive action programmes need to be set in the context of broader equal opportunities policies and procedures. For example, simply addressing issues of access to opportunities (through recruitment and selection, and staff development and training), does not deal with the less tangible forms of oppression and exclusion, such as hostility and rejection, questioning of credibility and authority, and systematic harassment within the workplace. Continuous experiences of this nature can impose high levels of stress and contribute to various forms of psychological disequilibrium and physical deenergisation (Cooper and Davidson, 1982; Littlewood and Lipsedge, 1982; Rack, 1982; Cox, 1986; Ineichen, 1989). This in turn, can have an adverse impact on employee performance and productivity (Jones, 1973).

Organisations need to develop mechanisms for monitoring such situations, and indeed to establish effective grievance procedures to respond to cases of racial and/or sexual harassment. Furthermore, such systems and accompanying procedures for activating them need to be widely communicated throughout all levels of the organisation. Simultaneously, people throughout the organisation need to feel a strong sense of relevance, commitment and ownership towards such facilities if they are to become at all effective.

Adequate degrees of commitment and ownership can be difficult to engender, particularly in organisations where the majority groups (predominantly white) perceive positive action as a vehicle for providing 'undeserving outsiders' (black people) with 'special privileges' and 'preferential treatment' at their expense. Positive action initiatives afford another 'visible' target (in addition to racial and gender differences) for attacks from those groups who themselves feel under threat in the context of government policies and resource cutbacks (Auluck and Iles, 1991).

Also, staff training and development opportunities, such as those previously mentioned, may particularly be perceived as promoting disruption of the organisation's equilibrium by radicalising the target groups. Some specific training programmes provide an opportunity for participants to share mutual concerns and frustrations (a process of psychological as well as verbal ventilation). Such programmes may also contextualise the problems experienced by black workers, and enable them to dismantle some of their internal (psychological) and external (organisational) blocks. Through this process of demystification and deconstruction of structural constraints, and of challenging, self-pathologising precipitated by the systematic internalisation of experiences of failure, such courses can promote greater self-confidence, stronger self-projection and enhanced effectiveness. This change in the self-presentation of some black staff may indeed be interpreted, by some, as a form of 'radicalisation'.

In parallel, black workers may view positive action initiatives as being tokenistic, marginalised and ineffective. For example, s.11 funded posts and specialist courses targeted at black staff only may encounter resistance, suspicion and rejection if they are seen excluding them from mainstream provisions. Such programmes may be devalued as being 'second rate', of 'poorer quality' and 'ghettoised', by both prospective participants and others within the organisation (Rooney, 1980). Also, these strategies may be rendered ineffective if the organisation is unable to respond to specific employee expectations that have been raised through, for example, recruitment publicity or staff development programmes. Unmet expectations can lead to increased frustration, anger, stress, and ultimately, disengagement and dysfunctioning.

CONCLUSION

Equal opportunity, in this context, is more than just transposing a black person into a white person's job. Obstacles have to be removed not just relocated (Jones, 1973).

Access and entry into employment are not the only problems. Black people tend to be under-represented in most organisations, particularly at middle to higher levels of the organisational hierarchy. Most mainstream organisations tend to be embedded with the values and ideologies of the majority (i.e. white) culture. These generally exclude minority (i.e. black) group values and orientations by dismissing them as being 'incompatible' or 'unfit' in terms of organisational needs and directions. Alternatively, black people may gain conditional entry into the organisation, that is, providing that they conform to established organisational culture.

To this extent, equal opportunities initiatives in employment need to go beyond issues of recruitment and selection, and staff development and training. Attracting and developing the individual is only part of the equation. Compatible change within all formal and informal structures and systems of the organisation is also essential. All of this needs to be managed within a strategic and integrative framework for change.

REFERENCES

Alban Metcalfe, B. (1989a). *The use of assessment centres in the National Health Service*, National Health Service Training Agency.

Alban Metcalfe, B. (1989b). Different genders—different rules? Paper presented to the British Academy of Management, Manchester UK, September.

Alderfer, C.P. and Smith, K.K. (1982). Studying intergroup relations embedded in organisations, *Administrative Science Quarterly*, **27**, 35–65

Alderfer, C.P. and Thomas, D. (1988). The significance of race and ethnicity for understanding organisational behaviour. In C.L. Cooper and I.T. Robertson (eds) *International Review of Industrial and Organisational Psychology 1988*, Wiley, Chichester.

Alderfer, C.P., Alderfer, C., Tucker, R.C. and Tucker, L. (1980). Diagnosing race relations in management, *Journal of Applied Behavioral Science*, **16**, 135–66.

Alibhai, Y. (1988a). The reality of race training, *New Society*, 29 January, 17–19.

Alibhai, Y. (1988b). Canadian Club, *New Society* September, 26–29.

Auluck, R. (1989). Black women and career development, Paper presented to the Creative Learning Forum, Women and Work Programme, Coventry Polytechnic, August.

Auluck, R.K. and Iles, P.A. (1991). The referral process: a study of working relationships between ante-natal clinic nursing staff and hospital social workers and their impact on Asian women, *British Journal of Social Work*, **21** (in press).

Banton, M. (1972). *Racial Minorities*, Fontana, London.

Bennett, R. (1986). How performance appraisals hurt women managers, *Women in Management Review*, Autumn, 145–53.

Ben-Tovim, G. (1978). The struggle against racism: Theoretical and strategic perspectives, *Marxism Today*, July.

BILT (1987). *Black in Birmingham*, Birmingham ILT Services, Handsworth Technical College, Birmingham.

Brennan, J. and McGeevor, P. (1987). *The employment of graduates from ethnic minorities*. Commission for Racial Equality, London.

Brennan, J. and McGeevor, P. (1988). *Graduates at Work: Degree courses and the labour market*, Jessica Kingsley, London.

Brenner, O.C., Blazini, A.P. and Greenhaus, J.H. (1988). An examination of race and sex differences in managerial work values *Journal of Vocational Behaviour*, **32**(3), 336–44.

Breugel, I. (1989). Sex and race in the labour market, *Feminist Review*, **32**, Summer, 49–68.

Brown, C. (1984). *White and Black in Britain*, Policy Studies Institute, London.

Brown, C. and Gay, P. (1985) *Racial Discrimination 17 Years after the Act*, Policy Studies Institute, London.

Cashmore, E. and Troyna, B. (1983). *Introduction to Race Relations*, RKP, London.

Clough, E., Drew, D. and Jones, B. (1989). Ethnic differences in the youth labour market in Sheffield and Bradford, *New Community* **X**(IV), 3.

Commission for Racial Equality (1982). *Massey Ferguson Perkins Ltd: Report of a formal investigation*, Commission for Racial Equality, London.

Commission for Racial Equality (1985a). *Beaumont Shopping Centre: Report of a formal investigation*, Commission for Racial Equality, London.

Commission for Racial Equality (1985b). *Positive Action and Equal Opportunity in Employment*, Commission for Racial Equality, London.

Commission for Racial Equality (1987a). *South Manchester Health Authority: Report of a formal investigation*, Commission for Racial Equality, London.

Commission for Racial Equality (1987b). *Chartered Accountancy Training Contracts: Report of a formal investigation*, Commission for Racial Equality, London.

Commission for Racial Equality (1988a). *Medical School Admissions: Report of a formal investigation*, Commission for Racial Equality, London.

Commission for Racial Equality (1988b). *Ethnic Minority School Teachers: A survey in eight local education authorities*, Commission for Racial Equality, London.

Commission for Racial Equality (1990). *Ethnic Minorities and the Graduate Labour market*, Commission for Racial Equality, London.

Cooper, C. and Davidson, M. (1982). *High Pressure—Working Lives of Women Managers*; Fontana; London.

Corby, S. (1983). In the Civil Service: looking back or held back? *Personnel Management*, February 28–31.

Cox, J. (ed.) (1986). *Transcultural Psychiatry*, Croom-Helm, London.

Cox, T. and Nkomo, S. (1986). Differential performance appraisal criteria: a field study of black and white managers, *Group and Organisation Studies* **11**, 1–2, 101–119.

Cross M *et al.*; (1988). *Black Welfare and Local Government: Section II Social Services Departments*, CRER, University of Warwick.

Davidson, M. (1985). *Reach for the Top*, Piatkus, London.

Davidson, M. and Cooper, C.L. (1984). *Working Women: an international survey*, Wiley, Chichester.

Davis, G. and Watson, G. (1982). *Black Life in Corporate America*, Random House, New York.

Deaux, K. (1976). Sex: a perspective on the attribution process. In J. Jarey, W. Ickes and R. Kidd (eds) *New Directions in Attribution Research*, Vol. **1**, Erlbaum, New Jersey.

Department of Employment (1988). Ethnic origins and the labour market, *Employment. Gazette*, December 633–46.

Dickens, F. and Dickens, J.B. (1982). *The Black Manager: Making it in the corporate world*, Amacan, New York.

Dominelli, L. (1988). *Anti-Racist Social Work*, Fontana, London.

Fernandez, J.P. (1975). *Black Managers in White Corporations*, Wiley, New York.

Fernandez, J.P. (1981). *Racism and Sexism in Corporate Life*, D.C. Heath, Lexington MA.

Fryer, P. (1986). *Staying Power—The History of Black People in Britain*, Pluto, London.

Glazer, N. (1975). *Affirmative Discrimination*, Basic Books, New York.

Gurnah, A. (1984). The politics of RAT, *Critical Social Policy*, **11**, 6–20.

Hammond, V. (1988). Women in management in Great Britain. In N.J. Adler and D.N. Israeli (eds) *Women in Management Worldwide*, N.E. Sharpe, New York.

Huck, J.R. and Bray, D.W. (1976). Management assessment center evaluations and subsequent job performance of white and black females, *Personnel Psychology*, **29**, 13–30.

Hunt, P. (1987). Coping with racism: lessons from institutional change in police departments. In J.W. Shaw, P.G. Nordlie, R.M. Shapiro (eds) *Strategies for Improving Race Relation*, Manchester University Press, Manchester.

Husband, C. (ed) (1982). *Race in Britain: Continuity and Change*, Hutchinson, London.

Iles, P.A. (1989). Using assessment and development centres to facilitate equal opportunity in selection and career development, *Equal Opportunities International*, **8**,(5), 1–32.

Iles, P.A. and Auluck, R.K. (1988). Managing equal opportunity through strategic organisation development, *Leadership and Organisation Development Journal*, **9**, (6), 3–10.

Iles, P.A. and Auluck, R.K. (1989). From racism awareness to strategic human resource management in implementing equal opportunity, *Personnel Review*, **18**, (4), 24–32.

Iles, P.A. and Robertson, I.T. (1988). Getting in, getting on and looking good: physical attractiveness, gender, and selection decisions, *Guidance and Assessment Review*, **5**(3), 4–6.

Iles, P.A. and Robertson, I.T. (1989). The impact of personnel selection procedures on candidates in P. Herriot (ed.) *Selection and Assessment in Organisations*, John Wiley and Sons, Chichester.

Ineichen, B. (1989). Afro Caribbeans and the incidence of schizophrenia: a review, *New Community*, **15**,(3), 335–41.

Jenkins, R. (1986). *Racism and Recruitment: Managers, organisations and equal opportunities in the labour market*, Cambridge University Press, Cambridge.

Johnes, G. and Taylor, J. (1989). Ethnic minorities in the graduate labour market, *New Community*, **15**(4), 527–36.

Jones, E.W. (1973). What its like to be a black manager, *Harvard Business Review*, July–August, 108–116.

Jones, E.W. (1986). Black managers: the dream deferred, *Harvard Business Review*, May–June, 84–93.

Katz, J. (1977). *White Awareness: a handbook of anti-racism training*, Oklahoma University Press, Oklahoma.

Kraiger, K. and Ford, J.K. (1985). A meta-analysis of ratee race effects in performance ratings, *Journal of Applied Psychology*, **70**, 56–65.

Lefkowitz, J. and Fraser, A. (1980). Assessment of achievement and power motivation of blacks and whites, using a black and white TAT, with black and white administrators, *Journal of Applied Psychology*, **65**(6), 685–96.

Littlewood, R. and Lipsedge, M. (1982). *Aliens and Alienists: Ethnic Minorities and Psychiatry*, Macmillan, London.

Lyon, S.E. (1988). Unequal opportunities: Black minorities and access to higher

education, *Journal of Further and Higher Education*, **12**(3), 21–37.
Manpower Services Commission (1986). *Survey of Job Centres*, Manpower Services Commission, London.
Manpower Services Commission (1987). *Annual Report 1986/7*, Manpower Services Commission, London.
McKeen, C.A. and Burke, R.J. (1989). Mentor relationships in organisations: issues, strategies and prospects for women. *Journal of Management Development*, **8**(6), 33–42.
Miles, R. (1982). *Racism and Migrant Labour*, RKP, London.
Moses, J.L. and Boehm, V. (1975). Relationship of assessment center performance to management progress of women, *Journal of Applied Psychology*, **60**, 527–9.
Nordlie, P.G. (1987). The evolution of race relations training in the US army in J.W. Shaw, P.G. Nordlie and R.M. Shapiro (eds) *Strategies for Improving Race Relations*, Manchester University Press, Manchester.
Oakley, R. (1987). *Employment in Police Forces: a survey of equal opportunities*, Commission for Racial Equality, London.
Penn, R., Scattergood, H. and Martin, A. (1990). The dialectics of ethnic incorporation and exclusion: employment trajectories of Asian migrants in Rochdale, *New Community*, **16**(2), 175–98.
Pumfrey, P. (1985). Some reflections on RAT, *New Community*, **13**(3), 485–9.
Purcell, T.V. and Cavanagh, G.F. (1982). *Blacks in the Industrial World: Issues for the Manager*, Free Press, New York.
Rack, P. (1982). *Race, Culture and Mental Disorder*, Tavistock, London.
Ritchie, R.J. and Moses, J.L. 1983). Assessment center correlates of women's advancement into middle management: a seven year longitudinal analysis, *Journal of Applied Psychology*, **68**, 227–31.
Robertson, I.T. and Iles, P.A. (1988). Approaches to managerial selection in C.L. Cooper and I.T. Robertson (eds) *International Review of Industrial and Organisational Psychology 1988*, Wiley, Chichester.
Robertson, I.T. and Kandola, R.S. (1982). Work sample tests: validity, adverse impact, and applicant reactions, *Journal of Occupational Psychology*, **55**, 171–82.
Rooney, B. (1980). *Active mistakes—a grass roots report*, *Multi-Racial Social Work*, No. 1, pp. 43–54.
Schmitt, N. and Hill, T. (1977). Sex and race composition of assessment center ratings as a determinant of peer and assessor ratings, *Journal of Applied Psychology*, **62**, 261–4.
Schmitt, N. and Lappin, I. (1980). Race and sex as determinants of the mean and variance of performance ratings, *Journal of Applied Psychology*, **65**, 428–35.
Searle, P. and Stibbs, A. (1989). The under-representation of ethnic minority students in post graduate teacher training, *New Community*, **15**(2), 253–260.
Singh R. (1987). Destination Bradford: Bradford's South Asian Community, *South Asia Research*, **7**, 13–24.
Singh, R. (1988). *Asian and White Perceptions of the Teaching Profession*, Bradford and Ilkley Community College, Bradford.
Singh, R. and Ram, S. (1986). *Indians in Bradford: the development of a community*, Bradford and Ilkley Community College, Bradford.
Sivanandan, A. (1985). RAT and the degradation of black struggle, *Race and Class*, **26**(4), 1–33.
Smith, D. (1976). *The Facts of Racial Disadvantage*, London: Political and Economic Planning, London.
Thomas, D.A. (1986). An intra-organisational analysis of differences in black and

white patterns of sponsorship and the dynamics of cross-racial mentoring, Unpublished Doctoral Dissertation. Yale University.

Thomas, D.A. (1989). Mentoring and irrationality: the role of racial taboos, *Human Resource Management*, **28**(2), 279–90.

Tomkin, B. (1987). State of the ART, *Community Care* March 17–19.

Toplis, J.W.C. (1983). Training Interviewers to avoid unfair discrimination, Paper to British Psychological Society, London, December.

Williams, R.S. (1989). Case study on fairness. In M. Smith and I.T. Robertson (eds) *Advances in Selection and Assessment*, Wiley, Chichester.

Wrench, J. (1989). Employment and the labour market, *New Community*, **15**(2), 261–8.

Chapter 10.2

Ethnic Minority Workers in the United Kingdom: Where is the Law Going?

Geoffrey Bindman, Bindman & Partners and University College London, UK

EQUALITY BEFORE THE LAW

The belief that in Britain all are equal before the law is hallowed by antiquity and repetition but—at least before 1965—it was true only in a narrow sense. Indeed the more closely one examined the notion the more limited its validity seemed to be. For the courts were always prepared to treat differently those whose circumstances were different—and there were all kinds of cases in which justice was tailored to differences or supposed differences in status, class, sex, or degrees of responsibility. The idea of equality rested on little more than an underlying axiom of popular morality: that the law should be applied equally in equal circumstances. The legal protection needed by ethnic minority workers, however, is not against unequal application of the *law* to them in comparison with white workers. The problem is that they need the protection of the law against unequal treatment by *other people*, especially employers and others in positions of power such as public authorities, estate agents, and the police.

Unequal treatment by these persons or institutions of black and other ethnic minorities had been largely ignored by the law. Before 1965 there was no statutory provision against discrimination and the common law provided barely an atom of protection for the victims of discrimination, while routinely providing redress for what were then more familiarly recognised injustices.

AMERICAN EXPERIENCE

In the United States racial segregation survived vigorously even during the Second World War: black and white soldiers fought in different regiments

Vulnerable Workers: Psychosocial and Legal Issues. Edited by M. J. Davidson and J. Earnshaw

and units. But after the war a powerful campaign against racial discrimination soon began. Legal measures had been introduced as long ago as the 1860s, during the Reconstruction period after the Civil War, but they had fallen into disuse. In 1945, Roosevelt decreed that discrimination on racial grounds should be prohibited in the public service and enforcement machinery was set up to investigate complaints of discrimination and, if they were upheld, to direct remedial action.

Outside the public sphere some of the state legislatures, beginning with New York and Massachusetts, set up Human Rights Commissions which had power to investigate complaints against private employers. If the complaints appeared to have substance ('probable cause') the employer was invited to make amends, either by offering the job previously denied or an equivalent one, or offering financial compensation. If he refused, a public hearing could be convened, followed if necessary by enforcement through the ordinary state judicial system. The publicity was unwelcome and the employers often backed down to avoid it.

THE FIRST RACE RELATIONS ACT

In 1964, the new Labour government introduced for the first time in Britain legislation to outlaw racial discrimination. The issue had become an important one as more and more of the newly arrived immigrants from the Caribbean and the Indian subcontinent met unexpected hostility. Racism within Britain had little room hitherto for practical expression. As the British people relinquished the Empire much of the racism previously directed at subjects overseas was turned inwards against those former subjects now enjoying legal equality in Britain.

Nevertheless, the first anti-discrimination law introduced in Britain in 1965 did not touch employment at all. Imposing legal restraints on the freedom of employers to recruit or promote at will was too big a step to contemplate until the idea of legislation had been tried out in a less contentious field. The Race Relations Act 1965 prohibited discrimination only in the provision of certain public facilities, such as hotels, restaurants, public houses, public transport and other public institutions (like museums) to which the public were normally admitted. A novel system of enforcement was adopted, based on the US model of the adminstrative enforcement agency. The Race Relations Board was established to investigate complaints of unlawful discrimination and seek to resolve them by conciliation if at all possible. Only if conciliation could not be achieved was there any provision for court proceedings and they could be initiated only by the Attorney-General, following a report to him by the Race Relations Board certifying not only that they had failed to conciliate but that the discrimination they had found was likely to be repeated if not judicially restrained. In effect, therefore, there was no sanction for the single act of discrimination and the sanction against persistent discrimination was never in fact invoked. In the three years before the Act was repealed not one single case was brought to court by the Attorney-General.

SECOND THOUGHTS

The first chairman of the Board, Mark Bonham-Carter (now Lord Bonham-Carter), had serious misgivings about the limited scope of the law and its cumbersome procedures at the time when he accepted the job. He stipulated that he should be allowed to recommend amendments and for this purpose two studies were commissioned: one from Political and Economic Planning (PEP) (now replaced by the Policy Studies Institute) into the extent and character of the racial discrimination which was actually taking place; and the second by three lawyers, Professor Harry Street, Geoffrey Howe QC, and the author of this chapter, into the structure and content of anti-discrimination laws in other part of the world. The Street Committee recommended new legislation and many of its recommendations were embodied in a new statute, the Race Relations Act 1968.

For the first time, racial discrimination in employment was brought within the scope of the law, as well as housing and the provision of goods, facilities and services. The Act retained the Race Relations Board as the exclusive resource for the investigation and settlement of complaints but gave the Board power to take proceedings in the County Court whenever conciliation failed, and damages could be claimed for any opportunity lost as a result of the discrimination. Unfortunately, an additional hurdle was erected for the victim of employment discrimination. If there was in existence a 'suitable body of persons' available to investigate the complaint then it had to be referred to that body instead of the Board. This was a compromise brought about by the opposition of the TUC and the CBI to the involvement of a statutory body outside the industrial relations field in the investigation of employment matters. The 'bodies of persons' were to be set up by unions and management to investigate discrimination cases in industry in the belief that the traditional collective bargaining machinery—or a variant of it—would have a better chance of reconciling the parties than an outside body. Only if no industrial body was available or if the industrial body failed to achieve a resolution of the problem could the Board become involved. In the latter case, the Board was given power to conduct a fresh investigation itself and it could ultimately use its powers to take a case to court. Industrial bodies were given no power to take legal proceedings. If they could not achieve conciliation their function came to an end.

This elaborate process—almost Kafkaesque—was hopelessly ineffectual. Although the Act had time limits built into the stages of the investigation and the Board had power to call in the case for its own investigation if the time limits were exceeded, it was naturally inclined to grant extensions of time to the industrial body while a possibility of compromise remained. Unfortunately what seemed a likely prospect of settlement rarely materialised.

It is now perfectly obvious, as indeed many people pointed out when the 1968 Race Relations bill was debated, that the collective bargaining system of industrial negotiation between management and unions could not be relied on to resolve complaints of racial discrimination. The fact was not faced that racial discrimination may benefit some workers as it harms others. White workers may side with management against black workers. Unions can only represent the dominant common interest perceived by their members.

When the law was re-modelled in the Race Relations Act 1976 this clumsy and ineffectual system for dealing with employment complaints was abandoned.

A NEW FRAMEWORK

The 1976 Act was a much more serious attempt than the previous statutes to make the law an effective weapon against discrimination. In 1975 the Sex Discrimination Act had been passed after pressure from a powerful lobby and it was impossible for the government to resist strengthening the law against racial discrimination to give it at least equivalent powers.

The new framework incorporated three important principles, all of which had been previously absent.

An Equal Right to Sue

The citizen subjected to racial discrimination should have the same right as the victim of any other wrong to seek redress by taking legal proceedings in the ordinary courts of law. It was patronising and even racist in itself to require black workers (the likely victims) to obtain the approval of a government appointed agency before exercising their legal rights when a victim of a car accident or a creditor could go to court against the driver or borrower without anybody's permission. Anyone complaining of racial discrimination in employment could now therefore take his or her own case to an Industrial Tribunal.

At the same time it was recognised that discrimination may not be easy to prove, because all the relevant information is in the hands of the employer. The Act provided for questionnaires to enable anyone suspecting discrimination to test out his or her suspicions before launching legal action. Suppose a black woman goes for interview and, when the employer for the first time has a chance to see her face, she is told the job has been taken. Or perhaps she is told this only the next day. She has no means of proving whether a better qualified candidate had turned up or if the employer has left the job unfilled or chosen a less well qualified candidate rather than take on a black employee. A series of questions can probe the facts. How many other people applied for the job? When did they apply? What were their qualifications? Was any of them selected? When? Are any other black people employed by the employer and in what capacities?

The answers to these questions will at least give a basis for deciding whether a case is worth pursuing. If employers prevaricate or refuse to answer it will look as if they have something to hide. If proceedings are started after that and the answers still do not emerge, the tribunal is given express power to draw adverse inferences against respondents from their failure to answer the questionnaire.

Indirect as well as Direct Discrimination

The second important new principle relates to the meaning of discrimination. In the earlier legislation it had been given what proved to be a simplistic definition. Those who drafted the law perceived discrimination as typically a conscious act of blatant injustice—a racially prejudiced state of mind acted out in practice by deliberately choosing whites in preference to blacks. And it was true that, before employment was brought within the scope of the 1968 Race Relations Act, black job applicants were openly rejected on quite explicitly racial grounds—and as often as not showered with racist abuse to add insult to injury. The definition was therefore articulated in terms of 'less favourable treatment' on racial grounds, which were themselves amplified to include grounds of 'colour, race, or ethnic or national origins'.

Of course such discrimination continued to occur and still does occur, but—as was becoming apparent in the United States in the mid-1960s but without influencing the draftsmanship of the 1968 Act—direct and deliberate discrimination is only part of the problem. Another kind of discrimination, less obvious but probably more widespread, is that which results from the delayed effect of past discrimination which has denied racial minorities the opportunity of competing on equal terms—even when the rules are ostensibly applied equally across the board. In *Griggs* v. *Duke Power Company* (401 US 424 [1971]), the Supreme Court of the United States in 1971 gave a broad interpretation to statutory language not unlike the 'less favourable treatment' language of the Race Relations Act so as to outlaw treatment which was equal in form but unequal in impact. The Duke Power Company tried to get round the Civil Rights Act of 1964, before which it had practised an overt colour bar, by demanding high school graduation as a minimum qualification for jobs which in reality did not need that educational standard.

It so happened that in the catchment area from which its workers came there were no black people who could meet this standard—black youngsters had been kept out of high schools just as their elders were denied well-paid employment. The Supreme Court was not prepared to allow a test which they considered irrelevant to the performance of the job in question to be used as a means of producing a discriminatory impact on a disadvantaged minority. Chief Justice Burger said: 'Under the Act, practices, procedures or tests neutral on their face, and even neutral in terms of intent, cannot be maintained if they operate to "freeze" the *status quo* of prior discriminatory employment practices'—unless, of course, they were essential for adequate performance of the job in hand. The Chief Justice continued: 'The touchstone is necessity. If an employment practice which operates to exclude negroes cannot be shown to be related to job performance, the practice is prohibited.'

Such broad and flexible interpretations of statutory language are not in accordance with the English judicial tradition, which tries (or sometimes pretends) to follow the literal wording of statutes and leaves major changes in legislation to Parliament. In order to widen the definition of discrimination to cover the indirect variety 'invented' in the Griggs case, the new Race Relations Act had to make specific provision for it.

Wide Investigative Powers

The third element of the new strategy of the 1976 Act was to give the new Commission for Racial Equality (which replaced the Race Relations Board) much wider powers of investigation, chiefly in order to probe for situations where indirect discrimination was taking place.

The PEP Report in 1967 had, by demonstrating the massive scale of discrimination in employment and housing, supplied the justification the government wanted for extending the 1965 Act. But a further detailed study carried out by PEP between 1972 and 1975 showed that the level of discrimination had not diminished notwithstanding the passage of the 1968 Act and other government measures designed to reduce inner city deprivation. So the conclusion was obvious that a law which could be enforced only by tackling a series of individual cases was never going to make a significant impact on the problem.

The characteristic of indirect discrimination which seemed to present a hopeful way forward was that it was typically a manifestation of a widespread pattern or practice affecting a large number of possible victims. While, therefore, it must be open to the individual victim to seek redress for indirect as well as direct discrimination, the major thrust of anti-discrimination strategy was to be the wide-ranging investigation which would attack the discriminatory practice itself. The object was to remove the source of the disease, not just its symptoms.

OTHER LOOPHOLES FILLED

The 1976 Act also filled several of the loopholes which had become apparent as the 1968 Act was interpreted. The 1968 Act applied to discrimination on the ground of 'colour, race or ethnic or national origins'. Did the latter expression cover discrimination on the ground of one's current nationality? The House of Lords held it did not. The 1976 Act added 'nationality' as a ground to reverse this interpretation. The amounts of compensation awarded under the 1968 Act were extremely low. In an attempt to encourage higher awards, the 1976 Act made it clear that awards could be made for 'injury to feelings'. (It was only after a Court of Appeal decision in 1988 that awards began seriously to reflect this: see below.) Considered as a whole, then, the Race Relations Act 1976 provided a sophisticated legal framework for a serious attack on discrimination, not only in employment, but also in housing and the provision of all forms of goods facilities and services. Its scope was broad: discrimination was widely defined; virtually all forms of employment discrimination were carefully included—recruitment, promotion, the treatment of employees and their working conditions, and dismissal. Even the meaning of 'employment' was expanded to cover 'contract workers' and workers who were not employed under contracts of service. The enforcement machinery was superior to that provided for litigants in other areas of law: not only had they the right to bring proceedings in Industrial Tribunals with the same rights of appeal as others; they had the additional advantage of assistance from the CRE (in its discretion), a questionnaire procedure which enabled them to test out the evidence before launching proceedings, and the benefit of a series of decisions requiring the respondent to give wide disclosure of documents and information. Monetary compensation and injunctive relief were also available in suitable cases.

Finally, the wide investigatory powers given to the Commission, including the power to require attendance of witnesses and production of documents and information for the purpose of an investigation, were there to enable patterns and practices of discrimination to be rooted out.

HAS THE 1976 ACT BEEN A SUCCESS?

So did this powerful new law dramatically reduce discrimination? Apparently it did not. The 1973 and 1974 PEP studies showed that black West Indian applicants for jobs were turned down at least four times as often as similarly qualified white applicants. This was a slightly greater level of discrimination than shown by the original PEP study in 1967.

In 1979 a test carried out in Nottingham by the CRE and Nottingham Community Relations Council produced a result about 50% less favourable still to West Indian job seekers. In 1984 and 1985 a much more detailed study than the Nottingham test, conducted by the Policy Studies Institute (PSI) (successor to PEP), showed a level of discrimination very similar to that revealed in Nottingham five years earlier.

Strictly, this is not evidence that the Race Relations Act has had a neutral or negative impact. If it had never been passed discrimination might be greater. But it is surely quite clear that it has failed to make a major impact on either public opinion or public behaviour. Indeed, if one adds up the number of individual cases which have successfully been brought under the Act and the number of investigations which can be shown to have ended discrimination in a particular situation, the disparity in comparison with the PSI findings and other evidence of the likely extent of actual discrimination is huge. For example, in 1988 the CRE supported 105 successful employment cases (either settled or decided in favour of the complainant), an increase over the 95 successes in the previous year. In 1989, the number of successful case fell to 102. In 1988, five investigations were completed and another seven were in progress at the end of the year. At the end of 1989, 11 investigations were in progress. In terms of direct impact there are no more than a few hundred individuals a year getting redress or being rescued from the consequences of discrimination by the law.

Is it worth trying yet again to strengthen the law or is one forced to conclude that its impact must remain marginal? Before answering the question one should reflect on what anti-discrimination law is designed to achieve.

THE PURPOSES OF ANTI-DISCRIMINATION LAW

A useful list of the objects of such a law was set out by the Race Relations Board in its first annual report in 1966 as follows:

(1) A law is an unequivocal declaration of public policy.
(2) A law gives support to those who do not wish to discriminate, but who feel compelled to do so by social pressure.

(3) A law gives protection and redress to minority groups.
(4) A law thus provides for the peaceful and orderly adjustment of grievances and release of tensions.
(5) A law reduces prejudice by discouraging the behaviour in which prejudice finds expression.

Have They Been Achieved?

It is obviously difficult or impossible to assess empirically the extent to which these objectives have been realised.

(1) The law remains a declaration of public policy but successive governments have put their sincerity in doubt by their failure to set an example or to provide sufficient resources to enable the policy to be effectively carried out.
(2) It is certainly likely that the law has been a helpful prop to those under pressure to discriminate who wish to resist the pressure. It has also provided a strong incentive to them to resist by making it clear that they would themselves be acting in breach of the law if they did not resist (see *R.* v. *City of Westminster ex parte CRE* [1984]IRLR 230).
(3) Protection and redress to minority groups has been supplied to an extremely limited extent, as the PSI studies show. Plainly the vast majority of those who suffer discrimination receive neither protection nor redress.
(4) Since 1965, there have been some serious public disturbances which reflect the existence of unsatisfied grievances and a build-up of tension in the relationship between black youths and the police in particular communities, such as Brixton, St Paul's in Bristol, and Broadwater Farm. Because of the limited impact of the law and a low level of confidence among black people in its effectiveness, it is unlikely that it has in fact done much to promote public harmony and order.
(5) The achievement of the last of the five objectives must also be in doubt. The findings of the Policy Studies Institute reinforced by common experience suggest that prejudice remains at a very high level.

Discrimination Must Be Made Expensive

Nevertheless, we know that anti-discrimination law has had important effects in the United States and even without legislative change the possibility of a significant attack on discrimination is beginning to emerge within the framework of the Race Relations Act.

The way forward must be to put sufficient pressure on employers to make them see major economic disadvantages in not having minority workers well represented at all levels. The weakness of the enforcement mechanisms of the Race Relations Act has been their failure to cause more than minimal anxiety to those whose decisions affect employment opportunities. Unless the discriminator faces a serious risk of being found out and, following discovery, a seriously worrying cost, he will usually find it more convenient to ignore his legal obligations.

THE CRE'S PROPOSALS

The CRE was given a specific power in the 1976 Act to keep the working of the Act under review and to recommend changes when it thought them necessary. The CRE did exactly that in 1985 after a thorough exercise in public consultation which lasted nearly two years.

Its most important recommendations go a long way towards a system which would increase the price of discrimination for the employer to an unacceptably high level. While retaining and indeed strengthening the machinery for individuals to pursue complaints, they would greatly increase the power of the CRE to press cases on a collective basis.

The greatest weakness of the 1976 Act, compounded by a series of restrictive court decisions, is the complexity and ultimate futility of the CRE's formal investigation powers.

The Act gave the CRE power to 'conduct a formal investigation for any purpose connected with the carrying out of [its] duties'. The courts narrowed the scope of this power in defiance of its literal meaning but the key question is: what happens if it investigates and finds or suspects discrimination? At present it can merely issue a 'non-discrimination' notice which cannot actually force a change of practice. What the CRE wants is a specialist tribunal to which it can go and get a ruling whenever it suspects discrimination and which can give wide-ranging directions to the discriminator to make changes which will prevent future discrimination.

Crucially also, the tribunal would have power to order the discriminator to pay compensation to all those shown to be victims of the discrimination without the need for them to bring separate proceedings as is now required. The effect of this proposal could be to replicate the impact of the class action in the United States, which has been the single most effective legal mechanism for improving opportunities for black workers. The potential cost of compensating perhaps hundreds or even thousands of workers, as has actually happened in the United States, is an extremely powerful deterrent.

Escalating the burden of compensation on the employer has of course a two-fold purpose; it acts as a penalty and an inducement to the employer to take active steps to introduce and implement appropriate policies; and it provides redress for the victim. In this respect it serves thc same purpose as the award of damages in personal injury cases, but in the field of racial discrimination assessing the appropriate level of compensation is more difficult because it is less tangible. Courts and tribunals have until recently placed a low value on the humiliation suffered by the victim of discrimination and have been unwilling to introduce a punitive element into their awards. Thus, ridiculously small amounts of compensation, such as £25 or even £5 in some cases have been awarded for injury to feelings. Fortunately the CRE's recommendation for a substantial increase, to be spelled out in a new statute, has been rendered superfluous by a forward-looking decision of the Court of Appeal, which increased an award from £50 to £500 and made it quite clear that courts and tribunals could award punitive or exemplary damages where they consider that an employer has deliberately flouted the law (*Alexander* v. *Home Office*).

Since that 1988 decision the level of awards has already gone up considerably and awards for injury to feelings now range between £500 and £4000—though it has to be said that the great majority are at the lower end of the scale.

WHAT SHOULD THE EMPLOYER BE REQUIRED TO DO?

Assuming that financial pressure will induce the employer to carry out appropriate action there remains the question as to what that action should be.

Plainly, there should be power, as there is not at present, for the tribunal to order the employer to introduce and carry out equal opportunity policies on the lines recommended by the CRE in its code of practice. Should it also be able to order affirmative action on the lines formerly available to US courts (though now drastically curtailed by a newly right-wing Supreme Court)?

The CRE has adroitly but perhaps too timidly side-stepped this controversial issue by recommending power only to order affirmative action to the extent that it is already made optional by the 1976 Act, e.g. where special training or special encouragement to seek employment may be provided for members of ethnic minorities in firms or institutions in which they are under-represented. This falls short of the imposition of ethnic minority quotas or targets which has been a feature of US affirmative action decrees. But the CRE does recommend that the Secretary of State be empowered to prescribe compulsory ethnic record keeping and that where it is prescribed the CRE should have power to call for returns to be made.

THE FAILURE OF GOVERNMENT

The CRE's constructive recommendations, already four years old, are of little value to ethnic minority workers unless they receive the support of a government which is prepared to put them into effect.

Sadly, the attitude of the present government has been almost totally negative. It has reduced the budget of the CRE to such an extent that it has had to refuse legal assistance in several serious cases which therefore cannot be pursued at all, because legal aid is not available for Industrial Tribunals.

By curtailing the power of local authorities to demand that those who enter into contracts with them demonstrate a commitment to racial equality, it has undermined a valuable non-statutory source of pressure on employers to end discrimination. Nor is it willing to consider a new more effective Race Relations Act. The government's only response to the CRE proposals has been to suggest that the CRE encourages the tabling of amendments to other legislation which is going through Parliament. This was done successfully by an amendment to the Housing Bill 1988 which has resulted in the CRE being permitted to issue a code of practice for the rented sector in housing. But in several other cases CRE-backed amendments have been opposed by the Government and have been rejected. Compounding the irony and indeed hypocrisy of the government's position is the paradox of the Fair Employment (Northern Ireland) Act 1989 which has enacted for Northern Ireland several of the major recommendations which the CRE intended for the rest of the United Kingdom, including the establishment of a specialist tribunal for discrimination cases, the introduction of compulsory monitoring (by religion, of course, not race—but where is the difference in principle or practice?), and a simplified procedure for formal investigations. Indeed, the Fair Employment Commission in Northern Ireland has been given far wider powers than the CRE has even asked for—it can direct employers to adopt specified policies, even involving affirmative action. There is no possible justification for accepting these sensible changes in one part of the United Kingdom and not in others. The government or, at any rate, the next government, must act on the logic of this position and give us a new Race Relations Act—preferably even tougher than that suggested by the CRE.

Index